THE SOLDIER

AND

THE BABY DOLL

MEMORIES OF A LOVE AFFAIR

BY

KATHARINE CASE FOURNIER

InstantPublisher.com

The chapters
'Eighty-Foot Driveway', 'Peril', and 'No Property Damage'
were previously published in
A Ribbon at a Time (Williamsburg, VA, 2004)
and are included here
by permission of The Wren Writers.

Thanks to the members of
Wren Writers and Williamsburg Writers
for their generous love and encouragement.

ISBN 1-59196-972-7

For
Douglas, Michael,
Adam, and Jenny

In the hope that knowing something
of where you came from
will help you to see where you are going.

On risque de pleurer un peu si l'on s'est laissé apprivoiser ... *

....from le Petit Prince by Antoine de Saint Exupéry

---

* One risks weeping a little, if one allows himself to be tamed.

CONTENTS

Sylvio 1941

Kati 1942

A FEW LIMBS FROM THE FAMILY TREE

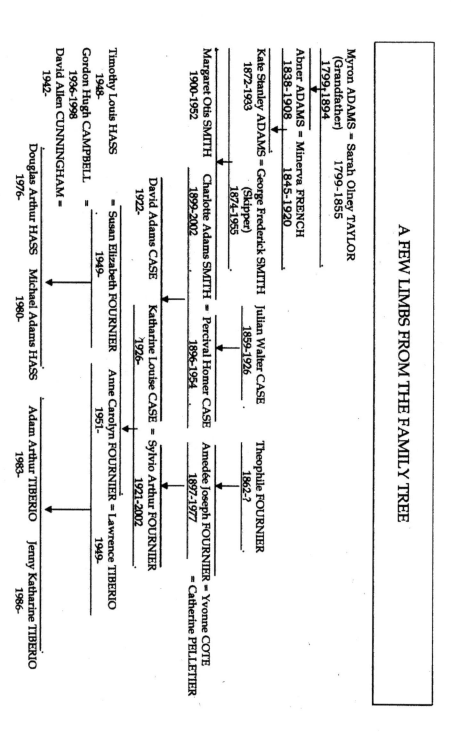

PRELUDE

When Art died, I wanted to die too. I thought by telling stories of our life, I might be able to find somewhere within them a reason to go on. Forget about Romeo and Juliet; each of them died over the other's death, but my choice is more complicated. They were very young. When you were very young, no one else mattered. There were no children or grandchildren to consider. If I cannot ignore the pain and guilt I might cause, does that mean I have to live my life for them? Or is there yet some unexplored dimension to my life, waiting to be discovered? I want to know.

৪০ ৪৪ ৪০

Before I begin, you need to know a little about where we came from. That our paths eventually crossed is one of the intriguing minor mysteries of fate; I would not have wanted to bet on it.

CƷ ꙮ CƷ ꙮ

He was Sylvio Arthur Fournier, though Sylvio was his
only name until I meddled with it.. But that is another story I
will tell you later.

His people came from Normandy, sailing in 1604 with
Samuel de Champlain up the St. Lawrence River. The first to
come was a pharmacist who knew something about healing
and also about agriculture. He was signed on as ship's surgeon
for the voyage. The French were interested in colonizing the
land, and accordingly the surgeon went back to France, found a
bride, and returned to establish a household. They settled on
the south bank of the river, and with other arrivals from France
spread out to populate the growing towns and villages.

In the early part of the 20th century, hard times prompted
many to migrate south to the United States to work in the
textile and shoe mills of New England. They continued to speak
the provincial French of their Québec villages. Sylvio was born
in 1921 in Lewiston, Maine. He attended Catholic parochial
school where he did not learn English, only a more classic form
of 'school' French.

When he was nine years old, his mother took his
younger sister and left Sylvio and her husband Amedée behind,
saying she did not love them and never had. For the next five
years until Amedée remarried, Sylvio and his father kept house
together. The young boy absorbed his father's strong work
ethic. On Saturdays, he helped Amedée clean the offices and
care for the buildings of the Central Maine Power Company
where Amedée worked as a janitor. They lived modestly, but
through the Depression Amedée brought home a pay envelope
each Friday. Sylvio's father never completed grade school, but
he determined that the boy would have a fine education.
Recognizing the limitations of a French-speaking parochial
school, he transferred the boy to public school. There, by total
immersion during the school day, Sylvio learned English.

He earned his spending money by delivering morning newspapers.

"Mornings were dark and cold," he told me, "and some of the apartments were on the third floor. No elevators in those buildings! I didn't mind, though, because at the end of my route was a bakery. For a nickel I could buy a jelly doughnut, still warm from the oven. I think the baker was sorry for me, coming in from the dark, shivering. He always squirted extra jelly into mine. They sure smelled good. Tasted good, too!"

Fournier House, Lewiston, Maine

In due course he graduated from high school as a National Honor Scholar. The entry about him in his yearbook, *The Folio* (of which he was business manager) said:
Nicknames: Stooge, Art, Silver, Fish
Time and tide wait for no man, and neither do I. Shall we ever forget 'Art's' wonderful personality and good sportsmanship? He has been

very popular among his fellow students. 'Art' is planning to study at a scientific college or be an apprentice for some successful businessman.

In 1939, Sylvio decided on the path he would take. He wanted a college education, but having no money, he settled on the U. S. Military Academy at West Point, which was free. His family certainly had no political connection to promote an appointment, so he decided to join the Army and enter West Point by examination. A few days after Sylvio's eighteenth birthday, Hitler invaded Poland. Europe was beginning to smolder. The military draft would be enacted later, but the recruiter readily welcomed the young man.

"Kid, you've got a wide choice. As soon as you go through basic training, you can see the world! What'll I put you down for--the Philippines, Hawaii or Panama?"

He stood there, heart beating fast, half afraid of this unknown world opening up to him. Two of the choices sounded far away, but Panama suggested easier trips home on leave, and certainly closer to West Point. .

"Panama sounds good, Sir."

"I'll put it down," smiled the sergeant as he finished the application, stamped it with an official-looking stamp, and waved the recruit inside. That choice might just have saved his life, although he did not know it then.

Following basic training, he was assigned to Camp Paraiso, Panama, named for Paradise. When he and his unit arrived at the camp site they discovered only large stacks of lumber there. They would build Paraiso and the army did not care that the rainy season was beginning. They slung their hammocks from trees away from the soggy ground and surrounded every post they dug into the ground with a moat of kerosene to discourage snakes and tarantulas. In a few weeks, the buildings were complete even to electricity, and the men took up residence.

Even in Panama, testing time came for West Point entrance. Sylvio scored high on the written part. As he expected, the physical was easy; he was very fit. At the end, the doctor said, "Take off your glasses, son, and read the smallest line you can." The room turned blurry, but he did his best.

"I can see the E at the top, Sir. If I put on my glasses, I can do just fine."

"I'm sorry son, but at West Point they require 20/20 vision. Didn't anybody tell you?"

"No, Sir, I'm afraid not, Sir." Sylvio swallowed hard. His long-held dream lay there in a thousand pieces. He took a deep breath, then determined to make the best of whatever came. He was dismissed to return to work.

The main work of the soldiers was to stand guard on foreign ships passing through the canal. For security, crews were confined below decks while an American pilot guided the ship and American soldiers stood watch. The canal was the vital link between the Atlantic and Pacific naval fleets and had to be guarded against sabotage. The work was important but boring.

Immediately after the Japanese attack on Pearl Harbor, the troops were evacuated deep into the jungle. The most likely second strike would be on the canal. In case of invasion, the troops could fight back, but if the Japanese dropped bombs the troops needed to be out of the way. The Canal was defended by a couple of aged airplanes, not much more. Although the attack did not come, the soldiers had to camp in the jungle for several weeks. One day, a half-ton truck came lumbering down the rough jungle road bearing hundreds of batteries, a mistaken oversupply.

"Cripes, leave it to the army to screw up. How are we going to get rid of these damned batteries?" The men grumbled at the stupidity. Not Sylvio.

"Look! What's Fournier doing now? With him, it's always something." That was true. Whenever a problem came up, Sylvio walked around it, thought about it, viewed it from the other side, and came up with something. Now he was rigging wires to connect several batteries in series. Then, he hooked up his electric razor and shaved in perfect comfort.

The food in the jungle was bad. They opened cans of rations actually left over from the first world war. The contents were green, but by cutting away all of the outside they were able to salvage enough meat for survival.

"Now," he explained later, "you can understand why I don't want Spam for dinner!"

Some of the men found native villages nearby and brought back canteens filled with 'pulqua' fermented from palm leaves. Sylvio's desire for alcohol never reached that level.

Even back at Paraiso, army life was basic. The camp communicated with the outside world on wire, by Morse code. Sylvio became a skilled key operator as well as an expert marksman. Lax supervision of the camp allowed the mess sergeant to siphon off funds intended for food. Instead, he bought cheap bananas and coconuts from the local market and served them for breakfast, lunch and dinner. Saturday nights the men would hike to Colón. Night life there was limited to bar-hopping or mattress hopping.

"Meester! You want my seester? She very pretty. I show you." A ragged little boy, not more than ten, tugged at a soldier's sleeve. Or someone's sister, usually teenaged, barefoot and dirty but not necessarily pretty, confronted them with a few explicit words in pidgin English. Usually, these girls carried a mattress strapped to their backs. When it was time to go back to camp, the men walked in the middle of the street in groups of at least three. They took off their belts, wrapped them around their fists with the heavy buckles swinging in front of them.

"That town was dangerous," Sylvio remembered. "The trip home was even tougher when we had to carry the guys who were too drunk to walk. Hard way to get an education but all part of regular army life."

In 1942 at the end of a three-year tour of duty, Sylvio, now a seasoned staff sergeant, was rotated back to the States along with many other men in the region. Having no naval escort, the troop ship zigzagged through German submarine-infested waters. Their ship was loaded with about twice its rated capacity; soldiers took their mess trays from the galley and carried them to the rail. Standing there shoulder-to-shoulder, they found it hard to eat when so many of their buddies were getting seasick over the rail.

Mississippi greeted them with a cold winter wind, blowing through their tropical uniforms right to the bone. At Camp Van Dorn, Sylvio was assigned to train raw recruits.

"They were so raw!" he remembered. "Crybabies. They had never experienced any discipline or hard work. That was a bad time for me and I had to find a way out. Whatever I was going to do or be, this was not it."

Desperately searching for an avenue of escape, the young soldier stretched beyond the limits of regulations and applied for three different assignments at once. When acceptances came on the same day for all of them, his commanding officer was furious.

"Make up your mind, Sergeant," he barked, "on the spot. You have one minute to make up your mind."

Officer's Candidate School was tempting. More pay, better uniform, more status. He could be a ninety-day-wonder lieutenant. Signal School would enhance his skills. The new Army Specialized Training Program would mean less pay—his sergeant's stripes had to go—but it would give him college courses. He thought, that's what I joined up for, isn't it? Eye on the goal.

"ASTP, Sir."

He was transferred to the University of Alabama for language school, but the army soon decided that engineers were needed more than linguists. He arrived in Yellow Springs, Ohio, at Antioch College to begin the engineering program in 1943.

My background was similar to his only in that my mother's family came to the New World in 1621, but from England to Plymouth, Massachusetts. The earliest immigrant was John Adams[1], a carpenter, and when he died in 1633, he left his thirty-five-year-old widow, Ellen Newton, with one little girl and two boys, all under the age of four. (Ellen lived to be eighty-four.) The inventory of John's estate speaks of the simplicity of their life: *¾ of a cow, one heifer and a cow calfe, 6 swine, 28 bushels of corn, 1 fether bed and bolster, 1 green rug, 2 blankets, 4 pr. Sheets, 2 table cloathes, 6 table napkins, 6 pillowbeers, 6 pillowes, 2 chests & a trunck, 2 cushions, 4 chairs, 4 small wool bed, 2 iron pots, 3 kettles, 2 frying panes, pewter vessel, 1 peece, debts due for goods sold, wooden vessel.*

The descendants slowly migrated westward. In 1686, John's great-grandson—also John—was born in Middlesex County, Massachusetts, but in 1734 he died in Windham County, Connecticut. His son—again John—was born in Connecticut but died in Berkshire County, Massachusetts, in 1782. His tombstone may still be found on a windy hillside near Alford. His son—known as Deacon John—took his family by horseback and boat to acres John had bought in New York State. They were the first settlers of the town of Bloomfield, Ontario County, south of Rochester. They rose from carpenters and farmers to owners of a small flooring business. As the brothers prospered and spread out, the firm expanded to branches in Boston, Syracuse, and Baltimore. The family became solidly middle class, reaching upward socially and financially through the Victorian age.

---

[1] Whose brother, Richard, arrived later and was the founder of the presidential Adams line

Adam & Jenny at the 1782 Alford, MA, grave

My great-great grandparents Hopkins welcomed Harriet
Tubman as a neighbor in Auburn, New York, and, Samuel
Hopkins Adams[2] recounts in his book *Grandfather Stories*, she
was more than a casual family adjunct. She frequently visited
the household and the children loved her for her entertainment

---

[2] Sam was a noted author of the early 20th Century; his *Grandfather Stories*
(NY, Random House, 1955) was a Book of the Month Club featured
selection, now republished by Syracuse University. He was my first cousin,
twice removed (meaning he was of my grandmother's generation).

value. She told them about the underground railroad, Sam recounted:

> Other "conductors" were seized, killed, mutilated, or jailed, and their charges haled back into servitude. Harriet never lost a passenger. If one of her band turned fainthearted and showed signs of wavering, she would draw the pistol that was always at her belt and exhort him, "Keep on, brothah, or die." Rewards totaling forty thousand dollars in gold were offered for her apprehension. "Dey might catch me," she would promise her Abolitionist supporters, "but not alive," and she would touch the butt of her pistol.

On the Adams side, two sons, Myron and Edward, were ministers. In the 1870s, when liberal religious thought began expanding, each preached a sermon on the same Sunday on the same subject, but in their respective Presbyterian and Congregational churches. The subject, a new definition of Hell, was so shocking that both men were tried and convicted of conspiracy and heresy. Their ordinations were revoked, then each minister took his congregation with him and formed a new Unitarian church.

My mother remembered going to Rochester Unitarian Sunday school in the very early 20th century and seeing a stern little old woman in a long black dress every Sunday; she was Susan B. Anthony.

These family threads of liberal thought and association influenced the formation of my character.

My father's people, better educated but less prosperous, were more recently arrived from Germany. His mother, Lucy Lorenz, was college educated at the end of the nineteenth century, when the education of girls was seldom taken seriously. His father, Julian Walter Case, was a Baptist minister with roots in Bremer County, Iowa.

My parents, Charlotte and Percy, met in high school. She told me she was fascinated with this boy who could write on the blackboard with the chalk in his left hand, switch hands when the writing reached the middle of the board, and continue uninterrupted with his right hand to the other side of the board. Evidently, there were other fascinations on both sides, for they became sweethearts. She waited for him when he went to France to drive an army ambulance in World War I. Miraculously, he was not wounded, although I sensed in him an inner wound from his terrible experiences. He never wanted to talk about it.

On September 11, 1920, Charlotte and Percy were wed in a ceremony conducted by Percy's father at the bride's Rochester home, at 24 Riverside Street. None of the parents looked with approval on the marriage. Charlotte's religious leanings were more liberal than her in-laws found comfortable; Percy showed a certain restlessness at his employment with Eastman Kodak that disturbed Charlotte's parents. All the reservations proved to be valid.

Percy was a self-taught engineer, very bright and curious. At Kodak he had learned some basics in the world of photography and now he would find his way out in the cold world. He was a *yuppie* before that word was invented to describe a young urban professional. He and Charlotte lived in Buffalo, Syracuse, and Denver, before settling at last in New York City. Along the way, he explored the technical side of photography and optics, becoming an expert in the field.

My brother David was born in Rochester in 1922, and I in Syracuse in 1926.

Charlotte continued her interest in music, studying voice at the Denver conservatory under the guidance of a coach who believed she had significant professional potential. For a time, she sang on the radio, but as her children came along she reached a decision point.

"Serious singing meant I had to compromise, put husband and children aside while I followed my dream," she told me in her retirement years. "My family was, in the end, more important. Percy was jealous of my music, too, and that helped me to decide. I gave it up, to sing only in amateur groups from that time on." Despite her firm statement that she took the right path, I heard the wistful note of yearning in her voice.

> **Opposite: Charlotte and Percy about 1936**

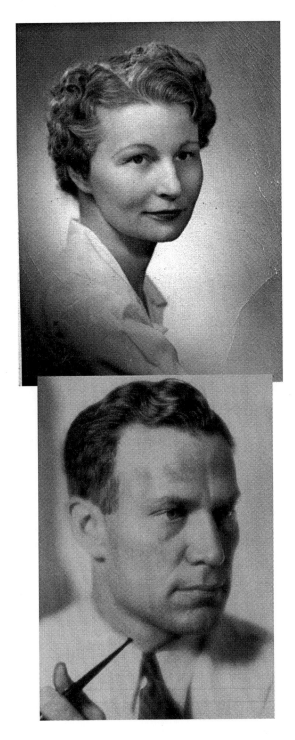

In New York during the Depression years, Percy rose to the position of general manager for the New York branch of Gevaert, the Belgian film company, then the largest in the world. While our family was never among the very rich, we were increasingly comfortable in our house on Grymes Hill, Staten Island.

70 Park Lane, Staten Island, New York

A sense of freedom marked my early life. I roamed through the thick woods, often alone. The few houses were dozens of yards apart. Our English stucco house, built into the side of the steep hill, looked out over the trees. In my bedroom—four full flights up from the ground level—I could survey the world below. Lower New York Bay spread out on my right, guarded by Sandy Hook; the Narrows separating Staten Island from Brooklyn—unsullied by the Verrazano Bridge, still to come—formed the waterway for great ships from all over the world; and to my left, if I leaned out precariously, just a hint of the famed skyline of Manhattan. Perched on that windowsill, I learned to hope and dream of my life to come. It seemed nothing wonderful was out of my reach.

My first five school years were in Public School #14 in the town at the foot of the hill. Surrounding the school was a settlement of Italian immigrant families, all poor and largely uneducated. In the depths of the Depression, some of my classmates had to take turns wearing the shared school shoes of their siblings. Although I was too young to take much notice of the difference between us, my teachers did. Imagine what a relief I must have been to those women struggling with unfamiliar languages and customs, coping with children who had eaten no breakfast. I wore starched and ironed dresses, my hair combed and beribboned. I spoke English well and came eager to learn. My house contained many books. Of course they indulged my every whim! I ran to Woolworth's at lunchtime to find the embroidery cotton they needed; they let me know I was very special. After school, I played Cowboys and Indians with gangs of ragamuffin kids, happily running in the side streets, galloping and shooting as I went.

Inevitably, I came home with the coarse language of the streets, upsetting both of my parents. The words are gone from my memory, but I can still taste the Fels Naphtha soap in my mouth. When my mother visited school one day and heard, two floors above, the teacher who would be mine in sixth grade yelling and cursing at her class, she made a decision. Before long, I was enrolled at the Staten Island Academy.

By this time, I had skipped two semesters of grades, so I entered private school the youngest of my sixth grade class, only ten years old. The class of about a dozen children had been together since kindergarten; I was the barbarian, untutored in the ways of the country club and Friday evening dancing classes. The circle closed to shut me out. At recess, both boys and girls ganged up to hurl playground balls in my direction. Sometimes, they reached their mark, and I returned to class with a bloody nose. In the locker room, girls giggled in corners and pointed toward me when I changed clothes. Puberty had not yet reached them, as it had me.

A personable young man, Henry White, taught sixth grade. All the girls had a crush on him. The year went pretty well academically, although in public school I had missed the more obscure subjects. My face still flushes when I remember reading a sentence aloud in class: "I hunted fossils in the dessert." The room exploded with derisive laughter. Poor me! 'Desert' had only one s, and I had never heard of a fossil.

Summer came at last. While the country club was foreign to me, I was entirely familiar with the sailing life, with the yacht club. This is a grand name for what was an old wooden building with a row of lockers, a hamburger stand, and a meeting room at the base of a long dock that reached into the small harbor. My delight was unbounded when I learned that Mr. White had a new boat, and my own mother was going to teach him the rudiments of sailing. In sailing circles, first names were always used, so he became Hank to me. I was to him, and to everyone except my family, Casey, derived from my last name, Case, and my initials, KC.

Like any novice, Hank was a little afraid of the sailboat. That made him a natural mark for experienced sailors, who taught him by scaring him to death.

"Keep your eye on the sail, Hank," said Mother. She sat beside him in the little boat. "Stay up in the wind. If it begins to luff or even get soft at the forward end, fall off just a tad until it's drawing full."

At the same time, another boat crept forward, coming up very close on Hank's windward side. When the boats were a few inches apart, rail to rail, someone made a noise. Hank glanced over his shoulder, caught sight of the other boat, turned pale, but heard mother say, "You're OK, Hank. Don't let go of the tiller for heaven sake, or you'll get hit. Just stay the course."

In this alarming way, Hank learned to stay cool. Eventually, he could hold his ground against competition.

As the summer wound down, Dad declared, "You're ready for racing, Hank." Back at school after Labor Day, my special relationship was obvious, even though I was careful to return to the more formal Mr. White. He would ruffle my hair and call me 'sailor', or ask whether I had been out on the water for the frostbite series.

I was an unattractive youngster, entering early puberty and beginning to fill out. By the time I was filled out in eighth grade, I was decidedly pudgy. The hostility of my classmates prompted me to assume the role of know-it-all. Accordingly, the social scene spiraled downward.

"Look at the baby! Here, catch this!" I tried to duck. It might have been a soccer ball or a hockey stick in the locker room. On the field, hockey sticks frequently tripped or bruised me.

On the bus, someone might push a boy into the seat next to me. "Oh no!" he would cry. "I'm next to Casey. I think I'm going to faint!" Then the boys collapsed laughing.

I was acutely aware of sprouting facial hairs that came along with my puberty but humiliated when a razor was left in my desk along with a bar of Lifebuoy deodorant soap. Hiding in one of the bathroom stalls for an hour, I wept tears of frustration and self-pity.

"I hate my body! Hate it!" Although I did well academically, I itched to escape.

One morning, toward the end of eleventh grade, I began my campaign.

"Dad, could I go to summer school this year?"

"What for? You having some kind of trouble in school?"

"Gosh no. It's going good. Only I realize that I already have all the credits I need for graduation. The only thing I'm missing is the fourth year of English, and there's going to be a class at school this summer. I could go to Cornell in September."

"But," Mother said, "you would miss graduation and all the parties next year. I don't think so."

"Mom, it wouldn't be the same." She could not guess that missing the parties was part of the idea. "The Academy is merging with the Day School next year. It will be all different, and the classes will be so big! I'd be lost there." The truth was that two very small struggling schools would join forces, expanding my class to nearly twenty. Why did they not point out to me that Cornell would offer a considerably larger class size? They never did.

I sensed something they did not. Knowing that Dad wished he had a college degree, I banked on arousing his pride in having so young a daughter in college. Before long, Dad and I were talking Mother into my plan.

, I was sixteen when I enrolled at Cornell University in the fall of 1942. The year began with an interview at the chemical engineering school. The office door swung open and I stepped into an imposing room, filled with bookshelves and a large desk. Sun shone through the ancient window.

"What makes you think you want to be a chemical engineer, Honey?" Dean Rhodes peered at me from under his thick dark eyebrows. It was more sneer than question and I sank into the brown leather chair. He leafed through my portfolio and conceded, "From your transcript, I conclude you could probably complete the work in good order. But why in the world would you want to do that? It's a long, hard five years, and we would never give you a diploma. We haven't graduated any girls from this school yet, and there are no plans to. What's wrong with home economics, anyway? You had better run along now, Sweetie." He waved me away as he put his glasses back on his nose and turned to papers on his desk. I rose from the chair and walked out of the office, my shoulders drooping.

My reaction was the most disheartening thing; I was completely intimidated. In my growing-up years, my parents had encouraged me to reach for any goal I desired, confident I could grasp it. I had been the academic star of all my classes — except Latin — and with a few short sentences from this man, I capitulated. My freshman year was an educational disaster.

At Thanksgiving, I went home for the holiday. Tired of commuting, and now that the nest was empty, Dad had persuaded my Mom to move to a Manhattan apartment. I pleaded with my parents to let me stay home. Even though I had nearly always been able to get my own way, this time they stood firm. I would finish the year. The one redeeming feature at Cornell was that boys and I discovered one another. There were many sailors enrolled in the Navy's V-12 program. In my eyes, all of them were handsome and manly in their crisp dress blues.

At the end of the year, my parents thought perhaps Cornell was too big for so young a girl, and they suggested a transfer to Antioch College, from which my brother had graduated. In September, 1943, I packed my suitcase and boarded the train for Ohio.

HELLO

The crowded train lurched to a stop, waited a few minutes, then began to back slowly into a siding. Groans rumbled through the car as the conductor appeared, striding briskly.

"Sir," I called to him, "are we going to be on time?"

He paused. "Honey, if we get there the day we're scheduled, we're on time. Where ya going?"

"Yellow Springs," I replied.

His rejoinder was a grunted "Hunh," and he disappeared through the other end of the car. Frustrated, I looked at my watch again. "We should be there by now," I thought, looking out at the Ohio fields of ripening corn. An inexperienced traveler — I was only seventeen — the uncertainty made me apprehensive. I checked again to be sure my suitcase was still overhead (Where would it have gone?) and settled back into my seat. At length, the train began to move again, each car jerking sharply as the car ahead tugged it into action. Lunchtime came and went, but I was not thinking about food.

"Next stop, Yellow Springs," cried the conductor. We must have been on time, because it was still Wednesday, September 29, 1943, although later than mid-morning. I hauled my heavy suitcase down from the overhead rack and lugged it toward the door where the conductor took it from me and set it down on the platform. As the train pulled away, I realized I was the only passenger to alight here, and I had no idea where to go. From around the corner, a young woman appeared, hurrying toward me. She was blonde, angular, taller than my five-foot-two.

"You must be Katharine Case?" I nodded. If she told me her name, I quickly forgot it. "I'm here to welcome you to Antioch College. I'm a senior, and we'll be living in the same house," she added. Together, we navigated a few blocks in the small town, taking turns with the suitcase. As we walked, she chattered on.

"I hear you're transferring from Cornell. This is better, I can tell you. They think they're so great, but it's a party school. Say, tonight after supper, you'll have to come over to the science building and meet my boyfriend. You'll just love him. He'll be there around eight." She showed me my space in a small bedroom and my bed on the screened porch, and left me alone. I unpacked my clothes, folding them into one of the small chests of drawers, thinking how different this would be from the two-girl room I'd had at Cornell. This big old house creaked with the steps of so many girls, crowded like sardines. The furnishings were old and few—a straight-backed chair or two, and three beds inside. I would be sleeping on the screened porch along with three others. At least the bedding looked ample for cold winter nights.

I would soon learn that the crowding in dormitories was caused by the presence of many Army men in engineering training. They had the regular dorms; we had what the administration could find. The women I met seemed friendly and the atmosphere was relaxed.

After supper, my welcome committee gathered me up to meet 'the boyfriend' at the science building. In front of the red brick building were cement steps and two low brick walls. Half a dozen men in uniform lounged about, smoking and talking.

"There he is!" She led me up to the one who was neither lounging nor smoking and made introductions. "Sylvio, this is Kati. She just arrived on the train this afternoon. Be nice to her."

As I shook his hand, I looked into his face and saw a serious person with a strange expression. His brown eyes fixed on mine and held my gaze firmly as he held my hand. It was not anything he said that caught me, but his gaze. In that moment, I sensed I had him hooked. In my brash and saucy way, I twirled my skirt and turned to one of the other soldiers.

"Where are you from?" I asked as an opener.

"Where do you want me to be from, Honey? I'll be from wherever you want." The others hooted in appreciation of this witticism. I glanced back at Sylvio whose expression had not changed nor his gaze wavered. I pulled out my old game.

"Well here, give me your hand. I can read your palm. In a few minutes I'll know where you came from and things about you that you never dreamed." His hand came right out, palm up.

"Tell me what you see. Am I going to live a long time?"

"Well," I pondered, staring intently at the hand, "your lifeline is pretty long, but there are jagged places in it, indicating pretty close calls. On the whole, I think you'll live to tell your grandchildren about your adventures."

Several more palms were thrust forward. "Tell me." "Tell me." It worked every time. I was always careful to find very long lifelines, knowing these were soldiers and possibly in danger. I played more with the heart line, and told them to behave better because their health lines looked a little wavy. They were enchanted.

When I tired of the game, I backed away and sat down next to Sylvio. The nameless girl was beside him on the other side, but he had turned away from her. Before I could speak, he said quietly, "OK men, time to go. Back in the barracks by nine." He rose to go, and the others did the same. Even though all of them were privates, I would learn Sylvio was an acting captain, leader of the platoon. Without another word, they marched off toward the dormitory.

The girl and I walked slowly back to our house. She told me that a week before she had taken his eyeglasses to be repaired for him.

"That meant I had to read his lessons to him. I kept the glasses for a couple of days after they were fixed, but he didn't know. I'm trying to get his attention, but he's so distant!" I thought I understood; she chattered on all the way home.

That night as I lay in bed, I thought it over. What was it about Sylvio? What had happened out there?

In the next few days, he telephoned me several times, asking me for a date. By this time, I was caught up in a flurry of classes and not really interested. The second week, a movie I wanted to see came to town, and he asked me again. I said yes. Although many details of that evening are still clear in my memory, I no longer remember what the film was. It could have been the latest Hitchcock movie, 'Shadow of a Doubt', or Ethel Waters in 'Cabin in the Sky'. Most of the war movies of the time held no interest for me, but I think Gary Cooper and Ingrid Bergman in 'For Whom the Bell Tolls' was probably the one.

On the walk home through the warm fall evening we spoke quietly of this and that. Autumn leaves crunched under our feet, and street lamps flickered through branches now preparing for winter. He grasped my hand.

In reference to nothing in particular, Sylvio stated firmly, "You're going to marry me."

"Oh, really!" I replied archly, "I am engaged to a lieutenant colonel!"

This was a bit of a stretch, although I *was* corresponding with such an officer, exchanging warm words of affection with a lonely young man in the Italian campaign.

"Hell," declared Sylvio, "I don't care if you're engaged to General MacArthur, **you're going to marry me.**" It was not a command, certainly not a question. He was telling me a fact in all seriousness. He kissed me gently on the cheek as we parted at the front door.

Once more, as I lay in bed, I thought it over. What was it about Sylvio? What had happened out there? I don't think I realized that although I was a girl playing games with boys, Sylvio was not a boy and he did not play games.

Little by little in the ensuing weeks we saw more and more of each other until we were a steady pair. On his small private's pay, he could only treat me to cartons of chocolate milk and bags of pretzels as we sat in a campus lounge. We talked non-stop; we exchanged personal histories. How different we were! He came from the French-speaking culture in a small industrial Maine town, born of Canadian parents. I was a New Yorker, the younger child of a prosperous engineer and his musical wife. Sylvio was not tall, was dark, not exactly handsome, except for a sensuous curve of lip. He was energetic, slender, with broad shoulders and skinny waist. I was not tall either. My hair was medium-blonde, and I was certainly not handsome. I was overweight and usually tired, but he told me I had an indefinable quality that came across as sexy, something of a wildcat to be tamed. I was flattered by his description, even if I did not understand it.

"Let me see your ID bracelet," I coaxed. "What does it say on the back side? Is it from your girlfriend?"

"I'll tell you what. If you can get it off, you can have it."

The tricky catch took me two days to decipher, but at last, in triumph, I slipped it off. The engraving on the back read: *Love, Lillian.*

"And who is Lillian?" I asked, taken aback.

"Oh, she's just a girl I've known all my life. My family picked her out for me, expects me to marry her, I guess. But it isn't going to happen. I have never asked her, never promised. I think I was waiting for you."

Sylvio's thrifty habits produced a little cache of funds, and he asked me for a date in Springfield for dinner and dancing. Yellow Springs offered no such luxuries, and I was excited. I donned my best pink cashmere sweater, adorned with the pearls my father had given me, a good navy wool skirt, dancing shoes, and even my one pair of silk stockings. The other girls in the dorm helped me with a dab of perfume; Mari Sabusawa, the exotic Japanese beauty in the house, provided a pretty pale green satin ribbon. She pulled back my hair and wrapped the ribbon around my head, tying it at the nape of my neck. Mari always knew just the right touch. She was a library major, but she looked like no other librarian I knew. In a couple of years, she would find her lifetime career, marrying an author and assisting him in research. He was James Michener.

Springfield lies about a dozen miles north of Yellow Springs, reached by public bus. When we arrived, Sylvio placed my hand on his arm and led me to the local hotel dining room. A band played swing music as three couples moved around the dance floor. White linen cloths draped over candle-lighted tables . The head waiter, seeing a romantic soldier and his girl, placed us at a small table in a discreet alcove. After discussing the menu with me, Sylvio ordered for both of us, and grandly added a bottle of wine. That accomplished, he asked me if I wanted to dance.

I was really nervous about this part. In spite of my high school dancing classes, I had never really learned to relax and follow. I smiled and took his hand as he led me to the dance floor. Within a few steps, I realized we were two of a kind; he couldn't dance either! I began to relax and we moved around the floor without stepping on one another very much. As our great-grandparents rightly feared, the point of dancing is holding each other close, close enough to whisper sweet words. The band was playing, the vocalist singing: *I'll get by, as long as I have you. Though there be rain and darkness, too, I'll not complain, I'll see it through. Poverty may come to me, it's true, but what care I, dear, I'll get by, as long as I have you.*

We sat down at the table again; his eyes met mine.

"What?" I asked.

"Nothing," he answered. "I'm just looking." There it was again, that gaze that looked right into my innermost self. I saw myself reflected in his eyes, and suddenly felt pretty.

Dinner was set before us, Sylvio poured the wine and he offered a toast: "To a beautiful evening with a beautiful girl." I think I blushed. Conversation continued at a good pace. He told me about his classes and described the physical training in Glen Helen, a forested nature preserve owned by the college.

"I'm a regular Tarzan. We have a timed two-mile course, mostly swinging from rope to rope over the glen, though there are walls to scale and at the end where the river is wide, a swim. All this with packs on our backs." Even allowing for natural braggadocio, I was awed.

What we ate is long lost in the mists of memory, but I think we finished the bottle of wine. (Typical of the times, no one asked whether I was old enough to consume alcohol.) By the time we finished dinner, he paid the bill, and when we were outside on the street once more, he glanced at his watch.

"Oh gosh, is it that late? I'm afraid we've missed the last bus back to Yellow Springs!"

"What now, Sylvio? It's a pretty long walk. Can we hitch a ride?"

"No, I wouldn't want to spoil a wonderful evening. I'll get a taxi." I was too naïve to guess this was part of the plan all along. When the cab pulled up, he handed me in, then followed into the back seat, gave the driver instructions, and turned toward me. The wine, the dinner, the late hour, all had combined; I laid my head on his shoulder and slept all the way home. In front of my house, he woke me and I sleepily stumbled out. As Sylvio paid the bill, I heard the driver say, "You ain't gunna let her get away with that are ya, Buddy?" He did, though, and I managed to float inside, undress, and fall into bed in a sleepy, romantic haze.

Temperance was not in my nature. The next day, I decided to replace his ID bracelet and it would say on the back:
Owned and Operated by K.L. Case
9-29-43
When I gave it to him, he looked at it and smiled. "We'll see about that!" but he let me put it on his wrist.

The following week brought bad news. For whatever obscure military reason, the troops were moving west to Purdue University in Lafayette, Indiana.

"No, don't cry, Kati. The world isn't coming to an end. I will be right here with you, sometimes in letters, sometimes in phone calls, always in my heart." He gave me his handkerchief, and I dried my eyes. At least we had until Saturday afternoon, two whole days. Sylvio never missed a class, and I may have attended to mine, but my heart was somewhere else.

At last, we young lovers stood on the station platform, locked in a long, hot embrace. An officer ordered, "Get on the train, Soldier." My eyes blurred as the train slowly gained momentum, and Sylvio was gone.

FINDING MY FEET

Left without a romantic distraction, I should have settled down to my studies. It did not happen. I was almost too tired to drag my overweight self—probably 170 pounds—around the campus; nothing captured my attention for very long. At last, the quarter was over, my sorry grades recorded, and I went home to my parents' apartment in Manhattan. This was to be the beginning of my job in Antioch's work-study program.

Despite my lethargy, I managed to send a letter off to Sylvio every day. He was a faithful correspondent, but sometimes his sense of humor brought strange messages. I retrieved the mail from the front hall of the apartment and took his latest letter to my bedroom to read it in private. Slitting open the envelope, I pulled out several sheets of paper. I gasped. All of it was in Morse code!

"Mom," I called, "where's the encyclopedia?"

"On the bookshelves in the front hall, Dear. What do you need?"

"I need a crib sheet for Morse code."

"What is a crib sheet, Katharine?"

"Never mind. I found it."

Dragging the big book back to my bed, I gathered paper and pencil and went to work. As the words began to appear, I realized they were—oh no!—in French.

"Of course," I groaned, "he's a fast key operator. This was probably much faster for him than script. And French is his first language. It's not even my second language any more! Oh Sylvio!"

The first line began:

-- --- -. -.-. .... . .-. .. -- --- -. -.-. --- . ..- .-.

The double translation entertained me for hours.

My first day on the college co-op job arrived shortly after New Year's Day. Probably because of my youth, I had been assigned to Mount Sinai Hospital in Manhattan, only a few blocks' walk from my parents' new apartment. I was assigned to the reception desk in the Private Pavilion, to answer the telephone and track down staff members or take messages.

The reception area was luxurious. My desk was fine furniture, well polished, hardly what I would have expected of a hospital. Soft carpeting muted sounds; even the telephone bell was melodious. Sunlight slanted in through south-facing windows. It seemed more hotel than hospital. On the second day, I lost consciousness.

Fainting was well-known to me. I had fainted several times at Antioch, once breaking a bone in my ankle when I fell down a short flight of stairs. For reasons buried in my mysterious mind, I had felt I needed to hide such embarrassments. I claimed to have tripped on something. This time, however, the adults took charge.

After an examination and an interview with a doctor, I was put to bed for a lengthy test. A mask was fitted over my face, and I was admonished to lie still and breath normally. Sleep overtook me almost at once. At that time, the only way to ascertain metabolic rate was to measure the amount of oxygen exhaled in a predetermined amount of time. The diagnosis was clear: severe hypothyroidism.

The doctor explained, "You're a very sick young lady. I'll write a prescription for medication you must take every day. And you will stay in bed, probably for at least two months, and then gradually you will gain strength. Within six months, you should be as good as new!"

The bright spot in all this gloom was that I could stay home from college. Actually, I was too tired to care very much. I fell gratefully into bed.

For a few weeks, I languished in bed, reading Sylvio's daily letters of worry about me and writing back reassurances.

Being young and basically healthy, I soon tired of playing Camille. To his surprise, the doctor discharged me to normal activity in about a month. That evening, my father took his usual place at the head of the family dinner table. He was forty-seven, a ruggedly handsome man, about six feet tall, trim, and undeniably distinguished looking. His features, his hands, everything about him was larger than life. At the other end of the table, Mother sat quietly, self-possessed. She was a pretty woman, slender, only about five feet four inches tall, but equal to any challenge. A smile flickered about her face as she listened to me, trying to stand up to this big man. I announced,

"I am not returning to college."

Now was time for a reality check. Dad responded, "What are you going to do, then?"

"Get a job, of course!"

"Oh? And what are you prepared to do?"

I had no idea. All my life, my parents had told me I could achieve anything I set my mind to; I was confident.

"Get this straight," my father went on, "you have wasted a good deal of time and made precious little progress. Now, to prepare yourself for at least minimal employment, you will enroll at Katherine Gibbs Secretarial School."

Since I could not think of a sensible rejoinder, I promised to get myself down there the following day. I signed up for typing and shorthand and endured several weeks of crushing boredom. Shorthand was tedious to learn, but I mastered the rudiments. Typing was no easier than piano practice had been, years before. I had little talent for it.

Eventually, certificate in hand, I set out to find a job. My Cornell friend, June, was working at the National Broadcasting Company, and she told me she liked it.

"Why not?" I thought. "I should be able to do anything she can do." I entered the RCA Building.

The application completed, I decided to walk home. The day was pleasant and I had nothing pressing on my calendar. Home was several miles away — forty-five blocks straight up

Fifth Avenue. The fountain in front of the Plaza Hotel sparkled in the sunshine, Central Park was still sleeping on this late winter day. I saw no hansom cabs trotting along with their usual cargo of visiting sailors. Traffic on Fifth Avenue was fairly light, going both north and south; few people who lived in Manhattan kept a car. Buses and subways were much more efficient, but walking was more fun. I smiled at the doormen as I passed, and they tipped their caps in response. In almost no time, I was passing the Metropolitan Museum. I could have jumped on one of the double-decked buses to speed my way, but I kept walking until I reached the doorway of number 1136.

"Good morning, Miss Case." Emilio held the door open, then stepped in to hold the elevator door for me.

"Lovely day," I smiled. "Thank you, Emilio."

I stepped out into the tiny tenth floor lobby and pushed a key into the lock of apartment B. There on the bookshelf in the hall was a yellow envelope—a telegram addressed to me.

"Mom, look! NBC wants me to start work on Monday morning."

Why a telegram? It was a fairly common mode of communication, fast and more confidential than leaving a telephone message. This was Friday, and a letter would have arrived on Monday.

At the appointed hour, I presented myself at the personnel department.

"Have you been fitted for a uniform?" the receptionist asked, looking over a paper that evidently held my assignment.

"No, what kind of uniform?"

"An NBC guide uniform. Take this request down to the second floor and find the guest relations office. They'll take it from there. And good luck!" She waved me toward the elevator.

My intense training program started at once. My head whirled with the script I had to memorize, the rules I had to know, the route I would take. By Wednesday, I went along with an experienced guide to see how he did it, and by Thursday morning, I found myself confronting a group of about twenty-five tourists and saying brightly, "Good morning and welcome to the National Broadcasting Company studios. I am Kati, and I will be your guide as we travel through the world of broadcasting. Step into the elevator and face the doors please. Our first stop will be the sixth floor."

I had entered a world completely new to me. My co-workers were, mostly, stage-struck would-be actors, volatile and dramatic. Every day brought another chapter of what might have been a soap opera called *Stage Door*. Although the Broadway stage was their ultimate goal, there were many opportunities in the casts of the many popular radio soap operas like *One Man's Family*. The guide job offered flexible hours, allowing time to haunt casting directors' offices during the daytime. Recruits came and went regularly according to casting opportunities.

Tours lasted until eleven at night. Our uniforms were light blue wool suits with straight skirts—trousers for the young men—the NBC logo emblazoned on the jacket pocket. Our shoes were plain black, high-heeled pumps and we took turns using eyebrow pencil to draw seams on each other's legs, neatly shaved and slathered with tan makeup. At least the seams never twisted like real stockings, unobtainable in wartime. The tan makeup came off on my slip.

In six months, I had outlasted everyone else and was senior on the staff. I was having a wonderful time, making ninety dollars a month—more than my friend June, who was typing in the business office. Even though half my salary went to pay my parents for board and room, I had plenty left over to satisfy all my needs.

Occasionally, I was assigned to the reception desk on the eighth floor, to give me a break from touring. The NBC Symphony Orchestra was one of the best in the world, alternately led by Arturo Toscanini and Leopold Stokowski. The men of the orchestra emerged from Studio 8H during their breaks, and I could tell just by watching them who was the conductor of the day. If they streamed out angry, swearing — in several languages — and threatening to quit, I knew they were playing for the great ego, Stokowski. But if they came thoughtfully, gesticulating in frustration, discussing how they could get it right, I knew they had been challenged to hear the same music that was driving Maestro Toscanini. This great man looked, when he came to work, like nothing so much as a bent, timid Italian greengrocer, with his too-small fedora perched squarely on his head. A feeble man? Oh no! A powerhouse. I sometimes peeked in during rehearsal. This small man was transformed on the podium into a giant, driving a hundred musicians at a furious pace, trying to catch up with his inner vision.

My tours were all about radio broadcasting. The guests were fascinated by the sound effects machines and delighted to hear their own voices carried over a microphone. By 1944, NBC had started broadcasting television programs a few hours a week. Very few people had seen TV, and most had never heard of it. Receivers were contained in large cabinets, the top lifted on hinges, and the small black and white images were reflected from the cathode ray tube to a mirror on the under side of the lid. Since the picture tube was very large, this was the only practical arrangement. When television was demonstrated to the tours, the reaction was always the same:

"What's it good for?"

"It's ugly. Who would want one?"

Even seeing themselves moving on the mirrored lid left them cold. They remained unimpressed, certain it had no future.

One day, during a break, I decided to stroll down to the street-level drugstore for a Coke. As I sat at the counter, and gave my order, I glanced to my left. And I glanced again. His eyes met mine. His head moved from side to side.

'No', he was telling me. I moved my head up and down in assent and looked away. As I sipped my Coke, I marveled, Wow. While hundreds of screaming girls jostle outdoors, here sits Frank Sinatra, peacefully drinking his coffee. He had entered the building for an evening broadcast, coming in a caravan of limousines through the secure underground entrance. Before television, the faces of celebrities were largely unknown. His shock of black hair and his skinny body were still his own property. Feeling a professional pride in protecting a fellow insider, I paid my bill and returned to work.

The real stars of the broadcast world were radio news announcers, bringing word from both war fronts into American living rooms. On June 6, 1944, I haunted the newsroom every moment I could get away. John Vandercook and Richard Harkness, both towering figures, read dispatches from the front as they were received by wire. The great armada had steamed from England to the Norman coast. Allied troops were storming the beaches. All ears turned east to hear little snatches of information coming back from those bloody landings. This was the heyday of H.V. Kaltenborn and Walter Winchell. Reception crackled and faded sometimes as Edward R. Murrow sent word from his post in London, with a backdrop of the tolling of Big Ben.

"Oh God," I prayed, "take care of David Kiesler and Johnny Domalakes. Keep them safe. Keep them all safe from this horror." David, my lieutenant colonel, and Johnny, one of the men in his company who wrote to me sometimes, were somewhere in the European theater. My brother, a new Navy officer, was steaming out in the Pacific Ocean on an aircraft carrier. I felt guilty gratitude that Sylvio was out of danger in Indiana, for now at least.

Pictures of actual war scenes appeared only in movie newsreels, after the cartoon and before the feature film. Life Magazine photos from the front never carried the immediacy that television would one day capture. For now, imagination mixed with fantasy, created a somewhat romantic picture of battle.

My working hours were long and my shift often ended at eleven, just time to race out of my uniform, don street clothes, and run down the street to catch the last double-decked bus up Fifth Avenue to home at Ninety-fifth Street. Wartime New York was glamorous, exciting. While street lights were dim, street crime was infrequent, although even then there were prohibitions against entering Central Park at night. No danger stalked the public bus. In fact, the last bus generally sounded like a scout camp by firelight; everyone sang. It was *Tipperary* or *When the Lights Go On Again* or *The White Cliffs of Dover*. War and heroism and romance were in the air.

COLLEGE – ARMY STYLE

Meanwhile, out in Lafayette, Indiana, Sylvio was having his own adventures. One winter day, his letter — this time in simple handwriting— expressed exasperation.

"Well, my dear, I'm packing again. Uncle's changed his mind one more time. Seems like the army doesn't need more engineers, after all. They're looking toward the invasion of Japan, and they expect it to be bloody."

Reading these words, my heart sank. Most of his classmates had already washed out of the program and been sent into combat. Was he next? To Japan? It had been a year since news of the Bataan death march had reached home, and I was horrified. But the letter went on:

"The other day, all of us were put through a kind of aptitude test. Uncle loves those. The next day, I was called into the commandant's office. He asked me 'Fournier, did you ever think about a career as a doctor?' Hey, I'm nobody's fool. Put two and two together real quick, snapped to attention, saluted and answered 'All my life, Sir!' (I know my way around the army by now.) So, this quarter's over and it's off to Urbana. I'll start the program at the University of Illinois in February and, believe it or not, I'll be a pre-med graduate by October! After that, I'll get an assignment to fill time before the med school class convenes in the fall of 1945. Tell me this, Sweetie: did you ever think about a career as a doctor's wife? Love, Sylvio."

Tears of relief coursed down my cheeks as I folded the letter back into its envelope. A doctor's wife! How would that be? I had to admit it did not have a very musical ring in my ear. Sylvio as a practicing physician? I could imagine him as a researcher, and perhaps that was the direction he would take. Somehow, I judged him unable to empathize with patients. His strongly voiced comments about those 'damned crybabies' in Mississippi echoed in my mind. Whatever lay ahead, it was not bombs and guns, at least for now.

That night at dinner, I tried — without success — to impress my father with the tale of this soldier-about-to-be-a-doctor.

"You say he's in the regular army? Not much of a recommendation."

"But Daddy, the regular army doesn't count any more. Everybody's in the service now. He's just more experienced than most, that's all. And he's going to be a doctor. Wait 'til you meet him, you'll see."

Dad had heard my protestations of love before and he usually paid little attention to them, but a young girl with stars in her eyes could not appreciate her parents' reservations. What did it matter if he grew up in a foreign culture? And five years' difference in age wasn't really much, was it? I was already seventeen.

As weeks wore on, Sylvio wrote me long letters about the classes he was taking, sixteen semester hours squeezed into a twelve-week quarter, including military drill and physical training. Of the two hundred who started classes, twenty-two would graduate. Competition was fearsome as the bottom of the class was cut every week.

He traveled on to Urbana, to the pre-medicine program at the University of Illinois. His letters were often sprinkled with quotations from the Shakespeare plays he was reading in class. The army was providing a surprisingly rounded education.

INTERLUDE

During the time Sylvio studied and drilled in Illinois, I spread my wings. Between daily letters to him, I managed an occasional one to the officer in Italy, 'my' lieutenant colonel, David Keisler. Now that the medicine was doing its work and I was growing thinner, I felt better about myself. I suppose that shone through, because I attracted attention from two young men, very different, and yet in one way the same. Both were looking for wives, and I was interviewed for the job.

Richard — I think there was a III after his name — was the scion of a millionaire from Long Island at a time when *millionaire* meant something. That summer, my dad, as an expert consultant about new directions in color photography, supervised an experimental photo shoot for advertising purposes, and just for fun, he invited Mother and me to go along. The locale was the East Hampton estate of Richard's father. Professional models lounged around the pool while shutters snapped, catching them in sunshine and in shade. My task was to keep out of the way and be reasonably unobtrusive, although I was invited to don a bathing suit and enjoy the swimming pool. While the photography was proceeding at one end of the pool and deck, I paddled around at the other end. Suddenly, I was startled to hear, "Don't you associate with those other beautiful women?"

I turned to look up at the diving board and saw the very image of what is meant by 'Adonis.' Brown eyes sparkled mischievously under a strand of light brown hair falling carelessly over his forehead. His muscular body was tanned to perfect bronze, set off by close-fitting white swim trunks. Not having cavorted on European beaches, I had never seen a swimmer so scantily clad.

"I'm only a spectator, not a participant," I returned, wishing I could think of something more clever to say.

"Well so am I!" and he dived into the water, scarcely leaving a ripple.

When he surfaced, flipping the errant lock from his eyes, I exclaimed, "Well done! You're good!"

"Oh, not necessarily good, but I can dive pretty well. Where do you keep yourself when you're not playing mermaid?"

And so it went, casual boy-girl banter. When it was time for me to dry off and get dressed, he had my phone number.

About a week later, he called and asked me to dinner and a show; of course, I accepted happily. When he came to fetch me, I was struck by the perfection of his tailoring. No ready-made Brooks Brothers' suit could possibly have been as flawless in every detail. The fabric was soft as cashmere. Of course! It <u>was</u> cashmere. His shirt cuffs extended exactly three-quarters of an inch below the navy blue sleeves; my seamstress eye was sure of that. His trousers were light tan, and his loafers sported tassels. I only hoped my dress was up to the company, but I do not think he noticed it.

It turned out Richard had a mission: he was searching for a wife, and he had very definite specifications in mind. He had his future all mapped out; now he was coloring in the details. While we were enjoying a marvelous dinner in the Plaza Hotel dining room, he held my hand and mused, "My wife will have a lot to live up to. First, she will need to be a gracious hostess, because I expect to entertain frequently. Of course, she will have staff to keep the household together, but she will need to be a competent manager."

"Whew! Sounds like a tall order. Think you can find someone like that?"

"I'm looking." He winked at me, pushed back that lock of hair, and then went on, "She will be the mother of my three sons. That's important."

"I guess so! What if she gives you daughters?"

"Won't happen. I intend to have three sons."

"Oh."

He told me a lot about his favorite sport, polo. I think his wife was to be an enthusiastic spectator while he played.

Richard was much better than this sounds. He was amusing when he wasn't laying down job descriptions. That particular evening, I was feeling pensive and sometimes fell silent. Twice, he tossed a penny across the table, saying, 'penny for your thoughts'. I came back to life then, but soon lapsed into quiet again. He pitched another penny, and I smiled. Suddenly, he glanced at his watch and exclaimed, "Oh god, we'll miss the curtain. I didn't realize it was so late."

He quickly paid the tab and we sailed off to find a taxi. During the intermission, he turned to me and said, "I hope you didn't want to go back to the Plaza again. I don't think I can show my face there."

"What? I thought you behaved like a gentleman."

"Well, not quite. We were in such a rush I forgot to leave a tip. All the waiter found was two pennies on the table." We looked at each other and exploded in laughter.

The exploration of my qualifications extended to several evenings. He took me to a delightful place called *Louis á la Fourchette*, an old speakeasy. It had retained the solid front door; you had to knock, and when the small window in the door slid open, announce your name. If you were on the reservations list, the door flew open .

"Monsieur! Mademoiselle! Bienvenu!" The maitre d', smiling a welcome, waved us in.

The menu had several choices, but the price of dinner was always the same: $3.95, not including cocktails or wine. You could choose *steak à poivre* or perhaps *saumon en papillote*. That was my favorite—I loved it when the waiter pierced the parchment and fragrant steam burst from the fish in a little white cloud. My parents had taken me there, and I was truly impressed to have a date who could afford such a luxury. As we were waiting to be seated, a man burst through the door and almost literally elbowed us aside. He was seated immediately, with much bowing and scraping. Richard whispered, "That's Brooks Atkinson, the theatre critic for the New York Times. They're probably afraid of him."

With my father's counsel, I had learned to handle the question of cocktails quite handily. No one ever inquired as to my age, but I wanted to be very conservative.

"I'll have a vermouth cassis, please. On the rocks."

I think I never had a date who had any idea what that was, but pretending sophistication, they let it pass. The bartender always knew; it was a nearly harmless concoction of vermouth and crème de cassis, a blackberry liqueur.

After dinner, we went to Madison Square Garden to see the Barnum and Bailey circus, but the litany of wifely duties continued. Poor Richard! He could hardly be expected to understand the world as most people did. His family really was very rich; he knew nothing but the finest of everything.

I must have failed the examination, because I do not remember that our dates continued for a long time. I certainly never met his family.

Pierre was another occasional date, but I did meet his mother. He was a page at NBC, and we frequently brought bag lunches to eat on the observation deck on top of the RCA building. He was slight, with dark hair and, I think, glasses. Pierre did not have the 'gift of gab' that makes a successful tour guide, but he was steady and reliable, with a nice sense of humor. We liked each other, and enjoyed swapping stories about the tourists or about the soap opera scenarios we witnessed in the locker rooms.

"Is Sybil still mooning over that producer? She has no idea what happened, has she?"

"No. Poor kid thought he was in love with her. Took her out a few times, laid her on the casting couch in his office, got sick of her mooning and went hunting for somebody else."

"Really? Is that what happened? She was throwing up yesterday in the locker room. She wants a part in the worst way."

We shook our heads. Neither of us had any interest in an acting career; in this, we were practically alone, and that gave us a bond of sympathy. When the Roxy had a good movie—like Bing Crosby in *Going My Way*—we sometimes took in the morning show together before reporting to work. By unspoken understanding, we each paid our own way; he seemed always to be a little short.

"Would you come to my house for dinner tomorrow night?" he asked uncertainly, adding, "My mother wants to meet you." Pierre seemed to think I might refuse.

"Of course, I'd be delighted. Tell me where you live and what time I'm to show up."

He wrote it down and handed me the slip of paper. The address was an apartment on Park Avenue in the Seventies, a very posh address. Since our work schedules were different that day, it was awkward for him to escort me, so I would come by myself.

At home that afternoon, I told Mother about the date. "What should I wear? I think a little black dress would be the best, don't you?"

Mother knew the only likely little black dress was hanging in her closet, and with my newly slender figure, I could probably fit into it.

"Oh, all right. Go try it on."

I did, and found it just a little matronly.

"Mom, what have you done with those curtains you took down from your bathroom window? Could I have them?"

"Yes, you may, but whatever for?"

"You'll see."

I cut the sheer white fabric into long strips and fashioned them into two ruffles, then basted one on each shoulder, from the neckline to the bottom of the elbow-length sleeves. I thought they looked fetching, but in retrospect I think they were possibly a little much. Mother smiled but made no comment, just said, "You look lovely, dear. Have a wonderful time."

Off I went in a taxi and arrived at the appointed hour. The doorman was obviously expecting me, and handed me over to the elevator man. We ascended to, perhaps, the fifteenth floor. Evidently, Pierre heard the elevator, for he opened the door before I could knock.

"Mother," he announced, "may I present Katharine Case? We call her Kati, though."

Mrs. de Valloniers was a slender fashion plate in a flowing gown of deep purple, her black hair drawn severely back to display elaborate jeweled earrings. I almost thought I should curtsey, but never having done that, I refrained, simply grasping her outstretched hand.

"Good evening, my dear," she smiled. "Won't you come in?"

The living room was lavishly furnished in what I took to be European style. She motioned me to a chair, and the maid offered me a glass of sherry. Delicate little tidbits were arrayed on a golden plate on the inlaid and gilded table next to me.

"What a beautiful table," I exclaimed. "Is it very old?"

"Yes it is," she responded with pleasure. "That table belonged to the count and countess—my maternal grandparents. It is French, as you may have guessed. You do have a discerning eye. Tell me about yourself. I understand you live on Fifth Avenue. Have you always lived there?"

We were called to dinner, and as Pierre's mother led me to my place, the questions continued unabated. Thinking she might be interested in my mother's lineage, stretching back to Pilgrim days, I outlined a little about the Adams family. At once, she made a connection with the Adams presidents, and she held tenaciously to her conclusion that I was one of those Adamses. Pierre busied himself with dinner, scarcely looking up from his plate. In the delusion that we were simply making polite social conversation, I babbled on. It seemed strange to me that she wanted to know details of my father's 'position', as she called his job. Finally, she observed, "That's such an unusual frock you are wearing. So original. Where do you find such interesting things, my dear?"

This is where I really put my foot in it. I did not want to say I was wearing my mother's dress, but I certainly enjoyed bragging about my prowess with a needle. As I described how I had cut up the curtains and constructed the ruffles, her eyes grew very large. One eyebrow arched high on her forehead.

Pierre lighted her cigarette, inserted into a long, black and gold holder. She rose slowly from the table and swept from the room, to be seen no more. Shortly thereafter, Pierre took me by the hand and led me to the elevator.

When we stepped into a cab, after Pierre gave the driver my address, he turned to me. "Please forgive my mother. She's always trying to match me up with somebody. I wish she'd just relax." He sounded so forlorn that I reached out and patted his hand.

"That's OK, Pierre. I gather I flunked." Both of us burst out laughing.

When I told Mother about the strange evening, she smiled and asked, "Don't you know what that was about? She was a European title trolling for an American fortune!"

"Oh. No wonder she dismissed me so suddenly. I think everything was fine until I told her about my home-made dress alteration. What a ninny I was not to know how to play along!" Both of us giggled.

Pierre and I remained friends, in spite of his mother. Looking back, I believe he was gay. I wonder if his mother guessed?

MILITARY LEAVE

"Mom! Mom! Look! He's coming!" Vibrating with excitement, I was shaking his letter vigorously.

"Good heavens, Katharine, keep your voice down. You make it sound like the Second Coming."

"No, Mom, it's the first coming—next week. Sylvio's coming. Oh gosh. We can put him up, can't we?" Suddenly, I realized my parents' apartment had four bedrooms, all occupied. My grandfather's room, though, had twin beds, one of them empty. Dear Skipper—grandfather—he would not mind. At least I hoped it would work out. And it did work out.

In the next few days, Mother and I put fresh sheets on the extra bed, I tidied up my room and dusted the furniture. Janie, the sweet young black woman who cooked for us, made a magnificent cake, thickly studded with coconut. (She couldn't know that Sylvio, after three years in the tropics, disliked coconut with much feeling. It was cheap in Panama, so the army fed it to him all too frequently.)

When the house was as ready as it was going to be, I had time to sit down and begin to worry. He had last seen me nearly six months ago and I looked different. I *was* different. Unless he really preferred fat girls, my new look would surely please him. More than that, working and taking responsibility had changed me. Would that please him? I wondered. Why had I been so forthcoming and detailed in letters about my social life? I railed at my insensitivity, but it was too late now.

When the day finally arrived, I looked in the mirror one more time. "There's the doorbell!" I tried without much success to keep my voice down as I ran to the front hall.

"Hi ya, gorgeous." His voice was soft and low. For a moment, we stood just taking each other in. His shoulders were broader than I remembered, his brown eyes sparkled behind his glasses. Then he stepped up and swept me into his arms. Wrapped in his embrace, I knew I was where I belonged.

Arms around each other, we walked into the living room to meet everyone.

"Family, here he is! Sylvio, himself." Then, taking him to each in turn, I introduced him to Mom, Dad, Skipper, and Aunt Margaret. After his duffel bag was put in my grandfather's room, I gave him a tour of the apartment.

"This is your bathroom to share with Skipper. Apartment bathrooms are always so small! And here's the dining room." The table was set and candles waited to be lighted. "Then that's Aunt Margaret's little suite over there, and mine is right here." I showed him my day bed and new desk and bureau, very Herman Miller, very stylish. The little window looked out over other roofs to the east. "Now I can take you through the kitchen, but Janie really doesn't like us to get underfoot when she's preparing dinner. We can sneak through the butler's pantry. We had a much nicer kitchen on Staten Island, but I guess these fancy apartments save all the best for the showy parts." Sylvio followed along, holding my hand and leaning over to kiss me as we walked the hallway to the living room. We returned to find Janie serving cheese crackers hot out of the oven, and Dad taking drink orders.

"A little scotch and soda would be good, sir, thank you." He spoke quietly but firmly, with confidence.

"How was your trip?" inquired my father.

"Long. I'm really glad to be here at last. Luxury has disappeared from rail travel; now every train has all the amenities of a troop train. You're nice to put me up. Thank you, sir." His voice still carried the broad A's and absent R's of New England, though he had been away for more than four years. He seemed completely at ease.

"How long is your leave?" asked Mother.

"I have to catch the train back on Sunday," he said. Already Thursday evening, we would have only two full days, and I had to work a half-day on Friday.

Mother directed us to our seats at the dinner table, Sylvio at her right side. Dad carved the roast; Janie served vegetables and passed the plates. Mom had saved up ration stamps to splurge for this occasion and would go meatless for the next week. As usual, most of the conversation was initiated and conducted by my father. Aunt Margaret and Skipper said very little; Mother listened to Dad with a look of worry and concern on her face.

"Today, I took on another manufacturing plant for the government," he told us. "I'll have to get it organized sometime soon."

At the end of dinner, Janie brought in the cake to be cut. She beamed when everyone exclaimed over its beauty. Mother cut the pieces and Janie passed them around as I poured tea. I wondered how Sylvio would react, seeing the frosting. I looked at him with a little frown, he winked at me and ate it all.

"Could I have another little piece, please, Mrs. Case? It's awfully good." Following dinner, and a little polite conversation afterward, we escaped for a walk down the avenue. As we walked through the front door, I stopped to speak to the doorman.

"Emilio, this is Private Fournier. He's the man I write to. I thought you should know who was taking you from your post every evening." Emilio tipped his hat, but Sylvio thrust out his hand. Emilio took it hesitantly.

"Thanks for looking after my girl, Emilio. She told me you walk her up to the next block to drop her letters in the mailbox. Above and beyond the call, isn't it?"

"No, Sir! Mr. Case has instructed me to see Miss Katharine to wherever she goes after dark. I'm glad to do it."

As we turned and strolled along, I whispered, "Golly, I didn't know that. That means Dad pays him to baby-sit me. I thought he was just being friendly."

"Don't worry about it," soothed Sylvio, "I have the impression your father knows exactly what he's doing. I'm sure he's right."

Although I wanted to know what he thought of my father and the rest of my family, I dared not ask. I was pretty sure Sylvio had encountered no life like ours, and I hoped he felt comfortable. I did ask him if he minded the coconut frosting very much.

"Honey, that coconut was so far from what we got in Panama that I would never have recognized it. The cake was really good." We talked about college life at Purdue and Illinois, about the other soldier-students I had met at Antioch, some of whom had washed out and been sent to the European campaign. After a few blocks, we agreed to go back. It had been a long day, and Sylvio was ready to turn in.

In the morning, I wondered how to juggle my responsibilities of job and guest, but Mother settled that.

"You go on to work," she told me. "I'll take care of Sylvio until you get back. There are a few things I need help with, and his muscles look just fine to me."

After breakfast, Sylvio agreed Mom's plan was the best one, and I hurried out to catch the bus. All morning as I led tours, his face swam before me. I could almost feel his arm about my waist, smell his after-shave lotion. I pictured him, again, listening intently to my father, storing up details. He was like that, would remember everything, I was certain. I wondered how he and Mother were getting along, whether he was restless, or annoyed at having to work. When I got home in the early afternoon, the two were sitting in the living room, drinking iced tea and talking.

"Well, your young man helped me put away things on top shelves and to clear out that big cupboard in the butler's pantry. I'm afraid I worked him pretty hard."

"Mrs. Case, I wish you could explain to my officers back in Urbana what hard work is. They seem to have a different idea. Honestly, I've had a very pleasant time."

The two of us spent the rest of the day exploring the upper East Side. He was curious about Gristede's, the neighborhood grocery store. "This is different from any I've ever been in. Seems sort of foreign, somehow, with baskets hanging from the ceiling, and all the exotic smells." He poked around and found imported sauces neither of us knew, cakes from Ireland, and barrels of fragrant coffee beans. Clearly, he liked grocery shopping.

We spent an hour or more in the Metropolitan Museum, and found we both liked Grant Wood's painting of Paul Revere's ride through the darkened village. Farther downtown, he was fascinated to see a shop with a large, very dusty 'Going out of Business' sign in the window along Madison Avenue.

"When, do you suppose?" he laughed.

"That's been there for years. Trying to snag out-of-towners, I guess." When we reached 57th Street, we caught the bus for home.

"C'mon!" I urged, "Let's climb up to the upper deck and get windblown." He followed me and we sat down in the middle of the bus. After a moment, Sylvio took me by the hand and led me to the first row, behind the windshield. That is how I learned that—although he could tolerate just about any weather—he really hated to get windblown. I was shocked to realize this was our first divergence. Would there be others? We seemed so perfectly attuned.

"Do you mind?" he asked me.

"No, of course not. However you're comfortable is how I'm comfortable."

"Don't you believe it," he warned. "We can give some without giving everything, you know." I puzzled over what that meant then, but now, in retrospect, I wonder where his store of wisdom stemmed from.

Except for an occasional "Please pass the butter" or "May I have a roll, please?" my father again dominated the dinner conversation. He gave us what news he had gleaned from the daily papers about the Pacific campaign and referred frequently to the big map on the dining room wall. He was planning yet another trip around the country to inspect the several manufacturing plants in the circle of his responsibility, recently converted to making war materiel. By now, he was also general manager of Universal Camera Corporation, but their wartime product was binoculars for the Navy. He was as surely a draftee as any of those young men in Army khaki or Navy blue.

On Saturday — May 6, 1944 — I guided Sylvio on a walking tour of mid-town Manhattan. When we strolled down Fifth Avenue, I noticed Sylvio was the object of considerable curiosity.

"Sylvio, why do people look at you so strangely? I noticed that soldier who just passed us turned to look at you again."

"Honey, he can't believe he's seeing the screw-up of the century. See these hash marks on my sleeve? They're service stripes. The gold ones are for when I was overseas. Now wouldn't you think anybody who's been in the Army that long could have advanced to at least PFC? And here I am a lowly private. They don't recognize my ASTP[3] patch; it's pretty rare. So they think I must be a really bad guy." He was grinning, completely unembarrassed.

As evening advanced, Manhattan acquired a soft sepia hue. Street light globes were painted to reduce their glow, taxi lights were very dim. We continued to Times Square, noticing store fronts were scarcely lighted at all. At 42nd Street and Broadway, we gazed up at the advertising billboards. The Camel smoker no longer emitted smoke rings, there were no cartoons flashing their messages. Darkness shrouded all. At this late hour, almost all the strollers were couples, soldiers and sailors with their girls. Suddenly, Sylvio walked up to a policeman.

"Excuse me. Can you tell me where I could find a jewelry store open?"

A grin of understanding spread across the Irishman's face. "Sonny, the best you're going to do late on a Saturday

---

[3] Army Specialized Training Program - college

night is right over there." He was pointing to a small souvenir shop across the square. "Good luck, you two!"

Leading me through the door, Sylvio began to search. I tried to look over his shoulder, but he was intent on his search. In a few moments, he found it, pulled out money to pay for it, and led me again to the street. Holding a little gold ring on his outstretched palm, he looked straight into my eyes.

"Kati, I love you. I will love you all my life. Will you take this poor token and keep it as a sign when we are apart?"

Not knowing what to say, I stretched out my hand for him to slip the ring on my finger, sure my thumping heart was audible ten feet away.

"Oh my dear!" was all I could murmur. He kissed me then, right there on the sidewalk, and whispered "some day." We went home then, saying nothing more. Why would we? It had all been said. He left in the morning to return for his second and third quarters at Illinois.

After dinner the next night, I sat down on the couch next to my father. "Daddy, Sylvio's the man I'm going to marry."

Dad put down his newspaper and peered at me over his reading glasses. "Why didn't you tell me that when he was here? I would have taken a closer look at him."

"Oh Daddy, I mean it. Be serious. Isn't he wonderful?"

"I don't know, my dear, and I doubt if you do, either. This is wartime and all the boys look handsome in their uniforms. When the war is over, they are all going to return home and put on civilian clothes. But your young man is a professional soldier. Do you have any idea what that means?"

"No he's not, Daddy. You don't understand. He's just in the army to get a college education. When the war is over, he's going to be a doctor."

"Hmm. Now let's just suppose for a moment that his idea doesn't work out. That happens sometimes. What if he, say, turned out to be a garbage man? How would you feel then?"

"I would love him just the same, really I would."

Dad shook his head and returned to reading.

The weeks wore on, letters continued to fly between Urbana and New York. A kind of panic crept into my reverie. Clearly, Richard and Pierre were a joke. Although I liked them, they began to represent my choices in the world. What if that was all there was out there? They were so wrong, and Sylvio was so exactly right. When I was with him, I felt different. In a mysterious way, he made me better than I was. He nurtured me like a precious flower bud. Although he was romantic, he was also straightforward and honest, and as he showed me on that first evening, he knew where he was going.

Nightmares haunted me. Somehow, I would get lost and not be able to find him again. I knew my parents were right about me; my serial infatuations were family legend. I understood my capacity for capriciousness and certainly mistrusted my ability to be patient and steadfast. It was his whispered 'some day' that chilled me. What did that mean?

Near the end of October, 1944, Sylvio graduated from the pre-medicine program at Illinois with the remainder of his Army Specialized Training Program cohorts. Northwestern University Medical School would admit him in the 1945 fall semester. For the interim, he was assigned to Vaughan General Army Hospital in Maywood, Illinois, where he would serve in the laboratory. The best news was he had fourteen days to report, and that meant he could make another trip east. This time, he wanted to go home to Maine and take me with him to meet his parents.

"Please, Mom, it's OK if I go?"

"Of course you may, dear. Think about what to pack and be ready when he comes."

Probably, both of my parents were hopeful this visit would dampen my ardor, help me to comprehend the meaning of the wide difference in our backgrounds, encourage me to wait. I was filled with cheer and blind optimism.

He arrived in Manhattan, and soon we were riding a train to Boston, changing from South Station to North Station, boarding another bound for Maine, and at last alighting on the station platform in Lewiston. His father, Amedée, met us there.

"How do you do?" I smiled. Looking him over, I marveled at his resemblance to his son. He was shorter and heavier—and of course his hair was gray—but the resemblance was unmistakable. He spoke a word of greeting to me and turned to embrace his son. This was the only expression of physical affection I ever saw between them. Sylvio had been away from home for nearly four years, and they had a lot of catching up to do. Although they were speaking English, Amedée's accent blended Down East with Québécois in a way that had me straining to understand. He pulled up into the driveway and we unloaded our suitcases. As Sylvio led me up the garden path, I saw his stepmother, Catherine Pelletier, standing bathed in light from the open kitchen door. As I put my foot on the bottom step, Sylvio leaned over and whispered, "I forgot to tell you - she doesn't speak English."

"Hello," smiled Catherine.

Whew! He was teasing me, I gasped. I took her hand and replied, but immediately realized she did not understand. 'Hello' would be the only word she ever spoke to me that I understood. The hour was late, and Catherine showed me to my room—Sylvio's, I think. It was simply furnished—no frills except the white window curtains. They were freshly laundered, ruffled, and well starched. Otherwise, there were just a bed, dresser, chair, and a little table. A small rug was the only covering over the wood floor.

In the morning, Sylvio toured me around the city. "There's the cathedral, up on the hill." He pointed to a grand Gothic structure of gray stone, surrounded by sadly impoverished little dwellings. I could see from whence the funds to build the church had been extracted. I hope I let it pass, but maybe not. "I remember," he went on, "one time when the priest came to make his annual family visit. Dad was unhappy with the church, as they didn't recognize his divorce, even though his wife had deserted him. The priest came to extract our tithe, and because the amount was less than satisfactory, he left us saying God would curse our house. Pretty primitive stuff, eh?" I was appalled. He drove on.

"When we were all little kids, we crossed the street when we came to this church. No telling what evil deeds went on in that place, and it was best to keep a safe distance." The building was the First Universalist Church of Lewiston; I remember giggling.

The four of us made a pilgrimage to Rumford and Mexico, two nearby Maine towns, to visit aunts, uncles and cousins. Although many of them spoke a little English — some were even fluent — all the conversation was in the local patois, which I could not follow at all. Sylvio tried for a little while to use his school French, which both they and I understood, but he soon abandoned it. They seemed to find it pretentious, as if the boy from Brooklyn had come home with an Oxford accent. I felt isolated and shrank into a private mental space. Sylvio, home from the war, was the main feature, and I mattered not a bit. Of course not! No one took me seriously anyway, or in fact took any notice of me at all.

Not unreasonably, Amedée took to calling me 'Baby Snooks', after a well-known radio character, parody of a spoiled brat. He meant no unkindness, but he must have thought this was a terrible mismatch; I was not French, not Catholic, just a spoiled child from the big city. And what about Lillian, the girl his family had paired him with, in the traditional way?

My perspective was a little different. Sylvio was at ease with these people, but they showed no sign of affection. In fact, the family showed little humor. Everyone talked at once, and they argued some. Sylvio might as well have been with strangers, and I was altogether invisible. The painful visit ended soon, and in a few days we were on the train, bound for New York.

"Good to see the old folks again," Sylvio told me. "Dad looks pretty good, don't you think? Did you like my cousin Jane?"

"Mm. Fine." Truth was, I had no idea which one she was. Their effort had been minimal, and evidently mine was even less.

"Well, anyway, that's over, and we can get back to business." Sylvio had left it all behind without a backward glance.

The trip had done nothing to assuage my fears, and my nightmares continued. What if all this evaporates, and I lose him? I don't care about his family; they have nothing to do with this. I know the timing is wrong, but I am so afraid if we wait, it may never happen. I cannot lose him.

We were back home in Manhattan, and these persistent thoughts swirled around in my head, but Sylvio said firmly, "We need to wait until the war is over, my dear. No telling what might happen to me—shipped over to Europe or Japan, killed or wounded. I can't burden you with that."

"But you're going to med school," I protested. "You will be safe."

"Ever hear of uncle changing his mind? No, I won't come home to my wife in a box or a wheelchair. Be patient."

I slid away, threw him a mischievous kiss and sat across the living room. It was not my nature to be patient. I flirted with him, teased, tempted.

"Baby, don't slip away from me like that. Come here and snuggle up next to me."

"Marry me," I purred.

"Make me," he said, grinning. "No, Honey, cool down for now."

"Don't be silly! I'm doing my best to heat you up, Handsome."

Although he loved the attention, Sylvio stood firm. His leave was over and we parted, both of us panting from the tension of our desire.

SIEGE AND SURRENDER

In 1943, my parents bought a farm, and that changed all our lives. The property comprised eighty acres in southwestern Michigan's fruit belt—Van Buren County—and eventually expanded to encompass about two hundred acres. In the summer of 1944, Mother was there for a few weeks, while Dad continued to work in New York. That left me to be the hostess in our house, to shop and manage the meals—though Janie was still doing the cooking. This most minor brush with juggling work and running a household prompted me to reflect on my growing sense of responsibility.

Ashamed to have waited so long, I finally found the will to write one last letter to my lieutenant colonel—now Colonel David Kiesler. He was engaged in a nasty, slow, and bloody campaign advancing up the spine of Italy. How to begin?

"My dear David," I wrote. I tried to picture him opening the envelope, reading—no matter what I might write—this 'Dear John' letter. I had been confident he would return and I would marry this gallant Southern gentleman. We met only briefly when I was fifteen, he a dozen years older. We had corresponded affectionately and even though no promises had been exchanged I had never mentioned anyone else. Now, I had to dump the truth all at once. I wanted to believe he would not care very much, and yet I suspected he had little to hold on to except letters from home. "I need to tell you that I've met someone else. I never meant for it to happen, but there it is." Those words were so stark! What was a gentler way to say it? No, it did not matter what I said. For the first time in my life I was aware of having committed serious injury to another human being. Asking his forgiveness would have been wrong; I was not worthy of forgiveness. I know I wrote something like, "Can we be friends, then?" Of course, I never heard from him again.

I wrote to another half-dozen or so young men overseas, but we were friends, nothing more, and we continued to correspond from time to time until the war ended.

Still, every day I wrote to Sylvio, now finishing his last academic quarter. The impending change in his assignment only reinforced my unease.

"Dearest," I wrote, "life is short. Why do we squander any of it in this separation? Even if your direst fears came true, do you imagine I would care less because my finger had no ring? Well, that's wrong. My finger has a ring."

Sylvio's response still counseled patience. The ring had become so important to me that I wanted to wear it always, but there was a problem. The ring had turned green within days — it left a green ring on my skin. Boldly, I took it to a fine shop in Rockefeller Center.

"Could you copy this ring in gold?" I asked the astonished jeweler.

"Yes I could, Miss. But why would you want to do that?" Obviously a man of little imagination, he showed a small spark of sympathy when I explained it had an important sentimental meaning to me.

"Oh yes," he explained, "and we can smooth it out on the inside. It will be a very nice piece."

"No," I protested, "duplicate the ring in every respect except one. I want a little plate inside engraved with the date 5-6-44." When it was finished, I wore it on my right hand, almost a wedding ring. I told Sylvio what I had done and he said he was pleased; I hoped that was true. I certainly was.

Still, he countered all my arguments by invoking that tiresome word, patience. This had become a campaign, and I needed a new strategy.

"Sylvio darling, patience is all very well, but are you just stringing me along? I have to know: do you really intend to marry me? Let's set a decision time, say the end of the month." With my heart in my mouth, I mailed that message.

Within a few days, the flood of mail from Illinois stopped. He had received my letter and was sending no reply.

Dad may have sensed the dumb fear gripping me. Surely he missed his wife, for bandaging up a breaking heart was not in his job description. He did the best he could.

"Kitz, how would you like to take in a show tomorrow night? I can get a couple of tickets for the City Opera production of *New Moon*. We could both use a little fun. What say?" He had two pet names for me, reserved for moments of great affection. Kitz was short for the Kitzidoodlebug he called me when I was a toddler; I have no idea where the other one, Sally McGinnis McGee, came from. Either one was as good as a hug to me.

"Daddy, I'd love it. Thank you."

The light opera suited my mood well. I was floating in a sea of romance, carried along on a wave of wonderful music. When the final curtain fell, it was hard to emerge into the world of reality again. We rode home in a taxi in silence, rode the elevator to the tenth floor, and opened the door to the apartment.

There it was. A telegram, propped up on the hall bookshelves. With shaking fingers, I tore it open and unfolded the yellow paper inside. There were just a few words typed on it, but I closed my eyes for a moment and held my breath. Reading it over my shoulder, Dad chuckled and waited to see what I would do.

"Oh no," I cried, "where's the Shakespeare?"

The words were, "Romeo and Juliet, Act II, Scene IV, line 72. Sylvio." Below on the shelf was a row of small blue books containing the works of the Bard. When I found the right one, and turned the pages until I reached the second act and then the fourth scene, I groaned, "No line numbers? I'll have to count." And so I counted to seventy-two and found this line from Nurse to Juliet: *Hie you to church.*

"Oh Daddy," I breathed, hugging him. "Oh Daddy." Delirious, I floated off to bed to dream.

In later years, Sylvio would tell two different stories about this. One was that I had counted wrong, and the line he had meant for me to read was: *Get thee to a nunnery, Go!* The other story involved 1944 being a leap year — when women have the power to propose — being cornered in front of a tenth story window, afraid for his life

DECEMBER WEDDING

"But that's only six weeks! The Saturday before Christmas? Impossible!" Mother had returned from the farm at the end of October to find me deep in elaborate wedding plans. Having no experience and no guidance had led me down the byways of bride's dresses and music to the exclusion of any practical matters.

"Mom, did you see the movie *Gaslight*? Ingrid Bergman wore the most wonderful Victorian dress of white velvet. Do you think I could have one made something like that?"

"In six weeks? Hmm. Where do you plan to have the ceremony?"

"At All Souls Unitarian church on Lexington Avenue, of course ."

"Is the church available December 16th? Have you spoken to the minister? Invitations will be a little difficult, dear. They must be out in two weeks. This is wartime. Where will you find good paper? That's a tight schedule for an engraver. Do you have a guest list? Where will the reception be?"

"Oh Mom, I was only thinking of a small wedding. We could have a simple reception almost anywhere." My sights were already being lowered.

"You start with the church, and I will see what can be done about a reception," she sighed doubtfully. Whatever dream I had, Mother always did her best to make it happen. I was still pretty confident.

Within days, I acquired an education in the meaning of reality. The white velvet dress was left behind in a burst of patriotism; it would be more in keeping with the times to wear something simple, right off the rack. My assumption that a small party could be held almost anywhere collapsed when the Waldorf, the Plaza, the Pierre all patiently explained that every available room was spoken for, long since. All I wanted was a place to serve fifty people a little cake and champagne, but the search was going to be hard. At last, with a call made by my father, the Carlyle Hotel found suitable rooms and agreed to provide refreshments.

Each day, I went off to work, led tours in something of a daze. Luckily, the spiel had become so automatic I could simply drop a virtual needle on the record and let my tongue roll on.

One afternoon, riding home from work on the bus, I saw the dress in a shop window on Madison Avenue. Quickly, I grabbed the cord to signal for a stop, jumped off the bus and ran back two blocks.

"Do you have the dress in the window in my size?" I was out of breath, gulping for air.

"Oh ma cherie. Do sit down and recover yourself. You're all aflutter!" The clerk led me to a chair and patted my shoulder until I was breathing normally. "There now. Do you feel better? Are you looking at the gray dress? That's the only one we have, but it just may be your size. Let me take it down from the window and we'll see."

While the elderly woman went to the window, another clerk led me into the dressing room. Soon, the three of us were admiring my reflection, turning first to one side then the other.

"Oh yes," I sighed. "This is it. He will love it."

"Ah, you have a rendezvous with a handsome young man, yes?" The older woman was enjoying her vision of sweet romance.

"Yes, I do. This will be my wedding dress. Do you have a hat to go with it? And gloves? It must be the perfect ensemble."

After debate, we settled on a small pink satin hat, studded with pearls and adorned with a little pink veil. The dress was carefully placed in a box, cradled in tissue paper, while Madam — I heard the other clerk call her that — scouted for the perfect hat box. When I had dressed and paid the bill, Madam insisted on sending the younger woman to hail a taxi for me. As I opened the cab door, Madam stretched up to kiss my cheek.

"Bonne chance, ma petite!" The car pulled away from the curb and we sped north up the avenue.

Daily letters from Sylvio helped me focus, at last. What did any of it matter, except we loved one another and would soon be married? He wrote, "I got leave OK. The major was pretty steamed, though. 'Why didn't you marry her when you had a fourteen day delay en route for godssake!' Of course, I told him it took me two weeks to ask you. He didn't think that was funny. But it turned out all right. When he demanded to know my serial number, and I told him, he calmed right down. I knew he was regular army and would recognize my number. It marks me as one of the elite, not a draftee. He signed my leave papers right there. I'll see you Friday the fifteenth, Gorgeous."

The day, December 16, 1944, dawned cold and sullen, threatening either rain or snow. Nothing so trivial touched me. A year of treatment for my thyroid problem had worked well and I had lost more than sixty pounds. Slender and womanish for the first time in my life, I slid the dress on over my head. It felt silky and soft, the hem falling below my knees. I pulled on a pair of silk stockings, hooking them to my garters. Lucite buckles decorated my black high-heeled shoes. After I pinned the hat securely to my hair, I pulled on long gloves.

"Well," I mused, "even if I'm not pretty, I certainly feel pretty today. And he calls me Gorgeous, so who am I to argue?" I turned to go, satisfied.

I rode with Dad to the church, the rest of the family, and Sylvio, coming separately. We had adhered to the old superstition that for him to see me before the wedding was bad luck. Most of the guests had already been seated, and Dad and I waited in the vestibule until the organist struck up the Lohengrin processional. Dad looked down at me with surprise in his eyes.

"You're really going through with this after all? I thought you'd back out at the last minute."

"No, Daddy," I smiled, "this is real. This is for always."

I took his arm and we walked down the aisle together. Sylvio stood at the chancel, erect and serious. His uniform was flawless, shoes shined to a mirror finish. His dark hair set off the sparkle in his eyes and he gazed lovingly into mine. Dad placed my hand in his and backed away to join Mother. Sylvio's hand was warm, and I trembled. Each of us repeated our vows, a soloist sang *The Lord's Prayer*, at the minister's signal, we kissed, turned to the congregation, and walked arm-in-arm to the vestibule.

"That's it?" Sylvio's question was more of an exclamation of astonishment. While the service had seemed very long to me, this fallen-away Catholic, accustomed to the full mass, could hardly believe we were really married.

I laughed, squeezed his arm and said, "Yep, now it's on to the champagne!"

We sped off with my parents for photographs at the Carlyle.. Since Dad was in the business, I thought pictures would be easy. Unfortunately, the man Dad had chosen to do the work was sick, and his replacement had little flair. It might have been his first wedding. Later, when the pictures were developed, it turned out the Agfa film was faulty and the colors were distorted. Color film was still experimental.

At last, we were turned loose to greet our guests, most of whom had already arrived. They were an odd lot, but this was wartime. Most of my friends were either away at college or fighting the war. My father's mother and sister had come, my friend Shirley and her mother were there, along with Dick Randall, a school friend from Staten Island. All of the others were friends or business associates of my parents, and I knew only a few of them. Never at ease socially, I dreaded having to introduce Sylvio to all these people. I need not have worried. My new husband was completely at ease talking with strangers. He charmed my grandmother.

"Here, try this," he said, handing her a glass from the waitress's tray. I stood stock still in agony. My grandmother was, I think, a charter member of the Women's Christian

Temperance Union. Strong drink had never passed her lips. She sipped.

"Oh, it tickles my nose," she laughed. "But it's good."

And she sipped more. I think she never knew what it was; I hope not.

When the cake was trundled in from the kitchen, everyone oohed and aahed. What a work of art! Sylvio and I stood by the cake while a few flashbulbs popped, and then I picked up the knife to cut. The knife rested on the frosting, but refused to penetrate. Thinking I was nervous, Sylvio came to my rescue and took the knife from my hand. He applied it to the cake. He pushed, he poked. We joined forces. The cake was impervious. Finally, the chef was summoned to cut the cake. He came with a large knife, but still the cake sat on the table unyielding.

Raising his knife high, he brought it down with a quick thrust. Pieces of brittle frosting splattered everywhere, but the cake was cut. In spite of all, the cake was delicious.

Having said our good-byes to the guests, Sylvio and I put on our coats. Mother called him aside.

"Behave yourself, young lady," she called to me. Turning to Sylvio, she continued, "If you have trouble with her—and you will—remember that you are always welcome at our house. And here's a little wedding present," she added, thrusting an envelope into his hand. The envelope contained the war bonds she had bought with my board-and-room money. None of Sylvio's family had even acknowledged our invitation, and I was moved by Mother's loving generosity and gesture of inclusion.

Off we went in a taxi to the corporate apartment Dad had loaned us for the night. The dull sky was spitting rain—every raindrop that falls on a bride will become a tear—mixed with snow—every snowflake that falls on a bride will become a dollar. The mix was about fifty-fifty.

Like children, we explored the luxurious rooms.

"Dad gave you two keys. What's the other one?" We rattled every door until we found the one that resisted. Sylvio inserted the key. The closet door flew open, and so did our mouths. The shelves were stacked to the ceiling with wine and liquor, cases and cases, bottles and bottles, unobtainable in wartime. We were awed. Strangely, it never occurred to either of us that we were meant to help ourselves. We closed the door, and he took me in his arms.

Following a long night of discovery and sweet ecstasy, we fell into a deep sleep. When Sunday dawned, I donned an apron and began my housewife imitation, preparing a breakfast of scrambled eggs for my husband. Suddenly, he strolled into the kitchen with a glass in his hand.

"What's that you're drinking?" I asked.

"Well," he replied with a grin, "the only open bottle in the whole closet was rum, and I found a Coke. So it's a cuba libra."

"Oh my goodness," I shrieked, "what kind of depraved monster have I taken into my bed? A rum coke for breakfast. Oh ugh." I shuddered in mock horror; he just grinned and drank it down. Thereby, rum and Coca Cola acquired a special meaning for us, lasting as a private joke for half a century.

Later in the day, we managed to pull away from each other long enough to tidy the kitchen, pack up our clothes and head for the train station. We spent our honeymoon sitting up all night in coach class on the Pacemaker, bound for Chicago. Sylvio was to report for work Monday morning. Married life had begun.

END OF THE WAR

"Where are we going now?" We had arrived in Maywood on the el, and Sylvio was gathering our luggage. I stood watching him, hugging my soft fur coat around me in the sharp wind. For my eighteenth birthday in May, my father had given me the gray coat of chinchilla rabbit fur. It had attracted second glances on Fifth Avenue, so like real chinchilla did it look.

"You'll see." He motioned me toward a taxi, loaded our bags into the trunk, and we were off to an address on Seventh Avenue. "It's Mrs. Milanico's establishment. Wait till you see what she's done with a little Chicago bungalow. We're lucky to have it—housing around an army base is hard to find. It's $40 a month, but still, it was good luck to find it at all."

I thought that was a hefty bite out of his $90 a month off-the-base allowance, but I said nothing about it as he led me down the walk to the kitchen door. I stepped in onto a worn linoleum floor. The gas stove was an old, black iron model; the ice box made of wood, with a bright nickel-plated handle; the sink and drainboard were stained white porcelain, flecked with the many nicks of time. A small metal table and two chairs clustered beside the window. The next room, I could see, had once been the dining room. An old-fashioned chandelier hung from the middle of the ceiling, providing the only light, other than two windows. This 'partially furnished' room boasted a small steel wardrobe, a small wicker table, two chairs, and a studio couch that might have been designed as a relief map of the western states.

I collapsed on the bed. As I pulled off my gloves, I began to giggle, my giggles grew into full-throated laughter, and soon I was holding my sides and gasping for air. Poor Sylvio. Had the poverty of these rooms so shocked me that I had come unhinged? He did not know what to make of it until I regained my breath enough to exclaim, "What a great adventure this is going to be! Oh, I do love you!"

We were to live there for nine months, though we did replace the bed with a friendlier studio couch and bought a lamp or two. Sharing the bathroom with our landlady and her husband was the major challenge for me. Mrs. Milanico used it for her kitchen sink, and never quite rinsed the spaghetti sauce from the bathtub. Mr. Milanico was senile and spent his days scratching out tunes on a violin, easily heard through the French doors separating our living spaces. I got the sense that nothing happening in our rooms escaped Mrs. Milanico.

The days grew ever darker and colder, but I felt cheerful and fulfilled, learning to shop and cook and clean. Actually, the cleaning was hit-or-miss, but I enjoyed exercising what I had learned in a cooking class. I could actually, with careful planning, put together a nutritious meal for two for much under a dollar. My copy of Fannie Farmer's Boston Cooking School Cookbook, a wedding present from my friend June, grew dog-eared. We were about a mile from the hospital where Sylvio worked, and sometimes I would leave supper simmering on the stove to go meet him halfway and walk back with him, hand in hand.

A week after our arrival came Christmas Day.

"You have to work on Christmas?" This was an unexpected blow, but of course the hospital ran every day, holiday or not. It happened that a cousin of my mother's lived in a far northern suburb and they had invited us to come spend the day and share their Christmas dinner.

"That's OK, Honey, you go. I'll be all right. I'll eat in the mess and they always have turkey for holidays. I can meet you at the train when you come home."

Crestfallen, but trying to put a good face on it, I packed up the presents I would take with me, kissed him goodbye before first light, and later walked alone to the train station. I found a seat next to a window and gazed out, seeing nothing. I tried not to cry. At the second stop, a soldier sat down next to me. I glanced at his khaki trousers and looked away again.

Soon, I felt his elbow in my ribs, and I swung around to give him a piece of my mind, only to find myself glaring into the mischievous grin of my husband. He kissed me right on the lips, then drew back and asked, "You were about to say?"

"But what? How?"

"Pure magic, Babe. I wasn't sure we could catch the train, but the sergeant in the car pool pulled it off. Don't ask me for details, just enjoy."

And enjoy we did. Our hosts were a family with four children and a big German shepherd. Four grandparents joined us for dinner, but the dining room was plenty large enough to accommodate twelve and a feast that would have made Dickens proud. As evening fell, my cousin Abner told us to pile into the family station wagon and he would drive us back to Maywood, a distance of thirty miles. At last, we tumbled out of the car, struggling to hold all our household presents, including a dozen pilsner glasses.

"Bye, Ab. Thanks for a wonderful day. And Merry Christmas!"

The days marched along. I waited eagerly for his greeting kiss and the long tales he would tell over dinner about his latest adventure at the hospital. Sometimes it would be a new parasite from a hapless soldier returning from the Pacific theater. He gloated when he could tell me he had identified it himself, remembering his parasitology classes in Urbana. His lab supervisor had been a prominent pathologist in civilian life; Sylvio was an earnest student, and the doctor took him under his wing, often inviting him to participate in autopsies. I found the detailed, graphic descriptions a little hard to take over dinner, but his scientific curiosity and enthusiasm overrode any squeamishness he might have felt. Only one autopsy he attended made him sick; it was a friend who had committed suicide by swallowing cyanide.

One day in the lab, Sylvio ran out of sulfuric acid and he hurried to the store room to refill his small container. In his haste, he became careless and poured the acid directly from a full, uncrated five-gallon carboy of the fuming liquid. It slipped, and a corner of the bottle hit the cement floor. Instantly, Sylvio was drenched in a chemical that began eating through his ankles. In a flash, he reached behind his neck to untie the lab apron, slipped out of his shoes, and into a big sink. Water flooded over his feet, but too late.

When I was summoned to his hospital bed, the doctor pulled me aside. "I can probably save his left foot, but it will be terribly damaged. I'm afraid the right one is . . ." His voice trailed off.

This young soldier had resisted marrying me during the war, lest he be wounded in battle, but here he was in the safety of a hospital, so badly hurt he could look forward to the life of a cripple. My mind went blank for a moment, then I turned and opened the door to his room.

"My goodness, look at you! What have you been up to?" I leaned over to kiss him, and he put his arms around me.

"Sorry, Hon, I guess I got a little careless. Doc says I'll be here awhile, but don't worry. I'll be back in the lab before you know it." He smiled reassuringly and I wondered how much he knew of the prognosis. I listened to every detail of the accident, holding tight to his hand.

"Well," I said, as the nurse came into the room, "I guess they want me out of here, but I'll come visit you again sometime if you like. OK?"

"You better, Babe. I want to see you a lot. These nurses are all right, but they can't hold a candle to you. Come back soon."

As I trudged home through the snow, I pictured myself in the role of the heroic nurse I had seen in a recent war movie. I think the drama of the situation insulated me from the reality. The Chicago winter of 1944-45 was the coldest within memory. The temperature dipped to twenty below zero, a new experience for me. Near the temperate ocean, New York never got so cold. Nevertheless, I bundled up and walked to the hospital every day for a month.

Sylvio liked to have me there when they were changing the dressings, so I could watch the healing process.

"Look at that bone!" he exclaimed admiringly during the first week. "Clean and white, just like it's supposed to be."

What I saw was red, angry flesh. I wanted to look away, but I drew in my breath and managed to say, "It's lovely, dear. Doesn't it hurt a lot?"

"Naw," he protested, "they give me this stuff. Makes me a little loopy, but it keeps it from hurting too much."

As the weeks went by, it became obvious his doctor had considerably overstated the extent of the damage. Before long, the wounds had closed, healed over, and Sylvio was beginning to venture out of his wheelchair long enough to stand up and stretch a little. The physical therapist came regularly to help him stretch his ankles, bear weight on his feet, begin to walk. Someone brought him his shoes to admire. They had been entirely disassembled by the acid and the laces nearly eaten away.

"Come on," he said, "push me down the hall and I'll show you the scene of the crime...Here it is. Open the door." I did.

"What a clean floor! And look at that radiator!" Supported only by a pipe coming through the floor, it had fallen over when the acid ate through the pipe.

"Boy," he said, looking at the wreckage, "I could have been hurt!"

In what seemed like an eternity, spring followed winter. The wounded ankles were entirely healed, leaving only a blush of red that would never fade.

During the long winter, I had taken a part-time job as a counter-girl in a local dry cleaning shop. This was my first encounter with a seamier side of society and my cheeks burned with the gossip of the other clerks.

"Rhoda, did you hear about Mrs. Murphy? Her Joe beat her up last Saturday, real bad. The neighbors called the cops and there was a hell of a ruckus. Watch for her when she comes in to get his pants. Her face is pretty battered.'

What's the matter with him?" asked Rhoda, "doesn't she give it to him when he wants to?"

"Nah, she's too busy giving it to the milkman, I hear."

"You must be kidding! I heard the milkman had eyes for another guy. I saw them together the other day, and well, they were. . .you know."

I did not know, and furthermore, I did not want to know. None of the comments were ever addressed to me, but I felt like a voyeur. I was glad when the job evaporated before long.

Remarkably, we could make do on his private's pay — augmented, I admit, with an occasional five-dollar bill thrust into my pocket when my parents paid us a visit. Sometimes, we walked back to the hospital and ate in the mess, where his dinner was free and mine only fifty cents. Movies at the hospital were a dime each, making for a pretty economical entertainment budget. I never did quite get used to the mess, though, with the large posters warning of venereal disease, illustrated with pictures of anatomy I had never seen in public, all oozing with disease. Sylvio laughed at my education; it was no news to him.

A brilliant idea struck me: we could ride bicycles! My bike was in storage in New York, along with my father's. In a burst of heroics when we still lived on Staten Island, Dad had vowed to save gas by riding to the yacht club. It had been short-lived—the trip was eight miles each way, and Dad was no athlete. I asked that they be sent, and they arrived one Saturday morning.

"Let's go for a spin to the hospital and back," I urged, as I pushed away from the curb. I led the way. It's true: you don't forget how to ride a bicycle. At once, I felt comfortable, breezing along, no hands. It never entered my mind that some people in the world do without bicycles. Bikes and roller skates had been a necessary part of transportation in my childhood. In Lewiston, Maine, Sylvio had not been one of the privileged. He had never been astride a bike before this moment. Actually, looking back, I can see he did pretty well. He managed to stay on board down the first two blocks, but then I signaled for a left turn, leaned into the curve, and slid easily into the intersecting street. He might have made it, too, if the telephone pole had been out of the way.

Two front teeth were broken off, and his face was very bloody. I got him to the hospital's emergency room, where Providence was on our side. A magnificently qualified dentist was available. He had left a fancy practice in Boston to join up, and fate had brought him here. The repair, caps on his teeth, left every dentist Sylvio ever consulted after that in awe of the beautiful work. They matched his own perfectly and never leaked or loosened in the next fifty-six years.

I wanted to put the bikes aside, but Sylvio rose above his humiliation, determined to learn. Eventually, one Sunday morning we rode to Glencoe, the distant suburb where cousin Ab lived. In those days, little traffic moved on the country roads on Sunday mornings. The route took us past farm fields and an occasional country store. Today, crowded housing developments and interstate highways make this route far too dangerous for biking. On this April morning in 1945, we arrived before Ab and his wife were out of bed.

"Get up, you lazies," I called. "We rode thirty miles to see your shining faces." We spent the day having a picnic in their backyard, while Sylvio nursed a sore knee. That was the first time I heard about his knees, but it would not be the last. As the afternoon wore on, I suggested we ought to be starting back, but Ab would hear none of it.

"We'll just pile the bikes in the back of the wagon and ride home in comfort. You've had enough for one day." We agreed that maybe we had overstretched a bit, but in fact we grew stronger in the coming months. The bikes were our only transportation for the next two years.

For months, we lived in a sort of cocoon, wrapped up entirely in the hospital. Sylvio rotated from hematology to parasitology to pathology, absorbing it all. He often ran pregnancy tests for the wives of servicemen, but he was distressed to sacrifice a rabbit for each one. He instituted careful surgical techniques, anaesthetizing the rabbit, cutting her open to examine her ovaries, sewing her up, and setting her in a cage to be nursed back to health. In that way, rabbits could be used numerous times without having to be killed. I wondered whether the rabbits appreciated the gesture. Sylvio became expert at extracting blood from the big sheep that was kept there. He could find the vein and thrust a needle into just the right place without hesitation. Later, I would call on this skill of his when I needed it.

I spent my days visiting injured soldiers and taking them books to read. The most disconcerting part of my volunteer days was playing ping-pong with men just returned from battle who had lost their ability to coordinate eye, hand, and mind. It was, I was told, an emotional effect of war, and trying to hit the ball was therapeutic. Some of the men had been very good at it, I could tell. The form was fine, but their timing was off by about a second or so. After the ball had whizzed by, they would make a wonderful lunge that, properly timed, would have slammed the ball back to my court. My heart ached for their frustration.

In 1945, the outside world began to impinge on our world. The war in Europe ended and now attention shifted to the Pacific. Suddenly — in late summer — the atomic bomb dropped. Everywhere else, jubilation reigned. At the hospital, joy was tempered by evidence of the ravages of war in every ward. For many of these young men, the war would never end.

For us, though, it ended right there. A point system had been set up to regulate the flow of veterans back into the civilian world. Those with the greatest amount of offshore duty would be the first mustered out. Ninety was the magic number of points for the first wave, and now Sylvio presented his records to the commanding officer.

"Sir, I want to claim my points and get my discharge."

"Are you crazy, son? You're going to medical school in just about a month. You wouldn't kick a free medical degree in the teeth, would you?"

"Yes, Sir. I've thought about it and I would, Sir."

"I can't believe it." Shaking his head, he bent over his desk and signed the order.

Whether my opinion played any part in Sylvio's decision I was not to know. This was the beginning of my understanding that his career decisions were entirely his own, though he usually discussed with me the process of his decision-making.

Outside the hospital grounds, horns honked and people waved at every uniform they saw. Sylvio burst through the kitchen door, waving his orders.

"Let's go, Babe! Let's leave this burg behind!"

"Wait a minute," I protested, "where are we going? What will we do?"

That was a question. With the flood of returning servicemen, the colleges were suddenly swamped. Applications from out of state would be discarded. You had to apply to your home state schools.

"Me? I'm not going back to Maine! Let's have supper and think about it awhile."

One clear choice emerged: the University of Michigan. My parents, Skipper, and Aunt Margaret had now moved from Manhattan to the farm. If we lived there for the six-months' residency requirement, we could go to Ann Arbor in the spring.

"Do you think they'd do it, though?"

"My parents? Of course they would. Remember, Mom said you were welcome."

"I think she meant without you, though, Sweetie. Would they take us both in?"

I poked him in the ribs then, and we went to make a rare long-distance telephone call, reversing the charges, I think. Mom and Dad readily agreed, Dad adding that extra hands were always welcome on a farm. We started packing.

Moving day found us trudging back and forth, carrying boxes from the back door to the street, along the narrow walk in the side yard. Mrs. Milanico spent the entire morning pushing a hand mower over the strip of grass bordering the house. Back and forth she went, evidently guarding against the probability that her tenants would abscond with the 'partial furnishings'. Actually, it did not happen. We were all too glad to leave Maywood and everything belonging to it and move on to the next chapter in our lives.

MARKING TIME

War brought restrictions to civilian life. More than meat and sugar were rationed; non-essential building was out of the question. There was no dwelling on the Michigan farm Dad and Mother bought in 1943, but to encourage agricultural development, building a basic farm house had been allowed. It was a Sears Roebuck pre-cut frame house of four rooms: a kitchen, living room, and two bedrooms, with one bath and a full cellar. By autumn, 1945, the family moved from Manhattan—father, mother, grandfather, and Aunt Margaret. The entire house could have been placed in the living room of the Manhattan apartment. It was to this family circle we were proposing to move for six months.

The original farmhouse about 1945

My father dreamed of establishing a farm to develop and breed a superior strain of Jersey cattle. Mother was never comfortable around farm animals, but—being a good sport and very much in love with my father—put a cheerful face on the enterprise and concentrated her effort on growing a garden. One day, she proposed to Dad that he buy the eighty-acre farm across the road and let her handle it.

"I can go into competition with you, and I believe I can do better with fruit." The other farm had been planted in peaches and apples. Delighted at her initiative, he answered, "You're on! We'll buy it and see what you can do." In that moment, *Peaches 'n' Cream Farms* was born.

This farm came equipped with a roomy house, large enough to accommodate the new farm manager's family of four on the first floor, with an extra bedroom on the second floor. Clayton Weeks—or Clayte, as he preferred—was experienced in managing orange groves in Florida and the migrant workers who came seasonally to pick the fruit. Michigan fruit was apples and peaches, but the migrant workers were the same. His wife, Juanita, sometimes helped in the orchards, but more often stayed home to care for her two little girls and to sew pretty dresses for them. She sewed them 'on her finger', meaning using no pattern, just making them up as she went along. The fabrics of cheap cottons came from DeHaven's general store in Lawrence. I used to wonder whether she paid a premium for what she bought there as our family did, for there was a two-tier pricing system that penalized outsiders.

Our farm's permanent designation as 'outsiders' probably stemmed from an unfortunate experience Mother had that first summer, when she was alone on the farm. Mother, like most women, had been raised on the 'Monday wash-day, Tuesday iron-the-clothes, Wednesday…' and so on. On the farm, however, with plowing and planting, harvesting, and hauling feed for the cattle determined by weather, household chores were sandwiched in between whatever else needed attention. Alone, and with only the neighboring farm boy to supervise, Mother coped as well as she could. Her previous agricultural experience involved raising pretty flowers in her suburban garden.

One Sunday afternoon, she finally gathered sheets, towels, and soiled clothing and lugged them down to the basement. She had just finished the first load of wash and was feeding it through the wringers to the rinse water when she heard a knock at the front door.

Who could that be? she wondered, as she climbed the steps, wiping her hands on her apron. When she opened the door, she faced a stranger, a man dressed in suit and necktie. "Good afternoon?"

"Good afternoon. I am Jason Beasley, pastor of the Lutheran Church in Lawrence. You are Mrs. Case?" He was looking her up and down in apparent distaste.

Mother realized that her elbows still showed traces of soapsuds, and damp locks of her hair hung over her forehead. She brushed them back and said brightly, "Won't you come in? I'm not very presentable, but I would be glad to stop for awhile. May I offer you a cup of tea?"

"Oh no. I had not expected to find you doing laundry on the Sabbath."

"I do laundry when I can, I'm afraid."

With that, the reverend Mr. Beasley turned on his heel and strode away, climbed into his car, and sped off. She did not see him again until many months later when she attended a funeral at the Lutheran Church for an infant daughter of the local banker. She was appalled to hear the preacher repeatedly refer to the baby as a sinner consigned to the fires of hell because she had died before a church christening ceremony was performed. Unable to bear such an assault on the grieving parents, Mother left the sanctuary and drove home in tears. *Peaches 'n' Cream Farms* and all its denizens were outsiders, objects of curiosity, but never members of the community.

Clayte's house was heated by a large stove in the generous kitchen. When winter winds howled up from the western valley, the girls gathered at the kitchen table to do their school work. Fresh gingham curtains and clean rag rugs made this a welcoming room.

The upstairs bedroom had a double bed, a plain painted dresser, and one chair. It would be our bedroom for the next six months; we would eat with Mother, Dad, Skipper, and Aunt Margaret in the tiny house across the road.

In exchange for room and board, we found plenty of work to do. Silos were rising at the back of the barn. Sylvio hauled wheelbarrows full of cement as the mason constructed the walls.

"Boy, you did good!" remarked the mason to Dad. "That son-in-law of yours is a real good worker. Nothing like a Mick for hard labor!" All of us were amused that the Swedish mason took this dark-haired stalwart Canuck to be an Irishman. Dad acknowledged Sylvio's diligence with a wheelbarrow, but apparently failed to notice much else about him.

Mom and I hauled bushels of tomatoes to the cellar of the little farm house for canning. There were two gas burners and a work table under the bare light bulb hanging from the low ceiling. We spent steamy autumn days down there, peeling and blanching the big red tomatoes, cutting and squishing them into Mason jars. Juice bubbled up to fill the jars. We twisted on the lids and lowered them into the boiling bath to sterilize. Little by little, the shelves along the walls filled with dozens of jars.

When the peach harvest was in, we followed much the same process, except the peeling was done with a weak lye solution. We cooked peeled peach halves in syrup, and filled the jars. After the same sterilizing process, those jars of yellow fruit joined the red ones on the shelves. When the apples came in, we peeled, cored, and cut them, cooked them with a little sugar and cinnamon, and filled still more jars with the fragrant sauce. I had read about 'putting by' for the winter, but I had never done it before.

"Look at those shelves! They're filling up nicely. Won't go hungry this winter, that's sure." We were proud of our accomplishment. While we worked together, drenched in steamy fragrance, Mother and I talked. She taught me about canning and about fruit farming, about life and love. She gave advice sparingly; she just talked about her experience. Now and then, she said something that stuck in my mind.

"Don't ever ask your husband to choose between you and his career. You might regret the choice he makes." I never knew whether this was advice or words out of her experience, but I remembered it whenever I opened one of those jars—and long afterward.

On the other side of this damp, dark basement stood two square wash tubs and the washing machine. No spin dryer here; every garment had to be fed through the wringer, one at a time. I learned to be careful with buckles on overalls, lest they damage the rubber rollers, and with buttons, lest they be broken. If the weather was fair, we lugged big baskets of wet laundry up the stairs, out the back door, to the clotheslines strung across the yard. We fastened the laundry with one-piece wooden pins, pushing them firmly onto the thick cotton lines to keep the clothes from flying away in the breeze, breathing in the freshness of soap and clean air. On rainy days, we hung the clothes row on row from the cellar rafters, making for an even more dank atmosphere. Jeans took days to dry. Once or twice, we misjudged the weather. After the clothes were blowing in the wind, a distant rumble stopped us.

"What do I hear? Are those clouds going to be serious?" Mother was dismayed. She gazed out over the valley where dark clouds had appeared on the horizon and were now rising higher in the sky. Another distant rumble. "Well, they've had five minutes to dry, anyhow. Let's get them in quickly."

As I struggled through the door with the last basket, the first raindrops hit my shoulders. When the screen door slammed, thunder cracked, and it began to rain in earnest.

In the evening, suppertime was something of a challenge. The kitchen, a good size for family cooking, was also the setting for family eating. There were six of us at the table.

Aunt Margaret always set it with a good cloth, pretty dishes, and silver napkin rings. Partly paralyzed from an early childhood disease, she had learned to make the best of her capability without complaint. In the early morning hours, Margaret watched for birds, writing down every new species she found. Her life list was very long.

My grandfather was called "Skipper" by everyone. I think it might have been because in his youth he had been the skipper of a sailboat at the family's summer cottage on one of New York State's small finger lakes. He took it upon himself to scrape the potatoes for dinner. He didn't hold with peeling them.

"Don't believe in peelers. I can scrape as fast anyway," he muttered as he patiently scraped away the skins. He could not, of course, but what was time to an old man? He was bedeviled with painful stomach ulcers, but complaint was not his style, either. Skipper and Margaret, both St. Louis Cardinals fans, listened to every game that was broadcast.

Mother cooked dinner, and brought it to the table for Dad to serve. I slid through the narrow space between chairs and wall when I cleared away the dishes, but that was no hardship. I was enthralled with farm conversation, all new to me.

"Louis Bromfield was right about the plow," mused Dad. "I think I'll try following his advice on that northwest field when I plant there. There's been some erosion damage and maybe avoiding a plow altogether will help the soil."

How can Dad know so much about farming, when he's always been a city executive, I thought to myself? He seems to have read everything. What a Renaissance man! I laughed at his jokes, admired his wisdom — regretting that my husband had neither his wit nor his sophistication. The weeks wore on, autumn came and went, winter set in. Although a stealthy wedge was slipping between Sylvio and me, it went unrecognized. I quoted: "Dad says . . . ," "Dad does . . . ," "Dad thinks . . . ." Sylvio had no defense but silence. Our bed grew cold.

Before we left the farm for Ann Arbor, I changed our names. Having tried on every conceivable variant of Katharine as if I were trying on hats, once again I tried a new one.

"Darling, would you still love me if I stopped being Kati?"

"What brought this on?" He was smiling a quizzical smile. "You couldn't stop being you if you tried!"

"No, I mean my name. What would you think of 'Kit', instead?"

"Sounds good. Doesn't cost anything does it?"

I poked him then. "And how about your name? Why don't we call you Arthur? Art! That's a great name!" Privately, I had a feeling that a foreign-sounding name was a disadvantage, and a little embarrassing. Anglo-centricity had not yet faded in America; I thought the change would be beneficial in the corporate world of the 1950s. Characteristically, he voiced no objection; whatever made his bride happy was all right with him. He knew who he was, Sylvio or Arthur, it made no difference. His steadfast indulgence and loyalty would hold us together in turbulent times to come.

COLLEGE — CIVILIAN STYLE

In Michigan, the calendar lies about spring. March may bring buds to the cherry trees in Washington — or even full blossoms — but it usually brings more ice and snow to the Wolverine State. In 1946, March brought us one hundred miles east to Ann Arbor for the spring semester.

We settled in a rented bedroom in the home of an enthusiastic university supporter. Paul owned a gas station on Packard Road, his wife, Marj, stayed at home and cooked for us and the couple who rented the other spare bedroom. I remember delicious dinners and lively conversations. The pretty colonial — style house stood on a side street only a block away from the football stadium, and within easy biking distance from the main campus.

Art showed me his class schedule when he returned from registration. He was aiming for a Bachelor of Science degree in biochemistry. "Yeah, one math course is a requirement, but I can slide through with a gentleman's C in calculus, I guess."

"But Art, math is not your subject. You know you don't do well, so you're going to have to hit the books."

"What's that supposed to mean? I got top grades at Purdue in analytical geometry!"

"Yes, but calculus is different. Some people have an instinct for number concepts. You don't. I'm telling you, you're going to need to work hard at it." I had insulted him. Did I tell the truth? Yes. But I did assault his self-confidence. "What else are you taking?"

"German, economics, and electrical measurement. I need to take the German if I'm going to read scientific papers. That's the hard one. It'll take the lion's share of my time I think." His eyes hardened, a little crease appeared at the side of his mouth, but he said no more.

Released from military discipline, Art struggled to fend off the distractions of marriage and campus life. I enticed him to watch the home team compete on the hockey rink, to see college plays. Our communal dinner hour, extended by conversation, cut into study hours.

To supplement our income from the G. I. Bill, I found a job as assistant to the diploma clerk. The tasks demanded very little thought, only meticulous accuracy. I had to verify the spelling of each student's name, be sure that full names were used. My first encounter with a different culture surprised me. Summoning a student to the office, I asked him to supply his real name on the form I handed him. The tall, burly young man hung his head. His ears glowed red as he filled in the form and handed it back. I frowned.

"That **is** my name, ma'am," he mumbled.

"No, I mean your real name, the one on your birth certificate instead of what you like to be called."

"Ma'am, I don't know what to tell you. I was Billy Bob Haggard the day I was born. What do you want me to say?" It was my turn to blush.

"That's O.K. I just needed to make sure. We can't use a nickname, that's all."

"Yes, ma'am." He disappeared through the door, and I looked down at his records. Kentucky. I learned to conceal my ignorance a little better.

As the semester began to wind down, I noticed Art was spending more time with his calculus text. My rude pronouncement was true, and he had to struggle for a bare passing grade.

"Don't worry," he grinned. "I'll make it up."

"How? You going to take more math?"

"No, French." His eyes had a mischievous twinkle. "I talked to the professor of the most advanced French conversation course. We had coffee and I convinced him to let me take it next fall. Bring my grade point average up a little." In his good-natured way, Art had once more sidestepped adversity.

When the summer session began, Art invited me to sit in on his biochemistry lectures.

"You won't understand much, but I hear the prof is a great lecturer."

"I might just understand more than you think," I answered with a sniff, and accepted his invitation. The diploma clerk's office was closed for the summer. Despite my bravado, I absorbed very little, and slowly I began to realize Art was developing expertise I would never share. He was devouring the course; academic life was a natural habitat for him.

Vaguely, I began to sense my own inadequacy. My father used to sit down with me to help me understand why the paper I brought home had only a 97 instead of 100 on it. I had longed for a simple "Well done." Now, after failing at college, I faced life in the shadow of a superior intellectual being.

By this time, we had moved to an apartment of our own. University Terrace offered a few lucky married students new, furnished one-room apartments. The complex, built next to the university hospital, looked out from the top of a hill over the rolling countryside. Each room was a rectangle about twenty by thirty feet. Two-thirds was occupied by the living room, furnished with a sofa bed, chairs, tables, and lamps, and even a built-in bookcase. The Pullman kitchen with a dining table and two chairs formed an L, and the remaining space was filled by the bathroom and a capacious closet. The apartment was new, sturdy, yet stylish, and it seemed like a dream come true.

Often, we ate dinner accompanied by the radio. The adventures of Hercules Poirot, Agatha Christie's Belgian detective, entertained us several times a week; the memory would make us smile for years after.

This scene, however, was too often punctuated by the anger over trivial frustrations that welled up inside me and then exploded. "The stupid squash is getting cold, the potatoes are still crunchy, and I don't know whether the meat is cooked or not!" I would slam down my hand on the counter and burst into tears. My bewildered husband's only defense was to take over in the kitchen from his baby doll, actions that only made me pout all the more.

Neither of us realized these were the first open signs of my inner turmoil. Soon I developed a chronic problem keeping food down, and I consulted the university doctors. But when tests failed to reveal any organic cause, and pregnancy had been ruled out, they suggested I consult a psychiatrist. Sweeping my inner feelings under the rug no longer served; I needed help. Art never shared his feelings about this development. He had taken on a juvenile, a wildcat to tame, he had said. In his pragmatic way, he now stood steadfast, supporting me when he could or standing by until the storms passed.

To my delight, an old school acquaintance appeared. He was the older brother of a boy I had known in high school, that place where I had felt so unloved and unlovable. Now here was John on my doorstep, certainly innocent of the crimes of old, but a trophy nonetheless, somehow a symbol of acceptance into that old circle at last. John was a soft-spoken young man, also a student. Art liked him, too, and we befriended him, often inviting him to dinner or to a campus event. We learned that his brother, the one I knew, had died by his own hand, and although John gave no details, he was clearly affected. He was lonely and vulnerable.

Art had Saturday morning classes, and John began to visit the apartment then. Sometimes he came early, finding me still in bed. No matter, he came in anyway. He and I talked about life and meaning. It should have been clear that each of us still had growing up to do; we were pursuing our own agendas, throwing caution aside. John admired me, was courting, even. I knew that, and I glowed. Although our pleasure never went beyond respectable conversation, I was inflicting damage on him and on my marriage. Did I know that? Maybe.

John grew increasingly unhappy, restless. One day in May, just before Art's graduation in 1947, he announced that he was leaving school and volunteering for military service. Suddenly, he was gone. Word later came that he died. Would it have been different if I had helped him find his way, rather than leading him down a dead-end road? Of course, I never knew, but guilt haunted me.

Through it all, Art was the adult. He knew; he endured. Whether I strayed or not, he would love me still.

In the psychiatrist's office, I engaged in the struggle to find out who I was. Whether out of his own conviction—he was a patrician—or at the behest of my parents—who were footing the bill—or as a tool to force the issue—I never knew—Dr. Dieterle slowly began to suggest divorce.

"You know, my dear," he began softly, "life sometimes takes us down unexpected paths. There is no shame in recognizing that you are on the wrong one. You can acknowledge the error, back up, and start again."

"No, it's too late for that. I'm here and I need to deal with where I am."

"But you are only twenty. It might be the best idea. There's still a lot of life out there ahead of you."

I knew that my parents still thought my 'find' (that's what they said to the doctor) was unsuitable. But I also knew that Mother's parents harbored similar doubts about Dad. I refused the bait because I knew that if I bolted and ran, I would take myself and my problems away with me.

"I will not run," I told Dr. Dieterle. "However long it takes, however much pain there is, I will stay in this marriage as long as he will have me." It was not that he was handsome, nor debonair, nor authoritative; he was none of these, just an amiable, intelligent, energetic man who loved me with an intense constancy.

The first effect of counseling was to settle my stomach. After that, benchmarks were harder to recognize.

After three semesters and a summer session, Art graduated in June, 1947. Because of my privileged position in the diploma clerk's office, Art received the only real sheepskin diploma awarded that year; the rest were paper. I thought he deserved it after his brilliant choice of college training in the army; Uncle Sam had provided five semesters' credit.

Many companies sent interviewers to campus to comb through the new graduates for likely prospects. As Art walked out the door, I teased him, "Don't take less than $3,500 a year, not a penny less."

"Sure. I'll tell them."

That evening, when he returned, I asked eagerly, "Well, did you get it?"

"Sort of," he answered. "Fact is, I'm getting the salary and housing thrown in. I'm going to be an analytical chemist for Upjohn." I hugged him in joy and disbelief. The job would be outside Kalamazoo, three miles north, on an Upjohn horse farm.

We packed up our belongings and headed west in our new red Jeep.

MARRIED AND TWENTY-SOMETHING

A few miles northeast of Kalamazoo, the Upjohn-Richland Farms stretched across broad meadows and over rolling hills. The wheels of our Jeep crunched along the curving farmhouse driveway. Gray wood clapboards and black shutters suggested a venerable age, but the house seemed in good repair. The sparse lawn was freshly mowed and sunshine spilled across the porch roof. We were excited; this was to be our first real home.

"Let's inspect it," said Art. He was smiling with satisfaction as we climbed the four steps of the front porch. Boards creaked a little under our feet. "Step in to your new abode, m'lady." He was holding open the screen door.

"Oh. This is the kitchen! I expected a front entrance." I soon learned that the real front door was unobtrusively tucked around the corner of the house. In the country, this was the most important room. We admired the large, old-fashioned kitchen with plenty of room for a table at the bay window, looking over the peony bed in full bloom. Art had moved through a doorway, and I followed him.

"Art! This is wonderful! A nice dining room—and look! The living room is right through this big arch. How spacious!" But he had already disappeared into the bedroom hallway. Two generous bedrooms and the bath completed our tour.

"Did I tell you that it's all going to be redecorated before we move in? You get to go in to town and pick out whatever paint and wallpaper you want. We can go this afternoon, if you like. They want to get started early next week. I'll be in the lab, starting work. Think you can handle this end of the deal?"

Boldly, I said I could, but I felt apprehensive. As a child, I had always been allowed to choose wallpaper for my bedroom, but this was a whole house—a lot of responsibility.

Outdoors, we explored the garden. Few plants grew around the house, save for some spindly bushes. Too much shade, I thought. Just behind the house, on the south side, trees had been cleared and peonies planted.

"Boy," said Art, "there must be at least four dozen plants here. I wonder if this was once a commercial effort? It's sure too many for a house garden."

By the time we reached the paint store, it was Saturday afternoon. The sign on the door said: Closed until Monday at 7 a.m. That left all the choosing to me alone.

Remembering the lovely garden, I chose a wallpaper splashed with large peonies in a soft, muted red. They would climb up the walls and right over the ceiling in our bedroom, where we could admire them in winter. Later, the paperhangers guffawed over the crazy woman who had insisted on flowers on the ceiling. I did not care what they thought, but I did hold my breath a little until the furniture and curtains were in place.

"You were right, Honey," Art said, "the effect really is beautiful. You did good!" His praise made me glow with pride.

We settled all the rooms, having liberally helped ourselves to the surplus furnishings my mother had saved from their move out of New York. Domestic tranquility reigned.

Late one afternoon, and quite without warning, Art's parents appeared at our door. After nearly three years, they decided the marriage might just be serious after all. They came to look us over. With them were Amedée's brother, wife, and daughter—five in all. After all that time, Art and they fell into easy conversation, just as if nothing had intervened since their last meeting. I hoped my amazement was politely masked, as I scurried around to arrange space for them. One way or another, we managed to bed down the whole crew. They brought us gifts of blankets and kitchenware.

This was my first attempt at hosting in my own house, and I nearly blew it. The first morning, I said I was going to cook eggs, and I asked how they would like them. Everyone shifted easily to English, except Catherine.

"She'd like hers poached, just one. I'd like two, soft-boiled," said my father-in-law.

"Fry mine. I could use a couple. Sunny side up."

"Oh I like mine over easy. Yes, two sounds good."

"Could you scramble mine? Don't cook them too much, though."

Art laughed until I shot him a look. Foolish me! I actually tried to fill all the orders, but ever after that, guests would get eggs scrambled.

They stayed for three days and then were gone as suddenly as a flock of birds wheeling away in the sky. While I had been insulted and hurt by their shunning our wedding and the years of silence, Art took it in good humor.

"That's just the way they are, dear girl. They wouldn't have wanted to waste good money on a marriage that wasn't going to last. We passed their scrutiny, that's all. " I sniffed and said no more.

My counseling continued for several years. I still drove back to Ann Arbor for fifty minutes in Dr. D's office every few weeks. My inner—and outer—life improved, but how can I tell whether it was psychotherapy or simply time and love? Maturing a little, I began to appreciate Art's easy way with people, his growing self-confidence. While I had been belittling him at *Peaches 'n' Cream*, he had been busy learning all he could from my father about farming, from my mother about horticulture. He soaked up knowledge wherever he went.

And the job at Upjohn? It stank. Oh literally, it stank. The horse farm collected the urine of pregnant mares, extracting from it the hormone estrogen. Art analyzed the product for the correct concentration. The penetrating odor permeated his clothes, his skin, his hair. After work, he came in the cellar door, stripped off his clothes, put on a robe, and went in to take a shower. He shampooed every day and put on clean clothes. Why did people move away from us in the movies?

"My belt!" exclaimed Art in a sudden eureka moment. "And my wallet!" Once you grew accustomed to it, you could no longer smell it.

Life on the farm was pleasant enough, and Art was fully competent at the lab work, but after nearly a year he observed, "This job is so routine I could do it in my sleep. And how am I going to get anywhere out here in the sticks?"

He read an advertisement in the classified section of the Chicago Tribune, answered it, and promoted a job offer from Swift and Company, the Chicago meat packer. He would fill an opening in the research lab. Strange as it seems, the stockyards smelled better. We packed up and headed for life in the big city.

MORGAN STREET

Most of the houses on the block were built of yellow brick in the solid 1920s Chicago style, but we would move into a third-floor walk-up in one of the few apartment buildings—the only one three stories high. Our address was 79-something South Morgan Street in a white working-class neighborhood that years later became solidly black. Our windows looked over rooftops, a private aerie. A generous bay window bathed the living room in morning light; the bedroom faced east, too. The bathroom floor was tiled with small white octagons and all the fixtures were white—colored sinks and bathtubs were still years away. Two windows in the ample dining room looked south, while the small kitchen gave out to the open back-stair landing to the west. The kitchen was equipped with elderly but working gas stove and ice-box—real ice. All else was bare.

"What do you think? Can you manage here?"

"Art, it's wonderful. I can just picture draw draperies across the bay to keep us cozy in winter. I can make them. I'll get sheer curtains to filter the light. Wait and see: you'll like it."

A day or two later, the moving truck bumped along the alley and stopped behind our building.

"This it, lady?"

"Yes," I said, "it's on the third floor, up those stairs." I pointed to an open iron stairwell, wincing at the many turns, but glad I wouldn't be struggling with those heavy loads. I climbed up to direct traffic from the apartment. When the last box was dropped in the dining room, the men collected their fee and closed the door behind them. Earlier, I had shopped for a few day's meals and had ice put in the ice box.

"Oh my! Where to begin?" I opened a box of linens, found sheets, and began to make the bed. "When he gets home, I want to have everything neat, dinner ready, the table set." Finished with bed-making, I hung towels in the bathroom and kitchen, humming as I scurried around.

"Hm. Here's a box marked 'kitchen' but I don't see any pots. Must be another one somewhere." I rummaged around, tossing packing paper on the floor, hunting for the pots. Chaos began to take over. I put knives and forks in the kitchen drawers, stacked dishes on shelves. Still no pots. The paper pile grew.

I heard a key turn in the front door and suddenly there he was, standing in the kitchen doorway looking down at me, cross-legged on the floor, digging through the boxes.

"Hi, Babe! Hard day?"

"Oh darn, I was going to be so organized when you got home. Is it really that late already? I'm bushed." I took his hand and pulled myself up, feeling a bit limp. He kissed me, took off his coat, and we fixed dinner together. We found the pots in the last box. By bedtime, we had washed the dishes and put our new home in order, more or less. Our voices echoed as we called from room to room.

In the next few days, I found my way around the neighborhood. Nearby, on Ashland Avenue, I explored the groceries and department stores that offered just what I needed. Before long, I had curtains up and flowered draperies finished. I made a striped cover of coordinating fabric for the studio couch, brought from Maywood, and my parents carried in more furniture to fill bare places. The rooms began to feel like home, and with curtains hung, certainly sounded softer.

When the Chicago Antiques Show came to town, Art took me shopping. Our eyes fell on a plain Pennsylvania Dutch dry sink, about a century old. As we should have expected, the price tag was high and we hesitated.

"Do you want it?" he said.

"Oh yes. Oh yes. It's just perfect, isn't it? I wish we could afford it."

"Well we can. We have just under $200 in the bank, so $185 is entirely within reason."

"But Art! To spend everything we have on this one thing? Can we do that?" I was torn between hope and fear. Although I loved the sink, I did not want us to empty our account for my heart's desire. What did he want, I wondered.

"If we don't spend what we have to buy what we love, what's the money good for? I love it, too, and I think we should have it." Art bargained to have the cost of delivery included, and I wrote the check. When, later in our tour of the show, we found china cups and saucers I really wanted, I sighed and moved on. Although they matched my grandmother's dessert plates that I already had, it was too late to think about them. We had made a choice.

Post-war Chicago was heated entirely with soft coal. Before the Clean Air Act, before environmental awareness, we suffered whatever effects the emissions visited upon us. Although I doubt they left any lasting bodily harm, they wreaked havoc with my lovely nylon curtains, which filtered more than light. Every ten days, I took them down and dropped them into the bathtub, filled with sudsy warm water. The water turned murky black, and when I drained the tub, a greasy, dark line ringed the porcelain. Another sudsing and two rinses brought the curtains back to white, but before I could hang them, I needed to wash the window sills. The whole process hurt my knees, but the result was worth the pain. I neglected dusting furniture and the floors, but — inexplicably — washing and scrubbing were easy to keep up.

Art settled into the laboratory with zest. His enthusiasm and skill prompted his supervisor to include him in a vitamin research project and, ultimately, in the editing of a standard text on vitamin assay. Art still held many more credits in the G. I. Bill, and he enrolled at night in the graduate school of the Illinois Institute of Technology, working toward a master's degree in biochemistry. His days were filled with absorbing work, his early evenings with classes, and his late nights with study, ad he bent over books at the dining room table.

"Art, it's late. You'll be exhausted in the morning. Come to bed."

"Just a little longer, dear. I'm not tired." In the morning, he was bright and smiling.

I had no friend but Art, and he was enough. My tendency to withdraw and live in my own inner world blossomed. The field of my life lay fallow and I was content to let it rest. Books kept me company and soon Art persuaded me to join a Great Books study group. Aristophanes, Plato and Montaigne opened me to a new world of thought. Without realizing it, both Art and I were evolving as intellectuals—or so we hoped. Our vocabulary was sprinkled with ten-dollar words, even when perfectly useful short Anglo-Saxon words would have served as well. Even while this phase of our lives felt right, my clock was ticking.

When Art had applied for the apartment, the landlord asked, "You don't plan to have children, do you?"

"No, we don't have children," Art equivocated. It was a silly question to ask a young couple.

Although I had never thought I was too young to marry, I knew I was too young to be a mother. That was then. Now we had been married four years, and I was twenty-two.

"Art, when do you think I should have a baby?"

"Is that a proposition?" He grinned as he looked up from his book.

"No, seriously. Do you think it's time?"

"If you're ready, I'm ready. We're settled, we're comfortable with each other. Or at least that's the way it seems to me. I can't think of a reason why not."

It was settled then.

AND BABY MAKES THREE

Within a few weeks, by February 1949, I was in the throes of morning sickness. I consulted a local obstetrician. For me, pregnancy was a miraculous condition; for him, it was routine. I asked him how he could tell when a woman was getting close to delivery time, and he joked, "We just plunk their bellies, like testing a watermelon for ripeness. When she plunks just right, then we know."

I took myself too seriously to see the humor and was repelled by what I thought was an attitude of factory production. The next time we drove to the farm for a visit, I stopped to see Dr. Paul Boothby, the local general practitioner. He believed he could take care of me.

"You come to visit often enough, and if everything goes without a serious problem, it will work. If there's a problem, though, be prepared for me to turn you over to someone local. And," he added, "you will need to live at the farm during the final month. Can you do that?"

I looked to Art for confirmation, and we both nodded in agreement. Then I asked, in a naïve way, "Doctor, what do you charge for pre-natal care and delivery?"

"Well, do you have insurance? Blue Cross? Fine. Let me look."

He began to rummage around in his desk drawer, and I wanted to know whether he was looking for a rate sheet.

"Exactly," Dr. Paul replied, " I have no idea. Here it is. You're covered. Won't cost you anything." I remembered the Chicago doctor telling me the charge was two weeks' wages. We returned to Chicago feeling confident.

The morning sickness persisted, and it extended into most of the day. I could manage to keep down a small dinner if I ate it very slowly while lying down. Everyone assured me it would soon pass. Five months passed, but the sickness continued. A few times, when I was in Michigan, I lay in Dr. Paul's infirmary while nutrition dripped into a vein in my arm.

That was when Art's skill came to my rescue. The attending nurse probed my arm with the needle, trying to connect with a vein until I planted my foot in her chest, pushed her gently away, and called for Art. Ignoring her protest, he took the needle and deftly inserted it into my vein.

"There," he said with satisfaction, "your arm is as easy as a lamb's neck." The nurse shook her head in bafflement, but I laughed. From then on, he was my needle man. Despite the misery, my pregnancy progressed well. The prospect of a baby of our own kept me going, as I hemmed a dozen receiving blankets with featherstitching and knitted pretty baby clothes in yellow and green. I hummed lullabies and rocked in the creaky old wooden family rocker. As suddenly as it had begun, the nausea evaporated in my fifth month, and my energy returned in full.

By mid-September, I moved to the farm, where my parents had remodeled their little house into a spacious home, more than twice its former size. Art, of course, stayed home to keep house alone, except for his Friday-to-Monday visits to *Peaches 'n' Cream Farms*.

The peach harvest was winding down and McIntosh apples began to show a deep red blush on the trees. I pitched in with the packing house work when Mother didn't say that I had to rest.

"Mom, I'm having fun!" I insisted, but she was from the generation that called it a 'delicate condition'. At my size, I sure did not feel very delicate; it was too hard to drive the big John Deere tractor. I could not even climb to the seat.

An October wind blew in from the northwest bringing snow flurries. My nose was red, my hands grew numb, but I kept on, having the time of my life.

"Get up to the house, young lady! It's too cold in here for you. Besides, no one can get any work done with you straining your body like that. Scoot now!" I did as I was told, but it was too late. I was coming down with a very bad cold, getting really sick. Shivering, I wrapped myself in a blanket and curled up in a chair by the fireplace. One of the house cats jumped into my lap and warmed me with her purring and affectionate kneading. She had claws, but luckily too short to poke through the blanket. I slept.

When I stirred again, I felt strangely damp, and I realized that something else was happening to me. I reached for the telephone and dialed the number penciled on the yellow pad.

"Art? I'm so glad I got you. I was afraid you'd be away from the lab."

"What's up, Sweetheart? You sound stuffy."

"Well I am. I'm afraid I got a cold. But there's more. I think I'm going to have a baby—soon. Could you come?"

"I'm on my way, fast as the law allows. Maybe faster. Hang on!"

"Art? Please drive carefully. You're going to be a daddy."

"Worry not, m'love, I'll get there safe and sound. Love you Mommy!" He hung up, leaving the sweet sound of 'mommy' ringing in my ears.

My next call was to Dr. Paul, and he said he would meet me at the hospital, eight miles away. My heart was pounding now. I sneezed and felt an alarming dampness growing inside the blanket. Using the intercom to the packing house, I called Mother to come right away. She bundled me into the car, blanket and all. We sped east to Paw Paw and the hospital.

It was a large home on the lakeshore, converted for use as the municipal hospital. Originally, it was said, the house had been built in the 1920s by the mayor of Milwaukee to entertain a woman to whom he was not married. The story was the only good scandal in town.

On the second floor, the maternity ward held six beds. A nurse helped me into a hospital gown, tucked me into bed, and brought a box of tissues for my bedside table. It was Tuesday afternoon. By suppertime, Art was there, holding my hand. Although my labor had started, it stalled. Dr. Paul was mystified, but being a conservative man, he decided to avoid intervening without clear reason. Labor continued through the night, all day Wednesday, and Wednesday night. Dr. Paul brought in his brother, also a doctor. Neither one could see any obvious reason for the delay. It would only be much later that I remembered being treated by an army doctor for a minor infection. He had created a ring of inflexible scar tissue.

By noon on Thursday October 13th, Dr. Paul sent Art and Mother out to the garden to wait. Tuesday's snow flurries had blown away, and the sun was shining brightly. Dr. Paul and his brother set to work, and within the hour Susan Elizabeth had entered this world. They showed her to me only briefly and from a distance, then whisked her away to the nursery. My sniffles developed into wheezing, sneezing and coughing; that was the most uncomfortable part of the whole procedure. I particularly hated sneezing.

"But doctor," I said, "I must begin nursing her! Why can't I hold her?"

"Because, dear girl, we're not going to risk two of you having pneumonia."

"I don't have pneumonia. I have a cold."

"The baby is getting bottle formula. Don't worry."

He shook his head, patted my shoulder and left the room, saying "patience, patience." Contrary to the new books I had read about nursing, no one there took it seriously at all.

Susan and I stayed in the hospital for ten days while I recovered from my cold, she in the nursery and I in my bed. On discharge day, the nurses gathered around while I dressed the baby in the pale green suit I had knitted. I pulled the bonnet over her dark hair and tied the bow under her chin. She was so beautiful! Suddenly, one of the nurses burst out laughing.

"Did you ever see a frog in a little green suit?" Giggles all around. I looked at Art. His mouth was set and his eyes had narrowed. One of the nurses carried the baby down the stairs while Art and another nurse maneuvered my wheelchair down.

We were packed into the waiting car and we sped off toward the farm.

"Art, what was wrong back there? Were you insulted that they were laughing at the baby?"

"No," he said. "I just don't want her called a frog."

"But in that green suit, she does look a little froggy, don't you think?"

"Listen. You wouldn't call an Italian a wop, now would you? Or a Jew a kike? Well it's the same thing with a Frenchman. Don't call us frogs!" He was still angry. One day, long in the future, his children would be so entertained by this story that they would begin to give him what became a large collection of frogs. There are stuffed frogs, stone frogs, glass frogs, tin frogs, wood frogs, even a stained-glass frog. Slowly, the word evolved from pejorative to affectionate, and he could laugh, too.

Eager to take his growing family home, Art soon bundled us all into the car for the ride back to Chicago.

"Honey, I can do that! You don't have to wait on me." Art set the tray of lunch on my chair-side table.

"Get used to it, Kid. I've taken vacation time for this project and it's going to work. You'll stay right there, play with Suzy and drink. And drink." He poured a steaming cup of tea and handed it to me. "Drink."

"But I'm gurgling! Enough!"

"Never enough. We're going to get your milk production up, just like Dad's cows." La Leche League, possibly not even established yet in Chicago, would have given him a medal. He brought glasses of milk, cups of tea, bottles of beer, every half hour.

"I've heard that beer is very effective. You'll learn to like it." No one in those times ever thought about possible effects from the alcohol.

I obeyed, and the treatment worked. Before his vacation was over, Suzy was drinking nearly a quart of my milk a day.

How did we know? We weighed her both before and after feedings, keeping a careful log. Parents of first babies tend to go overboard.

Our lives filled up with love and laughter. Baby Susan slept while I kneeled at the bathtub, washing diapers. If the weather was fine, clothes lines were strung on the back stair landing, but on rainy or freezing days, the dining room served. I bundled her up and took her walking in her handsome new navy blue perambulator. Even our landlord and his wife came out to exclaim over her. At night, Art rose to pick her up for her middle of the night feeding. He brought her to me in bed and held me close as the baby suckled. One night, captivated by her yawn, he snapped pictures of her.

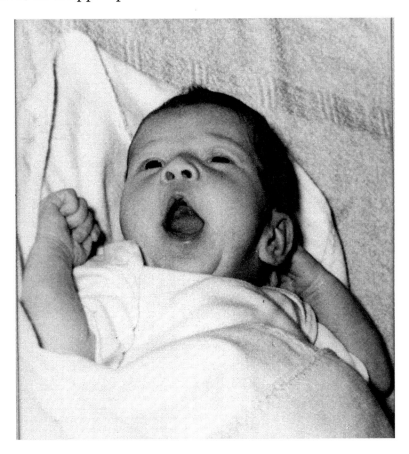

"Dear, it's three o'clock. Put out the light and stop acting like a foolish father!"

"But I am a foolish father."

Within a few weeks, this idyllic scene faded into colic. Oh how that baby cried! She cried in the day. She cried in the night. I walked with her, rocked her in grandmother's dear, creaky old rocking chair. She cried. Exhausted, I did a little crying, too.

One day, she awoke from her nap with a piercing scream. She was inconsolable. Desperate, I dialed the number for the pediatrician's office. This experienced man came to the phone and heard her cry.

"Get a cab and bring her to the hospital without delay. I'll meet you there." My hands shook as I looked up the number for a taxi. Best to wait until I know what this is about, I thought, before calling Art. My mind was racing nearly as fast as my heart. The baby's screams pierced the air as I ran with her down the flights of stairs and into the cab.

"To the hospital on Ashland Avenue," I said to the driver. One look at us, and he nodded, speeding off down the street.

At the emergency entrance, I paid the driver and hurried inside. The doctor met us and ushered us to a cubicle.

"What is it, Doctor?"

"Intussusception, probably. Excuse me. Telescoping of the bowel."

"But she seems fine now. Are you sure?" She had stopped crying and was cooing at one of the nurses.

"The pain comes and goes. Best way to find out is a barium enema. We can diagnose it through radiology. Sometimes the enema itself is the cure, sometimes not. If not, immediate surgery is indicated. This is life-threatening, mother." Blindly, I signed the papers thrust in front of me while a nurse made preparations to wheel the baby away. I asked for a phone, and dialed Art's number. He was away from the lab and I had to leave a message with a colleague.

Before the doctor emerged from surgery, Art was by my side. I explained what I understood and squeezed his hand. When he took me in his arms, my heart slowed down and I felt my breathing return to normal.

"Well," said the doctor as he strode toward us, "we were right. The bowel had a nice little telescope in it. You'll be glad to know the enema provided a diagnosis and a resolution, too. We could watch the bowel unfold itself."

The radiologist offered us souvenir pictures, but we declined. All I wanted was to get my baby back.

"Not today, dear lady. Sometimes these conditions recur in the first 24 hours. We'll admit her and keep an eye out. You can come back tomorrow to see her." With that, he turned and walked away. I asked a nurse, "Can't I stay with her? She'll be frightened."

"No, dear, she's in a ward with other infants. They'll take good care of her. Don't worry." Consideration for the emotional needs of patient and family came somewhere after efficiency in hospital priorities. We went home to wait. The following day, I returned to find Susan dressed and waiting. She seemed none the worse for her adventure; in fact, she laughed when a nurse made a funny face for her. If I could have peered into a clear crystal ball, I would have seen that this little girl was destined to be at home in most social situations.

When she was a little more than a year old, Susan developed a keen sense of time. Late in the afternoon, she dragged a little suitcase I had given her for play over to the bay window. Climbing on it so she could see up the street, she waited patiently. At last, Daddy strode around the corner. He looked up and waved, driving her into a storm of excited giggles. "Dere's Daddy," she cried. "Here come Daddy!" They had a bond.

Far away in Ohio, my brother David surprised us by sending an invitation to his wedding. Yellow Springs was a long day's drive each way. I wanted to go, but the trip with an eleven-month-old baby would have been hard for everyone. Thank goodness for nearby family! We pressed my cousin's housekeeper, Leora, into service as Susan's caretaker.

"Don't you worry, Miz Fournier, I've done this before. Took care of Miz Webster's babies, every one of them." She came with loving assurances from my Glencoe cousin's household.

Art and I headed for Yellow Springs. On the way, I asked him, "Do you suppose there's a Master Plan for these things?"

"I dunno. What do you mean?"

"The wedding date, dear. September 29th."

"So?"

"Darling, we met on September 29th, just seven years ago. Isn't that strange? And wonderful?"

"I guess so. How do you remember things like that?" His tone added: and why?

"Oh never mind. It's because I'm a girl I guess." Just the same, when we got there, Art walked me to the science building, sat me down on the brick wall and kissed me.

"What was that for?"

"Nothing. Just something I wanted to do then but didn't get around to."

True to her word, Leora had managed our household perfectly. All the baby's diapers and clothes were washed and folded in the drawers. Susan clung to Leora when we first entered. I felt a pang of jealousy, but Leora kissed her on the cheek and handed her to me. "She'll know you now. You feel right to her." She certainly felt right to me.

The colic that had plagued us all slowly diminished and disappeared. Suzy and I walked nearly every day. We stayed home in heavy rain or snow, when the temperature dropped below 20°, or when the weather was too blustery. On such days, Suzy sat in her playpen, surrounded by toys, content for ten minutes at a time. She really wanted me to turn her loose to explore her world, and protested firmly when I did not.

Before the end of January, I began to feel queasy. No rabbit test was needed this time. Our family was growing, but the apartment was not.

PARK FOREST

In the far south suburbs of the city, an entirely new kind of town was building, designed for young families like ours. Park Forest became notorious as *the* social experiment of the 1950s. William Whyte took up residence, interviewed the natives, and wrote *The Organization Man*.

Art applied to the developer for a rental townhouse. Entry rules were strict—minimum annual income was $4,300. Not missing a beat, Art wrote down that his income was exactly that.

"It's OK, Kit," he explained, "after my next raise I'll be making that much." We were accepted. Our July moving date started out warm and progressed to downright hot.

My morning sickness had again subsided after five months. Art's prescription of pyridoxine (vitamin B6)—brought home from the lab—mixed with peanut butter and spread on crackers speeded my recovery. His understanding of this use of the vitamin predated general medical practice by several decades. By the 1990s, it was a standard remedy.

"When is the baby due?" asked one of our new neighbors.

"Six weeks," I answered. The question startled me, because I thought I showed very little. It would be only the first in an unending string of questions about what I had always considered private matters.

Group living was new to me, and I embraced it at first. Lively companionship and easy acceptance lured me into the circle. We lived in each other's laps with no locked doors to deter drop-in visits. I was rarely alone.

We were divided into two age groups: 23 to 30 and 0 to 10, weighted toward the bottom of both ranges. No elderly residents tempered our perspective.

"Sally, was that a new diaper service I saw this morning? Didn't recognize the truck. Problems with Village Diapers?"

"Not exactly. Just the driver. That guy Terry finally got up his nerve and made a pass at me last Monday. I sent him packing, for sure."

"Yeah, he tries it sooner or later. If he was just better looking…"

Everyone laughed, and I made a note to myself not to use Village Diapers. Catty remarks about a neighbor spending too much money on clothes made me realize I should say nothing about anything I bought, lest I be the subject next time.

"How much does your husband make?" was a favorite question. My answer—enough to hold body and soul together—produced raised eyebrows and a few frowns. I began to withdraw a little the day a neighbor came in and found me reading—a book! A real book, not a pulp novel.

She began, "Kit, I've been meaning to tell you. To keep up with the current style in decorating, you really need to get rid of your bookcases. Maybe move them to your bedroom, at least. A few magazines on the coffee table would be OK, but it's really a bad idea to let people know you read books. They might think you're acting superior. Putting on airs, you know. Come on down to our level, dear." I must have looked as stunned as I felt, for she added, "No offense, just a word to the wise."

I decided to venture further into the larger community. Our small neighborhood was fine for mutual support, exchange baby-sitting, but it would not, apparently, provide real friends. Were there any other eccentrics like me out there?

ROUNDING OUT THE FAMILY

Right now, it was time to move to the farm to wait for a new baby. Suzy and I boarded the train for Michigan, leaving Art to fend for himself. At the farm, my grandfather and aunt offered baby-sitting, leaving me free to help with berry picking and tomato canning. Art drove over on weekends. One Saturday night, Dad, Mother, Art, and I were invited to an evening picnic at the Braybrooks' farm. I fed Suzy and put her to bed, leaving instructions with my grandfather. As I prepared to dress, I thought about the picnic. There would be thick, juicy hamburgers, barbecued chicken, maybe ribs, too. Corn on the cob would be plentiful, and sliced tomatoes. Would there be peach shortcake, with real biscuits and thick cream? Certainly. I knew how Ethel Braybrooks mounted a picnic. Mmmm. I could nearly taste all of it.

"Oops! What's this?" In the shower, I realized I was in the earliest stages of labor. What to do? Tell someone? No, they would make me stay home. This was going to be a major event of my summer, and no one would cheat me out of it. I padded myself as well as I could and said nothing.

Sure enough, Ethel outdid herself. About two dozen guests ate and drank and talked for hours. As the food and drink lulled us all into lethargy, we gathered in small circles of quiet talk. We sat, Indian style, on blankets and watched stars wink on overhead as the spectacular sunset faded. Lightning bugs blinked on and off among the grasses. Katydids provided evening background music. I slipped the watch from the wrist of one of the men, a doctor, but he took no notice. After awhile, startled, he asked, "Are you doing what I'm afraid you are? How far apart are the contractions?"

"About fifteen minutes, I think."

"What? Listen, girl, I've never delivered a baby in a corn field and I don't want tonight to be my first. ART!" he called, "come take your wife to the hospital."

The secret was out, and we were sent on our way, two miles down the road to Dr. Paul's house and infirmary. Art pulled the Ford station wagon into the yard. Dr. Paul hustled us into an examining room, and after a quick look sent us home.

"Not until tomorrow, I think. Get a good night's rest." He turned toward his bedroom to do the same.

We continued to the farm, but sleep eluded me. Every time I started to doze off, a contraction woke me. I got lonesome and woke Art. We lay side by side, talking, until another contraction began.

"It doesn't hurt particularly, just grabs my attention." Art grew anxious. Maybe he was thinking he had never delivered a baby anywhere, and he did not want to start here. Whatever it was, he insisted we should return to Dr. Paul.

Probably wanting to finish what was left of his night's sleep, Dr. Paul put me to bed with a relaxing potion, gave Art a slug of caffeine and an Esquire magazine and left us alone. I dozed.

Through a thick haze, I poked Art. "Wake Dr. Paul," I said.

"Let the poor guy sleep."

"No really. I've progressed."

Dr. Paul came, took a quick look, and said to Art, "You get her up and outside. I'll bring my car around. Do it now!" and he disappeared out the door.

Into the back seat of the doctor's brand new Cadillac I went. Art followed in his car. Later, Art told me he never dreamed our wagon could do 88 miles an hour. "And you were pulling away!" he added.

As we sped along U.S. 12 to Paw Paw, Dr. Paul called back to me, "Don't push! Open your mouth, pant, holler. Just don't push!"

Clearly, Dr. Paul had never been in labor himself. The next morning, a nurse told me they all thought the ambulance was coming in with siren howling. I did holler, but inevitably, I pushed. That night, I'm afraid I christened Dr. Paul's fine new car.

Picking me up in his arms, the doctor took me upstairs, two at a time. He was a short, stocky man, and he was breathing hard. I heard a nurse exclaim as we went by, "I bet I know who's going to contribute for an elevator in the new hospital!"

By now, Art was racing upstairs after us. As he entered the delivery room, Dr. Paul beckoned him to the sink where both washed their hands. Then the doctor poured a little liquid into a pad of gauze.

"Here, put this over her nose, just for a minute." The room went dark briefly, and then I woke again to hear the newborn cry of Anne Carolyn. The men had deprived me of that glorious moment of delivery. I was sorry for that, but nevertheless filled with joy. It was three o'clock in the morning, September 16, 1951. I drifted off to sleep.

"Here! What are you doing out of bed? You must still be drunk from that little sip of ether last night!" It was only eight o'clock. The nurse was trying to guide me back to my room, but I would have none of it.

"I feel wonderful! And I want my baby." I strode down to the nursery and picked her up out of the crib. "Please wheel her crib down to my room so I can see her all the time." It was an unorthodox idea, but the ward was empty, so why not? I held her in my arms in my bed.

I needed to put her down and go to the bathroom, so I gathered all my pillows and set Anne in the middle of the big bed, propping pillows on both sides and at her feet and head.

"And where did you think she was going? I know she's probably precocious, but most babies don't roll over, or get up and walk the first day." The nurse stood in the doorway watching me.

"Oh, I guess that's right. I was thinking a little ahead." I left her to watch while I went away.

Later on Sunday afternoon, Dr. Paul came to see us.

"Please, doctor, I'm bored. The hospital is fine, but it's boring. Can I have permission to go out?'

"I don't see why not. Don't drive yet—leave that to your mother. Stay close by to feed the baby and sleep at night. Otherwise, you're free to go." This time, there would be no languishing in bed for ten days. In three days, baby and mother left Paw Paw. On Friday, Art picked me up and we left for home Sunday morning. The family was complete.

How Anne Carolyn grew in one year!

A NEW CHURCH

The Park Forest developer provided for everything: homes, playgrounds, stores, laws, schools, and churches. The first religious group to form was non-denominational Protestant. Characteristically, most residents were breaking ties with their past. The single exception was the Catholic church, established in town very early

One town ordinance prohibited gambling. This seemed unremarkable to most, but bingo games in the basement of the Catholic church continued undisturbed as did troops of children selling lottery tickets door-to-door. Eventually, someone complained at a town meeting.

"If gambling is against the law, then they ought to be stopped," claimed one young man in the audience.

"That's right. The law's the law. I couldn't get away with that!"

A lively debate ensued, some taking that side, some dismissing it as all right for a church. I sat still, watching tempers rise.

"But the law makes no exception for churches!" I said out loud.

When the council voted, they came down on the side of the law, ordering both games to cease forthwith. Slowly, the local priest stood up to address the city fathers.

"You may have whatever laws you like. As for me, my instructions come from Rome, and I don't give a fig for your local laws. The games will continue." He sat down to shocked silence.

I had never thought very deeply about the pros and cons of gambling. In fact, I thought gambling was a rather vacant pastime and I scorned the suckers who would buy lottery tickets. Still, live and let live, I had thought. Now, the naked gall of this priest made me angry. To defy the laws by which we lived in favor of the narrower interest of the church was intolerable. In a fury, I wrote a letter to the editor of the local paper, defending the principle and ending "I dare him to send someone to my house to sell me a lottery ticket. I will go to the police and swear out a warrant for his arrest." Needless to say, sellers of lottery tickets made a wide berth around our house. Art observed that his wildcat was on the prowl. Nothing came of the letter.

Well, something did come of it. A handful of closet Unitarians read my letter and called me up. Like iron filings to a magnet, we gathered together sharing our unconventional views. Soon, eight or ten of us were meeting regularly in our living room.

At first, we simply enjoyed the freedom. In this company, we could talk about the religious education of our children without biblical constraints, ignoring what the neighbors might think if we taught them about Judaism, Buddhism, Taoism, or Islam. Even the atheists among us had concerns about the meaning of living a spiritual life. We yearned to give expression to our deeply felt religious thought. Before long, we were discussing the formation of a Unitarian fellowship. By general consent, I was selected to investigate with the theological school at the University of Chicago writing bylaws and establishing an official fellowship.

At first, Art stayed out of it. More conservative than I— and certainly less interested in religion than I—he sat in the dining room, ostensibly studying. In part, he was listening.

"We won't need much money," said Bernie. "We can just pass a collection plate on Sundays and use the money for expenses. Let's not get bogged down in bookkeeping. This is about religion."

"Yes, well we don't want to pressure anyone who might not be able to afford much, but maybe we need to set up a system of annual pledging." That brought shocked silence and then a change of subject.

"Can we continue to meet here, Kit? We could take turns bringing refreshments. What about Sunday mornings?"

What he heard convinced Art that none of us had any appreciation of money management. We were all vision and ideals. Eventually, he joined us in the living room and was elected our first treasurer. Much later, he told me, "I felt I had to get in there and protect my financial interest." I was never able to judge the depth of his interest in the spiritual aspect of the group, but he certainly joined in the camaraderie of what quickly became a thriving community. As the group's first president, I soon found myself negotiating to rent a schoolhouse for Sunday services and the burgeoning Sunday school. More people than we had dreamed were attracted to liberal religious thought.

One Sunday morning, a professor from the University of Chicago Theological School came as a guest preacher. He stayed for dinner at our house, and the three of us visited well into the evening. He was full of curiosity about our new town, about Art's vitamin research, about my family background. During that evening, he imparted wisdom and inspiration about church leadership. He was remarkably funny. Reluctantly, we ended the evening and I drove him to the train station.

As he left the car, a policeman approached me. "Evening, ma'am. Did you know you ran a stop sign back there?"

I gulped hard. "No, sir. If there was one there, I sure didn't see it."

"Well, there's one there all right. You usually skip stop signs?"

Oh just get on with the ticket, I thought, but slowly began to realize a ticket was beside the point. He was shaking me down for a bribe! I was furious, but had no idea how to handle the situation.

Just then, I saw that the minister had turned back to my car. "Excuse me, officer, is there a problem?" The policeman stepped back at the sound of his powerful voice. "This good lady is the leader of her church, and she has kindly driven me here to catch the train. I am a professor at the University of Chicago." With a frown, he handed his card to the officer. "Dr. James Luther Adams," he went on, "now — is there a problem here?"

Uncertain of the suggested influence of this commanding presence, the policeman mumbled, "No sir" as he backed away, climbed into his squad car and drove off. I had been rescued from harassment and probably a court appearance. Only later did I come to appreciate that Dr. Adams would be known as one of the greatest theologians of the 20th century.

The little fellowship prospered and expanded into every corner of our lives. We held an annual jazz festival that became a popular public event. Performers included rising stars of the day: Art Hodes, Big Bill Brunzy, and Pete Seeger. Every week, we square danced. Although neither of us was adept at the fox trot or the waltz, Art and I learned to do-si-do and right-and-left grand with enthusiasm and even grace.

"If we're going to be square dancers, don't you think we should dress the part?" Art was really getting into it. "I think I'd like a new shirt."

Soon, he was decked out in a turquoise cowboy shirt with black piping and string tie. I wore a twirling skirt to match, layered with petticoats, all products from my sewing machine. We were having fun.

Eight of us formed what we grandly called 'The Gourmet Club'. Once a month, we gathered to share a pot-luck dinner following a national theme. That's how I was introduced to Japanese seaweed.

"Oh this is great!" lied George Rosner.

"Yeah, terrific," agreed Art, pushing it to one side on his plate.

"Well, it's a staple in the Japanese diet," Maxine protested, "it must be good for something."

A few vulgar suggestions from the men about what it might be good for, and the matter was settled. No more seaweed. We four couples formed a bond that lasted to the ends of our lives, even though we scattered across the country. Joann and Will Zucker struggled to the death with her multiple sclerosis and his liver cancer. Elaine and Marvin McDaniel moved to San Diego. Our strongest bond was with Maxine and George Rosner, who would be the closest friends of our lives.

In less than two years, the fellowship grew large enough to seek a minister. With the help of the denomination headquarters in Boston, we found John Alexie Crane in British Columbia. Lex and his wife moved to Park Forest and became our two-doors-down neighbors. My feeling of being a cultural outsider began to fade away.

Although we soon moved from Park Forest, the church continued to thrive. In a strange coincidence, more than half a century later the minister of our church in Williamsburg, Virginia, would be called to the Unitarian Universalist Church of Park Forest, Illinois.

POLITICS

It was 1952, a presidential election year. Most of our neighbors were indifferent to politics and made no effort to be informed about issues. A few were, as the phrase went, 'madly for Adlai'. Adlai Stevenson, the Democratic candidate, should have been a natural for my support, but I believed his strong academic credentials and little charm made him unelectable.

"He's too liberal for me," said Art. "The thing is, it doesn't make any difference. After twenty years of Democrats in the White House, the country is ready for a change. Mark my words, our next president will be a Republican."

"But *what* Republican? The clear front-runner is Robert Taft of Ohio. Do you really want a head-in-the-sand isolationist in Washington? We should be able to do better than that. He scares me."

"Me too," admitted Art. "Well, let's wait and see. There's talk about drafting Eisenhower. He's been around the block. He'd be a better bet."

Soon, Art got wind of a small group in our town that was organizing to campaign for Ike. We joined them. Around the country, similar groups were growing, but the editorial writers and the newscasters gave little hope. The nominating convention would be held in Chicago, where Taft's support was solid. Midwesterners gave their loyalty to this senator, son of the 27th president.

We threw ourselves into the fray. I, the stay-at-home-mom, produced flyers from a mimeograph machine in our basement. Pushing the baby carriage, I delivered "I Like Ike" buttons from door to door.

"Good evening," I said brightly, gathering my courage. "I have information for you about General Eisenhower. This is going to be an important election year, so I hope you'll read about him and support his nomination for president. Just in case you do decide, here's a button for you to wear. Let's let our neighbors know where we stand."

Although my sales skills were a little weak, my enthusiasm seemed to come through. Nearly everyone smiled and took the materials I offered.

As I walked along the buildings, I glanced through each living room window I passed. Without exception, the children in every household stood before the television in rapt attention. Each head sported a pair of large black mouse ears. Little voices intoned the anthem: *M I C, K E Y, M O U S E, Mickey Mouse, Mickey Mouse!* Not just some living rooms—every one. In unison. It was the national anthem of 1952.

Art took vacation time and rode the train to Chicago every morning to join about fifty others. The president of the Union Pacific Railroad provided minute-to-minute information about the arrival of delegates at the three major rail stations in the city. Racing from station to station, fifty people began to seem like mobs everywhere. With banners flying, a small band playing, they chanted "I like Ike! Ike for president!" as the delegates streamed from the trains. On the evening news, we heard, "It's amazing. This should be Taft country, but there seems to be a ground swell for Eisenhower. His supporters are everywhere. It's going to be a horse-race, folks!" Art organized the communication links between pay phones in the stations and the office phone at Union Pacific.

The Taft camp expressed confidence. "Wait until we get to the convention floor. You'll see where the strength lies."

As the delegates prepared to begin balloting, the doors to the hall were flung wide, and the claque—now about doubled in number—surged through, waving their flags and chanting for Ike. In the end, the vote went overwhelmingly for Eisenhower.

On election night, we partied with our compatriots in Park Forest.(Let it be said that we remained in the Republican camp until Barry Goldwater ran in 1964. Neither of us could stomach the failure of the right wing of the party to disclaim the John Birch Society or the saber-rattling speeches of the candidate. Lyndon Johnson scored the greatest landslide since Franklin Roosevelt's 1936 sweep.)

When Art stepped forward to take a leadership role in the 1952 Eisenhower campaign, another campaigner took note. "Art, would you come down to my office on Wacker Drive for a talk with our people?" The man was sales manager for International Minerals and Chemical Company.

Art's Wacker Drive office talk developed into a job offer with IMC, a major producer of agricultural fertilizers and industrial chemicals. Art would join the sales team, covering a territory that included southern Michigan, Ohio, Indiana, and part of Illinois.

"This entails a lot of travel, Kit," he explained. "I'd be gone from Monday to Friday most weeks. They'll give me a company car and more than half again as much money as I'm making now. The travel might be hard on you, though. What do you think?"

Having not a clue what travel might mean to me, but sure the salary would be great for us, I answered, "Go get 'em, tiger!"

Art tried to give notice to his superior at Swift.

"Never mind, Fournier. If that's the way you feel, you can go right now." Art was stunned to be cast off without a second thought, but it taught him to protect himself first.

In the beginning, Art traveled to the office in downtown Chicago every day, undergoing orientation and training. Along with the job change came Art's painful decision to leave graduate school for awhile. That while turned out to be forever, leaving him with half a master's in biochemistry and half in business administration. The academic life of a medical researcher had appealed to him, but now he had caught a glimpse of the cosmopolitan world of commerce. It set him on fire.

"Kit, by the time I'm thirty-five, I will be pulling down $10,000 a year. Promise."

I was nonplussed by his bold declaration. At thirty-one, Art was pledging an increase of one-third over his new level in four years, in addition to the leap from his Swift salary. When I remembered General MacArthur, though, I knew it was a cinch. And so it proved to be.

Life became more comfortable as our affluence grew. Art insisted we buy a washing machine, and when it was installed in our basement, I washed the first load of clothes in it. In that dark, damp basement the clean white porcelain box shone like a beacon. The thrill of that moment has never left me. A washing machine is, for me, a treasured luxury.

Soon, Art graduated from training and set out on the road, driving with a senior sales representative on a tour of his new territory. Since Eisenhower's interstate highway system was still only a plan in Washington, they traveled narrow two-lane roads that crept through every town on the way. Art's mentor was an enthusiastic patron of good restaurants; he knew every one. Who could have guessed the tiny hamlet Red Key, Indiana, boasted a world-class French restaurant, hard by the railroad tracks? Wine glasses sloshed when freight trains rumbled through, and all conversation stopped. Dinner was superb. Marshall had the original Schuler's, pride of Michigan. The all-you-can-eat lobster place near Cleveland was a real find. They ate their way from one end of the territory to the other. After that, Art was on his own.

Life on the road is a lonesome business. Although there were established clients, Art had a quota to meet that called for new customers. He had to make cold calls, gleaned from the local Yellow Pages. He was a stranger knocking on the door of a tight little world. His product line was fine chemicals and bulk commodities, the same line offered by competitors at the same prices. It was Art's credibility for sale, his ability to convince strangers that he was reliable, a problem solver. Although bribery and kickbacks were commonly expected, his customers would do without these perks from him. They had to like him, that was the bottom line.

Years later, Art confessed to me, "After dinner, I would go up to my little hotel room and pull out the phone book. I made notes for tomorrow's trolling and practiced what I would say. Usually, before I went to bed, I had lost my dinner. I was really scared. But in the morning, I put on my sincerest tie and set out again." He smiled in remembrance. "Kit, did I make you cry? I'm sorry. It's all in the past now."

Tears rolled down my cheeks as I pictured this earnest, determined young man who would rise above his fears and make it, all alone. I hugged him. "You're quite a guy."

His first quota was met, then the next, and the next. He was on his way. In time, the territory became routine and the evenings more comfortable, though too long. Movies appealed only some nights. Ever resourceful, Art bought the parts for a Heathkit and built a radio tuner, amplifier, turntable—a complete music system. The finished product occupied an important place in our living room for many years.

"I wonder if I left a string of hotel electric bills along the territory that spiked according to my schedule?" He laughed. "After all, I soldered hundreds of connections, hour after hour."

ON OUR OWN

For about two years, the children and I were on our own. Art traveled from Monday morning to Friday night nearly every week. The neighborhood baby-sitting cooperative gave me a chance to join the League of Women Voters and accept an appointment as a commissioner of traffic and safety, but most of the time, I stayed home to cook and clean and launder. And to take care of sick children. Living as close together as we did, our children freely shared germs with one another.

"I could consider," joked Dr. Rosenbloom, "group rates for the neighborhood. Just pitch a tent in a front yard and pile all the kids into the infirmary." None of the illnesses was serious; it was their unrelenting presence that led to burn-out among us young mothers.

My new friend, Maxine, told me, "I knew we were destined to be friends when we kept meeting at the League and at city council meetings and then at church." She was right, and in those times, we preserved each other's sanity. Her boys, Kent and Andy, were each a year younger than our two. We lived about a mile apart and, both housebound, survived on our telephone conversations. Many an afternoon we ironed as we gossiped and discussed our philosophies for hours. That is, I ironed. Two little girls went through many starched, puffed-sleeve dresses in a week. While she talked, Maxine busied herself with her favorite diversion: cooking.

Susan was nearly four and had developed a severe skin reaction to foods. The patches of eczema in the bend of elbows and knees itched terribly; I taught her not to scratch, fearing scars. But she itched, and she needed to scratch. I watched her from a distance as she sat in the sandbox circle. She began to squirm.

"Suzy!" I called sharply, as I ran toward her, but it was too late. Susan could stand it no longer and reached over to scratch the child next to her. Screams erupted. Mothers came running from all directions. What a commotion! I gathered up my little girl and retreated, bending under the shouts of infuriated parents and screaming children.

"Take her away from here!" shouted one mother. "If she can't behave herself, she is banished from the playground." My explanations blew away in the wind. Inside the house, I sat and rocked my baby until her sobs died away and my heart stopped pounding.

In a few days, I enrolled Susan in nursery school, directed by a compassionate older woman. I needed her calming, mature influence, so sadly missing in our town. Sure that her first day would be traumatic for Susan, I stopped the car in front of the building.

"Hold my hand, dear. Let's find Mrs. Waldman." As the woman approached, Susan slipped her hand from mine and ran into the school yard, pigtails bobbing up and down. She had discovered swings. Mrs. Waldman put her arm around my shoulders and led me back to the car.

"She never said goodbye or even looked back," I said.

"The first day is hard, but you will survive. I seldom need to worry about new children, but the mothers have some pain. It will pass."

I gulped hard and drove slowly down the street.

Susan loved the first year of nursery school. Her reaction was a harbinger, for she was to have an outgoing and independent nature all her life.

Anne, approaching two, knew no problems—life came easily for her. Her delicate blonde hair and sweet face charmed everyone on whom she smiled. She was a sunny youngster, but adventurous even then. She was alarmingly fearless.

When Friday night finally came, the three of us waited eagerly to see the red Ford come around the corner and into our courtyard. Art opened the door and two little girls wrapped themselves around him.

"Daddy! Daddy! What did you bring me?"

"Come see what I have!"

"Me first!"

"No, me first!"

Poor Daddy had just driven three hundred miles after a full morning's work. Nevertheless, he staggered up to the back door, four little arms wrapped around his legs. He gave me a long kiss that promised better for later and dropped into a kitchen chair.

"What's for dinner and when?" he asked wearily.

LESSONS IN GRACE

Peaches 'n' Cream farmhouse expanded

In April and May, we visited *Peaches 'n' Cream* three times. That my parents were experiencing serious financial difficulties never penetrated my consciousness. When Dad took another job away from the farm, I assumed this meant the old war horse was hanging on to the world of business. Even when Mother took a job in a department store in Kalamazoo, thirty miles distant, I did not get it. In a very naïve way, I thought my parents' wealth and comfort were unassailable. What did I know of the ups and downs of agriculture?

Dad was experiencing a mysterious numbness in one hand, and had come to Chicago for evaluation, weeks before. The doctors thought he had suffered a small stroke from which he would soon recover. I was reassured, as a child would be, by soothing words. The Baby Doll still lurked in my nearly twenty-eight-year-old body. My father, the pillar of my existence, would be fine. I needed him to be fine.

On May 24th, I answered a call from the farm. Mother needed my help. I phoned Maxine. "Tomorrow's the nursery school pot-luck, and I'm heading the committee. Could you possibly take my place?"

"Of course I can. What's wrong, Kit? You sound upset."

"Well, I'm not sure yet, but Dad's sick and Mother is asking me for help, that's all I know. Thanks. I'll call you when I get back."

I packed clothes and children into the car and set out on the three-hour drive for the place I still sometimes called 'home'. My heart raced and my palms grew sweaty on the steering wheel. My parents were my bulwark; I called them in time of need. That they now called me filled me with dread.

When I arrived, the scene was worse than I could have imagined. Dad was sick, but that happens to everyone sometimes. It was his eyes. I climbed up on his bed, leaned close to him, took his hands in mine, and looked directly into his eyes. Once I saw a rabbit caught in a box trap. His eyes were like that.

He whispered, "Stay with me. I am afraid."

"Afraid of what, my dear?"

"The seizures. I don't want another one. It's awful." I put my head on the pillow next to his and caressed his hair.

When the ambulance came and they carried him out the door, he called to Clayte, the farm manager. "Take care of things for me, will you?"

"I sure will do that. You can count on it."

Then they were gone. Mother and I followed in my car. She spoke very little, only telling me that Dr. Paul had sent them to a neurosurgeon at Bronson Hospital in Kalamazoo. Her face was bleak.

How long was it—hours? days?—before the surgeon called us into his office. He showed us x-rays of Dad's brain.

"This shadow here—I'm pretty sure it's cancer. I need to operate, try to remove all of it. I have to tell you, I'm not optimistic."

Mother put her signature on the papers he thrust in front of her, and we went up to see Dad. What followed was a nightmare that I promised myself no one I loved would ever again endure. His lawyer came to discuss with him his last will. The secretary took away notes and soon returned with a typewritten copy. Dad sat up in bed to sign it while I fought back bitter tears. Soon, nurses came to transfer him to a gurney and wheel him to surgery.

Mother and I waited, each wondering how long a person could hold her breath.

When the surgeon came from the operating room, his face was somber. His worst fears were confirmed. "We removed the tumor, but the disease has spread. More than half his brain is so compromised by disease and surgery that, if he lives, he will not be a thinking, aware person."

"Will he live?" I heard myself ask.

"He may. We'll give him what support we can and wait to see what happens next."

"But why?" I cried. "Just let him go!" I remembered my father's eyes; he would not want this.

The surgeon explained with patient logic that he was a doctor, pledged to preserve life as best he could. Because he performed only brain surgery, many of his patients were in danger of dying. Making daily decisions to allow this one to die and that one to live were beyond his realm.

"I struggle to keep them alive as long as I can."

Long afterward, I wondered whether this young doctor ever changed his perspective, whether he ever came to know it was not about him. For now, I accepted his prognosis.

Twelve days in June crept by, Mother and I rotating in the chair next to Dad's bed. He breathed in and out, nurses turned him, changed his intravenous tube. Sometimes, when no one else was in the room, I talked to him, told him I loved him, sang his favorite songs to him. Silently, I prayed for him to die. I was afraid that one day his eyes would open and he would be gone.

This strong man had challenged me to do my best, to use my intellect, to strive always for excellence. This was the gentle man who remembered that I once declined his offer of orchids because I was too young for orchids. On my 21st birthday, though he was far away, orchids arrived in a little box; before I looked, I knew his name was on the card. This was the young man who started out with little education and narrow cultural experience, who parlayed them into a life of brilliant self-education, sophistication, and affluence. Now this powerful father figure, this giant who had always taken care of me, lay in his narrow hospital bed, cut down, breathing slowly in and out, in and out.

At last, in the fifty-seventh year of his life on June 12, 1954, Percival Homer Case stopped breathing. In a way, I had stopped breathing days before, only to resume many days after. I had abandoned my children to the gentle ministrations of my grandfather — thank God for 'Skipper'. My mother, Charlotte, shattered by the loss of her loving partner, was so self-disciplined that she kept moving through her pain. Years later, I read her farm journal. That day's entry read: *Planted lima beans, snap beans, zucchini, parsnips. Perc died.*

My brother, David, took over the duties of visitation as the family gathered from afar. On Monday, Ed Palmer, the Unitarian minister of Kalamazoo, conducted a service in Paw Paw. Neither Mother nor I had any idea who came nor what was said. We only clung to one another. Her journal entry for that day noted that 598 pounds of strawberries were picked. The following day, she swam in the pond with the children, the farm crew picked 744 pounds of strawberries, and all went to the Braybrooks Farm for dinner.

Mother was teaching me profound lessons in grace and forbearance; Dad had been only a part of the family strength.

THE FARM

Death has a way of rearranging life's chess board. Now that my father was gone, I found myself in a new role. No longer the dependent daughter, I entered into a partnership with my mother.

The Internal Revenue Service challenged the farm's return, demanding an additional thousand dollars in taxes, with penalties to be added. Mother had always kept the books, but now she needed to delve deeper into the abstruse field of accounting.

"I just don't think they're right, Kit. Perc set this up with his accountant, and I've followed the instructions he set down. A thousand dollars would be hard to come up with right now. Can you help me?"

"Mom, I know nothing about depreciating cows and fruit trees, but I guess I can learn something. First, let's get them to send an agent to the farm to help us." It may seem a little peculiar to ask the IRS for help in such a situation, but it worked. They sent an agent to spend the day with us, going over accounts and pointing us in the right direction.

"Yes," said the agent, "cows get depreciated same as fruit trees. After all, both have definite productive life spans. Here's how you figure the formula." I wrote everything down. For the next week, we buried ourselves in a blizzard of papers, discovering overlooked exemptions, recalculating depreciations, correcting mistakes. Then we called the IRS and asked for a complete audit.

"You're asking us to audit your books? That's a new one! Oh, your case is pending, and you want to get a reassessment? Bring in your evidence." We did that.

After several weeks, Mother received a call from a surprised IRS agent in Detroit. "Ma'am, we have gone over and over your figures and we cannot find any discrepancies. The regional director has ordered a refund check to be sent to you. You should have it within a week."

Beating the IRS on its own turf was a heady experience for both of us. Neither Mom nor I would ever again be intimidated by the tax man. When Art heard the news, he took it in stride.

"But Art! We did it! Two little ladies and we did it!"

"Of course you did, Kit. I never doubted you would. You're not just 'little ladies', you're two very bright women who can do pretty much whatever you set your minds to. I knew that." To temper any swelled head, he added, "and you're pretty sexy, too." I shot him a black look.

'Skipper' died the following year, leaving Charlotte alone on the farm, save for Clayte, the faithful farm manager. Spurning offers of better pay elsewhere, Clayte held fast to his promise to 'take care of things'. He and his family would stay as long as Charlotte owned the farm. Together, they sprayed and harvested the fruit and managed the migrant workers. This was a formidable responsibility for a woman who, until ten years ago, had only gardened a little for pleasure. That summer, and for several following, her Aunt Maie came from Syracuse to keep her company, help with the house garden, and put up the jars of pie cherries, peaches, tomatoes, and applesauce.

As often as possible, we piled into the family car and drove to Michigan. In summer, the girls plucked hollyhock blossoms and fashioned dolls with frilly pink and white skirts. I could hear laughter as they competed to see which one could fly higher on the swing that hung from the tall elm tree on the hill. The honey-locust just outside the kitchen door was a favorite climbing tree. Anne scrambled up to the tallest branches to peer over the house and garden and down the valley. From there, they could see Clayte's house, across the road. Susan followed up the tree, but at a safer height.

One rainy afternoon they tortured the barn cats on the screened porch. "Look, Mommy, we dressed them up in our doll clothes and they're having a tea party!"

"Girls, don't hurt the cats. They have sharp claws, and you would be sorry."

"No, they like it. Fluffy's purring."

As I turned away, I heard the scraping of chairs on the cement floor. The cats, perched on chairs, were pushed up to the table to take their tea.

Sometimes, when squabbling broke out, Clayte took Susan with him to the orchard. She liked to hear the workers calling to each other in Spanish as they moved the apple ladders from tree to tree. One day, they surprised a fox as it streaked across the orchard and was gone.

"Mom, why won't Clayte take me on the big tractor? Grampa did."

"Because Grama didn't approve of it then and she wouldn't like it now. She's afraid you might get hurt. Be satisfied with the Jeep."

Clayte taught the girls to hunt gophers in the lawn. "Here, take this jug and fill it half-way up with water. That's right. Now find a hole, turn the jug into it and watch what happens."

Squeals of delight broke out when they spotted one of the little varmints emerging from another hole and scampering off.

"Girls, the idea is to catch one. Keep on trying." They doubted him when he said a gopher would swim right up against the current and land in the jug.

"The neck is too small, Clayte. They couldn't fit. You're just teasing."

"Keep on. You'll see."

Sure enough, the astonished children watched as eventually a gopher did struggle into the glass jug. They brought the jug to me.

"Look! He's swimming, Mom! What should we do now?"

"Take it to Clayte and let him deal with it." I tried to conceal my disapproval of this method of ridding the lawn of these pests. I knew the holes they dug caused twisted ankles and a bumpy lawn, and I supposed this was no worse then poison. Clayte would dispatch the creature quickly, I knew. Out of sight of the children, I hoped.

As evening fell in late summer, the children chased fireflies with mason jars to make a night light for their dormitory. How many and what gender his grandchildren would be was yet unknown; Percy built one very large room as the second floor of the house addition. He planned to divide it according to the eventual number of boys and girls, but all six grandchildren were to be girls. When it was dark, the girls trudged up to bed with their night lights. Apparently, Anne felt sorry for the little blinkers and both girls opened the jars to let them loose. At first, the flickering points of light were enchanting, but suddenly a "yeeeaaahh" of alarm and disgust rang out.

"Quiet down, children."

"Mommy! They're bugs!"

"Well what did you think you little geese? You've got them now. Get used to it." In the morning, we swept up the remains, scattered over floor and beds.

Aunt Maie introduced Anne to the art of picking currants in the garden. They picked more than we could eat or make into jelly, so baskets of the tart fruit went off to market. I favored carefully tucking a currant into each raspberry that went to our table. We gathered for breakfast on the porch where we could hear the buzz of bees and the chirping of chickadees. A little sugar and a pour of thick cream turned bowls of fruit into ambrosia.

When the weather was fine, we often set up a game of croquet on the lawn—I have not played the game since then. Swimming in the pond took a special kind of bravery; I stayed dry. The water flowed from underground springs and had been dammed up to make a pond of about an acre. The water, summer and winter, was fifty degrees—too much for me. Mother and the girls enjoyed it, and might come home with their hands full of watercress they had gathered in the stream below. On Sunday, Clayte sometimes piled his children and ours into a car for a ride to Lake Cora's sand beach and warm water. If Art had come for the weekend, he donned his bathing suit and went along.

The girls and I spent many summer weeks at the farm and Art joined us when he could. I drove to meet him at the midnight train in Watervliet many Friday nights. His summer vacation was all planned for him. He drove the tractor, hauled crates of fruit, and carried sweet corn and beef steaks down to the picnic tables under the trees by the pond. He was skilled at building a fire and cooking the steaks, and he ate sweet corn with abandon. He filled the role of head of household with new assurance.

Some days were rainy—not many—and the children were confined in the house. They chased one another around the raceway, shouting as they went. The raceway was the path from living room to dining room to kitchen to back hall to master bedroom to front hall to living room and around again. They drove us crazy, until Mother sat down at the piano and began to play. Drawn like bees to honey, the girls climbed on the bench beside her.

"Play the Volga Boat song, Grama, please?" She did, and they all sang lustily.

"Play it again!" She did, again and again, with gentle patience, until at last she shooed them off and tried a little Chopin. Then the jigsaw puzzle came out. We spread it on the dining table and spent hours sorting out edge pieces, hunting for all the blue pieces that seemed to go just there. Art liked to hide one piece and at the right moment declare, "I finished the puzzle!" as he fixed it in place with a satisfied look.

In the cellar, Mother washed and ironed. The cellar, down steep stairs, was damp, a little dark, and Susan declared it spooky. Still, she ventured down when the mangle was hot to watch Grama feed sheets and pillowcases into the roller. The smell of linens fresh and ironed smooth was a sensation to store away for later memories. At such times, Anne was likely to perch herself on the dressing table bench in the master bedroom and play with Grama's jewelry. She dressed herself in rings and bracelets and admired her reflected finery in the mirror.

We marked Thanksgiving at the farm. Dave and Barbara came from Yellow Springs, bringing Janet, Martha, and tiny Sara — only a few weeks old. Polly was yet in their future. Snow covered the dormant garden and ice was beginning to form around the edges of the pond. Sleds came out of the barn and four snowsuit — encumbered girls stamped down a path on the hill below. While they and the fathers cavorted, we farm wives brought turkey and all the fixings to the table. Rosy-cheeked girls and tired fathers gathered to count our blessings.

"Barbara, I think your two could do with a nap," said the experienced grandmother. "They look a little feverish, don't you think?" Chicken-pox was developing among all the Case girls. For the following days, sick children turned the farmhouse into an infirmary. Sue and Anne had already suffered the nasty disease, and we took our leave for home.

In winter, Mother closed up the farm house and drove to join us in Park Forest until spring broke through the clouds. Late winter weekends found her in Michigan, pruning fruit trees. Several unusually severe winters and late frosts had taken a toll on the fruit crops, and many farmers in the area went bankrupt. Art worried that the strain on both her body and her bank account were too much. Quietly, he broached the subject of selling the farm and casting her lot with the Fourniers. He knew it would be hard but that she needed to come to a decision herself.

Although abandoning civilization to live in the hinterland had been difficult for her, now the prospect of giving up the incredible beauty and deep satisfactions of farm life wounded her even more. But without her partner, that life had lost much of its spice. In the end, she agreed that Art's advice was sound, and she moved to put the farm on the market.

Art did not consult with me. He was dealing directly with his mother in this. I was satisfied with that.

Selling *Peaches 'n' Cream* was no simple matter. Surrounding properties were modest, but this farm offered a large and imposing house, faced with Indiana limestone. The living room had a great stone fireplace, mahogany paneling, cork floors warmed with radiant heat, and a thirteen-foot picture window overlooking the valley to the west. The barn, silos, machine shop, all were of the finest construction and reflected the latest developments in agriculture. The interstate highway system was yet to be developed, placing the likeliest buyer — a Chicago executive — at least four hours away, and the country was sliding into recession. After agonizing months, a buyer arrived. He was a dreamer with no significant experience and way too little money. The farm sold for less than the machinery had cost. Everything went, except the most personal contents.

While Mother and the realtor were closed in the office, taking care of final paperwork, I wandered down to the packing house. In the dim light with the big barn doors closed, I could see the apple grader standing still and quiet, apple crates stacked neatly against the wall. Memories of happier days came flooding back — the day I lifted crates of apples that cold October day. It could have been yesterday...

The peach harvest had seen the last of the Elbertas. Hale Havens went to market weeks before. McIntosh apples began to show a deep red blush on the trees. Two grades of fruit left the farm in big semi-trailer trucks, bound for the Chicago market. A local cider mill bought the bottom of the line. In Chicago, the wholesale house called La Mantia absorbed all of our top grade peaches and apples. They were packed in special containers, each fruit cradled in its own nest. They brought a deliciously high price, sometimes as much as seven or even eight dollars a box—only four-fifths of a bushel. Both peaches and apples rolled through the brusher machine, to remove the fuzz or shine up the skins. All the fruit was graded, that is, passed through an inspection line for rejects, and then sorted by size. After that, packers went to work. Top fruits were laid in the Kyes Packs, fiber trays with individual depressions. Less than fancy, but still number one grade, were packed in bushel baskets.

Migrant workers, a team of half a dozen, worked in the packing house under Mother's supervision. The noise of the machinery and of the tractor bringing boxes from the orchards was so great that no one could make conversation. Most communication was by hand-signal. Those days were long before the establishment of OSHA (the federal Occupational Health and Safety Administration). Today, everyone would wear ear protection, but then no one thought about it. Mother's deafness may have stemmed from those times.

Large as I was, I remember pitching right in with the work. One woman taught me how to pack a bushel. After I got the hang of it, I sometimes raced with her, but she was much more practiced and won easily. Whenever the tractor came in with a load, I helped carry filled crates into the packing house. Sometimes, I had to thread my way between stacks of crates; when I did, everyone stopped to watch to see if my bulging body would get stuck…

My eyes blurred in the dimmed packing house as memory flowed through my veins. I trudged back up to the house to see how the business was progressing.

"Kit, would you walk around for a final inspection? Be sure we haven't forgotten anything?"

"Sure, Mom." In the kitchen, I ran my fingers over the mosaic tile counter that Mother and I had spent so many weeks making. The red barn, the big rooster, the rows of fruit trees, all had been created from colored ceramic tiles that we cut and ground into shapes and put together like a jigsaw puzzle. The dim cellar still housed the laundry equipment, but the dozens of jars of fruit had been taken away. I walked around outdoors. A glass jug leaned against the wall near the spigot.

Coming in at the front door, I gazed at the avocado tree, growing in the stone window box inside the living room. It had come from a cast-off seed that Mother planted in rich compost. The box actually had no bottom, and the roots had spread under the foundation. The tree, which had to be pruned to keep it off the nine-foot ceiling, provided shade on summer afternoons.

I smiled as I remembered the girls sliding down the slanted end of the huge, maroon bathtub. The color of the fixtures was eye-catching, but I recalled how difficult they were to keep free of soap and water stains. Upstairs, four beds and a crib were lined up against the wall. I stooped to retrieve a forgotten crayon drawing.

"Nothing is forgotten," I reported to Mother.

As we walked down the front path for the last time, I stared hard at the California poppies spilling their yellow profusely over the lawn and walkway. The rope swing still swayed to and fro from the big elm tree on top of the hill.

My father's dream of a gentleman's farm was gone, along with the considerable fortune it had devoured. We drove back to Park Forest in sad silence.

TRANSITIONS

'Grama', as the little girls called my mother, squeezed into the larger of the two Park Forest bedrooms with the children, while Art and I moved into the smaller one. Rivalry between the girls often erupted in struggles and tears.

"Get your stuff off here. This is my side of the room."

"Tisn't! I can too stay here! Grama!!" Anne ran to bury her face in Grama's lap.

"Oh Susan, don't be like that. She's not hurting anything. Tell you what. Anne, you find the Parcheesi board and Sue you bring the little table. We can play a game before it's time to set the dinner table."

And so it went, my patient mother helping them calm down, work it out, and have fun. She taught them to play Old Maid, War, double solitaire, and eventually Gin Rummy, Hearts, and Cribbage. She taught them to lose without throwing the cards, to win with reasonable grace. She was, for Art and me, a welcome baby-sitter.

Much later, Charlotte observed that the social atmosphere in the community was stultifying. Conversation revolved around children, diapers, teething. She probably looked forward to the return of apple blossoms, but she never complained.

For me, the days stumbled along in a blur of grief. I could manage the daily routine, but reaching out to my family or community was beyond me. For Art, it must have been disheartening to see his wife's preoccupation with the loss of another man. Never inclined to show deep emotion, he kept his eye on his goal. Slowly, carried along by gentle Art and generous Maxine, I emerged again into the light.

Eventually, Art stopped traveling. His success on the road led to a promotion into the home office. Now he became regional sales manager. Every day, he commuted an hour each way, usually on the train. That gave him time to shift gears from the chaotic world at home to the bustling world of commerce, but it made for a long day.

This was a time of the corporate soldier, and Art knew how to be a soldier. In fact, he was bucking for senior officer. The nation had suffered through a protracted depression, fought a war on two fronts, endured deprivation of consumer goods, and at last emerged into the light of rising prosperity. Now every man had a chance to conquer the world. He needed only to don a gray flannel suit, learn the rules of the corporation, and rise to the top. Loyalty was still a serious quality in both employed and employer. The wives of rising young hopefuls did not question the rules, they only sought to learn what they were. A corporate wife dressed smartly, attended command performances, engaged in witty conversation. Not too witty. She did not dream of chafing at her husband's long hours or at the pressures he encountered. If the boss needed something unexpectedly, a family vacation might be postponed. It happened. Good corporate people understood.

Art understood; he played the game superbly. His accomplishments in the technical sales department were widely visible. One evening, after the children were in bed, he told me, "Honey, I have a decision to make. The head of the purchasing department approached me today about moving over there."

"But Art, you're a great salesman! Is that a good idea?"

"Well you see, the truth is, commodities are in surplus right now, and selling is an uphill road. Momentum right now is with purchasing. If I jump over the desk and deal with sales from the other chair, I think I could do pretty well. Besides, I've served my time. I should move on."

"Sounds like you've already decided, Dear."

"I guess I have. Besides, my new salary will match that goal I told you about."

"So now it's on to the next milepost? And what might that be?"

"Just wait and see." He grinned.

By this time, Susan had reached a puzzling stage. She began to resist going to school. Mrs. Waldman told me, "Last year, Susan related mostly to the teachers and to me, and that seemed to suit her well. Now, she has advanced to a stage of wanting to make contact with the other children, but it's a little daunting to work her way into the group."

Curiously, the anxiety and grief that had surrounded the children never connected with any of the adults involved. In a conservative, if less than insightful move, we withdrew Susan for the remainder of the year until kindergarten in the fall of 1954. The birthday boundary for kindergarten enrollment was December first; the general belief at that time was that the sooner children advanced, the better.

Anne, now approaching three, was forming strong friendships with neighborhood children. She craved approval from them and allowed them to dominate her. Younger than many, she toddled cheerfully after them. They were happy to have her, and for a very good reason. The back porches were covered by flat roofs, supported by stout pipes about three or four inches in diameter. Frequently, balls bounced up there and failed to bounce back. One day, I glanced out the dining room window and caught a glimpse of two chubby little legs dangling from the roof.

In a panic, I ran to the kitchen door and called, "Anne, come down from there this minute! Here, I can get you, just hang on." I reached for a kitchen chair to stand on.

"It's OK, Mommy! I can get down." And she wrapped her legs around the post, slid to the ground, and grinned at me. "See? I can do it."

"Kids," I scolded them, "don't let her go up there. She can get badly hurt. You are all big enough to know better." They nodded soberly, but Anne continued to climb for the balls that older children were afraid to retrieve.

Charlotte's Aunt Alice gave me a very basic sewing machine, a 1926 model Singer. Mother had tried without success to teach me sewing when I was a child, but she observed, "It's very hard to teach someone who already knows it all!"

Foolish me! Now I had to teach myself. For the sake of thrift, and eventually for enjoyment, I made dresses for the girls, and matching ones for their dolls. I thought it was fun to dress the girls alike, as if they were twins, although their size and coloring were very different. Many years later, Anne told me what a torture it had been for her.

"Mom, did you ever realize how long I had to wear the same dress? First I wore mine, then you let the hem down, and I wore it some more. Then you took up the hem on Susan's dress, and I wore it, and you let the hem down again, and I wore it even more. Boy I got sick of the same old dress!"

"But why didn't you say something, you silly girl? It never occurred to me, but now I see. I would never have done that if you'd just told me how you felt!"

"I don't know, Mom, I guess I just thought that was the way it was." I learned, eventually, that she dreamed of clothes more intensely than I could have imagined.

I created clothes for myself and shirts for Art, all costing about half the price of ready-made. Ever since, I have felt guilty about buying anything I could sew myself. It was a knowing gesture when, several years later, Art gave me a lavish Christmas gift. It was written on a large fragment of birch bark:

To Cinderella Fournier
Payable on Demand
$500
toward your wardrobe.
Account subject to audit upon
complete fulfillment
By order of S. Arthur Fournier

Ever the professional purchasing agent, he had specified an audit to insure that I actually spent it all. I was overwhelmed.

Susan entered kindergarten and Anne began her first year of nursery school. The Rosner boys were interleaved in age with our girls. Kent rose to senior nursery school, while Andy waited for next year to follow Anne. The parents' friendship was mirrored in the children, and they were miscreants together. One evening we gathered the children at our house and hired a high school baby sitter while the four of us spent an evening out. As far as we knew then all went well, but years later they let us in on their secret.

"We had a ball," said Kent. "Remember how we lured that girl outside? And then we ran back and locked her out."

"She was really mad," agreed Sue. "Pounded on the door. But we had turned on the television to watch a show we were forbidden to see."

"Why that's terrible! You bad kids! When did you finally let her back in? She never said a word."

"We made a deal. If we let her in, we'd watch the show and she'd never tell. Worked great. She didn't say a word. I don't remember that we ever had her again, though." I imagine not.

A LITTLE HOLIDAY

By lucky chance, Art and I chose Williamsburg, Virginia, as our destination for a holiday in early autumn, 1957. He needed to be in eastern Ohio on business and I needed a change of scene. We hoped our children would be a welcome diversion for Charlotte.

"We'll cross the bridge at Wheeling, and then the Tidewater is just over the mountains. Easy trip." Art was confident.

On the morning of our last stop in a small Ohio town, Art went to the hotel cashier for his bill. After looking it over, he passed it back to her with a broad wink and quick glance at me..

"Could you give me another bill, please? One without the little lady?" His voice echoed across the small lobby. Immediately, all eyes turned to assess me from head to toe. As they exchanged wise smirks, I stood there with reddening cheeks. How could I explain about hotel receipts as business expense? Anger would have been stupid. I simply stood there, promising myself a future payback. Now that I think about it, why did I not laugh?

'Just over the mountains' proved to be much farther than either of us had imagined. Art's extensive driving experience was on flat land; the mountain roads were curvy and narrow. Seat belts were a new feature, included in our red Ford sedan, and I learned to be grateful for them. Art was a fast and confident driver, and he took the sharp mountain curves faster than I would have done. The belt held my body securely as it was pressed from side to side on the switch-backs of West Virginia. By dusk, we had reached Winchester, Virginia, and Williamsburg was still a long way off. We sped down the Shenandoah Valley in the dark, finally realizing we would not make it tonight. At last, a lighted motel sign beckoned, and we fell gratefully into bed, visualizing our new concept of mountainous terrain.

In the morning, we stopped briefly at St. John's Church in Richmond to hear a re-creation of Patrick Henry's 'liberty or death' speech. Since both of us, growing up in the northeast, had learned that all American history stemmed from Boston and all early colonial settlement was in Plymouth, we were a little surprised by exposure to a new perspective. We had thought of Virginia as a vague blur of backwater tobacco plantations.

By evening, we settled into the bed-and-breakfast right next to Williamsburg's Catholic church. Our host was the widow of a professor at the College of William and Mary; through her we learned to pronounce the name of the college with awed respect. The extraordinary good luck of our choice was that this was the 350th anniversary of the landing at Jamestown, thirteen years before the anchor of the Mayflower touched down in Massachusetts. Though Queen Elizabeth and Prince Philip had already returned home, echoes of the festivities still reverberated.

For the one time in my life, I looked at the Magna Carta, not a replica, but one of the original documents, actually signed by King John on the Runnymede meadow. The years 1066 and 1215 had been cornerstone dates in my high school studies. Mrs. Clark, the English teacher, came into class every day with questions. One day it would be "Battle of Hastings, class?" and we would chant in response "1066." Or it might be "Magna Carta, class?" and we responded "1215." Mrs. Clark believed these were the two most crucial dates in the history of the English language and culture, and here I was right in front of the real evidence. My heart actually skipped a beat and I felt a catch in my throat.

Art and I drank in the experience of early colonial history in Jamestown and of eighteenth century life in Williamsburg.

"I've never felt history come to life before, Kit. It's awe-inspiring."

A gentle, misty rain fell every day, but it failed to dampen our spirits, only enhanced the rich color of the leaves on the great maple tree next to the Powder Magazine. Crowds were thin after Labor Day; we almost felt we were alone in a lost world. We discovered Brunswick Stew and biscuits at Chowning's Tavern, elegant dining at the Inn. Delicious Virginia ham and Sally Lunn bread at the King's Arms were exceeded only by peanut soup, a new taste experience for us Yankees.

We looked over the provisions in one of the shops, and I said, "What a pity we can't take home one of these hams!" A clerk heard me.

"Madam, you certainly can take one. Which shall I wrap for you?" She was dressed in 18th century style and stood there, hands on hips, smiling at me.

"Oh, I'm afraid not. You see, we're driving all the way back to Chicago, so of course we couldn't keep it cold. Too bad."

"Madam, how do you suppose hams come across the ocean? They are salt-cured and will keep well, do not fret."

We bought a ham and a recipe book, as well as ginger cakes to munch on the way. When we reached home, I soaked the ham twice and simmered it, and gave a dinner party. Our friends, accustomed to the mid-western style sugar cure, did not think much of the salty, stringy ham from Virginia.

A darker side of American history, one that I had naïvely thought long gone, struck me like a physical blow. Jim Crow had been only a quaint phrase to me until I saw signs on doors that read "Colored Women" and on drinking fountains that said "White Only." Only with firm restraint on my arm did Art prevent me from walking through the wrong door and drinking from the wrong fountain.

"But Art, it's wrong! Wrong! We cannot just let it go!"

"No Kit, we are visiting guests. We are in no position to change the world here, only to cause trouble and embarrassment." Art had a matter-of-fact approach, but I should have grasped the futility of a dilettante's gesture. Martin Luther King, Jr., was twenty-eight years old.

"Well," I said, "this is a great place to visit, but I wouldn't want to live here." Not guessing what the future would hold for us, we pointed the red Ford toward the west and home.

FIRST HOUSE

Art had an announcement for us. "IMC is moving corporate headquarters to Skokie. It's too far to commute from here, folks, so we will need to regroup." And so we opened a new chapter of our lives in the northern suburbs of Chicago.

How do you choose the place to live? We always knew Park Forest would be temporary for us, even if the company stayed on Wacker Drive. Now, in 1957, the search was on in earnest; the company would relocate in only a few months.

"If we could pick any place, where would it be? What's the most important thing?" I was looking for a starting point.

"Schools," said Art, "everything else is secondary, isn't it?"

"That's hard. Because New Trier High School is one of a handful of the best schools in the country. Only we can't afford to live in that district. So what's next best? Do you know?"

"Wait a minute. How do you know we can't afford to live there? Sure, Winnetka and Kenilworth are in the district, but maybe there is another corner we could manage. Let's get a map of the district and sniff it out."

Sure enough, a little slice of Glenview was in the district, and furthermore, they were building a new elementary school right in that slice. We drove the sixty miles to see for ourselves.

Nearby, the school was under construction. It was surrounded by new houses going up, and the models were open.

"Look, Art, this is the latest thing in homes. Tri-level. See? Half of it is two-story, the other half is one. An efficient way to increase floor space without a great increase in cost. What's the price? Is it in our range?"

I gulped when Art said, "It's less than twenty thousand." He might as well have said less than a million, for I was sure that was way beyond our budget. We would have to add the cost of landscaping, as the builder was scraping topsoil into a pile at the back of the lots.

"I know, honey. It looks like a lot. But we have enough saved up for the down payment. The monthly mortgage and utility bills will be manageable. We can do this." And we did. We chose a house that was already framed up and roofed over right in a sharp curve of Heatherfield Lane. That gave us very little frontage on the street in a pie-shaped lot that broadened generously in back.

"Look, Art, we can put the picnic table right here!" I was standing in a mud puddle behind the house. He laughed and invited me in to look over our new house.

On the entry level, the living room—with a dining alcove— looked out large picture windows toward the street. On the other side were a powder room, then the light and ample kitchen. Up a half-flight of stairs were three bedrooms and a bath, while down stairs were the utility room, a second full bath, and another spacious room.

"Will this lower level be OK for Charlotte?" asked Art. "It would give her privacy and her own bath."

"I'm sure it will be fine."

Before we made the contract final, we drove up again, this time with the entire family. Mother approved heartily and began thinking about developing the garden. The girls ran around, trying to put themselves into this new place.

"Now, girls, we'll need to decide about the bedrooms. Want to draw straws?"

"No, Daddy, we'll figure it out."

I shuddered at the conflict to come, but to my surprise they had it ironed out right away. Susan took the smaller corner room. Anne hesitated over giving up the room with a laundry chute, but Susan persuaded her that the larger room would suit her to a T. We signed the contract and drove home with a handful of brochures outlining choices we would have to make. What color paint? Kitchen counter? Wanting to follow the current fashion, we chose turquoise for the counter and black for the refrigerator and stove.

As construction progressed, Art and I followed closely. Every weekend, we drove up to inspect, write notes to the builder, and improve what we found. Fiberglass insulation covered the exterior walls, but in the kitchen, we thought the area around the sink needed extra. We scrounged up parts of batts left lying around on the floor and stuffed insulation around all the pipes. It was an itchy business, but later in frigid winters, we were among the few houses without frozen pipes. Art found me busily writing.

"What's that?"

"I'm asking them to insulate the interior walls around the powder room."

"Not in the plans, Honey. It'll cost more. Why?"

"Sound absorption, Art. This room is stuck right in the living area."

"Good thinking! Wouldn't have thought of that."

The day came when, amid hugs and tears, we bid farewell to our Park Forest neighbors and headed north in the family station wagon. In an hour, the big moving truck lumbered up the driveway right behind us. The girls, now six and eight, were bouncing up and down in the back seat.

"Can I help unload my furniture, Daddy? Can I? I'll be careful, I promise."

"No, sweetie. I have a special task for you. You'll be up in your bedroom telling the men where to put the furniture. You decide. We'll see that everything gets to the right rooms." Both girls scrambled up the half-flight to wait, each in her own doorway. When the truck finally backed out and rolled away, I collapsed into the big blue wing chair.

"Whew! What a mess! Will we ever get it straightened out and put away?'

"Probably not. We'll just live among the boxes forever." Art grinned and stretched out on the couch.

"O.K. Enough of that. Everybody get to work. Girls, I'll help you find linens and make your beds." And I headed for the stairs. Far too late, we all fell into our beds. When the morning sun hit my eyes, I woke and rolled over to look at Art. He was staring up at the ceiling, smiling.

"What?"

"I was thinking about a Christmas tree. With our two-story living room, can't you just see it?" I stared at him in disbelief.

"Are you the same man who fussed over my spending five dollars on a tree last December? The man who wanted to know why we always have to have such a monster tree?"

No garden yet, station wagon in the driveway

"Yeah, but just think! It'll be much easier to decorate. We can put it next to the stairs. And the star on top? Pop it on right from the balcony. We could do a twelve-foot tree." He had not heard a word. Scrooge lost in his fantasy.

Art's new office was only ten minutes away, in a very new, very modern, very spectacular, architectural-award-winning building—that worked poorly. The receptionist at the front door sat with her feet on a warming pad, shivering in the cold winter. Everyone on the sunny side sweltered in summer. The helicopter pad on the roof made travel to O'Hare airport for business trips a true delight. A delight, that is, until the day the chairman was aboard when something went wrong and the craft dropped to the second floor before the pilot had it under control again. The heliport was closed on the spot. Nevertheless, Art enjoyed the proximity that gave him time for home chores.

There were prodigious chores. Moving all that soil to level the yard was too much for one man; the work was hired out. More real topsoil was added. Art smoothed the ground and spread grass seed. I moved sprinklers, turned water on and off, until in a week or two a faint green haze appeared over the lot. At night, we perused nursery catalogs, selecting the shrubbery that would grace the borders.

"Art, can you believe this? Today, the mailman dropped off this little bundle. I don't think this is what we ordered, is it?" Opening the package, I began to read off the label on each spindly stick.

"Syringa? What's that?"

"Lilac," mother assured me.

"Philadelphus?"

"Mock orange." I read them all as Art checked off the list: forsythia, buddleia, azalea, viburnum.

"That's the lot. They do seem a little pitiful, though. What do you think, Mom, will these things grow?"

"I think so. You need to plunge them into a bucket of water until tomorrow. Small ones usually transplant much better than big ones. The big ones are set back by the shock and take time to recover. The little ones get right to work."

Saturday morning, we got right to work. Mother stood by, coaxing us to be more optimistic.

"Farther apart. More. No, digging the holes ten feet apart is minimum. These are big shrubs." Shaking his head, Art moved over more and started to dig. Twigs planted ten and twelve feet apart seemed ridiculous, but he followed the horticulturist's advice with faith. To give us more sense of progress, we drove to the local nursery and bought larger crabapples, a Kentucky coffee tree, a thornless honey locust, and a clump birch. With experienced advice from Charlotte and the local nurseryman, we dodged many amateur mistakes, and soon our garden acquired a spare beauty.

Some lessons are learned only painfully. It developed that we were the lowest lot in a cluster of six; all the others drained into ours. After any significant rain, unwelcome Lake Fournier formed in our backyard. We managed to drain it by laying garden hose from the lake through a window to the sump in our crawl space. The pump emptied it in several days, but a more permanent solution occurred to Art. He rented a gasoline-powered trench digger and cut deep trenches in a radiating pattern through our beautiful lawn. After he lined the trenches with gravel, he laid perforated pipe, leading the water to the perimeter drains around the house, from which it would drain into the sump and get pumped out. He fabricated a one-way valve for the outlet from the pump, just in case it backed up. As a final touch, he planted a willow tree at the lowest place. After repairing the extensive damage to the lawn, we stood and surveyed the result.

"You're some guy," I said, putting my arm around his waist.

"We make a pretty good team," he answered, satisfied.

Within several years, the project developed into a showplace. We added a garage and paved the driveway, had a room built at the back of the house with a wood-burning fireplace and gas-fired heater. We built a wood fence between our house and the close neighbors on the driveway side, then between the driveways planted a rose garden, all the way to the street.

"Shame to waste all that sun," Art declared. Even though their care was a constant round of dusting, fertilizing, and watering, they rewarded us with spectacular displays in spring and autumn.

GIRLS, DOG, NEIGHBOR — LIFE IN GLENVIEW

The neighbors on the other side from our rose garden, Barbara and Bob Berman, became good friends. Despite similarity to my Park Forest experience, my relationship with Barbara had more distance between our kitchen doors, and that made all the difference. Barbara had been a night club singer before she settled down to suburban life. Her blonde hair usually needed a comb, she padded around in slippers, housecoat covering her ample body, a cigarette dangling between her fingers. Her smoky voice, a little reminiscent of Julie London's, frequently rang with laughter. She regaled me with stories of a seamier side of life than I knew.

"Oh the club in Galveston was some hole. The best part was that it was a building way down at the end of a long pier out into the bay. They had a lookout stationed at the entrance to the pier, and when the feds came, he signaled the boss at the other end of the pier. By the time the fuzz reached the club, all the gambling stuff was in boxes hanging under the pier. Never got caught. The customers were the most notorious Mafia people."

"Weren't you scared, Barb?"

"Nah. It was my job to sing, that's all. I saw what was going on, but I wasn't part of it. The hardest part was learning to belt out a song while everybody was talking and drinking and smoking, not paying any attention to me." Barbara washed dishes from the day before while I plied my knitting needles at her kitchen table. Both of us smoked and sipped coffee. Both of us were raising children, all of them girls. In that setting, I finished knitting Christmas hats, scarves, and mittens for all the little girls.

Susan and Anne were developing very different personalities. Sue had solved her problem of socializing with her peers by becoming a strong leader. I intended to reach home every day before my girls arrived from school, and I was almost always successful. One day, however, I was fifteen minutes late.

What in the world? I drove around the corner to our house, and saw the police squad car pulled up in front. One officer gave me a hand signal to stay back. I rolled down my window to hear what the policemen were saying to three boys from Susan's class. One officer barked out, "Awright youse guys. I wancha ta scram outta here real fast, see? Before I run youse in. An don' lemme catch youse coming back, neither." It was a pretty good rendition of a scene from a B movie starring Edward G. Robinson or James Cagney. The boys skedaddled, kicking up their heels as terror lent them wings. The squad car drove off in the other direction as the men laughed and waved at me. I was speechless.

I raced into the house. "Girls! What in the world?" Susan stood in the middle of the living room, hands on her hips, a satisfied look on her face.

"I called the police, Mom. They came really quick."

"Tell me from the beginning." I sat down.

"The boys chased us all the way home from school, but we were faster than them. When we got inside, I locked the door. Then they started yelling and throwing stones at the windows, so I called the police, that's all."

"I was scared." This from Anne, who inched closer to me on the couch.

"Not me!" declared Susan. "I was mad though. What else do we pay taxes for?"

I promised myself to redouble my efforts to reach home first, every time.

Anne had discovered her affinity for every living creature. A little mouse was caught by the schoolyard door and squeezed. Anne wrapped it tenderly in her handkerchief and carried it home to nurse it back to health.

"Mommy, can we take it to the doctor? I think it's really hurt."

Unfortunately, the accident proved fatal and amid tears of regret, we buried the soft gray body in the garden.

Tears, in fact, proved to be Anne's trademark. Each night, either Art or I would stop by her bed as we retired, to see that she was comfortably covered. Each night, we found her pillow damp with tears.

"What's going on?" Art wanted to know.

"Oh she brought up the business about getting a dog again, and I said no again. Honestly Art, I have enough without taking care of a dog. I've never had one, wouldn't know what to do with one. You know it's Mother who'll wind up walking the dog, cleaning up dog hair. . ."

"You're right, I guess. Until the girls show a little more tendency to take responsibility." Art did not sound so firm, but of course not. It was always the mother who got stuck. The father tends to be vulnerable.

And so it was. Art convinced me that we should all go to the annual Chicago Dog Show, a major national exhibition. Knowing nothing about dogs, we debated about the best breed. We would persuade the girls of the rightness of our choice and that would be that.

On the appointed day, off we went to inspect the dogs. Susan was excited, but Anne was strangely quiet. When we entered the amphitheater, I was daunted by the sight. Row upon row of benches, stretching through several buildings. Art and I pretended mild interest in each breed we passed.

"Don't touch, children," sternly admonished every handler. We trudged up and down the aisles, looking at everything from collies to St. Bernards. When we had finished the rounds, Art said brightly, "Well, Anne, how about going back to take another look at the dachshunds. Or maybe the Dalmatians?"

"Oh no, Dad. I want to go back to the Corgis."

"The WHAT?"

"Corgi. Oh Daddy, they're wonderful dogs. They come from Wales and they herd sheep. C'mon. I'll show you." As she led us unerringly through many rooms of dogs, she chattered on about the stellar qualities of this breed we had never heard of. Clearly, our six year old had made good use of the encyclopedia.

"Just what we need to herd our sheep, Art," I whispered. He grunted.

"There they are!" Anne was bubbling. The handler invited them, "Sit down on the bench girls and pet the dogs. They won't hurt you." Immediately, the girls were swamped by four dogs, wagging all over and licking their faces. We parents knew we were doomed; it was hardly a fair contest.

The Pembroke Welsh Corgi is a short-legged dog with no tail. It has a long luxurious coat that sheds. People have called it a collie with its legs cut short, and that is a fair description. Weighing about twenty pounds, it is a small dog, not tiny or fragile, but quite sturdy. Within a month, we visited a Corgi kennel in Indiana and bought Sandunes Lady Gay, a nine-month-old puppy we called Gay. She was mostly black on top and white underneath, with splashes of tan. Being a young pup, she chewed. Art found that a little smear of Tabasco sauce on the edges of her wooden bed worked well. One taste, one sharp yip, and the bed was saved.

The girls did better than we expected in accepting responsibility, although of course I did take care of Gay when they were in school. When Gay reached her first birthday, Anne undertook her obedience lessons. Before long, Gay was a responsible member of the family. Each day brought a new lesson. It was 'Heel' and 'Stay', but she also learned to balance a dog biscuit on her nose and wait for the signal to toss it in the air, catch it in her mouth, and crunch it happily. At the end of a leash, Gay would wander the back yard. When she was about to step over the line into a neighbor's yard, Anne would tug the leash and say firmly, "Home, Gay." Soon, Gay knew the boundaries and stayed reliably inside, except when Barbara's

West Highland Terrier, Cricket, barked a welcome. Then the two friends would run and tumble together, heedless of any boundary at all.

Cricket, a true reflection of her family, knew no discipline. Cricket's white coat was wiry and always dirty. Wiping was useless. Barbara shampooed her frequently, after which she was a thing of beauty for a little while. However, Cricket liked to walk under the car parked in their driveway, and that left her the mirror image of a skunk: white with a black streak down her back.

Gay's coat was smooth and silky. On rainy days, she came in from her walk dripping, and because of her low-slung undercarriage, sometimes muddy. At the command, 'wipe feet, Gay', she rolled over on her back to be rubbed clean and dry. In every way, she was a very satisfactory addition to our family circle.

PERSPECTIVES

Father Knows Best, a popular television series that ran from 1954 to 1963, reflected perhaps the last gasp of traditional family roles in middle-class America. That was a time when mothers were moms, children were just kids, and fathers were in charge. In spite of our growing restiveness, we were part of that culture.

"What's for dinner and when?" Art had caught me, exasperated, in the middle of correcting a mistake in my sewing project.

"You're home early. What's up?" My eyes were glued to my work.

"Nothing much. But again, what's for dinner and when?"

"Hey it's four o'clock. The answers are, in order: I don't know and later."

"You need a new watch. It's after four-thirty. How come you don't know? Do you at least have a plan?"

"Honest to god, I have a problem not a plan. I'm trying to undo my last hour of work." This through clenched teeth.

"Babe, your Job One is to keep us all properly nourished, the dusk is gathering, and you tell me you don't have a plan?"

"I don't notice that you've starved yet. Quit hectoring me." I liked it when I could catch him with a word I was fairly sure he did not know. He turned on his heel and stomped upstairs. When he returned, dressed in gardening clothes, he threw over his shoulder, "Let me know when you develop a plan," and disappeared out the back door.

Damn him, anyway, why couldn't he be late when I'm in a mess! A stealthy shadow of guilt spread across my work table. After all, it wasn't his fault that I made two left sleeves, now was it? No, but why does he have to come at me with that tired old thing about what's for dinner? He knows I hate it . I know he's right about planning—I don't do much of that. But why is it always my job to . . . Good lord, I sound like one of our children. Folding up my unfinished work, I pushed my chair away from the sewing table and headed for the kitchen, still steaming.

Soon, the vegetables were simmering on the stove. I sliced the leftover ham and took a jar of mustard from the refrigerator. At least my early-morning dessert project had set up properly. I filled the teapot and poured milk and juice.

"Girls, come set the table, please. And tell your father dinner is ready." Sue went to look for him.

"Mom, he says he's in the middle of something and will be in when he's done."

"Oh that's just swell. Well, girls, sit down while I dish it up. No need for us to eat cold food." Soon, the back door slammed and I heard his shoes drop on the rug beside it. He stopped at the sink to wash his hands and took his place at the table. Without a word, he spread his napkin on his lap, lifted his fork, and started to eat. My guilt was covering me like a blanket.

"Sue, did you have a violin lesson at school today? How did it go?" My heart was still beating fast, but I kept my voice light.

"It was O.K." She sounded wary.

"Mommy, don't you feel good?" This from Anne, and my defeat was complete. I looked at my husband.

"I'm sorry, dear."

"Me too." Only his voice still sounded grim. "Anne, finish your vegetables."

"But Daddy, they're yucky. I ate one bite. Isn't that enough?"

"No, I said finish."

"I'm finished. Don't care for any more, thank you," as she pushed away her plate, lima beans still sitting there.

I got up to clear the table and bring in dessert. On the way by her chair, I leaned down and whispered, "Take another bite, honey. Won't hurt you." She pulled the plate closer and maneuvered one bean to her fork. Glass of milk in one hand, fork in the other, she lifted both toward her face. First the bean, then a gulp of milk.

"It didn't go down. It's stuck in my mouth. I can't eat it."

"You will eat it," declared father in a low voice. Now they were eyeball-to-eyeball.

"Mother, may I please be excused?"

"When you have finished your vegetables," repeated father in an even tone. "No dessert until they're gone."

When everyone—except Anne—had finished the tapioca pudding, a family favorite, Susan helped me finish clearing away the dishes. The stubborn little girl still sat there, grimly staring at the offending beans.

In the kitchen, I tried to intercede with Art, but he was adamant.

"Fussy eaters are a pain in the neck. She has to learn to eat what is put in front of her."

"They will hate you when they grow up if you can't learn to bend a little," I pleaded.

"It's not a popularity contest, Babe. Whatever they think of me, they will learn to eat their dinner."

When loneliness in the dining room weighed too heavily, Anne brought her empty plate to me. I smiled and gave her an affectionate squeeze, but I did not want to know where the lima beans had gone.

In the end, Annie had her own perspective. Decades later, as she mourned Art's death, she wrote through her tears in memory of her father:

. . . The memories have been both somber and humorous, which reflect that Dad had both a serious and very silly side.

Some things I learned from my dad:
- How to eat corn on the cob properly, and in quantity

- On Saturday mornings after the chores, sardine sandwiches are great while listening to Russian music
- Even though I never thought of Dad as an avid athlete, I found out when I was young and *very* athletic, he could outsprint me, no sweat
- At the Daddy-Daughter Dance in high school, he was an OK but not really great dancer. I know he went just to be with me and my sister, not to dance.
- How to pack suitcases in the car artfully and scientifically
- Learning about finances and investments doesn't have to be boring if you just give it a chance. Really.
- Learning new things is a lifelong pursuit
- Community service is part of everyday life
- To be honest and ethical is . . . simply to be
- There is no higher calling than to be there for your family, always and forever.

THE EIGHTY-FOOT DRIVEWAY

Who's talking? I was barely half awake, eyes not yet open. Oh, it's the radio. That time already?

Slowly, I swung my feet over the edge of the bed, feeling sorry for myself as I always did when the other side of the bed was empty. The clock read seven, time to start breakfast, wake the girls, let the dog out, and survey the situation. I slipped my feet into cozy lambskin slippers and reached for my blue wool robe lying at the foot of the bed. Sliding it over my shoulders, I pushed my arms into the sleeves, zipped up the front, and tied the sash.

At least I don't have anything on my schedule until ten. After the girls are gone, I'll open the *Chicago Tribune*, pour another cup of coffee, and have a quiet time, just me and the dog. Oh boy.

Without opening the curtains, I padded downstairs quietly to let the girls have another five minutes. The living room waited in the dark, heavy draperies still closed against the winter chill. Down another flight, I opened the utility room door.

"Good morning, Gay! Good dog. Time to go out." Her soft body wiggled all over with happiness. She raced me up the stairs and stood panting at the back door. I opened the door.

Omigod! Was this supposed to happen? The weatherman said flurries. Gay bounded out the door and immediately disappeared. The powdery stuff was at least a foot deep. The foot-high Corgi reappeared as she jumped up and was immediately engulfed again. She made her way to the corner and back.

"OK, kiddo, wipe your feet." Obediently, Gay rolled over, all four feet in the air. I wiped her dry and turned her loose. "Go get Anne," I coaxed, "get Suzy." Smart little dog she raced up the stairs to wake the children while I started a pot of oatmeal on the stove. Now time was short; I had not counted on shoveling. Quickly, I set the table, sliced melon, poured juice.

"Girls! Hurry now!" I called up the stairs, "and dress warmly, pants on under your skirts. It snowed last night and you'll need something sensible on your feet. No Capezios. Your feet will freeze, even in boots." I sighed. Flimsy little ballet slippers were the rage, and I braced myself for the sight of four disobedient little feet barely covered. Should I fight this one, or heed Mother's advice to cultivate blindness when it really did not matter? The thing is, I was never quite sure what mattered and what did not.

Lucky that Art's gone. He'd make them change. What was I thinking? Lucky? He could be clearing the driveway!

"Morning girls! Don't you look nice! Sue, don't complain about the pants. They look perfectly all right and you can take them off when you get to school. Try not to get too wet, that's all. Anne, can I help you untangle that hair? Give me a brush. Sue, do you have your homework in that bag? Good. Sit down and eat, please."

"Mom, can we stay home? Maybe there's no school anyway. We can shovel out the driveway for you. Please?"

"No, thank you very much; but I really appreciate your generosity. Maybe after school, you could clear the patio and a path for Gay. That would really help."

Groans.

"Oh Mom, you always make us go to school when it snows. No fair!"

"Button up those coats, girls. And Sue, put your hat on. Quick kiss and you're out the door. Bye. Have fun." I watched out the window as my two girls, seven and nine, slogged along, the hems of their winter coats dragging against the deep snow. School was only three blocks away, just around the corner; they would be fine.

I hurried to put the dishes into the dishwasher and milk, jam, and butter back into the refrigerator. Gay sat safely out of the way under the breakfast table, watching my every move. When I turned to go upstairs, she raced me to the top.

I had just finished lacing up my boots when the phone rang.

"Hello? Oh, Barbara, hi." It was my neighbor. "How did you know that? Art just left for Lakeland, Florida, yesterday, and I haven't talked to you since then. Oh. It snowed. And when it snows, you always assume Art's gone to Florida on business. Very funny. But you're right, it does seem that way. No, I'm not mad, not really. Can't be helped. I just wish we didn't have an eighty-foot driveway, that's all. See you over the snowdrifts!"

The first thing I had to do was figure out how to move the snow away from the side door of the garage. I did not want the drift to fall in and make a mess inside. A broom from the kitchen closet helped me brush the door clean where the wind had plastered it, and sweep most of the snow away from the sill. Inside the garage was dim and cold, but I found the big shovel. I heaved up the heavy door, and in front of me stretched eighty feet of pristine powder, crossed by the two tracks the girls had left. I shivered and set to work.

At first, the powder fairly floated off the shovel onto the side garden, but as I progressed toward the street, the snow seemed to get heavier and heavier. I pushed it, I dug it, I threw it, I panted. Sweat ran down my face and stung my eyes but my toes were getting numb. I could hear the scraping of other shovels and see puffs of snow flying, but there was no neighborly chatting. Everyone who needed to go somewhere was intent on the work.

Two hours later, the way was cleared. Winded, I leaned on my shovel and admired the effect. Already, the sun was beginning to find black pavement under the footprints left by the girls. I hung the shovel back on its hook, stamped the snow from my boots, and entered the house. Already ten o'clock, I should be at a committee meeting across town. Dripping snow onto the kitchen floor, I picked up the phone.

"Carol? This is Kit. Sorry about the time, but it has taken me until now to get the snow cleared off the driveway. Is everybody there?...Nobody yet? Anybody called? Oh, we're scheduled for eleven now? OK. I'll hurry through my shower and see you then. Bye."

As I toweled myself dry, I thought about Art. Sunny Florida. He did have to visit the company offices there, I knew, and weather didn't have anything to do with it. But it was odd that the snow and his trips came at the same time, every time. Oh well, he'd be home Friday night and we'd have the weekend.

Art called. "I understand Chicago had a little snow?" I gritted my teeth without comment.

Days passed in a usual, routine way, until at last it was Friday. This time, the girls would visit with Barbara while I drove to O'Hare Field to meet the plane. I dressed carefully, glanced at the mirror to see if I looked like a proper suburban wife, and went to start the family Ford station wagon. I drove west on Dempster Street, then turned south on Mannheim Road; the late afternoon traffic was light, and I arrived in time to park the car.

I checked the board for arrivals and walked to the gate just as the plane was taxiing up to the jetway. My shoulder muscles were still aching; maybe I would give Art a piece of my mind. I peered down the slanting corridor until I spotted him striding toward me. He put down his briefcase and folded me into his arms.

"How're you, Babe? You look great! Good to be home. What's for dinner and when?" That old query always managed to get a rise out of me. I started to sputter, but he reached into his pocket, drew something out, and popped it into my mouth.

"Fresh off the tree outside the office door." He grinned as I bit down and the lovely juice flowed in my mouth. A kumquat. He knew that would get me every time. I forgave him on the spot, handed him the keys, and we walked arm in arm toward the baggage claim. There were more fruits where that one came from, and he doled them out as we drove home, chattering happily.

I did get back at him, though. That Christmas, I gave him a snowblower.

SAVI NG THE WORLD

In September 1961 when our daughters were ten and twelve and settled in a new school year, the Fourniers and the Rosners decided to save the world. Change was in the air as the sun set on Joseph McCarthy and rose to illumine Rachel Carson's global anxieties. Our concern surrounded the political apathy of German citizens.

"If they don't wake up, it could happen again," worried Maxine. She and her sister had recently visited Germany. "The young people in particular just don't want to get involved."

" Maybe they'd find out what their parents did in the war, and they don't want to know," offered Art.

"Exactly! Only extremism has a way of creeping up unnoticed when you're not paying attention."

The extravagantly named American Foundation for World Youth Understanding was about to be born. We would establish a cultural exchange between young Germans and Americans, with the mission to engage them in the political and civic affairs of their respective countries.

As I look back on these plans, I am astonished that we accomplished so much. Although the recruitment of American youth was less successful, we did put together a working group that brought many hundreds of European young people to our shores. Willy Brandt, the mayor of Berlin, signed on and helped raise funds that supported air travel. Senator Paul Douglas, a Unitarian, lent support in Illinois, in Washington, and in New York.

I remember a chartered plane arriving one night at O'Hare Field. The international terminal building was a dark and noisy metal structure, set apart from domestic traffic. A stair ladder was rolled up to the door of the propeller-driven plane, and out tumbled a hundred tired, wrinkled, bewildered kids. Most of them were in their early twenties and had not traveled before, at least not across an ocean.

After the customs business and baggage retrieval were done, I stood at the door of one of the buses. "Bring your bags here to the sidewalk, and get on the bus, please. We will leave as soon as everyone is on board." I was beginning to feel right at home, just as if I were leading a tour at Rockefeller Center. The adventure had begun.

On the way from the airport, I encouraged them to talk about their expectations, about their attitudes toward the United States.

"What makes you Americans think you're so special?" asked one in a somewhat belligerent tone. General murmurs of agreement from the crowd.

"Well," I answered, "hold on to that question. I see that you are skeptical now, but try to hold an open mind. Later on, we will take up that question again."

Until we reached the Congress Hotel in downtown Chicago, I did not realize the full extent of the word *adventure*.

"What do you mean you have two large beds in each room?" I was facing a flustered, defiant night manager. "We contracted for four adults in each room. You were supposed to move in four single beds. No, they cannot double up in beds. Are you nuts? These people are strangers to each other. Let's get cracking and straighten this out."

We had to face a large group of people who had just endured an eleven-hour flight over the ocean and ask them to wait while the hotel's furniture was rearranged. Suddenly, the project was developing into a real challenge. Our good fortune in attracting influential sponsors extended to Albert Pick, the owner of this and other large hotels. Accordingly, the reluctant manager assembled his staff and started moving beds. By midnight, we had everyone bedded down.

Maxine, her sister Barbara, and I collapsed onto couches in the hotel lobby.

"Kit, this is not going to make it. We need more structure in our organization to manage these details. You're good at this, so you're elected." Maxine was the decisive one. From that time on, I negotiated meals and lodging in Chicago, Washington, and New York.

"Well," I said doubtfully, "I'm not sure I can do it on the budget we've laid out. I told you it was too tight!" Tight or not, I was assigned to house and feed this horde somehow. Later that week, I sat down with the general operations manager of the chain. Mr. Pick had evidently briefed him on our organization and his enthusiastic endorsement of our aims.

I started the conversation. "We will need three meals every day. Let's look over menus. These young people need a good breakfast with meat. Plenty of coffee. Of course fruit. Maybe bagels or Danish?"

"And what is your budget for breakfast?" His pen was poised over the menu.

"Less than a dollar should do it, I think. We still have lunch and dinner to figure, and the total for a day's meals and lodging cannot get above seven dollars, tops." The poor man was sweating.

"Seven dollars! But this is a first-class hotel! Please!"

"Yes, I know. We would not ask them to stay in anything less and we are so grateful that Mr. Pick has seen the wisdom in that!"

We worked out menus for each day and arrived at a final total of $7.50 per day per person, food and lodging. I shook hands with the wilted man.

"Mrs. Fournier, I know this program will be repeated again and again. Could you possibly see your way clear to spread your business around a little more? I'm bleeding from every pore!"

"Don't count on it." I smiled, and escaped while I was still ahead.

The plan was to keep the group together in Chicago for a week for initial orientation. Their command of English was excellent, but they had no idea about the American language. American culture was new to them; someone had to tell them a few hard facts, and that someone was, by general agreement, me. As I rose to speak to them in the hotel auditorium, I noticed a row of news reporters in the back row.

Good!, I thought. We'll get local coverage. I launched into my cautionary speech. "You will soon be traveling west for a three-week visit in the homes of families in Iowa and Nebraska. They are looking forward to welcoming you, and I know you will have a wonderful time. Just a few little things you need to know. This is July and you will want to take your swim suits with you for a dip in the community pool in the town where you will be staying. Ladies, before you go to the pool, you must try on your suit in front of your hostess. Probably many of you will need to replace your suits with American models. The bikinis you are used to wearing at home are unknown here and more modest models will be needed." Gasps all around, while the German women looked at one another in consternation. The men smiled broadly at their discomfort.

"Now men, wait. Here's a message for you. Drinking beer in public places may be prohibited by law in some of the towns." I heard loud exclamations: *what!?! how can that be?!* And phrases I could not translate exactly but whose meaning was quite clear. "Seriously, fellows, beer may not even be found in many of the homes. The general rule is this: some of the American Mid-West associates alcohol with morality. Forget beer unless it is offered to you." I wondered privately whether they would miss beer so much once they tasted the American brands. Probably not.

I thought I should find a way to lighten up my offering, but I needed to cover still another issue. "One more thing I need to tell you. Unmarried American men often have a 'line'. They say sweet things to pretty women such as yourselves, but they may not really mean it. It's a generally innocent game played here. Just be careful to believe less than everything you may hear about undying affection! We tend to have freer exchanges between men and women than you may be used to.

If you find yourself in an awkward situation, trust your hostess to guide you, in this and other matters."

Following my cautionary discussion, Dr. Milton Rakove launched into a lively lecture on the rise of American urban society. His talks over the next three days gave an overview of our cultural history, a condensed version of the course he taught at the University of Illinois.

There! We had covered it all, but I wondered how much of it sank in. And I wondered whether the reporters had stayed for it all; they were gone now. In the morning, I found out. On page three of the Chicago Sun-Times blared the headline: **Beer, Bikinis and Bachelors!** The article gave a very funny account of the collision of two cultures. I hoped our young guests missed it.

The next three weeks gave the officers of the AFWYU (even that was a mouthful) a little time to regroup and plan for the next phase. The Germans were living with very generous Kiwanis families, demonstrating by living the American life. Our itinerary would take us next to the nation's capital.

In Washington, Senator Douglas had arranged for a special conducted tour of the White House. After breakfast, Maxine and Barbara led our group to walk the four or five blocks, and I brought up the rear. Incredibly, even though the leaders tried to keep up a brisk pace, the line stretched all the way from the White House gate to the hotel front door. I learned that although Europeans say they like to walk a lot, the truth is that they stroll, Americans stride. Later, we filled the gallery at a session of the House of Representatives.

I found myself fielding questions about the structure of our government and its practical workings, digging into my own education and reading for the answers. Sometimes, it was pretty funny. An historic battle was raging over an issue about privatizing satellites. A filibuster had gone on for days, and now a frantic struggle raged to raise a quorum in the Senate and the real possibility of a successful cloture vote, for the first time in history. Our guests caught the excitement and tension, but they were bewildered. We gathered in a small auditorium where one of Senator Douglas's aides tried valiantly to explain.

"Any questions?" he ended. A hand went up, hesitantly. "Yes?"

"This is all very confusing, but I think you could clear it up for us. Just tell us: who is this Mr. Phil A. Buster?" The effect on a very tired office staff was electric, and they all lunged for the doors, faces barely concealing hilarity. One of our staff ended the matter with the announcement that everyone was now free to take the rest of the day for shopping or sightseeing.

The end of our tour took us to New York, where we visited the United Nations. Our guests knew next to nothing about it, and I admit that much of it was a revelation to me, too.

One of many facts I learned was the homogeneity of the German nation. It came home to me when we walked through Chinatown, on our way to a restaurant. For the first time, our guests kept in a tight little knot, a few even holding hands. The Germans were surrounded by Chinese faces and they were scared!

"Madame Direktor (that was me), I've never seen a real Chinese before, except in the movies. Are they dangerous? They look like they might be." When we sat down for dinner, I moved from table to table, asking questions about their experience of foreigners. They had none. Most of them had never experienced any culture except their own. Jews, of course, were mostly absent, and North Africans had made no significant entrance. It was an insular society. To them, the jars of peanut butter they had stowed in their luggage were the most exotic food they had ever encountered. I was sobered.

At last, departure time was at hand. Our band of Germans now looked nothing like the people we had welcomed only five or six weeks before. They wore jeans and polo shirts, and had even acquired cowboy boots. The men sported American haircuts. And everybody talked at once, American slang was rampant. I had trouble quieting them down on my bus as we approached the airport.

"Listen, everyone. Do you remember the question somebody asked when you first arrived?"

"No! Too long ago!"

"I do! It was what makes you Americans think you're so special!"

"That's it," I said. "Now have you figured out any answers?"

Silence. Then one voice chimed in, "But you are special. I don't know why, but you are. I'm going to have to go home and think more about it."

"O.K.," I challenged, "what's special? What do we do that you did not expect?"

"You volunteer. I couldn't believe you were not getting paid for what you do. Then when I went out to Nebraska, my hostess did it, too. She worked at the hospital, led a Girl Scout troop. Never got anything for it."

Everyone had a story like that and it mystified them. Would they take this idea home and apply it there? I never knew, but hearing the warmth in their voices filled me with hope.

As they headed for the plane, I called out, "Go home and save the world!" They shot back "Ja wohl."

THE THIRD DAUGHTER

Art liked Sunday mornings in church. Not that religious practice was any more attractive than it had ever been, but we sat there for an hour; being together close and quiet was enough. Sometimes he nodded off and I had to nudge him a little, but he claimed that he was only 'resting my eyes'.

This Sunday, as I sat forward, listening intently, I became aware that he was fixed on the minister's story, too. The message, probably something general about rips in the fabric of society, was not what caught our ears. He was telling about a young girl, a runaway from a troubled family, a child falling through the cracks. She was a youngster from our own town, no one wanted her, and she had been sent to a juvenile detention facility. Her crime was to have run away, and no one had emerged to save her from hopeless descent. Art looked at me and I looked back into his eyes; we knew we would step forward.

After the service, Art spoke to the minister, asking for more information. Other members of the church gathered around—I remember a psychiatrist and a social worker. We learned that Sandy, 14—just our Susan's age—had been deserted by her mother when she was a little girl, and had been living with her father and his new wife, along with several step-siblings. Recounting of her physical and psychic abuse touched our hearts, especially Art's. He may have been connecting to his desertion by his own mother, but he never said so.

The minister said with sympathetic assurance, "If you want to shelter her, I would certainly be there to offer whatever resources I could muster."

The psychiatrist nodded in agreement. "She might need counseling, and you two could certainly use guidance. I'm here."

I forget whether anyone else spoke up, but Art was writing down information about the court that oversaw her case.

When we gathered our family together, we talked over what we wanted to do and asked whether everyone else was on board. Mother, as was her custom, expressed no opinion. The girls were excited, though.

"She could sleep in my room," offered Anne.

"No, she's my age and she should be with me," objected Susan.

"Are you sure, Honey? It would mean crowding another bed and dresser in your small room. What if you two didn't get along?"

"Of course we'll get along," said Susan confidently, "we have to. She needs us."

"We're going to have another sister!" both said together.

"Well, maybe for a little while at least," cautioned Art. "We'll see. There's a court hearing tomorrow and Mom and I will go find out what's up."

The process of investigating us and accepting our offer to shelter Sandy was outrageous. The court knew only that Sandy was a loose end that needed tying up and here was a likely-looking pair willing to take her away. It was done in only a moment. The judge's gavel fell, the deputy handed her over to us, and the court's next case on the docket was in session.

Sandra was a tall, slender, pale girl with rumpled hair and a withdrawn demeanor. She looked us over with sullen eyes and followed us out of the courtroom.

"Sandy, I'm Mrs. Fournier and this is my husband. We want you to come home with us for awhile. You'll be in a family with our two girls and my mother. We have a little dog, Gay, too. And you'll be in New Trier High School, where you have already started. Our daughter Susan is a freshman, too." I babbled on, trying to fill the silent void as we walked to our car and drove toward Glenview. Sandy was polite but distant.

We had managed to find temporary furniture to make her feel at home; she brought pitifully few belongings with her. When we arrived, Gay greeted us at the door with joyful wiggles. Sandy's face softened a little.

The three girls trooped up to show Sandy her room and they vied to see which one could offer her more shared clothing. Before long, they were sitting on a bed showing off family albums of pictures. At least Sandy did not have to carry her end of that conversation.

When dinner was ready, I called, "Girls, wash your hands and come down to dinner please." As they came down the stairs, Sandy stopped in hesitation.

"Here's your place, dear. This is your napkin ring." Sandy stood still. "What's wrong? What do you need?" She shook her head in bewilderment, but came and sat down.

"Sandy, you need to know that we are not very good at mind reading. If something bothers you, you need to say what it is. Can't be sure to fix it, but we can try. So what is it?"

"It's just that . . . I don't know. Do you always have dinner together, or is this just for today?"

"Sandy, whatever else we might be doing, unless someone is away from home, dinner time is together time. That's the rule."

"And breakfast, too, by the way," chimed in Art, "Mother really likes breakfast!" Everybody laughed, knowing how firm I was about eating a good meal to start the day.

As usual, the dinner conversation revolved around the day at school, at the office, and in the neighborhood. I could tell that Sandy had little experience with table chatter, or with table manners, for that matter.

As I undressed for bed that night, I reached for a cigarette. The minister's words rang in my ears: *only fourteen years old and already she smokes a pack of cigarettes a day.* The match nearly burned my fingers. I blew it out and threw the unlit cigarette into the wastebasket. How could I address the child's habit without first putting out my own? After twenty-one years, that was my last cigarette.

One day, I took Susan aside. "Sue, dear, I know you want to make Sandy feel at home, but imitating her table manners is not the way. Please try to be a model for her so she can learn the right way."

"But Mom, I know you don't want to scold Sandy. And you don't mind scolding me. So that way, she can learn what not to do!"

I laughed. "I guess I do correct you pretty freely, don't I! Let's not call it scolding, though. It might take a little longer, but just do right and let Sandy catch on. I'm sure she will. Thanks for helping."

In the next few days, I found that Sandy had no interest in talking about her classes in school, or in fact, anything else. She seemed to talk with the girls better than with the adults. I decided it was time to go to school and talk to her advisor there.

"Mrs. Fournier, good to meet you. Please sit down. How well do you know Sandy's situation? I thought not. Well let me tell you, it's not going to work out. I can see right away that you are the wrong people for her. You obviously have very high standards for behavior, for academics, for your children's future. This girl is never going to live up to your mark and the whole thing will blow up in your faces. I advise you to retreat from this before someone gets hurt."

"Oh?" I was astonished. "And what would you recommend then? No one else seems interested in her."

"Mrs. Fournier, it's a nice altruistic gesture but it's not grounded in the realities." Having relieved herself of the bone in her throat, she dismissed me briefly and went on to other things. I sat there, stunned. My next call was to the minister; surely he could help me get a sense of direction. That, too, was an unhappy encounter. He told me that he regretted having sounded as if he had something substantive to offer, that in fact he had no idea. The psychiatrist turned out to be too busy to talk to me. I turned to another psychiatrist who had offered me personal counsel. We met in his office, where I outlined the situation. After a long silence, he began, "Well, you really are into something, aren't you! It sounds to me as if this youngster is pretty badly wounded. I have to tell you that in these cases, a favorable outcome is very unlikely."

"But, doctor, we expect to be in this for the long haul. If Sandy needs help, than we want to get it for her. Would you be willing to take her on as a patient? We would cover the bills, of course." His characterization of this as one of 'these cases' alarmed me. Sandy wasn't a category, she was a child who needed all of us.

"Let's talk about why you want to do this, then," he continued, without answering my question. Then he gave me his theory. "Your daughter Susan has become distant, hard to communicate with. Isn't that right?" I had to agree with that. "In fact, you've lost contact with her, and Sandy seems like a good substitute. You think maybe you can reach Sandy instead."

Susan and I had, in fact, grown apart. I ascribed it to her beginning adolescence, her grasping for independence. My hands grew sweaty—was I deserting her, turning away because I had given up? While I wanted to deny it, here was a respected authority accusing me. I asked again whether he would take Sandy—or our whole family, for that matter—as a patient. He tried to sound kind and gentle, but his 'no' battered my ears. I left and drove home through a blur of tears.

That night, after everyone was in bed, I turned to Art. "I guess we're going to go it alone in this. We have only instinct to guide us now."

Art gave me a long squeeze and murmured, "No, we have love on our side. Let's hope it's enough." He turned out the light.

The next two or three weeks settled into a familiar routine of meals and homework, television and walking the dog. Sandy loosened up with me, occasionally showing me an assignment she needed help with. We grew hopeful, until the day the school called. "Mrs. Fournier? Is Sandy sick? This is the third day she has been absent from class." I replied only that I would look into it, and I hoped that the panic in my voice did not come through.

When Sandy came home at the usual hour, I confronted her. "Sandy, where did you spend the day?"

"In school, why?" Her answer came smoothly, her face betrayed nothing.

"Sandy, I want to give you a chance to talk to me, to tell me what's on your mind. Or in your heart. Don't tell me lies! Tell me the truth." I was pleading with her, trying to maintain a motherly stance, but tears of frustration began to roll down my cheeks. Sandy turned on her heel and walked away.

After dinner, Sandy approached me in the kitchen. "I'm sorry, Mom. It's just that school got to be more than I could stand. I wasn't doing anything bad, honest."

I led her to the kitchen table, and we sat down facing one another. "Tell me."

"It's not worth telling, I guess. Just didn't want to go. Only now you upset me."

"How's that?"

"Well, nobody ever cried over me before, that's all. I guess nobody ever cared what I did or where I went. I hurt you, Mom, and I'm sorry."

There it was again. Mom. She had never called me that before. "Dear girl, the next time you feel like doing something you shouldn't, try talking to me first, will you? We can't make life easy but if you let us, we can help you stand up to it. Running away really isn't the answer." We stood up and she actually hugged me before she disappeared up the stairs. I closed my eyes and exhaled slowly.

The girls made a little trio, held together by different things. Anne was apparently fascinated to learn something about Sandy's adventures before she joined us. Anne was awed by tales of beatings and food deprivation; she had read tales by the Brothers Grimm, but this was real life. Sue was, I think, attracted to Sandy's rebellious side, her affinity for trashy companions. Sue found allure in the forbidden side of life.

Sandy seemed to respect Art; she obeyed his exacting expectations of sharing in the family work on weekends. She never exhibited any affection, though, nor called him Dad. It was a little awkward, but she simply referred to him as 'he'. She did not connect to my mother at all, not following the other girls in their limitless love for her.

I continued, suspended on a breathless string of hope. Until the phone rang one morning. It was Susan.

"Where are you, Sue?"

"I'm at school, Mom. Listen, I just called to tell you to lock up the liquor before we get home, O.K.?"

"What are you talking about? What's happened?"

"Nothing, Mom. Only I found out that tomorrow is Sandy's turn to bring the booze. A bunch of them get together before classes start and pass booze around. They're pretty out of it by the time school begins. So, like I say, just lock it up. Gotta go." I stood there holding the phone, the dial tone ringing loud in my ear, my heart beating fast.

After that eye-opener, family life began to unravel quickly. Sandy avoided Art's questions. She was non-committal with me. Her promises to go to classes and to stay sober were violated regularly. At last, tension, suspicion, anger filled the house. Art was ready to throw in the towel and I could not find a contrary argument. All the nay-sayers had been right; we were not up to it. Art admitted to feeling physically sick, too.

"Don't feel guilty, darling," he soothed, "it's not our fault. We didn't start the trouble, but by god we will bring it to a decent conclusion. She's not going back to be punished by the legal system." That vow became our crusade as we searched for weeks for a suitable sheltered environment for Sandy. We couldn't even get her into a State psychiatric hospital. Evidently, troubled teens were in plentiful supply.

We returned to the court to plead her case. Although we had found a good placement for Sandy, it was full and they refused to take her on our application. After spending time persuading the judge, we went away dejected. The following day, a call came and we learned that the House of the Good Shepherd had found a bed for her, after all. This was a home for girls such as Sandy, locked, as they said, to protect them from the world.

Sue and Anne were tearful at the farewell, but Sandy remained stoic. Whether she felt pain at this development—or maybe even relief—we never knew. She packed clothes I had made for her along with those the girls had shared. We drove downtown in silence.

A nun greeted us at the door, and ushered us into a small reception room.

"Will you come to see me?" asked Sandy. Before I could answer, the nun said, "No visitors for a month. You can receive one letter a week, that's all. After that, you may have family visitors briefly from time to time. You will get used to thinking of this as your home, and you will forget about the rest." I hugged Sandy hard, Art shook her hand, and she disappeared through the door with the nun.

Our relationship resumed after the required month, but of course on a very limited scale. Of the family, she wanted to see only me, even though Art went with me sometimes. Children visitors were forbidden anyway. Mostly, I wrote to her and I was a peculiar correspondent. In my childhood, one of my favorite books was *Daddy Long Legs* by Jean Webster. It was a tale about a girl in an orphanage who corresponded with a somewhat imaginary and fantastic Daddy. Whatever it was that charmed me so long ago now took hold of my imagination. I would be that imaginary and fantastic parent. Since Sandy had never experienced a good mother, I would become the Perfect Mother. It was pretty easy, since I never had to be tired or cross or unreasonable. I modeled The Mother, in a way that I suspected the nuns were not able to do.

After three years, convent life overwhelmed her but Sandy found her escape. The one impossible sin for the nuns to cope with was homosexuality, and when Sandy made overtures to one of the nuns, an out-placement was quickly found. She was placed in a family with young children as a mother's helper. When her natural tendencies were revealed in a flirtation with the young father, Sandy was once again on the outside. I worried helplessly. We were in Texas when we received an invitation to her marriage to someone she had never mentioned, and her last name became Stachel. We sent her a wedding gift with our best wishes. She bore three children, Denise, Dawn, and David, and soon after David came, she was divorced. She stayed in her modest house and brought up the children alone, apparently successfully. David joined the air force and was stationed in Japan; the girls married and had children of their own. She was a devoted mother. During these trying times, Art and I sent money to help out, but it was always returned firmly but with thanks. All she ever accepted from us was clothing that I sewed or knitted for her.

In a disastrous misstep, Sandy then married someone she knew from the post office, where she had worked for twenty years. He insisted she stop working when they married. She told me he was personable, and had promised to stop drinking. Predictably, he took everything she had, house, money, furniture, even her seniority at the post office. Her health began to deteriorate from years of heavy smoking; she developed serious heart disease.

I think I succeeded at least a little. One Mother's Day, she wrote me a note, saying I was the only real mother she had ever known. I think my letters were all she knew of how to be a mother.

CHANGING TIMES

"Suzy, please leave the table and go comb your hair. I'm really sick of seeing it in your face." Without a word, Susan shoved her chair away from the breakfast table, stamped up the stairs, and slammed her bedroom door. Anne bent over her cereal and stayed quiet as a mouse.

"Honestly, Art, that child!" I shook my head. "What's on your schedule today, dear? Are you home for a little while or off on another lecture somewhere?"

"Have to tend the home fires some of the time, I guess. Nothing on the boards right now. How about you? When's the next mob from Germany set to land?" We continued checking in with one another, leaving parental care aside.

Anne gathered her books, kissed us goodbye, and started for school. She and Susan had their own friends now and seldom walked together any more. Art tied his necktie, picked up his briefcase, and waited for me to go start the station wagon. I drove him the three miles to work.

"Bye, Beautiful. Keep it going for me, will you? See you tonight. I'll ride home with Con." Con Mers, who lived just down the street, worked with Art in the purchasing department. He was a good friend as well as being, as Art told me, one of the nation's best experts in packaging, especially multi-wall bags—whatever they were. I was glad to be relieved of taxi service, even though Art's commute was miniscule; my day was filled with comings and goings.

When I put the car back in the garage and went into the house, I noticed Susan's books still sitting on the ledge near the front door. Darn. She forgot them and that meant an extra trip to drop them off at school. I sighed. When I turned around, the sight of Susan on the stairs startled me.

"Susan! You're going to be late for school. Why haven't you left? Now you've missed the bus and it's too late to walk. Get into the car and I'll drive you there. Honestly!" I did not wait for an explanation; experience suggested I would not get one anyway. Just sullen looks. I was not disappointed.

Susan's friends worried me. They had an indefinably dangerous air about them. If it had been an issue, I might have refused to allow them to visit in our home, but Susan never offered to bring them there; she met them somewhere else and left me with an uneasy feeling. She was developing her own interests, whatever they were. At home, she was growing more and more withdrawn, sometimes angry, often defiant. Art and I operated on an efficiency theory: in our busy world, the only way to keep everything together was to get everyone marching in the same direction.

On the way home from dropping Susan at school, my mind wandered back to another era. I could picture the scene clearly, although it must have been ten years ago.

I had taken Great Aunt Alice Christmas shopping at the Marshall Field store in downtown Chicago. She was eighty years old, and arthritis made walking painful for her. I carried a wheelchair in the trunk of my car. When I pulled the car up to the curb on Wabash Avenue, the uniformed doorman stepped over to open the door. He lifted the chair from the trunk and helped Aunt Alice into it.

"I'll find a place to park and be right with you," I said to them. An empty space waited less than a block away, and by the time I returned, Aunt Alice was waiting comfortably inside the store.

"Let me get my list out and we'll begin," she said, rummaging through her purse. A small black hat on her crown of white hair, her rimless glasses, the triple row of pearls at her neck, ladylike white gloves, sensible black shoes, and bright twinkling eyes, she seemed to me the picture of Mrs. Claus down from the North Pole for a little shopping spree. We looked for toys for her youngest grandson and clothes for the other three. Just for fun, we examined beautiful Irish table linens and Battenberg lace-edged cloths.

"Time for lunch," she said, and we headed for the Walnut Room. The traditional Christmas tree rose to the ceiling, several stories above us, Christmas carols playing softly in the background. When our lunch was finished, we set out for a final round, but not before she carefully placed the morning gloves in her purse and extracted a clean pair for the afternoon.

I smiled ruefully at the memories that flooded my mind. By now, in 1964, the world had moved on. Marshall Field's doorman was gone. And a parking space on Wabash Avenue? Forget it. Aunt Alice was gone, along with the hat and gloves; no one wore them any more. Girls had begun to wear jeans — although not to school. And they called them dungarees. Skirt hems were rising, and the concept of a 'ladylike appearance' made young women roll their eyes. They wanted to be cool, they wanted to soak up the lyrics of Beatles songs. Listening to their parents was out of the question.

My busy day ended at home in the kitchen, preparing dinner. The table was set and we gathered in the dining room. One place was empty. The front door opened.
"Susan, you're late for dinner. Where in the world have you been? You know dinner is on the table at six-thirty." Sue looked down but had no answer; she seemed to be hiding behind untidy long, dark hair that was perpetually in her face. Ever since Sandy's departure, she had been increasingly troublesome. Punishment and groundings had become the norm; still we persisted in our march ahead.

Although Susan, at fifteen, was reaching forward for the 60s, Anne, and the rest of us, were stuck in the 50s. At thirteen, Anne spent her summertime volunteering at the local county forest preserve.
"Mom, the naturalist asked me if I could bring home mallard eggs to hatch. Can I, Mom? Please? The foxes are

getting all the eggs over there and we might lose all the ducks! Please, Mom?"

"You mean the world is suddenly going to be without ducks any more if we don't act? How terrible!"

"Aw Mom! Can I please?" Well, I thought optimistically, they might not hatch, so I said yes. We took the eggs to the high school biology lab where they rested in the incubator. Of course they did hatch, all but one.

"O.K., smarty," Art asked me, "where are you going to keep the little guys?"

"I thought you could build them a duck run, Dear. Shouldn't be too hard—just a little fencing, that's all."

Anne and Dad took the station wagon over to the hardware store and came back with fencing and posts and staples.

"How about water, Dad? Ducks need water."

"Simple. Go get your mother's canning bucket while I figure out a ramp." At last, the rest of us were summoned to survey the final effect. My canning pot was filled with water, a narrow ramp made of wood was firmly attached. A tarpaulin draped over one end offered shelter from the wind and a little shade.

"Now bring the ducks!" Anne carried the box of fluffy little yellow balls from the garage and, one by one, gently lifted them into their new home. At first, they skittered together to the corner, under the cover, but after a while the more adventuresome poked around the food dish. Before long, one brave little bird found the ramp.

"Look! He's going swimming!" And sure enough, up he went, toddling uncertainly up to the top. Plunk! I caught my breath and lunged to catch him before he drowned.

"Don't worry, Mom, he knows how to swim." He did. Then followed a duck parade up the ramp. Plunk! Plunk! Plunk! Small as they were, the pot could accommodate them all swimming at once. Gay was so excited, she barked and ran around the enclosure, trying to herd them.

From then on, my days were punctuated with sudden departures from wherever I was meeting, PTA or scouts.

"Excuse me, I have to go. It looks as if it might rain and I can't let my ducks get wet." The naturalist had explained that little ducks in the wild were protected by running under their mother's breast and picking up her feathers' oil. Without a mother, a duck could get soaked through to the skin, contract pneumonia, and die. So I left my bewildered cohorts to save the ducks from rain.

Some weeks after they arrived, the ducks had grown to almost full size. Only one duck could swim at a time, they were forever getting out of their pen, the dog was busy noisily trying to herd them, and I was getting tired of the game.

"Anne, it's time to return the ducks to the forest preserve. Remember, that was the whole point of this project. Let's find big boxes and deliver them tomorrow after school."

Anne gave one more try to own the ducks. When we arrived, she beseeched the naturalist, "Couldn't we band them, so we'll know which ones they are?" As she spoke, he was busy taking the boxes out of the station wagon and setting the ducks free among the others in the flock. In only a moment, they were all milling around with their cousins.

"The last thing I need," he confided to me, "is a crying girl trying to find her missing duck. Better this way." The duck episode was now just a cherished memory.

Where was Susan in all this? She was a spectator, but not a participant. It was not her show. Did anyone notice? I don't think so.

YOU CAN'T GO DOWN IN THE MINE

It was Art on the phone. "Can you clear your calendar for a few days right after the Fourth of July?"

"Not the easiest thing, dear, the Fourth is this Sunday! What's on your mind?"

"Oh, it's not vital, but I'm taking a little trip and I thought you might like to come along."

Instantly, I pictured the kitchen of my childhood, with a mop and pail sitting in the middle of the floor, abandoned. My dad had summoned my mother for a sudden business trip, and after she had departed in haste to join him, I remembered seeing that pail just where she had left it. It's a little peculiar to have a clear vision of the origin of your priorities, but I said quickly, "Sure I can. How soon?"

"You haven't asked where!"

"Oh, I guess I'll need to know that, won't I? But I've told you: I'll follow you anywhere. So where?"

"Coatzocoalcos."

"No, really. Where?"

"O.K., Mexico City first and then Coatzocoalcos. You'll need mostly city clothes, but bring your bathing suit. I'm going to be hunting for sulfur mines."

Since my mother was right there to take care of the household, going away was pretty easy. Deciding what to take was the hard part; I had not traveled out of the country before, unless you counted a couple of visits to Niagara Falls. The only thing I knew to assume was hot, and I was right about that. In less than a week, I had stocked the pantry, packed my clothes, kissed the girls goodbye, and stepped into the big, black limousine that came to pick me up at our front door.

The driver headed for Art's office where we found him waiting at the door, suitcase in hand. Then it was off to O'Hare Field and sulfur hunting. Art explained to me that the world-wide shortage of sulfur was a serious problem, since it was a major component of agricultural fertilizers. He had to locate a source that would provide hundreds of tons of the stuff and he thought he had a line on a mine in Mexico that could work for him.

In good time, we settled into the Mexicana airlines plane and took off. The flight was uneventful, boring. We were too high to see anything and I dozed some. Shortly after we had crossed the international border, I noticed a stewardess carrying a tray forward. On it stood two open bottles of Dos Equis beer.

"Art! Did you see that? She took the beer right into the cockpit!"

"Welcome to the wide world, Babe." I was more than a little startled. Despite my misgivings, we arrived safely at the Mexico City international airport and were soon inside the terminal. Crowds were milling around and I had no idea what to do. It looked as if we would need to find our way to the crowded customs officer's desk to gain entry into the country.

But no. A man came up to Art, introduced himself, bowed to me, and said, "Señor Fournier, please follow me." He led us through the crowded room to a side door, pressed something into the hand of a uniformed guard standing there, held the door for us, and we were out on the street. The man handed us into a waiting limousine, spoke briefly to the driver, and we were off. At the hotel, we found a huge bouquet of red roses with a card addressed to me. It said: Welcome to Mexico, Señora.

"Whew!" I exclaimed. "What happened? Who was that man?"

"That was a representative from the mining company. In two days, he will be back again to take us to the mine. Did you see how we got around customs? The tip he gave to the guard is called 'mordida' and that translates to 'bite'. Don't look at me that way. Get used to it; it's a way of life here."

In the two days we had to explore the city, we discovered the floating gardens of Xochomilco. It was fun to glide along on the water among the tropical flowers, serenaded by Mariachis. Even realizing that it was what we would have termed a tourist trap back home did not spoil the romance. I did my part for the Mexican economy, buying delicate hand-woven shawls in every color from the vendors who came alongside in their flat-bottom boats.

The next day, we found the archeological museum. We were awed. The building was breathtaking, a deft combination of pre-Columbian and modern architecture, but the presentation of history of the region was like nothing I had ever seen before. It rivaled the great museums of New York and Chicago. No, I think, surpassed them.

"Some day," said Art as we reluctantly walked away from the building after hours of exploration, "we'll come back here and spend a week, just learning in this one place." I came away with a beautiful silver bracelet, decorated with the same calendar stone we had admired there. But we never did return.

The third day dawned bright and hot. Our limousine was waiting at the hotel to speed us away to the next leg of our flight to southern Mexico. This time, the plane was small and cramped. It was a puddle-jumper and we stopped at many towns on the way. I remember Vera Cruz, although we made only a brief stop there. The terminal was a small adobe building, ancient and stained. Dust swirled around the cactus. A man lounged against the building, large straw sombrero tilted over his face and I half-expected to see a laconic Humphrey Bogart appear from around the corner. We took off again, still winging southward. Soon, we had arrived at Coatzocoalcos and it was time to get off. A different escort met us there. He was dressed in a polo shirt, open at the neck. After greeting us in a very formal manner, he led us to a taxi waiting at the curb.

"Oh look," I said, "what a lovely beach!" Our escort ordered the driver to stop and invited us to get out and admire the view. The white sand stretched for perhaps a mile, wide and deep and not a soul in sight, only the blue water lapping at the shore.

"Where is everyone? Here it is summer, and no one to enjoy this?"

"Señora, it is too hot. This is a popular place in winter, but no one comes here now." We continued the ride to the next town, Minatitlan. The taxi stopped at the curb, but all I could see was an iron railing along the sidewalk. We got out, and our escort looked at me in dismay. He was looking at the way I was dressed, in high heels and stockings. When I realized that we were going to climb down a ladder on the other side of the railing to reach the river, about thirty feet below, I understood.

"Oh don't worry," I smiled, as I took off my shoes and looped the sling-backs over a finger, "I'm a sailor. I'm used to this." Showing off a little, I clambered down the ladder, clenching my teeth when the rungs dug into the soles of my feet. The men followed and we climbed into a waiting motor launch. As we proceeded up the Coatzocoalcos River, the lush forest soon closed in behind us. I shuddered a little as I looked up to see vultures in the treetops watching our passage. Hope we don't get shipwrecked, I thought. The river seemed to be largely uninhabited, but once Art pointed to a long canoe by the bank. It was a log that had been hollowed out and shaped by hand, a very primitive craft. I laughed when I saw that a big Johnson motor was hanging on the stern. In a little while, we passed a woman doing her laundry in the river. She was actually pounding the clothes with a rock, but she had carried them down in a plastic pail, and put down a big box of detergent by her side.

After an hour, we rounded a bend and saw a large wood dock ahead. We landed there, and I was handed out to climb into a military Jeep.

"Welcome to Salinas," said the tall young American driver, who turned out to be a mining engineer. When we were seated and our bags put into the back, we started through the little village. About a dozen houses made of mud and thatch were clustered around a square. The buildings had only openings for doors and windows.

"Excuse me," I said to the driver, "did I see what I thought I saw in those houses?"

"Oh you mean the electric stoves and refrigerators? Sure, everybody has them. We have plenty of power left over from the mine and the appliances are barged up here from the city. No roads out of the jungle, just the river."

We arrived at a fine-looking tiled building; it was what they laughingly referred to as the Salinas Hilton, and we would be housed there overnight. The day was hot and steamy, but the guest house was cool with subdued light in the spacious bedroom.

A Mexican man-servant carried our small bags in and unpacked them, folding everything neatly in the drawers of a large carved wood chest.

"Would the Señora like to enjoy a swim before dinner?" I thought I would. Art had disappeared to confer with the mine managers and I was on my own. I slipped into my bathing suit and padded out the door to the patio beside the pool. Everything was tiled, the walls, the floors, the roof; even the pool tiles were brightly decorated with flower designs. Of course, the placid blue water was as warm as a bath and I swam the length. When I looked up, I noticed that the servant was standing nearly hidden behind a pillar between the house and pool. It made me uncomfortable to be watched like that, until I realized that he was only standing by to serve me in whatever way he could. Later on, when Art joined me in the pool, he laughed at my 'life guard'. Art knew I was a poor swimmer.

We toweled dry, lay down on the big bed for a siesta.

"Want to make this an international love affair?"

I had already rolled away, and I murmured, "I'm asleep," but in a moment his arms were around me, his lips on my neck.

"International is good," I sighed, rolling back. And then we really slept. We woke and dressed for dinner.

"Well," said Art, "I think we've got a deal. This little gem seems to be mostly unknown and they haven't much idea about international marketing. So they're pretty much languishing. I can swallow up their entire output, and it will be just about enough." He was triumphant. "Now don't embarrass yourself tonight by asking for a tour of the mine!"

"Why not? Is it something about my being a woman?"

"No, they'll try to tease you into asking, though. You need to know that this isn't that kind of a mine. Sulfur is extracted by pumping super-heated water underground. That turns the sulfur into a slurry, and then they pump it out. It's all done with pipes and pumps, dear. No caverns."

"Oh. Thanks." We ate dinner with four American mining engineers and their wives, but no one tried to tease me. The women were too glad to have a new woman to talk to; it was a lonely life for them.

In the morning, we packed up and prepared to leave.

"We're flying out in about an hour."

"Flying? How can that be? We're in the middle of the jungle! An amphibian couldn't take off from the river, because it's too twisty. Where's the air field then?"

"Wait and see." Art was smiling at my perplexity. We ate breakfast on our patio, brought on a tray from the kitchen. I thought I could live like this for at least a little while longer, but soon it was time to move on.

We were led to a small clearing in the dense growth where several cows were grazing. Suddenly the roar of an engine filled the air, and a small plane dipped into sight. It buzzed the 'runway', sending the cows loping off into the underbrush. Quickly, the pilot turned and glided in, before they returned. We were handed up into the cabin and our bags stowed. Two soldiers appeared, grabbed the wings and slowly pivoted the small craft until it was facing the runway, but by this time the cows had reappeared. The soldiers ran after them, shouting and brandishing their rifles, while the pilot gunned the engine, sped down the grassy space, and we were airborne. Some kind of a ride!

We flew directly to Vera Cruz, where we picked up a commercial plane for Mexico City. From there, we were non-stop to Chicago.

And Art had his sulfur.

PERIL

Susan lay in her hospital bed, waiting for the surgeon. Almost sixteen years old, she was going to have a lumbar laminectomy and fusion. Until just a few weeks ago, neither Art nor I had ever heard those words, but by this time we were all too familiar with them. Three or four years earlier, Susan had slipped on the ice. She fell hard on the end of her spine, and that incident was probably the onset of a deterioration that continued until she was nearly disabled. The doctor doubted she would be able to carry a pregnancy successfully as the condition worsened, and that decided the matter for us all.

"Don't worry," Dr. Scheman had assured us, "it's a fairly common surgery that I have performed many times, although usually on older patients. That's an advantage. She will recover faster and suffer fewer lasting effects than the average patient. All I need to do is release the pinched nerve and then fuse two vertebrae together so they won't move and cause her further trouble." Other doctors had agreed with the plan of action, and now here we were in the Highland Park Hospital. Don't worry, he said, and in fact, we *were* soothed by those words. In 1965, the doctor still carried an aura of infallibility that would survive for another decade or so.

"I'll see you in a little while!" Susan was relaxed and cheerful, waving goodbye as we held on to one another. Worry or not, this was our little girl, our first-born.

As the hours dragged on, Art dozed and I knitted. A volunteer brought us steaming mugs of coffee. "I'll let you know as soon as I hear anything," she assured us. The minute hand of the clock seemed to have stalled. My hands began to tremble. Suddenly, the door to the waiting room swung open and a masked stranger, clad in white, strode into the room. When he lowered the mask, I breathed a sigh of relief. It was Dr. Scheman after all.

"It went well, Mom and Dad. Everything is going to be just fine. Dr. Rosenblum is closing and then Susan will be wheeled into recovery. When she's alert, she will be back in her room and you can see her then. I'll have someone take you there now." He shook our hands, turned on his heel, and disappeared again.

When we first saw her, Susan was groggy but able to talk. "No, I don't feel any pain at all. Just a little fuzzy." Soon, she dropped off to sleep.

"Why don't you two go on home and get a little dinner?" urged the nurse. "She will sleep most of the time until tomorrow, though if you like you can stop by around eight to say goodnight." We followed her advice.

At home, Susan's sister and grandmother were eagerly waiting for more information. Although we had phoned to say the surgery was over, they wanted all the details. I was shaking and cold, so Art did most of the talking. Really, there was very little to say. She was on the road to recovery.

We did return that night and were not reassured. Shouldn't Susan have better color by now? What was her blood pressure? Why was she not awake?

"Dr. Scheman should be stopping by before long," assured the nurse. "We've been in contact." Was that usual, I wondered? It was almost nine o'clock. We sat down to wait.

When the doctor came in, he was accompanied by another staff person trundling an IV stand. That seemed odd, since a drip was already going into Susan's arm. The man went to work, setting up a drip for her other arm, then he hung a bag of whole blood on the stand.

"What's the story, doc?" asked Art.

"Simply routine," came the reply. "She lost some blood, you know, and this will replace it. We will keep a close eye all night, so you two can go home now. If there's any change, we will let you know. Go on, now. You need your strength, too. We already have patients a-plenty!" We did as we were told, but carried dread home with us through the dark, hot July night.

At first light, we were at her bedside. She was still asleep, if asleep it was. I could see that her color was a little better. The blood was still dripping from the stand, drop by slow drop. Art's instinct was sharper than mine. He spoke to the nurse. "How many units of blood has she had so far?"

His question was perceptive enough that the nurse did not think to stall the answer. "This one is four."

I was about to insist that the doctor be summoned at once, when he walked into the room.

"She is bleeding internally," he explained. "We are pumping blood until we can get more information."

Before breakfast, the doctors had decided to go back in, find the offending 'bleeder' and tie it off. More time passed. More blood dripped.

By nightfall, the situation had not improved; they had failed to locate the errant blood vessel which had retracted somewhere and was still spraying her insides like a fire hose. Still another attempt failed. The crowd of physicians was growing thicker, their faces growing longer. They made no attempt to conceal their concern, and one of them said, "She's sinking fast. I say we go back in and make a last-ditch search from the abdominal side. We gotta move."

"No choice," agreed another. Dr. Scheman looked to us for approval. I was frozen to the spot, but Art said, "Go get it."

"It's grave," the doctor countered. "She may not make it."

"Go!" And they went.

It was a long night. As my mind rejected the situation, my body rejected everything that was inside it. I emerged from the bathroom pale and shaking. Art held me tight while I cried in despair. Still the soldier, he clenched his teeth and endured.

By morning, Susan was transferred to a room in the intensive care unit. She lay there pale and unmoving, but at least breathing. More blood dripped into her veins. There were thirteen units in all, donated by unknown benefactors. I breathed a silent prayer of thanks and I counted each precious drop. Dr. Scheman soon came in. He looked older, tired as a soldier dragged from combat.

"We found it," he said. "It had pulled all the way back into her belly. It's safely tied off now. If she can make it through the next couple of hours, we'll be O.K."

At lunchtime — though neither of us could eat — Susan woke. Although she was weak, she could talk to us a little before she drifted off again. Her few mumbled words gave me immeasurable comfort. I stayed with her the rest of the day, even as Art left briefly to check in at his office. By nightfall, as Susan seemed to gain ground, we were urged to go home to rest. We did that, somewhat reassured.

Anyone familiar with the laws of probability knows what happened next. Susan had undergone four surgical procedures, and her number was up. The next battle would be against streptococcus infection. In her fragile condition, another battle posed terrible peril, but there it was, soon in full flower.

I learned that her high-school friends were phoning the hospital to find out how she was doing and were learning that her condition was listed as 'very grave'. Like all adolescents, they believed they were immortal, and this phrase scared them. We arranged for the hospital to change that message to the familiar 'as well as can be expected'. What were they thinking!

The battle for Susan's life continued for weeks. She drifted in and out of consciousness, delirious, fearful. Her recurrent terror was that the wet tea leaves in the hall were swelling and rising and would soon flow over the transom and smother us all. Her room was a barren white box, stripped of all extraneous embellishments, its only redeeming feature the large window that let in the sunshine. Inside walls were of glass to allow the nurses to observe her at every moment. No flowers or cards were allowed in intensive care; it was all business.

I hoped that her mother's presence would help, even when she did not seem to recognize me. I stayed there without cease, except when a nurse ordered me out of the room for a while, and when Art came to lead me home. We needed to bring more weapons to bear in this battle, but what could they be? Susan had grown passive, lethargic. The light of her spirit had dimmed.

Every morning, before he saw any other patient, Dr. Scheman came in bearing a flower from his garden at home. His devotion reflected his deep sorrow over the medical stumble and its disastrous consequences. No one ever admitted error, but his genuine contrition spoke volumes.

"I think we need to bend some rules around here," he declared. "Let everyone know she is ready to receive greetings." When that word got out, the cards and little gifts poured in.

"Tape the cards to the wall," he told the nurses. "Yes, yes, I know the rules, but tape the cards." Before very long, the wall filled up, with hardly an empty space for more — stuffed toys came, too.

Meanwhile, the medicines and Susan's inner strength began to turn the fight our way. Although the surgical wound in her back remained unsutured, it was slowly healing from the bottom up. Now the pain medication could be reduced and the terrors began to recede. She was getting well at last. One day, she asked, "Mom, what's the date? How much more time until school begins?"

The joy in my heart mingled with caution. "Don't worry about that, dear, just continue to gain strength. The future will take care of itself."

The doctor disagreed. "Her desire to get back to school is a great instrument of healing. Let's not discourage her. If there is a way to get her back there, we should do it. A wheelchair could work."

A little more than a month had gone by, and classes were about to start for fall semester. The school was on a modern campus and students moved from building to building, a poor prospect for a weak girl in a wheelchair.

Nevertheless, Sue was determined and her friends willing to help.

She did return and with help moved from class to class. In only a few weeks, she had tired of the arrangement as too slow. She was allowed to shift to crutches, but was on her own two feet largely unassisted by the time Thanksgiving rolled around.

Thanksgiving? You bet! And maybe the children were not so wrong about immortality.

BLIZZARD

It was snowing when I got up on Thursday, January 26th, 1967. I looked out the window and realized it was snowing hard. Art grumbled, "Oh great! Was this predicted? How bad does it look?" He was in bed as I peered out the window at the street light. The sky was still dark, but I could see big flakes swirling around the pool of light shining down on a white blanket below.

"Honey, I don't think I heard about anything like this! It doesn't look good. If we're driving to Ann Arbor, we'd better get cracking." Luckily, we were already packed. Art swung his feet over the side of the bed while I padded down the hall to wake the girls.

Susan had decided to apply to the University of Michigan for early decision, and she was expected to appear for an interview on Friday morning. Art agreed to make a family excursion of it, taking a couple of days off and driving over to his old alma mater. It would give Anne a chance to get a sense of the campus too, preparing for her college quest a year later. Grama would keep the home fires burning with our dog, Gay.

"Come on, girls, time to roll out. The weather doesn't look so good, and we ought to get on the road as fast as we can." They tumbled out quickly and before long all four of us were gathered in the living room, watching the weather report on television.

". . . front moved in from the northwest and this storm is gathering strength. Traffic in Minneapolis at a standstill . . .all secondary roads in southern Wisconsin closed. Stay tuned for your local forecast." Snow was coming down in thick clumps as if the very clouds were falling. Art looked grim.

"Please, Daddy, let's go! You know it's never as bad as they say!"

"I don't think this is a day for driving, kids. Let's call O'Hare and see whether it's a day for flying." A few minutes on the phone gave us the bad news: the airport was closed. "O.K.

then, I bet the trains are still running. They never stop." He punched a few numbers into the phone, listened, then hung up. All anxious faces were turned to him. His face was set in that stubborn way that I knew well; this was a challenge.

"Repack light, kids, just what you can carry yourselves. We're going to catch the noon train for Detroit. Chop chop!" Quickly, we dumped our bags, found smaller ones, repacked, and reported back to the living room. This was exciting—even Gay caught the spirit, running around and barking at everyone.

Our trip downtown was surprisingly easy. Buses and commuter trains were running on schedule. We reached the La Salle Street Station just in time to board the noon train for Detroit, with one stop in Ann Arbor. We should be there in time for dinner. Art pulled open the door to the coach to let us enter.

"What in the world. . .?" Half the population of Chicago was already in that car; we could barely squeeze our bodies into the aisle. Stow our suitcases? No, the solution seemed to be to sit on them. Noon came and went, but still we sat there. A few passengers struggled to get off, a few more came on board. At last, about two o'clock, the doors closed and the train began to move very slowly. A cheer went up from the crowd. We gained speed until we heard the comforting clackety-clack, common to train wheels everywhere. Chicago's South Side slid past like a white ghost from a half-remembered dream. A low hum of conversation and the occasional slap-slap of cards on a suitcase card table blended with the rhythmic wheels. A young man, finding no place to sit, climbed up and stretched out on the overhead luggage rack and went to sleep.

Once, the door opened, a conductor stuck his head in and called out, "Tickets please!" When he could not even get his body inside the coach, he muttered, "Oh never mind," and he disappeared, not to be seen again. Daylight faded, but we could still see snow swirling around street lamps. The roads were deserted, not a headlight to be seen. Several times, we lurched to a stop and waited while a crew outside used blowtorches to defrost switches and let us through. We had crossed the state line into Indiana, a long way from Ann Arbor.

"Art," I whispered, "I'm worried about Susan. Maybe we were foolhardy. How's she going to withstand this hardship?" She was only a few months beyond her back surgery and the brush with death. We watched the girls, who had inched their way into the center of the aisle. Sue seemed subdued, but her color was good. She was perched on both the girls' suitcases. Anne alternated between leaning on the arm of a seat and standing up. She was talking animatedly to whoever was sitting there. I was too far away to hear, but it was obvious that Anne was telling a story, selling something. After a little while, I was astonished to see a middle-aged man stand up and change places with Sue. She smiled wanly and sat down. Anne looked back at us and winked broadly.

Later, she explained to us that she had sought out a likely looking couple and began to tell the story of her sister's ordeal in the hospital. They listened sympathetically, and the man got up to offer Sue his seat. Anne had accomplished her mission.

Our progress was slow, until we bumped to a full stop somewhere in Gary, Indiana. A semi, loaded with steel, had turned into what the driver thought was a road into the steel mill. It turned out to be the railroad right-of-way. He continued for a few yards, jumped the tracks, turned over, and spilled his load. We waited there until a crane could be trucked up from the mill and eased into place. It off-loaded the steel beams on the side of the tracks and somehow towed the truck out of the way. A weak cheer went up from the assemblage as we again lurched into forward motion.

Somehow, passengers managed to doze off. The few who had brought something with them to nibble on the journey divided it among the others. I imagined loaves and fishes; certainly the impulse to hospitality was the same. Art and I rested against one another and closed our eyes. I had folded my winter coat under me for a cushion — the coach was very warm and steamy and odorous. The night grew deeper and we slept.

"Ann Arbor! Ann Arbor is next! Five minutes to Ann Arbor!" I woke with a start and looked at my watch. It was nearly five o'clock. The train slowed and finally came to a stop. We struggled to the door, handed down our suitcases, and stumbled into the snow. To our surprise, we were the only ones getting off. The train picked up speed and was gone.

"All right, let's see if there's a taxi anywhere around." Art strode forward and looked in all directions. Darkness covered everything, the snow silently filtered down and covered our shoulders. Only a few street lights showed us the way up the hill toward the campus. "Let's climb!" Art led, and we pushed our way wearily up to the top of the hill, through knee-deep snow. By a small miracle, a taxi did appear, cruising for train passengers, but afraid to risk the steep hill.

"To the University League," instructed Art as we all piled into the cab. When we finally fell into our rooms, Art told us, "Only three hours until wakeup call. Sleep fast." I don't remember undressing; I think I just collapsed and was unconscious before I hit the pillow.

Not one of us remembers how we managed to get up, dress, eat breakfast, and appear at the student admissions office at nine o'clock, but we did. The three of us sat and waited while Susan went in for her interview. After an hour, she emerged smiling.

"Hey, coming was a great idea! The committee was so impressed that we actually made it through the storm that I was accepted on the spot! I'll be getting a letter of admission to the School of Nursing next week." Elation carried us through the day, but we nearly fell asleep at the dinner table that night.

On Sunday morning, we boarded the train for Chicago. The tracks had been cleared and we returned to the city on time. Getting home was another story. Chicago was slowly digging out from what would be termed the greatest blizzard of the 20th century. Our commuter train moved north very slowly and stopped at every station, although few people were traveling. At our station, we found a taxi that would take us to the main street, about two blocks away from our house. No car could get into the side streets. We held our suitcases over our heads as we slogged through the waist-deep snow. The first-floor windows of the house were buried half-way up in snow and the driveway had disappeared under the drifts. At last we tumbled through the front door.

"Hi Gay! Hi Grama! We're home! Home at last!"

MOUETTE

"Let's go down to the boat show Saturday."

"Art, are you serious? What sparked this?" For as long as I could remember, sailing was a part of my life, as it had been for my mother. My family sailed and raced in the summers, and even built a fleet of frostbite dinghies in our basement to be sailed most of the winter in New York. All my talking about sailing, my urging to 'just try it' had fallen on deaf ears in our house. Now the boat show?

"Well, last summer's little experience at the AMA kind of intrigued me, and I thought we might go see what all those boats look like." At the American Management Association's 'camp' in Saranac Lake, New York, Art had been bitten by the bug. It was ostensibly a business trip for executives at the association's luxurious mansion on the lake shore, but during play time, someone invited Art to go along on a sailboat race. That's where it all started.

I said, "Sure! I wouldn't pass up a chance to kick a few tires."

Boat shows are generally predominantly either power or sail. Oh, a few of the odd kind, just to satisfy the maverick. This was a sailboat show. There were the real sailors — you could tell them by their Topsider shoes (with no socks), their tanned bodies, and usually tousled blond hair. They moved with lithe grace and they all knew each other. Then there were the young wannabes, climbing aboard big racing sloops. They had no money, but they had dreams. Salesmen paid no attention to them. The scarcity of gray-haired, overweight, cigar-smoking men was explained by posters advertising the power boat show next week. (My bias showing?)

We were prime marks for the sales force — late thirties, looking fairly prosperous, and taking notes on the smaller craft.

"Here you are, sir, here's just the thing! She's small enough you and the missus can handle her easy. A sailor are you? Not yet? Well, this little beauty will start you off right. Made in Nova Scotia, where they know about boat building but they haven't learned about high pricing yet. Believe you me, you couldn't go wrong with a Mouette."

"What's a Mouette?" I whispered to Art, suspecting the salesman would have no idea.

"A gull."

"Oh. Sounds more glamorous in French." Art shook his head, always baffled by the tendency of Americans to find French words glamorous.

She was a pretty little sailboat, about sixteen feet long with centerboard and a small cuddy up forward, just large enough to keep life jackets dry but available. Art and the salesman danced around a little, negotiating the price and amenities. Within half an hour, we owned a Mouette, to be delivered next week.

On the way home, I exclaimed, "Art, I can't believe we did it! We bought a boat! After all this time. Finally." He was grinning.

"I've been giving it some thought lately. Joined the Power Squadron and signed up for courses in boathandling." Just like him, I thought, to get education right up front.

On the shore of Lake Michigan, in Highland Park sat a small beach club. No building was included, just a stretch of beach where small boats lay on the sand lined up in two neat rows. Between the rows, about a hundred feet of metal-grid ramp led from the beach into the water. Our Mouette took its place in line.

"Hey, who wants to go for a sail?" Three female voices answered. "Me!" "Me!" "I do!" Grama thought it sounded a little strenuous, so she passed. We drove the family station wagon to the beach, loaded down with new sails and an assortment of different sizes of rope.

Art, fresh from Boating 101 at the Power Squadron took us in hand and instructed us in mounting the rigging, and tying sheets and halyards on the two sails.

"Now what?" asked Sue. Our little boat was sitting on the beach, all dressed up and no place to go.

"Got muscles?" asked the skipper. "We're going to back the trailer down the ramp until the boat floats. Mom and Anne, you hang on to the boat when it's in the water while Sue and I drag the trailer back up. Got that?" All nodded, and the exercise began. Pushing the trailer was harder than it looked, and all four of us grunted and heaved. Slowly, the wheels began to move and the craft picked up momentum—a little momentum. At last, the boat was afloat. My feet were freezing in the lake water.

"Hurry up before I turn into an icicle," I complained. The Mouette had begun to buck in the water; Anne and I struggled to control her. Art and Sue put their backs into their job, and at last the trailer was secured. They ran to join us.

"Now what? The water is trying to push the boat back on the beach. How do we do this?" My feet were numb.

"We push it out into the water at the same time we jump on board, take in the sheets, turn the tiller away from the wind, and sail away. Simple!" Not so simple until you got the hang of it, but at last, scrambling to climb and fall into the cockpit, we managed to do just what the skipper had described.

"We did it! We're sailing!" Cold feet and bruised knuckles were forgotten in the elation of the moment. There are no words to capture the sublime sense of joy and freedom that comes with skimming along under sail. It was a perfect afternoon.

No one really wanted to head for shore, but the hour was growing late and we needed to practice the technique of beach landing. With commendable coordination, we managed to approach the beach head-on, pull up the centerboard, and scrape bottom. All of us scrambled into the water, holding on to the hull.

"You kids come with me. Mom, you hang on until we get back with the trailer." They ran up the beach, pulled the trailer into position, and attached the winch cable to the tongue. Then they rolled the trailer down to the water. This was the tricky part. The trailer had to be far enough into the water to receive the floating boat, and we had to maneuver the boat onto the trailer. Not just tricky—darned hard. I thought the four of us did not have enough strength to accomplish it, but there was no choice. When the boat was tied to the trailer, Art and Sue ran up to crank the winch while Anne and I stayed behind to be sure the boat and trailer stayed together and on the ramp.

When the boat was put to bed, all of us fell on the beach, certain we could never move again. When we caught our breath, someone said, "That was fun!" We laughed until our sides ached.

In the next months, we improved our skills, though the launching and beaching never became routine or easy. Sometimes, high waves prevented our launch into the surf, but the sheltered cove was usually pretty friendly. The water never warmed up; Lake Michigan is cold in summer and colder in winter.

Every now and then, we would be out on the lake when the wind died. Although we were equipped with paddles, the Mouette made a very poor rowboat. Art solved the problem neatly and gained the girls a formidable reputation at school.

"O.K., gals, who wants to swim?" I certainly did not, but Anne and Sue were always game. They braved the chilly water as Art tied a mooring line around each waist and commanded them to tow the boat home. They dived in, we secured the other end of their tethers, and slipped home through the water in style. At school, the girls described how Captain Bligh made them walk the plank and swim for shore, towing that big boat! Their friends were impressed, but in reality, towing was pretty easy; the boat offered little resistance in the water.

Our family introduction into the world of sailing proceeded happily for two summers, and then we sold the boat. The family was heading for a new adventure.

HEADING SOUTH

"C'mon now, tell me the truth! Was it the blizzard that pushed you over the edge? Was it?"

"Of course not!" He bristled. Art was sitting on the edge of the bed, taking off his socks. "Do you really believe that?" I pushed his shoulders hard and he landed on his back, looking up at me. I was crouched over him, scowling.

"What was it, then!" I abandoned the scowl. Sinking down to lean on his chest, I said, "Darling, why Houston?"

"'Cause I always wanted to be a cowboy, that's why." I had seen Art on a horse once, and the memory sent me into peals of laughter. Whatever type he was, it was not cowboy. He was laughing now, too.

In contrast to our adventures at home, Art was beginning to feel stale at work. IMC was basically a stodgy business; it is hard to find glamour in fertilizer and bulk chemicals. The founder's son, now CEO, was making a zealous effort to inject excitement into the company, but he was doing it in ways Art found imprudent. The showy building was becoming a backdrop for expensive Japanese artwork, aspiration for more vigorous growth in the stock price was prompting less-than-conservative practices. The company motto was 'Grow' — perfectly reasonable for a fertilizer company — but Art had taken to muttering, "Cancer is growth, too." One officer of the company battled Art repeatedly over Art's refusal to engage in unethical business practices. The office atmosphere had taken on the attributes of trench warfare. More than all this, Art's vision of the future included a serious slump in agricultural commodities that he predicted would extend well into the future. His enthusiasm for challenge began to search elsewhere for satisfaction.

After fifteen years with IMC, Art had acquired a national reputation in his field. He was a regular lecturer for the American Management Association throughout North

America, the Chicago Tribune consulted him for business forecasts, and he often appeared as a guest for radio and television business types. Staying where he was offered security of position and the possibility that he would be elevated to the level of vice-president; nevertheless, he polished up his résumé, hooked it to the line at the end of his pole and confidently dipped it into head-hunting waters. Very quickly he had a nibble.

"I didn't want to tell you before in case nothing came of it, but now it has. Headhunter called me and asked a few questions, then wanted to know if I was available. I said 'hell yes, for the right thing' and then he asked me how I would feel about relocating to Texas. That was yesterday. Today, he called me back and said they were interested, so we set up an interview for next week."

"How much do you know? Is it hush-hush?"

"Not really. They're trying to play it close to the chest, but I figured it out. It's a specialty food company, privately held, major in its field, and it's in Houston. So it's Uncle Ben's."

"Rice? You know about rice, too?"

"Sure I know about rice. Comes in bags and boxes, white and brown. What more do I need to know?" I giggled as he rolled me over on the bed. "Sweetie, it looks like a deal to me. There are warning flags up all over the place, but I can handle it."

When I thought about it, I realized there had been signs I had missed. The greatest hint of his restlessness was that he was doing everything he could to promote his number two man, Tony Longhini. Replacing himself, I had thought, but for what? Now I was finding out.

Following a whirlwind of phone calls and interviews, Art had an offer: vice-president of the commercial division at a salary nearly double his current one. Before making a final decision, Art called two men who had once worked for Uncle Ben's; they warned him that the company was strange, marched to its own tune, had peculiar ways. He mulled it over for about ten minutes, then accepted the offer. We were going to Texas.

Somewhere along the line, I think he asked me if it was all right with me. My view was that it was his career, he had to show up at the office every day, not me. I knew I would follow him anywhere. But south of the Mason-Dixon line? I had not counted on that. And now we needed to tell the girls. And Mother.

"But Mom! I'm going to be a senior next year. I don't want to move now! Couldn't I stay here, maybe with the Bermans?" Anne was no more thrilled. Both the girls had friends, boy-friends, too. I laid down the law.

"Don't you dare try loading guilt onto your father. You will put a smile on and you will go along, got it?" In the end, I made a deal with them. I would stay behind until the current school year was over, no more. After that, we were moving to Houston. I have to give them credit; they swallowed their own misgivings and prepared to separate from their friends. My mother, as was her way, smiled and asked when we were going. I never knew her true feelings.

Within two weeks, Fran and Tony Longhini put together a gala farewell party that included all the purchasing people from IMC. Men like Con Mers—and women too—people Art had mentored came for a touching tribute to his friendship and leadership and, among other things, presented him with a real Stetson ten-gallon hat. Now Art did like to wear hats, but given his short stature—about five feet eight inches—the cowboy image was an improbable fit. Who knew that it would forever be his favorite hat?

In late February I think it was, in 1967, Art loaded up the family Ford station wagon with everything he thought he needed to take with him, we kissed him goodbye and watched him disappear around the corner. My heart remembered the goodbye on the station platform in Yellow Springs, and a tear rolled down my cheek.

The following evening, the phone rang.

"Hi, Darling, where are you? Everything going O.K.? . . . What? Where's Friendship? Arkansas? Why are you there?"

The dear old Ford wagon was threatening to cough its last. The doctors, in the form of two mechanics, were examining the patient and shaking their heads. A vital part had to be obtained; it was absent in this town of fewer than 200 souls. True to the promising name of the town, those two kind men drove to the next large city, returned with the part, and stayed up the better part of Saturday night to make the repair. They had introduced Art to the local motel keeper and left him to get a good night's sleep before continuing the long drive to Houston.

"I'm going to turn in now, Sweetie. Keep me in your thoughts tomorrow, because they tell me the fix will be partial, that the old tin lizzie will only tolerate slow speeds the rest of the way." The road to Houston was two-lane, and I could only imagine what tomorrow would bring. Later, Art told me that by evening, Sunday traffic was backed up behind him for twenty miles. He was exhausted when he finally rattled into the parking lot of a Houston Ford dealer. There, he parked lizzie against the wall and called a cab to take him to a nearby hotel.

In the morning, his adventure began again. He arrived at the dealership when they opened their doors expecting to either buy or rent a car on the spot.

"Not that easy," he told me. "Trouble was, I only had cash. I had no business card, only my good looks. Of course, I didn't have a check from a local bank. They wouldn't take my cash; it wasn't enough to buy the car outright and they weren't going to let me drive away with anything less."

"What did you do?" I asked.

"It was pretty embarrassing, but I had to call the company. They sent somebody down to vouch for me. While I was waiting, I found the car I wanted and now we own a Ford Falcon. We got straightened out finally, but it certainly wasn't the best beginning in a new company. At least it can't get much worse, so it's going to have to get better, isn't it!"

I ached for him. He was humiliated, so far down that his usual spark of upbeat cheerfulness had dimmed. What could I say?

"I love you."

"Me too." He hung up. Of course, it did get better. Art was soon engrossed in learning about rice and Texas and Uncle Ben's.

FOR SALE BY OWNER

Meanwhile, back at home, I had my hands full; it was all up to me now. Selling the house was my first imperative, because I had no idea how long it might take. The more I thought about it, the more I believed it would be a good idea to sell it myself. Why pay a broker 6% of the selling price? At least, I could give it a shot, because I had three months. If it failed to sell soon, I could always back-track. Actually, I was kind of proud of my decision. Art, having no more experience in this arena that I did, agreed that I should do as I thought best. This turned out to be a very expensive mistake.

I dusted the house, tidied up every room. Because snow still covered the ground, I set up a slide exhibit of pictures of the beautiful garden in bloom. Then I placed a small advertisement in the local paper.

The morning the ad appeared, our doorbell rang at seven o'clock. Still in robe and slippers, I opened the door to find a woman standing there.

"I've come about your ad," she said. Well, this was quick response, I thought, as I ushered her in.

"I am sorry not to be better prepared to receive you. Not all the beds are made yet, but do come anyway and look through the house." She was, I judged, a little older than I, well-dressed and exuding an imperial manner. When she had taken what I thought was only a cursory look around, we sat down together in the living room.

"What are you asking for the house?"

"Forty-two thousand dollars." (I am uncertain now exactly what the price was; whatever it was, it represented all the money we had put into the house plus a very modest profit margin — maybe two thousand.)

"Well, I think the house will do very nicely, the price is satisfactory, and I want to buy it. Before I do, I want my husband to see it, just to be sure, although I have no doubt about it." From her manner, I deduced that he had better not object. "Will you hold it for me until I can bring him early this evening after work?"

My second mistake: I said, "Yes, of course." I felt lucky to have had an interested buyer on the very first day and never imagined what happened next. After we shook hands on it, and she left, I hurried upstairs to dress, just in case. Today, I have no recollection where the girls or my mother were while this was going on. Very soon, the doorbell rang again. And again. The driveway was filling up with cars and the house was filling up with prospects. More than one couple wanted to make an offer. I told them that I had promised the right of first refusal to someone, but if the deal was not made by tonight they were welcome to bid. I took down names and phone numbers. Traffic was getting thick.

One family, a father, mother, and two children, kept going back to look again at details. They gathered in a corner to talk excitedly, then the father came to me.

"You say the house is already sold?"

"Well, not for sure," I said, "but I have promised to hold it for someone until her husband can see it this evening. If they don't want it, then yes, it's still for sale." He went back to confer with his team, and they again went over the house. Father approached me. His voice was businesslike this time.

"How much do you want for it, really?"

"Well, I told you, it's not a matter of price so much as it is an obligation. You can just wait until tonight and then call me."" He went away again, but the family gathered in the garden room. At length, the man came back to me. This time, a genuine pleading crept into his voice.

"Look, I have to buy this house. I've got an anxious wife and two crying kids out there. They have fallen for the house, no two ways about it. What am I supposed to do? Please! Name your price! We can come to a number both of us will be happy with. Please!"

My heart was beating way too fast—I was in over my head. I knew I had made a stupid mistake, but I *had* made it. I wanted to make this family happy, and I wanted to make more money. How much more, I wondered? Stop that! I told myself. Is your word worth anything?

"I am very sorry, sir," I said. "Call me later this evening, and we'll see if there's anything we can do." They went away in tears — even the father looked as if he would cry.

The imperious woman did return with her husband that evening and they bought the house for exactly what I had asked. When my lawyer was drawing up the papers, I told him my sad tale.

"Did any money change hands?" he asked me.

"Not then. Not until the husband came back that night."

"Then you didn't have a deal, Kit! You didn't have to go through with it. You could have made, probably, ten grand more!" His voice was gently scolding me.

"Yeah," I said sadly, "I had a deal." It occurred to me that if we had been staying, we would have needed to find a new lawyer. I had no doubt what Art would say when I told him, and I was right.

"Damn! Well, it's only money, honey. You did the right thing." I knew that, but we never again tried to play in a market we had no means to measure.

HOW WE GOT THE ELECTRA

A rt understood that he had a problem: his daughters were reluctant to move away from friends, especially those two boys they currently favored. He knew what to do. March in Illinois may bring spring break, but it never brings spring. Winter was still dragging on.

"Kids," he said on the phone, "why don't you bring your mother and grandmother down and have a real spring break in Texas?"

"Oh Daddy! What a great idea!" For the first time, they were excited, especially to hear that we would go all the way south to Brownsville, and even slip across the border for a visit in Mexico. It didn't hurt that there would be a national surfing contest in the waters off Padre Island.

With Gay safely settled in a kennel, we all flew to Houston.

"Daddy, this is a neat little apartment! But it's so small!"

"Well I don't give a lot of big parties, so it does fine for just me."

"But where will we sleep?" they asked. Art had reserved space in a nearby hotel for Mother and the girls; I would stay with him. We enjoyed dinner in a local restaurant and fell into bed to wait for morning and the start of our journey even farther south.

It was hard to stuff our luggage into the trunk of the Ford Falcon, but we managed somehow, and headed south on route 59 toward Victoria. As usual, Art drove, I sat in the front passenger seat, and Grama sat in the middle of the back seat. Mile after mile, we sped past nondescript countryside, occasionally seeing a few cows grazing. At the next rest stop, the three in the back seat changed places.

"My," said Mother, "that back seat is pretty hard!" Susan took a turn in the middle. Before long, Sue was asking that we stop and shift again. It was Anne's turn. Now we were driving south on route 77 into ever drier land. At the next stop, I said,

"Mom, you take my place in front and I'll sit with the girls." We set out once more. Oh, they were right. I don't know much about the anatomy of a car, but whatever that bone was down the middle, it was coming right up to meet my tailbone.

At the next stop, I declared firmly, "We are going to rotate seats every hour. Art, you get in back and I'll drive for awhile." The girls offered him the middle seat, and he took it in good humor, even though it was unusual for the father in the family to be assigned an inferior seat. From there, he conducted a tour of the country we were driving through.

"Dad, why is there a rail stop out here in the middle of nowhere?"

"Those ramps are for loading cattle into cattle cars. We are now passing though what I believe is the biggest ranch in the world, the King Ranch."

"How big?"

"Bigger than Rhode Island. I think it's about 850,000 acres, all in one family. You can imagine that the King family wields a lot of power in these parts."

"How big is that anyway?"

"Well, they say driving from one side of the property to the other is farther than driving from New York to Philadelphia, or Pittsburgh to Cleveland. Listen, when Texans tell you stories about big, believe it. Everything here is big."

After an hour or so, he said, "O.K., time to shift again. Let's stop for a cool drink and then everybody move." Thus we made our way south, each taking a painful turn in the middle of the back seat.

At last, we pulled into the motel at Port Isabel on Padre Island, just outside Brownsville. In no time at all, the girls were into bathing suits and out on the beach. As far as we could see, north and south, the blue waters of the Gulf of Mexico curled up over white sand. Few people were on the beach, though some surf boards were bobbing about offshore. Light breeze ruffled the water; the waves were disappointingly small. Toward evening, enough tanned young athletes were eyeing our daughters — their gaze frankly returned — to satisfy expectations. The next day, we headed for the border.

"That's it?! That's all?"

"Yep, that's the Rio Grande all right. More muddy than grand, isn't it!" We crossed the bridge, stopped for a cursory check by the Mexican police, and looked for a parking place in the town of Matamoros. The novelty of the shops, bright colors, and cheap prices compensated for the undeniably tawdry tourist junk for sale. We bought a few souvenirs to remind us of our first visit south of the border, and headed north for Houston.

A few days after we had returned to Glenview, Daddy called. "I just wanted you to know I bought another car. Thought you'd be pleased! I tried out all the back seats, and I think you'll find nothing to complain about. I'll take the Ford to work and the rest of you can have the Buick Electra."

I wondered, what's an Electra? It turned out to be a light blue, fully loaded, block-long, supremely comfortable gas guzzler. It got as much as seven miles to the gallon, but with gas selling at less than a quarter a gallon, who was counting?

SECOND HOUSE

"Honey, come on down next week. We can go house hunting."

"Are you trying to subsidize the airline?… No, of course I'm not reluctant! Just concerned about mounting costs, that's all."

"O.K. I understand. I'll pick out a house and send you a picture. You like surprises, right?" The next week, Art met me at the airport and took me to meet the realtor.

We had researched the school situation in Houston with dismal results. As another displaced Yankee put it, the best schools were comparable to average mid-western counterparts—thirty years ago. Experience proved that assessment optimistic. Both girls were adamant about private school—they refused to go. In Chicago suburbs, private schools were thought to be only for the self-important rich or for incorrigibles. I knew that view was inaccurate, but try to convince two teen-age girls! Memorial High School appeared to be the 'least worst'; accordingly, our housing choice was confined to that district.

Art left me in the hands of a very experienced salesman for a preview of the neighborhoods. In one after another, I tried to hide my naïve astonishment. The houses were palatial, comparable to the best of the Chicago North Shore, certainly nothing like Heatherfield Lane! We noted the addresses of likely choices and waited until Art could join us. I was too timid to bring up prices.

"Art," I whispered as I met him at his office door, "I think he's got us in over our heads. Keep a leash on him, will you?" Art smiled. He knew better.

After a few false starts, we entered the one I knew I wanted. In the front yard stood a magnificent old live oak tree on one side, and an equally impressive magnolia on the other. The brick, one-story house had a gracious, settled look. The double front door was sheltered by a circular portico with large white columns. Inside, the terrazzo-floored hallway boasted a remarkable chandelier. To the left was an unexpectedly modest living room, and beyond, separated by a wide arch, was the dining room decorated with a second crystal chandelier, this one not to be believed. The ceilings were nine feet high. The back of the house was for real living: a spacious family room, with a stone fireplace, that flowed into a generous breakfast room and bar. These rooms looked out on the patio and pool beyond. The kitchen was as large as our living room at home, with ample pantry and endless cupboards. The laundry room included a half-bath, just right for swimmers coming in from the forty-foot pool in the back yard. On the other side of the house were three bedrooms, two baths, an office, plus a master suite comprising bedroom, dressing room, bath, and a closet large enough for a six-piece band. Large windows in the master bedroom let in sparkling reflections from the pool. The patio overlooking the pool was partly sheltered under a roof and partly open to the sun. Loquat and orange trees flourished around the pool. At night, soft blue lights in the pool lent the scene an ethereal, glamorous air. A very wide and deep two-and-a-half-car garage completed the offering.

I was torn between falling in love with the house and backing away from what was clearly a wild extravagance well beyond our means.

"Excuse me? The asking price is…? Did I hear that right?" He was trying to tell me that this dream house was, incredibly, about fifteen percent more than the price I had taken for our little house on Heatherfield Lane. Our offer for 12222 Rip Van Winkle Drive was accepted and I flew home in a daze.

I had taken careful measurements of each room, and now we four women bent over my sketch of the house plan. Most of our furniture would move, of course, though some of the least could be discarded. I determined to have every piece refinished so that we could move in with style.

"Mom, our drop leaf table can go in the breakfast room. Don't you think the Dutch sink should go there, too?" She nodded in agreement. "O.K., then what goes in the dining room?"

"And what in the world can you put in that big front hall?"

"My dears, Dad tells me he will introduce us to a dealer in the Chicago Wholesale Furniture Mart. We can do better here than in Houston. Let's go shopping!"

What a good time we had, choosing new dining room furniture, finding a wonderful carved wooden Mexican chest for the front hall, a whole new bedroom for Mother and for Art and me, too. At last, our house would be spacious.

The down side to all this soon struck. One evening, during one of my visits to Art's Houston apartment, I cooked dinner for us and took a pie out of the oven. It was too hot to eat, so I set it on a cake cooler and Art and I went to the movies. When we returned, I turned on the kitchen light and screamed.

"Ugh! Get it out of here!" The pie was crawling with the biggest roaches I had seen since leaving Manhattan. Bigger. Dozens of them.

"Here, I'll just brush 'em off," said my dear husband. "No use wasting a whole pie."

"You will not! Put it in the trash and take it outdoors." I felt a little sick.

"Welcome to Texas, m'dear!"

After the house on Rip Van Winkle was vacated, Art hired an exterminator to seal and fog the house. He suspected the owners had stopped having an exterminator as soon as the contract was signed. The weekend following treatment, Art went to the house with grocery bags, broom and dustpan. In the dressing room were banks of built-in drawers which he had left partly open. Now he dumped the dead roaches into bags, swept the floors, cleaned the kitchen.

"Filled two big bags right to the top," he told me.

"Please! There are things I really don't have to know." The exterminator became a regular visitor after that. Everyone had one on a monthly contract, just to keep the bugs at bay. Getting rid of them was impossible, it was a matter of backing them off. I was about to find out that meticulous, perfect housekeeping is a survival skill in Texas.

On Heatherfield Lane, boxes were filling with books and china, old furniture was coming back buffed and polished. Spring had arrived at last and farewell parties were in full swing. Susan dressed for the junior prom and Anne packed for a trip to Massachusetts.

Anne's Mariner Scout troop was embarking on a spring shake-down cruise on the schooner *Shenandoah*, sailing out of Martha's Vineyard. For a much-reduced price, the girls would ship aboard to help get ready for the tourist season. They scrubbed and polished, swam in cold Atlantic waters, sailed in the fog, and had a marvelous time.

Susan, Mother, and I swept out the last of the debris from the Heatherfield Lane house and locked the door behind us. Amid tears of farewell to Barbara Berman, we sped off to the airport. Mother's car traveled by moving van; Gay flew in a special crate.

In a few days, I drove to the Houston airport to meet Anne. As she came down the stairway from the plane, I could see she was crying.

Poor baby, I thought, she has been homesick after all. Well, not quite; she was crying because she had left New England. Anne had developed a serious love for that part of the country, just as we had suspected she might. Even when she was a small girl, we joked that she would one day leave us for New England. Something about her evoked that culture, that way of living. We had been right; New England was in her bones.

For now, we were all at home in Texas.

12222 Rip Van Winkle, Houston, Texas

EDUCATION – TEXAS STYLE

What were we thinking? After the moving van had driven away, after the beds were made, after the dishes and crystal were in place, books arrayed on the shelves, an ominous quiet settled over the house. Ten weeks of summer stretched in front of us and the girls were without a single friend. This was not a good beginning.

During his enforced bachelorhood until we came, Art found the Emerson Unitarian church. The minister, Frank Schulman, and his wife Alice, made special efforts to welcome him into the congregation. By the time the rest of us arrived at church, Art could introduce us around; he was already part of the Unitarian family. Evidently, Frank guessed that the transition would be hard for two teenagers, but he took care of that.

"A couple of good-looking high school girls are moving into the neighborhood," he told the LRY[4], "and they have a big swimming pool in their back yard. You might want to check it out." When the youngsters started to arrive, they discovered the extra refrigerator filled with snacks and cool drinks, along with stacks of fresh towels in the laundry room.

"Art, that fridge was a stroke of genius! Now we don't have to wonder where our daughters are in a strange town; they're right here." Day after day, and into the evenings, splashing and laughter filled the air. Tanned bodies stretched out on towels at poolside, catching rays, as they said. One of the boys, Roy something, came just about every day. He was a waif, blond, shaggy-headed, barefoot, and altogether dangerous-looking. The indefinable aura about him would have made his fortune in Hollywood — he reminded me of James Dean.

---

[4] That's what Unitarian high school groups were called then: Liberal Religious Youth.

"Mom, of course he's attractive, but he's pretty heavily into drugs, you know!" No, I did not know, but in the next months I would learn about such things.

One afternoon, I worked at my desk in my bedroom overlooking the pool, glancing up from time to time to see what the kids were up to. One big hulk of a boy bounced up and down on the diving board. He was reaching for something. With every bounce, he came a little closer.

"Omigod, he's trying to catch the electric wire that's strung high across the pool!" I opened the window to shout at him, but it was too late. Repeated stress on the board from that great weight had finally overpowered it, and board and boy plunged into the pool with a great crack. I ran to see whether everyone was all right. They were, just startled and now laughing. I was shaken.

"What in the world did you think you were going to do with the electric wire if you caught it, young man? You would have carried it into the pool and electrocuted everybody!'

"Oh gee, Mrs. Fournier, I never thought of that! I'm sorry about the board."

"Never mind, at least nobody got fried. Try to use your head, kids, will you? Watch each other." It was going to be a long summer for me, I could see that.

In fact, I crowded my summer with acquiring curtains and redecorating parts of the house to enliven the dull background. My favorite tendency to spill bright flowers over the ceiling worked effectively in the girls' bathroom, and I papered panels in the master bedroom with navy blue paisley. Mother busied herself on a lavish Jacobean design for the piano bench, done in crewel work to set off the red damask at the other end of the room. By September, the girls were registering for school and my house was in order.

I looked at the proposed class schedule that Susan presented to me. Oh Lord, deliver me from another battle with this girl. Four music classes, one English, and precious little else.

"Susan, do you find this an appropriately challenging program?" She rolled her eyes.

"Mom, it's what fits the time schedule."

Oh well, I thought, let the school battle this one. They will never allow such foolishness and for once I won't have to play the villain. The school never turned a hair, accepted it on the spot. This was a different philosophy — if philosophy was the word. Art's reaction was pragmatic.

"Let the kid alone, Mother. She's had a tough couple of years, she came back handsomely, and she deserves a sabbatical." We let it ride. After all, she had an acceptance to the University of Michigan, so why should we worry? In the next months, we traveled with Susan to several other colleges, notably Vanderbilt, in Nashville, and Texas Woman's University, in Denton, just to make sure there was not another better place to study nursing. She confirmed her original decision.

Susan's report of her first day in class at Memorial High School provided little comfort for the academic year ahead.

"At the end of the class, my English teacher passed out a reading list of the books we would read during the year. So I went up to her when the class was dismissed and asked her what I should do, since I had read every one of the books in my previous high school years."

"What did she say?"

"She said, 'Good. Then you should be able to get an A in this class without cracking a book.'"

"No! She said that?"

"She did." At least the teacher's powers of prognostication proved accurate: Susan got an A and never cracked a book.

Anne's problems developed more slowly. She was floundering in Chemistry, and her reports of her teacher's puzzling lectures caught Art's attention. He told me privately,

"I'm going to take a day off next week and visit the class. I need to see for myself what the real problem is."

Art did that, and when he arrived back home, I asked, "Well? Did you identify the problem? Do you know how to solve it?"

"Yes. And no. I have no idea how to solve the problem, because the problem is that the young lady doesn't know enough chemistry to be teaching a high school course."

Anne's experience in Biology was no better. Her lurid tales of how the boys killed frogs for dissecting horrified us all. They took them by the back legs and smacked them on the edge of the lab counter. Most of the time, the frogs were badly wounded but seldom killed. Several of the boys seemed to take particular delight in assaulting the defenseless creatures over and over again.

"It isn't right!" declared Anne. "How should they be dispatched, Dad?"

"With a quick, deft snip of the spinal cord, right behind the head," he answered. "There's no excuse for encouraging brutality in a science class." We sent a note to school asking that Anne be excused from this exercise until a more appropriate way to kill the frogs could be instituted. She was excused.

I conversed with the school principal on the subject of separation of church and state, pointing out that the daily Bible readings and prayers read over the speaker system were in violation of the United States Constitution. He responded that he refused to interfere with a generations-old tradition for the sake of politicians in far-off Washington. I was learning that Texas ways were a thing apart, and that upstart Yankees should hold their tongues.

Although that first summer introduced our girls to many young people, they soon learned that liberal youth represented little of the local culture. Girls came to school dressed as if they were attending a tea party, displaying fine jewelry and carefully coifed hair. Their goals seemed to be graduation, a new car, and a husband, in that order. If college entered the picture at all, the choice would be in Texas. When Anne offered her collection of catalogues from colleges across the country, the counselor told her that Memorial graduates attended Texas schools, so the catalogues would be discarded.

Of course, Susan's classes produced a musical program. Art and I cleared our calendars, remembering how important such productions were at New Trier. I asked about getting tickets, fearful that all would be gone if we delayed. On the appointed evening, our family arrived early to find good seats. Only a few parents of performing students had bothered to note the occasion; the hall was mostly empty.

Football? That was another story. Friday nights found most of the population of Houston, whether connected to high schools or not, in attendance at the astonishingly enormous stadiums. The game seemed almost a state religion.

"Have you thought about going back to college?" Art noticed that my flurry of activity in the house had subsided.

"No, in fact, I wondered what I would do with the rest of life, and I suppose I should make my degree a goal, shouldn't I?" The next week, I enrolled at the University of Houston as a sophomore, right along with all the nineteen year olds. I was forty-one.

I was annoyed on learning that I would have to endure the second semester of freshman English. Even though good grades earned me the right to omit the course at Cornell, Houston had an absolute requirement. Any embarrassment from being lumped in with eighteen years olds evaporated when I began to read Homer's *Odyssey*. The story was certainly captivating, but more than that, a whole world of cultural reference opened up to me. Wow! So that's where Scylla and Charybdis are! They became real places instead of just hard-to-spell mysteries. The young man who slouched in the chair next to me in class kept muttering, "It's not relevant." "Oh shut up,"

I said gently, "read it, store it. It will mean more than you can imagine." He remained unimpressed.

In those days, the Viet Nam War breathed down the necks of my male classmates. Their mantra was 'Flunk, Get Drafted, and Die!' — strong motivation to keep grades up, but not necessarily to learn. My professor of Analytical Geometry took full advantage of his power position to intimidate the boys.

"I know you," he ranted, "you draft-dodgers. Well, I'll have the pleasure of flunking any of you who don't measure up. You can get sent to Viet Nam and see how you like it. I've been teaching for thirty years and I have never given an A to anybody. You won't get one either, but you could easily get an F."

I held my breath. In other parts of the country, students were on the march, demanding their rights. The classroom fell silent. Surely, I thought, simple decency and respect were their right here, but they did not seem to know it. They were thoroughly cowed.

An innovation among colleges was to give a seat on the governing body to a student. I was about to find out what the University of Houston would do about this.

"Mrs. Fournier," said my English professor, "it has been decided to give students a voice in governance here. You would be an excellent representative of the student body and I would like to propose your name for that chair. Would you accept?"

Looking at him in disbelief, I restrained my impulse to punch him. My anger and frustration bubbled out in words: "Student body? You think I represent the student body? The college is copping out here. These kids are being abused daily by fusty, incompetent, dreary has-beens. I don't wonder the establishment is afraid go give them a true voice. Will I front for them? No! Offer the chair to a typical student if you dare!" I turned on my heel and strode away, shaking. To give him his due, my professor give me an A anyway. My math professor stuck to his guns; I had a B.

After Susan and Anne had left home for college, I wrote them a letter about a friend I saw on campus. "Guess who I saw yesterday? It was Roy, you remember, that waif that I thought was so attractive and you warned me he was taking drugs. Well, apparently he has reformed. What a transformation! He was wearing shoes—polished loafers. And jacket and tie. His hair was cut and combed. I tell you he looked absolutely respectable. And you thought he was hopeless. Never give up, dears."

Both of them, hundreds of miles apart, answered me in the same vein. "Mom, that's not reform. What you saw was a user graduated into a dealer. He's adopting camouflage so he won't be picked up by the Narcs." Oh. I had a lot to learn. The Woodstock festival happened about this time.

A PECULIAR PLACE

Some say that only Texians really understand Texas. You can live there a long time and call yourself Texan, but to be a *Texian* you have to come from generations of Anglos born and bred to it. The term stems from the early nineteenth century, the time of Texas independence. Texas is independent still.

"Don't call us Southern," warned my new acquaintance, "say rather Western. Or if you must, Southwestern. Just not Southern."

In 1967, the Houston city limits encompassed several fields of feeder cattle and even a few rice paddies. No true downtown held government and commerce like Northern cities I knew—everything scattered across miles. Lack of zoning put gasoline stations next to mansions, and no one seemed to think the worse of it. Mexican faces outnumbered black, and while neither was welcome in more upscale stores, Mexicans seemed to be less welcome.

Driving from our house to the new music theater, Jesse H. Jones Hall, was a tempting twenty minutes, far different from Chicago theaters. We bought season tickets to the symphony and opera, and on opening night all of us piled into the Electra. Since this was 'an occasion', we were dressed to the nines. Mother even wore her mink stole. I certainly had no idea what a grand occasion it would turn out to be.

Art drove into the underground garage, and because it was a pleasant evening, we came out on the street level to walk across to the hall entrance.

"Oh my goodness, did you ever…" My jaw dropped. Pulled up to the curb all the way down the long block was a row of white Rolls Royces. Each one disgorged passengers at the entrance and then slowly moved on to make room for the next. They kept coming around the corner until I believe I had counted twenty before we crossed the street. Improbably, an occasional pickup truck crept along in the line, rifle securely fastened into the gun rack behind the driver. Formally dressed ladies alighted to join the throng. The hall's marble columns eight stories high framed great glass walls, glowing with light.

Art pointed out the fire hydrant on the corner. "Don't want to miss the sights," he said, smiling broadly. All of us tried not to gawk, but how could we not? The fire plug was chromium! "It's a Texas statement, Honey."

Inside, a spray of shooting stars reached toward the ceiling, many stories above our heads. We were surrounded by rich red velvet and golden mahogany, our feet sinking into the finest carpet. All around us were elegantly dressed patrons literally dripping in diamonds. It was a black tie affair, and suddenly I felt entirely out of place in my short skirted wool suit, even if the jacket was lined with mink fur. It was dowdy against the sparkling evening dresses everyone else wore. Oh well, I reminded myself, we came to hear the music.

Actually, I forget what the music was, but I know André Previn was conducting. As we took our seats, we realized that everyone was turning around to peer at the boxes in the first balcony. I could see that a young woman had entered the center box, but I did not recognize her. The girls did.

"That's Mia Farrow!"

The air was heavy with general disapproval. Fingers pointed, and I heard someone say, "Cheap woman! Who does she think she is!" Although Texas men might keep mistresses, they kept them in Conroe, a town decently distant from Houston; they did not display them in public. Previn, one of the talented musical geniuses of the century, had been captured by Houston as its principal conductor, but before long he and his lady had disappeared from the scene. On the whole, appearances trumped musical performance; Houston was not such a big town after all.

During intermission, we strolled among the glittering guests. One woman was starkly dressed in a very short black and white gown, almost as if she were a painting by Piet Mondrian; she was the wife of André Courrèges, the famous

Paris couturier. An elderly woman gathered a crowd of respectful admirers, paying court to royalty. She was Texas royalty: Ima Hogg. This name evoked no smirks in Texas. Her father had been a revered governor and she was among the richest patrons of cultural projects in the state.

Entirely congruent with the peculiar ways of Texas was Art's employer, truly one of a kind. Uncle Ben's marched to its own tune, being privately held by the Mars family, with no publicly held stock. Instead of executive offices, everyone at every level, worked at his desk in a large room. The desks were arranged in columns and rows; the one concession to rank was the president's desk, at the end of a row, somewhat buffered by potted palms. Art's desk was, I think, in the third row, second column from the right.

Although he was vice-president for the commercial division, he had no secretary. When he wanted to write a letter or memo, he picked up the phone and dictated to the clerical pool. Purchasing requires a level of confidentiality in contract negotiation that was impeded by such a system, but Art created ways to work with it.

He, like everyone else including the president, punched a time clock every morning. It was to his advantage, since each day that he reported on time he received a ten percent bonus on that day's salary. Latecomers got no bonus.

"What about when you're out of town on a business trip?" I asked.

"I have to phone in. On time, or I don't get the bonus."

"Oh." I was amazed that Art seemed to take it all in good humor, feeling that none of this was central to his main objective. Once he had learned the ropes, he was eager to spread his wings. The company expressed grand plans for new products and Art was bursting with ideas. He traveled to Minnesota to help solve the puzzle of growing wild rice, and successfully shepherded the agricultural development of the crop. As a result, prices plummeted. He traveled to eastern

Oregon and Washington, encouraging research on freeze-dried potatoes for marketing to fast food companies.

"The one nut I can't seem to crack is prepared packaged rice dishes," he told me. "The company is dead set against the idea. Apparently, plain converted rice is all they will consider; they don't see prepared foods as the wave of the future." He was sure that his persistence would finally pay off there, too.

Art did not fit the inner circle of the company, of whom there were only two or three. Politics was not his game and he was repelled by intrigue, although he was well aware that the real strings were pulled from McLean, Virginia, the Mars family headquarters. Art was one of seven vice-presidents, a surprising number for a relatively small company. All of them took this to mean there were plans for great expansion, although none of them knew for sure what the direction would be. For now, Art was content to continue lowering the costs of procurement while polishing employee skills and systems. His very handsome salary papered over any bumpy places.

OUR TEXAS LIFE

Now that all the family had succeeded in catching up to the 1960s, harmony prevailed among us for the most part. The girls had found special boyfriends. Susan joined the choir of a Presbyterian church to benefit from the leadership of the director; Anne assumed leadership of the Emerson Church LRY, serving as its president. Mother was appointed treasurer of Emerson Unitarian church. I found Taping for the Blind, and volunteered to record books for the Library of Congress.

None of these activities kept us from the sailing life, however. Before long, we owned a boat of the Ensign class, named the Pulver. (Those who remember the play *Mr. Roberts* will recognize the name.) We kept it at the Houston Yacht Club on Galveston Bay, a considerable step up from the poor little sailing club on the shores of Lake Michigan. Art became a racer, sometimes in the Pulver, sometimes in another boat with his new friend, Herb Bailey. Since I hoped never to see another starting line, I was glad to let him go, and hear of his adventures later in the club bar. In summer, it was too hot to sail during the day (unless you were a racer); we usually waited until the sun was close to the horizon. Not a breath of air stirred.

"You can't sail in this calm," complained the men, as Dorothy Bailey and I coaxed them into the boat and cast off the mooring lines, "Where's the wind?"

"Be quiet and paddle," we said. "We can get out into the channel and wait for wind." Sure enough, just as the sun sank out of sight, a gentle breeze struck up. The sails filled, and we slid silently along the glassy surface. The wind hovered for a time just above the water, propelling us along like magic without rippling the water. We turned our bow south toward Kemah as dusk settled about us and the breeze freshened, filling the sails and setting up a harmonic vibration in the rigging. We four were suspended in time as the stars winked on and cares of the week fell away.

In about an hour, we arrived at our destination, a waterside restaurant. Sliding up to the dock, we attracted the attention of diners looking out the windows. Boat secured, we gathered our duffels and strode into the building to find the lavatories. When we swept into the splendid dining room — to scattered applause — we were all properly dressed, combed and polished. After a delicious shore dinner, we reversed the process, casting off and sailing home. The moon danced on the waves and even stars reflected, sparkling like tiny diamonds on dark satin water. We were bewitched in the silence, each woman cradled in the arms of her man, content with the world.

One evening, at a party at our house, Dorothy encouraged my mother to try quilting.

"I'd really like to make a quilt like the one in this beautiful needlework book the girls have given me, but I've never done any quilting," said Mother. "I'm not sure I could."

"Of course you can. I make quilts. It's quite easy, and you do beautiful sewing." Mother had just finished making the crewel-work piano bench cover. With this little nudge in the right direction, Mother set out on what proved to be a nearly lifetime avocation. She was then almost seventy years old, and in the next twenty-five years she created more than four dozen quilts, leaving an incredible legacy of beauty.

In September, 1968, Susan flew off to college on her own. After Christmas recess, she wrote to us that she was working as assistant to the director in a student production of *Camelot*.

"Let's fly up there and see it," suggested Art. "We haven't seen Sue in her new environment and I think Mommy is yearning for her little girl." He was right, and I was delighted to go. On Saturday, February 15th, we sat in the Lydia Mendelssohn Theatre, treated to a remarkable performance, especially of a very talented senior in the role of Morgan Le Fey. She was Gilda Radner, clearly destined for theatrical fame. Sue took us on a whirlwind tour of the campus; neither of us remembered many details of our life there. Our apartment, brand new twenty-three years before, was gone. We went away satisfied that Susan was happily settled in the right place.

Annie's[5] turn came the following autumn; she had chosen the University of Massachusetts in Amherst. It was in New England, naturally, but she was also attracted by a course that would have her raise and train a young horse. The heart has its reasons. Mother and I determined to drive Annie to Amherst, detouring on the way to find old family landmarks. In New York State, we found the summer cottage of Mother's childhood on the shore of Conesus Lake and the house where she was born in Rochester.

Annie's dorm room was on the seventh floor of a very tall dormitory; even the library was high-rise. It was hard to leave my youngest child all alone so far from home, but I swallowed the lump in my throat and kissed her goodbye. Mother and I headed west in the Electra.

"What would you think about swinging by Ann Arbor on the way home?" I asked Mother. "Would you like to see Sue in her new habitat?" Mother was game, and we sped toward Michigan.

Does everything have a reason? We arrived late in the evening to find Susan a little tearful and in a quandary. Having no idea we were on our way, she had poured out her problem to a friend, lamenting "if only Mom were here." She fell gratefully on our necks.

"Oh Mom, I'm in such a mess! Here I am starting my second year and I don't want to be in nursing school. I want to change my major. What can I do? What will Dad say if I bail out!"

"Dad will say you need to decide what you're going to do and then do it. The only thing he wouldn't approve is if you stopped moving forward. Believe me, dear, we don't care what

---

[5] It was, I think, her LRY friends who changed Anne to Annie. It stuck for the rest of her life.

you choose for a major. That's your life decision. There's no shame in changing your mind, only in failing to go after what you want. There now. Dry your eyes and find us a room at the League. We'll talk again in the morning before Grama and I head for Texas."

Of course, life seemed brighter in the morning and we left Susan smiling and plotting the next move in her college career. She shifted to English as a major and eventually graduated *cum laude*. Mother and I continued the long journey to Houston, satisfied that another crisis had passed. Art, glad to have us back again, listened to our tale of Susan's dilemma and, as I knew he would, agreed with my approach.

In a few days, the phone rang. It was Frank Schulman. "Are you lonesome, Mother? Nest empty? Yes? Good! I've been waiting for this." Pretty strange when your own minister feels glad about your sorrow, but soon he made me understand. "I didn't want to intrude on your busy family life, but now the church needs a new employee and you would be just right for the job. I need someone to help me develop programs—a men's group, for starters. We can't pay much, and it would only be quarter time. Would you do it?"

That evening, I told Art. "Only quarter time means I can continue going to school and recording books, too. Would you mind if I took on this one more thing?"

"It's up to you, Babe. If you want it, go for it. Just don't let it eat up what time we can carve out for the two of us." I promised, and called Frank back.

Despite a few cultural dissonances, our life was rich and fulfilling. Art's thirst for wealth was finding satisfaction. For him, money was a personal measure of his career achievement; he was not inclined to flaunt it, and he was generous with it. From the beginning, we agreed on conservative management, saving and investing. We had never quarreled over money. Art felt the satisfaction of building a really secure, debt-free future for us. Then, with little warning, the axe fell.

HARD TIMES

Mid-afternoon that Friday I was working at my desk in our bedroom when Art came in and closed the door behind him.

"Hey, you're home early! What's up?" Turning to find him ashen, drooping, I rose and put my arms around him. My heart skipped a beat. "What's wrong?"

"Sit down. It's a long story." He led me to the bed, where both of us sat, arms around each other. He drew in a breath. "I got fired."

Time stopped. A little green gecko slithered along the windowsill, then disappeared in the garden. I could hear the circulating pump in the swimming pool click on. I could hear my blood coursing past my ears as my heart lurched into high gear. Art held me close.

It had begun a few weeks before, when the first of the vice-presidents went. Another soon followed. Rumor had come down from on high—McLean, Virginia—that the boss wanted to buy a California pet food company and needed cash. The quickest way for Uncle Ben's to generate cash was to unload extraneous executives. The process had started and was moving through the company.

Clearly, the core of any business was manufacturing, sales, procurement, and personnel. At the time, Art predicted to me that his friend in advertising might be next. Art had guessed wrong. Today, it was his turn. Every one but personnel would go; the vice-president was a close friend and ally of the family that owned the business.

"I thought it was odd when the company president called me out on the sidewalk in front of the building. When I got there, he said I was separated from the company. I should get in my car and leave. And no, I could not go back into the building for any reason. My desk would be cleared and the contents delivered to my home on Monday."

As Art was speaking, I drew away to sit with my back to the headboard, leaning on a pillow. I wanted to look at Art, to judge the impact, but my body began to shake uncontrollably. I clenched my teeth to keep them from chattering. *Stop it! This isn't about me.* Eventually I was able to say, "My god, you must feel awful. What a terrible thing to do. What's the matter with those people anyway!"

"I don't know and I guess I don't care. I need to develop a plan, get organized. Unfortunately, the country's in bad economic shape right now. A lot of people are getting the shaft" In truth, the nation was sinking into a recession that would last for many months.

After more than twenty-four years of leaning on my husband, I began to realize that I would need to stand on my own feet and help him regain his confidence. Was the last of the Baby Doll finally slipping away?

He told Mother at dinner that night. Characteristically, she took a positive attitude. "So what's next," she asked, "And what can I do to help?" In a few days he called the girls to let them know.

"Don't worry, Sweetie," he told each one, "I'm pretty good at landing on my feet. It will take a little while to sort all this out, but in the meantime just keep on doing what you're doing. No, there's no problem about tuition money or anything like that. Just leave it to me." He managed to sound upbeat, confident, and after the first two days of alternating between anger and humiliation, he appeared to be.

In the next days, Art made a call or wrote a letter to every contact he had developed over the years. He made no attempt to conceal the fact that he was unemployed and seriously looking. Pride, he said, had nothing to do with it, lots of people look for jobs. In short order, true friends were sorted from the rest, some acting as if Art had a contagious disease they needed to avoid. Others came forward. One of these ran a struggling consulting firm in Houston.

"Art, this is a great opportunity for me. Will you join the company and give me the benefit of your experience? I can't pay anything except a share of whatever business we bring in, but while you're looking you'll have a base, a title, and a letterhead." Of course, Art accepted, even though he knew there would never be enough business to support both of them. I remember that the company's initials were AIM; Art took that as a good omen. He was taking aim at the nation's management levels.

Every day, we drove into town to buy out-of-town newspapers. I parked at the curb while he chose—sometimes San Francisco and Pittsburgh, sometimes Phoenix and Los Angeles. But always the *New York Times* and *Chicago Tribune*. I developed a filing system for clippings and typed the letters he dictated to likely possibilities. Head hunters across the nation heard from him by letter and phone.

As time passed, Art learned of other men he knew in Houston and Chicago who were in a similar position. They formed a network, exchanging tips and encouragement. After a few weeks, some of these men began to fall aside. Art watched helplessly as some sought escape in drink. Redoubling his efforts of support to those who hung on, Art seemed to get even stronger and more determined as time slipped past.

Some feelers were extended, but only a few. Art complained that he would consider anything at any level, but he was 'over-qualified' for most jobs.

"What does that mean?" I asked, exasperated.

"It means nobody wants to hire somebody they think is just parking until they can land something better. I'd pump gas, but that option doesn't seem open, either."

I heard him tell his friends, "Looking for a job is a full-time job, a 9-to-5 job, every day. You cannot take days off. You have to keep yourself in shape by eating and sleeping right, staying in training. And believing in your quest. Believing in yourself. If you don't, who will?" He followed his own advice. During our prosperous time, Art had allowed himself to gain quite a lot of weight, but now he turned that around. His weight began to drop, helped along by a loss of appetite, the only overt sign of his distress. He even dyed his graying hair. Every day, he dressed for business, sometimes spending time researching in the public library, sometimes calling on head hunters, sometimes meeting friends to exchange reassurance.

Of course, we sold the boat and resigned our membership in the Houston Yacht Club; that had been our one real extravagance and we regretted having to let it go.

I did what I could to continue my life as it had been, but college seemed superfluous right now. I stopped that. Bill Cameron, the president of the board of Emerson Church, was an insurance agent with his own business in town. He came to me.

"Kit, this doesn't seem quite ethical for me to do, to try to steal you away from my own church. But I need full-time help in the office. Would you consider taking the job?"

Nothing was ever said about Art's situation and I never knew whether this was more an act of charity for me or of necessity for him. Art, focused on his own quest, let me decide on my own. I took the job, of course, determined to be the best I could be, in gratitude. Though still at the beginner's level, my new salary was much better than the stipend I had been getting from the church and would help our cash flow at least a little. I worked in Bill's store-front office from eight until five, and was glad to have both Mother and Art keeping the house tidy and the kitchen stocked for me.

The adding machine baffled my fingers, just as piano keys had when I was a child. Somehow, my fingers and brain seem to work at different speeds. Bill was patient and he worked hard at training me to the insurance business. I was an eager student at our daily hour-long sessions; the knowledge base he provided for me proved more valuable than either of us could have guessed at the time.

One day, Art got a nibble, but it was from a company that mined uranium. How much did he want to find work?

What kind of work would he take? Just then, a headhunter called with a contact with a German chemical firm, and Art gratefully let go of the mining company. An interview was set up in Pittsburgh, where the U.S. operation was based, and Art flew north.

"Looks good, Hon," he said when he returned. "They said they liked me and we got down to details, like compensation and contract provisions. All that remains is for them to convince the home office that an American would be a better idea than a German to fill that chair." In subsequent conversations, they even referred us to a real estate broker. I was elated; Art was cautious.

"Careful now. This thing about importing a German national is serious, and I think my French background does me no good here. Wait and see. Don't start packing yet." He was right; they brought in a boy from the home office. The weeks wore on.

Sadly, I realized that our twenty-fifth wedding anniversary was coming up. I wanted to give him a token of my love, but I knew it had to be something in keeping with our circumstances. I chose a handsome but modest gold ring with a jade cabachon set in it. I just hoped he would not be upset at my extravagance.

The night of December 16th, he took me to the theater. During intermission, we kept our seats.

"You know what? I've been meaning to buy you something you've wanted ever since I've known you. You sure deserve it now." He handed me a jeweler's box, tied with a gold ribbon.

I caught my breath when I saw what was inside. "Oh my god." It was a watch bracelet made of gold mesh, with a hinged cover over the watch face. On the cover was a lovely star sapphire, and on the back of the watch was engraved:

Owned and Operated by SAF 12-16-69

"Here, take my handkerchief."

"Art, you really shouldn't have! It's so beautiful, but…."

"I love you," he said, kissing me right there in public. "And how many times are we going to have a twenty-fifth anniversary, anyway?"

He wore the ring I gave him every day after that. I told him jade would bring him luck.

In all the concern about our own affairs, we were still parents, a fact that came home to us in the middle of one Saturday night. The phone woke me.

"Hello? Yes, this is Mrs. Fournier. Oh my goodness. Let me put my husband on the extension, please." I shook Art awake, handed him the phone and ran to the office extension. "Yes, I'm back. Doctor, tell me your name again? You want to admit Susan to the University Hospital?"

The doctor's voice said, "Yes, she has had an accident, but she's going to be just fine. I want to assure you that the x-rays indicate her spinal fusion is undisturbed. She has a broken bone in her pelvis."

"What happened?" asked Art.

"I don't have all the details, but I understand a group of students were taking advantage of a snowfall by sliding downhill on cafeteria trays. Susan collided with a tree and was brought to the emergency room by the young men she was with. Really, we just need to keep her overnight. We'll have her back in classes on Monday. Don't worry, mother and dad."

After we had hung up, I climbed back into bed, shaking. Art held me close, but soon I realized he was laughing.

"What?"

"Oh nothing, I guess. She's a bit of a wildcat, that's all. Must take after her mother."

"Well at least I never — oh never mind. Go to sleep."

The early 1970s were hard times for the country in more than economics. Unrest over the Viet Nam war was causing turmoil on campuses; in May, 1970, Kent State University suffered a terrible loss of life. At Michigan, the SDS and the Weather Underground were active; we knew Susan was at least acquainted with these radical groups, and hoped she was not too involved with them.

Annie telephoned in terror from her dorm room at U Mass. "Mom, they're shooting!"

"Who's shooting, Dear?"

"I don't know, but bullets are flying." She was crouching on the floor of her dorm room and crying. I could hear the distant crack of gunfire. How comforting it was to know that she was on the seventh floor. My heart raced and my hands shook as I tried to talk my little girl down.

"Just stay in until morning, Annie. By then, tempers will have cooled and it will be all right to go to your classes." I hoped I was right. I had been glad the girls were away at school, not at home to witness their father's distress and frustration. Now, like a mother duck, I wanted my little flock right here under my wings. I did not think I needed to share this latest crisis with Art.

Later that same semester, out of the blue, Susan called from Ann Arbor. "Dad? Mom? I'm an emancipated minor!"

"What in the world does that mean?" I asked. "I always thought you were pretty emancipated, but did you make it official?"

"Yes I did. I figured out the rules on financial aid. You are no longer responsible for my college expenses—I'm on my own. And don't send any more allowance because I've figured that out, too. I've arranged for work-study with college support and I'll be fine." Our first-born was no longer just a fledgling; she was out of the nest and soaring.

Out of his association with the consulting firm, a new contact developed. A partnership was forming to offer to companies psychological profiling and testing of their executives. The partners were impressed by Art's background and experience.

"Honey, would you mind if we had three of them for dinner at our house? I think they want to look both of us over." Of course I didn't mind.

When the evening came, I was ready. The table was set with my nicest linens and silver, flowers were arranged and the bar set up. Art greeted them at the door and introduced me to the president, Mr. Smith, his wife, and the psychologist. Mrs. Smith's dress caught my eye: it was bright blue, too bright. There were pleats and ruffles, showy jewelry filling a too-low neckline. Mr. Smith, a small, thin man, wore a gray striped suit topped by a red striped necktie. His diamond ring was gaudy. They telegraphed 'cheap' when they meant to exude 'rich'. The mustached psychologist gave me a penetrating look that unsettled me.

During dinner, I said little but watched closely as they courted my husband.

"How can we best approach some of the big corporations, Art?"

"In fact, I know most of the middle and top management people of the corporations you have on your list," he said.

"Hear that, Joe?" said Mr. Smith to the psychologist. "I told you this guy was really top drawer. Art, you're a prize! We knew you by reputation, but seeing the real thing … Well, I can tell you, we really lucked out!"

These people made me very uncomfortable. They were too much — too admiring of Art's every word, too charming, too complimentary. I had the feeling they were appraising the furnishings of our house. Mrs. Smith turned over a spoon. Yes, I wanted to tell her, it's sterling all right, and my mother taught me that you never do that!

My mistrust must have come through because suddenly they proposed to take Art away, fly him to California to meet one more person. After the guests departed, I tried to express my misgivings, but Art became defensive.

"Art, they were fawning on you! They hung on to every word you said."

"Well, maybe I had something to say, Babe. I do have a reputation and I do have the connections I said I did, you know."

At least I knew when to stop.

On his return from California, I met Art at the airport. "How did it go, Dear? Did you find out more about them?"

"Sure did. It looks really interesting. They have an excellent business plan — that is, we have."

"We?" My pulse was beginning to speed up.

"Yes, we. I've joined the firm. And, by the way, I wrote a check you'll want to record. Investment. Makes me a full partner."

"Oh? How much?" It was several thousand dollars. I was livid. "How could you? Without a word to me? Telephones out of order in California? What was the rush? We have never done anything big financially without talking it over first."

"Well, kiddo, that's too bad. You need to understand that this is my career, my judgment, my decision. Live with it." We drove the rest of the way in stony silence.

I had hurt him by challenging his judgment; who was I to think a woman's intuition trumped executive judgment? But, I thought, it did. I clenched my fists. He was so naïve! A little flattery, some smooth talk, and he got sucked right in. I thought we had a partnership, but now? What was I going to do — hurl a grenade and blow up everything? For what? Because he did a stupid thing? I never mentioned the money again.

Little by little, the truth was revealed. To develop a cash-flow stream, the partnership was conducting a very questionable dating-matchmaking service, using the psychologist's scientific-sounding jargon as window dressing. This came as news to Art. He, of conservative New England upbringing, was stunned. In fact, they never had a genuine plan for the legitimate side of the business. Within weeks, the trio had absconded with Art's money and the money they had extracted from other distressed, unemployed executives in Houston. They had moved on to mow greener fields.

Art managed to identify other suckers, but all were too humiliated to take the case to the police. Not Art. He was stung and he was mad. The prosecuting attorney was delighted to meet Art. He already knew about Mr. Smith and gang but had never been able to obtain any formal complaint or evidence. Art supplied both. The offenders were caught—in Arizona, I think—brought back to face Texas justice and take up residence in a state prison for a long stretch. This outcome brought a little satisfaction, if not profit.

Art did not apologize to me for any of this, but I accepted his willingness to humble himself by going to the police (when others would not) as an act of courage. It was enough for me.

Still more time passed with no real prospects, and we decided the next move had to be the house. I wanted to sell most of the furniture, too, but Art said no. We found a decent apartment a few blocks away with enough space for the three of us and our furniture. We had one extra bedroom piled to the ceiling, but we got it all in.

This time, we had a broker sell the house. The market was very slow and depressed in concert with a failing economy, but Shell Oil was relocating its headquarters from New York to Houston; executives were house hunting. We realized a very small profit on the sale and walked away without looking back.

Art's intermission lasted about a year and a half, but nightmares do end. Baxter-Travenol, a major medical equipment company in a Chicago suburb needed a new purchasing director. Art was hired, and we prepared to move back to Illinois.

Mother and I saw to the packing of furniture while Art was traveling on business. The two of us started north in two cars, but left Mother's little yellow Rambler in the airport parking lot for Art to retrieve that evening. The distance to Chicago was over a thousand miles, and even though Mother and I rotated the driving, we were glad to put our heads down each night. All the way, I kept looking in the rear-view mirror. Art was somewhere back there, chasing us. We had a considerable head start, but he was a fast driver. Maybe, maybe—could he catch us?

By March, Texas had already seen its blossoms, but we chased spring all the way to Illinois. An hour after we arrived at Maxine and George's house, Art rang the doorbell.

"Hi ya, Gorgeous. Sorry I took so long. You drive fast." I was in his arms again, and all was well.

LAST HOUSE

415 Carlisle Avenue, Deerfield, Illinois

In Deerfield, the perfect house waited for us on a quiet, curving suburban street. Upstairs, four light and airy corner bedrooms, gave us space to spread out. Downstairs, the living room faced south, overlooking a small side yard, just enough garden for Art. The east-facing dining room looked out on the steep slope behind the house that ended in several acres of forested public park land. The kitchen, breakfast room, and laundry gave me plenty of space for all the dishes and silverware we had collected. The slate-floored front hall led to the den wing, a cozy wood-paneled room with a welcoming stone hearth, connected to the large garage. Our furniture fit the house as if it had been bought especially for this place. We three celebrated with a festive candlelit dinner and toasted a new beginning with a bottle of really good wine.

"Here's to no more garden-building!" Art raised his glass. Within weeks, though, he and Mother were digging in thousands of pachysandra plants on the embankment to hold it firmly in place. Other than that, very little grass needed mowing.

Squirrels scampered up and down the ironwood trees in the north yard, just outside the breakfast room where I had hung a bird feeder. That's when the war began.

"&%($! little varmints! They've found a way to get to the bird feeder and they're eating up all the seeds. Shoo! Scat!" Art thought about it awhile, then said, "I've got it! They need to climb the tree that holds the feeder. I can just nail a sheet of thin aluminum around the trunk. That'll fox 'em." And it did, for a little while, at least. Soon the most agile were scrambling fast over the slippery surface and lunching busily.

"Not slippery enough," Art declared. "Where's the Crisco?"

"You're going to do what?"

"Keep those blasted little furry rats out of that tree, that's what!"

It was comical to watch them try, slide down the slippery surface, land on the ground, lick themselves clean, and try over. Eventually, of course, they licked off enough that they could again make it to the feeder. I was afraid all that fat would make them sick, but my warrior was grim and determined.

"Eureka! I know how to do it!" Art went to the hardware store and came back with a roll of wire, hooks, and a strong cylindrical spring. He spent an hour drilling the hooks into tree and house and stringing the wire.

"Come see," he called.

"Why the spring?"

"The tree moves in the wind. Don't want to break the wire. Now I'll just hang the feeder in the middle and we're done with thieves."

Sure enough, we sat there and watched the squirrels. It was too far to jump, although one did try it. Bounced off the feeder dome and landed on the ground. They sat in a circle, looking up, switching their furry tails and scolding us. Art strutted as if he had just won the Nobel Prize.

The following morning, I called Art. "Come see what your engineer friends have done! They switched to ballet." One of them was walking the wire! Was Art defeated? No. He had one more trick.

"Bring me all the empty spools you have." Since I hate to throw away anything, I found more than a dozen tucked among my sewing things. He strung them on the wire. "Now let them try that!"

"You're more stubborn than the squirrels."

"You betcha!" Within minutes, a squirrel was tightrope walking toward the feeder. He put a paw on a spool. The spool turned. The squirrel picked himself up off the lawn. Triumph at last. They never did figure that out.

Art's office was only ten minutes' suburban drive away; he was a happy man. The new job at Baxter gave him a chance to do what he loved most of all: build a team. In the business mode of the day, companies were gathering their far-flung procurement functions, earlier scattered to all the branches, back to the home office. No significant purchasing team resided in the headquarters — Art would build it, at the same time mollifying all those people in distant offices whose buying power had been taken away. The company was straining to grow, to grow explosively. Top management decreed that the bottom line would grow twenty percent every year, and so far it was. Even though it was a pressure-cooker environment that made ulcers, Art kept his equilibrium, enjoying the excitement, but not trapped by it. He liked to say, "I don't get ulcers, I give ulcers."

DAUGHTERS AS FRIENDS

The girls were away at college and once again, my life settled down into a comfortable routine. I should have realized that part of our family routine was interruption from the younger generation.

Susan called from college. "Mom, I'm doing a paper on urban history and I need to do a little field work."

"That's nice, Dear. What city?"

"Williamsburg."

"Williamsburg, Michigan?"

"No, Virginia."

"How are you going to do field work in Virginia, Susan?" Why did I not guess? In a few days, she and I were driving down U.S. 60, on the way to Tidewater Virginia. Susan did most of the driving, until I ran out of patience.

"Not so fast, Sue. This road is a little curvy for such speeds."

"Oh Mom, you worry too much Just sit back and relax."

"I mean it. Slow down." In a few minutes: "Sue, it's my turn to drive. Pull over." My daughter was over twenty-one now, but she was still testing me, I was still mothering her.

When we settled in Williamsburg, Susan's energy and seriousness in pursuing her subject impressed me. I began to see her, not as my daughter, but as a young woman with goals and direction. In those few days, we began a real friendship. She got an A on the paper.

I had barely settled back into home life when Annie called from Amherst. "Put Dad on the phone, too, Mom." I did. "You know how a lot of students spend their junior year abroad?"

Art rolled his eyes at me and turned his pocket inside out. "So?" he asked. "What do you have in mind?"

"Well, the University of Wisconsin is opening a new school for environmental studies, and I'd like to go as an exchange student for one semester. In the fall. Do you think I could?" She waited.

"Sounds good to me," said her father evenly. "Find out more."

When we hung up, we both howled in relief. "Whew! Got out of that one easy! I was thinking Paris."

It was settled. Mother and I made the trip, shorter this time, to Amherst to collect Annie and the things she would need for the fall semester. She would be at home for the summer; Susan was working at the university.

On the drive home from Amherst, I recalled my childhood impression of the Delaware Water Gap. "Annie, we're going to take a little detour so you can see an amazing sight: the world on its ear. When I was little, my parents took me there and I never forgot it. When I think geology, I think Delaware Water Gap." It was just as I remembered, layers of rock stacked like pancakes, the whole plateful tilted toward the sky. We stopped. Annie took her camera and climbed steps to an overlook. After a few moments, she came back down and we headed for home. That was an unfortunate detour; it must have been on her climb that she encountered the poison ivy.

One of Annie's goals that summer was to brush up on her chemistry in preparation for college chemistry later. She enrolled in a local community college. After the first class, she came home cursing her own foolishness.

"I never should have piled all my hair on top of my head. How does Susan do it? It has given me the worst headache!" I advised her to take aspirin and go to bed, but something about her manner made me uneasy. Just too much mothering, I decided, and let it go.

In the morning, she called me from her bed. "Mom, could you bring me another aspirin? My head still hurts. A lot." I picked up the phone and called the pediatrician who had cared for her years before.

"Dr. Harris? This is Katharine Fournier…oh how nice of you to remember me. I'm calling about Annie." I told him the problem, said it was unlike her to fuss over nothing. What could it be? He asked me if she could touch her chin to her chest; I checked and told him that no, she could not bend her neck.

"Listen to me carefully, mother. I don't want to wait for an ambulance, I want you to drive her to Evanston Hospital right now. Do you think you can get her into the car? This is important, so if you find you can't, call me right back and we'll get her there."

"What is it, doctor? What do you think it is?"

"It sounds like a possible meningitis. Now don't waste time. Move." He hung up, and I moved.

Arriving at the emergency entrance, I saw a man with a face mask waiting at the door with a wheelchair. Someone took my car away to park it, and I followed my daughter in the wheelchair through the door and down the corridor. The elevator door was open and we flew in, closed the door, rose to the third floor, rolled out and down the corridor. As we passed, staff members pressed back against the wall, staring curiously. We wheeled into a room with a big 'QUARANTINE' sign; Dr. Harris followed and closed the door. He and the nurse were wearing masks, too.

The nurse ushered me out as I said, "I'll be right outside, Baby." I paced. Four steps this way, four steps back, up and down, until the door opened and Dr. Harris emerged.

"Yep, looks like a full-blown meningitis, all right. When did she get that poison ivy? It's circling her trunk."

"Doctor," I pleaded, "is she going to die?"

"Absolutely not! She's my patient and I cannot afford to lose a single one. Hard to come by. No, absolutely not."

Mine was a senseless question, but his was an inspired answer. His reasoning made no sense but his unconditional certainty gave my heart the answer I needed.

Though there were medications to make itching from poison ivy less intense, none of these could be ordered because of the complication they might have caused her brain. The only remedy was to keep her on a bed of ice to deaden the nerves. Her other discomfort was the parade of doctors. None of the younger doctors in this teaching hospital had ever seen meningitis before. They came in twos and threes all day long, until Annie begged Dr. Harris to make them go away. Another doctor wanted to do a second spinal tap, just to reconfirm the diagnosis. Dr. Harris declared Annie's room off limits to everyone.

The disease ran its course, the rash subsided, and Annie was discharged to return to home and chemistry class. Art threatened to write his own book called *Six Crises*, but I suggested he wait for a little while. There could be more to come. I was right.

MICHIGAN WEDDING

Brrrrp. Brrrrp. Somewhere in the fog of my mind, I knew it was the telephone. A sudden stab of fear shocked me awake.

"Hello? Susan! What is it?"

"Hi Mom." She sounded excited. "It's something good! Tim has asked me to marry him!"

"That's nice, dear." I sank back on my pillow.

"What kind of dress are you going to make for my wedding, Mom?"

"What time is it?"

"Three o'clock. Only two your time."

"Susan, could we possibly take this up again in daylight? Tell Tim I said hello. I love you, dear."

"I love you, too, Mom." We both hung up. Art was looking up at me with one open eye framed by an inquiring eyebrow.

"Tim proposed."

"Hmmmph." The eye closed and he was asleep again.

Over breakfast, we reminisced about our first meeting with Sue's young man. The two had come up our driveway, fresh from a camping expedition with his parents, carrying a cooler filled with fish. Tim was medium height, powerfully built, sandy hair. Oh yes, the hair—a lot of it—I remember the mutton chops. We led them back to the patio where Art fired up the barbecue, then poured cool drinks for everyone. Tim set to work cleaning fish.

"Tim," said Susan, "I think if you would cut it right there..."

"Sit down, Sue. Sit down and be quiet. I know how to do this." His voice had been firm, authoritative. Susan sat down. Art followed me into the kitchen.

"So what do you think?" he asked me. "Is this serious?"

"I think so."

"Well, it's a good beginning. I never heard anyone tell her to sit down and shut up and make it stick."

"Hush! They'll hear you!"

"She has some wildcat in her, you know. And I think I see where it came from." He gave me a quick squeeze before we returned to the patio.

Tim was a law student at the University of Detroit, having his undergraduate degree from the University of Michigan. Both his parents, of solid Polish extraction, were ardent Catholics, and their reservations about this union would loom large over the couple. The wedding date was set for June, soon after Susan's graduation.

Some months before the appointed date, when Sue was at home for a holiday, Tim came to Deerfield for a visit. They disappeared to Susan's room for a conference, and it was clear that something was wrong. Art and I were summoned.

Tim spoke. "We need to postpone the wedding. Just for a couple of months, that's all."

"What's the story?" asked Art.

"It's my parents. They need a little time to get used to this. I'm sure that if we reschedule the wedding to, say, August, I can talk them into it."

My heart sank. Had this decisive young man turned to jelly? I looked to Art, who was shaking his head. "Tim and Sue," he said, "this is your decision. Your impulse to bring harmony is fine, but do not let go. Whatever you decide, you must live with. We will stand by whatever you choose to do." That is how the wedding came to be an August event.

Sometime that summer, I met Tim's mother. Her conversation about her son was like nothing I could have imagined. She told me that he was studying at University of Detroit because he was too dumb to get into Michigan. She recounted his failures, his faults, his stumbles. In an eerie way, her tone was that of a mother boasting of her son, but the words were terribly destructive. I was speechless.

Slowly I began to understand Tim's contacts. That last semester, he had phoned several times to tell me of his grades, the progress he was making, the paper he had written.

"What does your mother say about all this?" I asked.

"Kit," he answered, "I have not discussed my grades or my papers with my mother since I was in high school." He offered nothing further, and I did not ask. I ached for him.

By this time, Susan's childhood friends were scattered to the winds and their mutual friends were in Ann Arbor. They decided on a ceremony in St. Mary's, the Catholic student chapel. Susan would write the words and the chaplain would read them. We doubted that the Pope knew of this arrangement.

I set to work on the white satin dress, listened with trepidation to Susan's dream of a long, laced-edged veil. There would be two bridesmaids and her sister, Annie, as maid of honor. Luckily, the desired dress styles were quite simple, for I would do the construction of most. I found a beautiful silk sari cloth of yellow and gold for my own mother-of-the-bride gown.

Art did the appropriate thing, acting as father of the bride. He waited to be told what to wear, where to stand, when to show up. I envied his role sometimes, although it was true that most of the burden fell on Susan. She chose everything: the location for the reception, the baker for the cake, the supplier of the flowers, the invitations and guest list. Art stood by with a checkbook.

I suggested to Susan that she make contact with everyone involved in supplying elements of the wedding to be sure that all was in order.

On Monday, before the Saturday wedding, she called in a panic. "Mom, disaster! The man who agreed to make the cake is nowhere to be found. Somebody thinks he's gone fishing in Canada. No one knows anything about a cake. What can I do?" She was near tears and I admit to wiping a damp spot on my cheek.

"Susan, in all of Ann Arbor, there is someone else who can bake a wedding cake. Go find him—or her." Poor bride! It's hard enough when she's surrounded by family, but to handle all this alone? I was comforted to know that she was fully capable, yet I worried along with her. She found two ladies who sometimes created wedding cakes in their kitchens.

When the wedding day arrived, Annie, Mother, Art and I were settled in our rooms in Ann Arbor. The bridal couple, defying all the gods of tradition, met and traveled together to attend a friend's morning wedding near town. Sue had returned to our room to rest, when Art answered a knock on the door.

"It's your bride's bouquet, Sue. Shall I take it?"

"Of course, Daddy! Don't be silly." She sat down and pulled the white satin ribbon from the box, slipped off the lid, and burst into tears. "They're the *wrong kind*. Oh I hate catleya orchids! They're supposed to be cymbidiums!" She sat there, sobbing hysterically. When the storm subsided, we left her in our bedroom to nap and closed the door.

"What the hell is that all about?" asked the nonplussed father of the bride.

"Nerves, Dear, bride's nerves. She will be just fine." I hoped it was true. It was an omen when Sue tore her veil on a corner of the car door, as she alighted at the church. Thank goodness for a more experienced friend who had cautioned me to carry a little handbag with emergency supplies. Three hairpins to tuck the veil back into her cascading hair did the trick, and I hoped she did not realize what had happened. If she did, she never let on.

Family photographs were to be taken before the ceremony, and we waited for Tim's parents to arrive. And we waited.

Tim began to pace. "Maybe they've been in an accident." He was distraught. "Should I call the police?"

"Wait just a bit longer," counseled Art.

Forty-five minutes late, the parents arrived. They offered no real explanation, and the process began to move forward again. The ceremony was expressive and lovely, derived mainly from the writings of Kalil Ghibran.

We offered a simple reception of champagne and light refreshments, along with tiny white boxes of 'groom's cake', slices of our favorite fruit cake from Texas. For those too young to know the custom, Annie constructed a sign explaining that the box was to be put under your pillow to dream on. But, she added, watch out for the dreams, because the fruitcake was from Texas and might promote very big dreams.

Tim's mother declared firmly that with that ceremony it hardly seemed they were married, and I knew the postponement had done little good. She spoke of gaining another daughter, but Tim's sister heard and told her mother, "I'm the only daughter you have, and don't you forget it."

Later, I told Art that I was going to do my very best to forget as much as I could of the ugliness I had witnessed. He told me to concentrate on Susan's and Tim's possibilities. Mother, Annie, Art and I drove home the next day.

Grandmother with the Bride

I TAKE A NEW DIRECTION

"What are you going to do with the rest of your life?" It was a question I had begun to ask myself in moments of reverie, but this was Art quizzing me. Sitting on the boundary of what was and what was yet to be, I had no answer.

"Why? You don't like me as I am?"

"I like you fine. How do you feel about it?"

"I've been thinking about looking for a job, but there isn't anything I'm fit to do. This week's want ads don't look very promising for a dumb housewife."

"Inexperienced in a particular field is different from dumb. What's offered?" We looked in the local paper. "Here's one right here: *secretary to school psychologist, full time, benefits.* See?"

"Sure. My shorthand is long gone, such as it was, my typing's abysmal. I'd be a shoo-in."

"Honey, you have exactly what they need. Those skills can be polished up, but what they need most is responsibility, strong work-ethic, intelligence, flexibility. Life experience is a long way ahead of a kid who doesn't know what time it is. They'll be glad to see you. Go for it."

With my heart in my mouth, I called for an appointment. The woman who answered sounded friendly, and I was encouraged. The next morning, I drove to Winnetka and pulled up in front of the Skokie School. It was an imposing brick structure, probably half a century old, with a white-columned entrance.

Just inside the door, a smiling woman walked toward me. "Mrs. Fournier? I'm Judy Crowell. Welcome." It turned out she was the psychologist. In her office, she asked me a few questions, reassured me about the typing, and asked if I thought I would like to work there. I thought I would. A boss who laughed a lot seemed like a good beginning. Judy was tall, large, motherly, although in truth she was younger than I. She made a very good impression, and I suppose I must have, too. I got the job.

At home that evening, Art was unimpressed. "Honey, I've hired a lot of folks and I'm here to tell you if you walked in my door I'd hire you in a minute. I could teach you all the nuts and bolts you need. You already have the important qualities."

My daily tasks included filing and answering the phone and typing. My biggest problem was orienting myself to the five schools, learning the names of the players—secretaries, principals, special education teachers. Remembering faces was, as it had always been, very hard to do, but I progressed. Judy was unfailingly supportive, and her sunny disposition infused the office with laughter.

Several months after I started, a tall, dark-haired woman came into the office, closed the door, and sat across from me. She introduced herself as Dr. Peterkin's secretary.

"This conversation must remain very confidential," she told me, in a conspiratorial tone. A fleeting thought about the FBI darted across my consciousness, but I pushed it aside. I sat up very straight and promised to be discreet. "I am resigning, and Dr. Peterkin wants me to recommend someone. I have been watching you and I believe you have the qualifications. Would you be interested in having Dr. Peterkin interview you? It is a very important and responsible job that would require your ultimate attention."

"Yes, I believe I would be interested." Although the Winnetka Schools were nationally famous as leaders and innovators in the field of education, and Dr. Peterkin was the superintendent, I felt that she was puffing the position a little. The address was not 1400 Pennsylvania Avenue, after all; I had the impression she thought it was nearly as significant.

Within a few days, I was summoned. Even with Art's cheer-leading fresh in my mind, I was intimidated. I walked across the secretary's office, opened a door, and stepped down three steps into the inner sanctum. Gordon Peterkin was a slender man with gray hair and commanding presence. He rose and motioned me to a comfortable chair at the side of the room and came to sit beside me.

As we talked, I began to put the scene into perspective. He was an executive, but I dealt with executives all the time. Art was one. We mixed socially with his colleagues. What in the world was I so afraid of? I smiled. Dr. Peterkin smiled back, and I think our bond started building at that moment. I got the job.

What a shock to discover that my new boss was a skilled and rapid typist! I had the latest IBM Selectric machine at my desk and stumbled along as best I could. Sometimes, he gave me materials already typewritten and I needed only to produce many copies for the board of education or for parent groups or for the press. Luckily, my typing held a low priority. He gave me much more complex tasks that required a bit of brain power. More and more, I was asked to compose letters for him with only a few clues as to what to say. He seemed to like them well enough.

One day, after my particularly frustrating struggle with the Selectric, Dr. Peterkin came into my office holding a sheaf of papers. "Kit," he said, "you are really a rotten typist."

I braced for the inevitable termination talk. "I know. I'm sorry. I guess it just isn't in me to be a typist."

"Exactly what I was thinking. But as you already know, we have to put out a scandalous amount of typed material. You are much too valuable to me to be wasting your time on that stuff. Will you please insert an ad in the local paper for a part-time typist? She can sit over there. Have a desk and typewriter brought in, and maybe a good lamp. You will supervise her work." He turned on his heel and walked back into his office. You have to love such a boss.

Was I lucky? The advertisement produced a perfect typist. Esther had retired as an executive secretary but either too much time on her hands or too little money in her bank account prompted her back into the job market. She was a gray-haired, tall, angular woman who spoke little. But could she type! Esther could sit for four hours at a stretch, her fingers darting over the keys too fast to follow. Mistakes? She simply didn't make any. I learned that she had won a competition, years before, as Illinois Secretary of the Year.

My job got better after that, with the drudgery reduced. I turned my attention to installing systems, cleaning and organizing files, and discarding paper that should have gone long ago. I developed and wrote copy for a newsletter for the staff members of all the district schools. Taking and transcribing the minutes at school board meetings became routine. In fact, all of it was becoming routine. My position had no potential for advancement; I was doomed to meet myself coming around the same corner for the remainder of eternity. After four years at that desk, I began to wonder, once again, what I was going to do with the rest of my life.

THE JOUST

With Susan married and living in Michigan, me settled in my job, and Art in control of his, Art decided to indulge himself a little. Long bothered by a persistent and worsening but somewhat embarrassing medical difficulty, he decided to undergo surgery.

"I might as well do it now," he told me. "Doc says the surgery is routine but the younger I get it out of the way the better."

I had heard routine before and it turned out this time much the way it had the last: a synonym for harrowing. In the aftermath of this adventure, I needed to send letters of thanks to the dozens of friends and colleagues who had stood by, near and far. In my relief, I indulged in outrageous whimsy, as follows:

Let it be recorded in the annals that on July fifth Sir Arthur descended into the valley to do combat and slay the monster Hemorrhoides. The battle was joined on July sixth and Hemorrhoides done in. But then other monsters in the valley, their territory threatened, counterattacked the sorely tired Sir Arthur. First came the minor pesky monster Bladder Infection. He hit the Hero Arthur but was disposed of easily by trusty lieutenant Sir Urologist, using a new potion brewed by Merlin. Hah! In retrospect this may be seen as a diversionary action. Another monster, Abcessa, was discovered lurking in the surgical site and was run through by Sir Surgeon.

Onward to recovery! But wait . . . The worst monster had yet to strike, and strike he did with a vengeance. The Black Knight Septicemia, the meanest and sneakiest of them all entered the field. Sir Internist was summoned and a war council convened. The great battering ram, Chloromycetin, was moved to the front. (to the rear, actually) Murky medications, intravenous solutions, and mysterious machines were brought to battle. Sir Cardiologist was held in reserve on the hill, continually monitoring the battle.

When the dust settled over the battlefield, all the monsters were slain and peace once more reigns in the valley. Sir Arthur, his wounds healing, is on the way to total recovery and will soon resume his regular pursuit of the Holy Grail and other vital purchases.

To all his friends who lent support with their concern, calls, cards, and cheer, Sir Arthur expresses his gratitude.

Subscribed by the Lady Katharine,
   who also helped with the hand-wringing.

MASSACHUSETTS WEDDING

Christmas in Williamsburg conjures up visions of groaning boards, holly wreaths studded with lemons, and perhaps just a dusting of snow on picket fences. After a long year of planning, we gathered to test the truth of those fantasies for ourselves. It was 1973. Annie was home for the holiday from her senior year at college; we four came from Illinois. From Michigan came the newlyweds, Sue and Tim. The four Rosners came, too. We occupied—rather, overwhelmed—a local rooming house near the Restored Area.

By now, Annie was engaged to Larry, who came to join us. He was six feet tall, good-looking, and personable. Like most young men of the time, his light brown sideburns were prominent. I liked him. In fact, everyone liked Larry. We would eventually learn that being liked was an overriding value for this young man. Annie was defensive about his Italian background, but Art and I, knowing better, passed it off as nothing important.

We spent the days sightseeing and eating, the evenings talking into the morning hours. At the milliner's shop, Annie found a broad-brimmed straw hat for her wedding.

Maxine got lost in the maze in the Governor's Palace Garden. "Just turn left, Mom!" called Kent. "You'll be fine." He knew it was a right turn. Maxine kept circling, calling out, "Somebody come rescue me. I can't find my way out." Her wicked sons doubled over in laughter. George was no better.

The Cascades Restaurant saw us at the champagne brunch, enjoying our last meal together. Accustomed to girls, I was hugely embarrassed by the men, young and old.

"You've got to perfect the technique," said Tim. "You make a dike of rolls and muffins and then pile the food in the middle." Their plates were a scandal. The waitresses were no help at all. They egged them on and found partly finished champagne bottles on deserted tables for them.

Art and George, who might have been setting a mature example, were too busy beating a path back and forth between table and buffet. Maxine, Mother, and I were awe-struck at the capacity of all those men. There were hugs and kisses all around and then we took our separate ways back home again.

One more time, I was the wedding dress seamstress. This dress was to be made of a homespun linen-like fabric, and I spent the winter crewel embroidering foxtails, mushrooms, and other wild things around the hem, the sleeves, and the neckline. Susan was to be Annie's only attendant, and I made her dress also. This was another long-distance adventure; the wedding would be in Massachusetts.

Annie phoned home often. "Mom, could you make shirts for Larry and his brother, please?"

"Annie, I have no idea what you want. Be more specific if you can."

"Poet's shirts, Mom, you know the kind. Big sleeves and open collar." I didn't know any poets, but I started looking for a pattern.

"Do I have to wear something strange?" This from Art.

"No, dear, slacks and a sport jacket will be fine. Maybe an ascot!" He looked alarmed at that, but took it under advisement. I made a practice shirt for Larry, just to see if I had the right idea. When it passed muster, I found two fine Swiss cotton fabrics for the real shirts. My costume took a far-back seat in all this, but one day I called Annie with, "Honey, I've found just the thing for me. Would you believe orange paisley stripes with polka dots?"

Bless my dear daughter, she never turned a hair. "I'm sure it will be lovely, Mom." Or did she really hear me? It was as I described—a long skirt with white silk blouse, prettier than it sounds.

I found the perfect wedding cake instructions and sent them off with a picture. It involved layers with mocha frosting, decorated with many little mushrooms made of meringue dusted with cocoa. The bride would carry a sheaf of wild flowers—Queen Anne's lace, foxtails, ferns.

On the wedding day, it rained. The sullen sky promised nothing good for an outdoor wedding in a rose garden. While a pavilion under roof was available, its atmosphere was marred by large posters advertising the company that owned the lovely park, loaned for the occasion. The women were housed together in a motel, the men nearby.

Early, the men drove down to survey the grounds and set up folding chairs. We were to follow just before noon. The drizzle continued, sometimes pausing, sometimes not.

"Oh Mom," moaned the bride, "I think we're gong to have to be under roof. Darn this rain anyway!" *Every raindrop that falls on a bride will become a tear*, I thought, then put it out of my mind.

"Just wait, dear. We left that decision in the hands of the men and we'll know when we get there." Near the noon hour, we four women piled into my car and headed for the park, a mile away. The men were setting up chairs on the lawn, as the rain had abated for the moment.

Frank Schulman, our dear minister from Houston would perform the ceremony, looking impressive in his scarlet-trimmed Harvard robe. A trio of string musicians would play Italian folk tunes. An arbor, pink roses cascading from the arch, would be the backdrop. Now, if the rain would only hold off!

About forty of Larry's family arrived from Boston in a bus, hired for the occasion. Lina, Larry's mother, had fed everyone before they started and would host a big dinner when they returned. Their culture centered around food, and Lina was never sure there would be enough for any occasion.

Tim ushered me to my chair, everyone found a place, and an expectant hush fell. I think we expected a deluge. The bells in the clock tower rang twelve times, the trio struck up a tune, and Susan came forward at a stately pace. What was this? Susan was near tears, in fact I thought I saw one sliding down her cheek. Susan, our self-possessed little girl who never exhibited an unintended emotion. Surely Annie, our emotional one who cried at every ceremony, would be sobbing. I turned to look. On her father's arm, she was serene and relaxed, the picture of contentment. A wonder! We all looked up at the sky again, hoping the rain would wait.

Dr. Schulman began to speak. As he asked them to repeat their vows, the clouds parted. A single ray of sunshine, surely sent by an angel, pierced through the clouds and fell upon the bridal couple. I think I heard everyone reaching for handkerchiefs. If Hollywood had tried such a stunt…. Never mind, the clouds soon began to retreat, and by the end of the ceremony, the sun was shining warmly.

The reception line was a revelation to me. I have never been kissed by so many people, men and women alike. They were strangers to me, but in the Italian way, they welcomed us into their family.

We sat down for lunch in the pavilion, and I walked over to view the wedding cake. Oh oh! Wait until the bride catches sight of this! The cake had been transported in a pickup truck thirty miles and by now had taken on the posture of the tower in Pisa. But on this day, nothing could upset the bride.

"Come take pictures of this before we cut it!" She was laughing. The cake tasted wonderful, despite its tipsy appearance.

All the while, I had noticed many people moving around taking pictures of everything that was happening. I assumed one of them was the hired photographer, until Annie came to us, near the end of the festivities. "The darn photographer just got here," she said. "He was lost." She was exasperated but still smiling; eventually, we had copies of snapshots from many amateur photographers.

All Larry's family from Boston piled into the bus for the long ride home and the rest of us stayed to gather up presents and say goodbye to the last of our other guests. The bridal couple, both school teachers, started on a summer-long honeymoon that would take them from Lisbon to Athens along the northern shore of the Mediterranean. Art and I put our things into the car and drove south to our next adventure.

The Bride and her Father

SAILING THE SOUND

We drove to Connecticut in silence. I was exhausted, from the bustle of the wedding and from the realization that both my little girls were now all grown up and gone. Art drove the whole way, settling smoothly into the late Saturday afternoon traffic; as always, he was comfortable behind the wheel. After a little while his hand reached for mine, he gave it a gentle squeeze, and I knew he understood me. We found a motel in New London.

In the morning, the ferry took us to Orient Point at the northeastern tip of Long Island, where our friend Herb Bailey met us. The thirty-foot Pearson sailboat, John Jay, was waiting in Greenport. With Herb's father-in-law, the crew was complete, and in the afternoon we set sail in a brisk wind. I retreated for a brief nap.

Emerging from the cabin still rubbing sleep from my eyes, I took a line the skipper handed me to hold.

"Here, Kit, hang on to this while I free up the jib. It's jammed." He moved forward while I stood there, still half-dazed. The line slipped from my grasp and swung away, just out of reach. This was very unfortunate; the line was the jib halyard.

"Get that line!" Art and Herb lunged for it, and Herb managed to retrieve the bitter end as it swung wildly in the wind. Now the other end had slipped from the masthead block. We had to return to the marina. What a humiliation!

Only later did I realize that my sleepiness and mental confusion were subtle signs of seasickness, my first experience of it. I thought that if the line was going to jump out of the block, it was just as well to discover it close to home, but proper protocol demanded that I say nothing in my own defense. Having committed the unthinkable, I could only resolve to be alert and responsible for the remainder of the voyage.

Our week-long sail took us along Long Island's north shore and across the sound to Connecticut. In Mystic, Art and I spent the day strolling through the maritime museum there, marveling at an entire culture that was now gone.

"Look at this, Kit! Everything centered on whale oil." He was looking over the grappling hooks, the knives, the spears, all used to capture and kill the great animals and to render their flesh.

"And then petroleum came. There must have been terrible hardship when all these people lost their livelihood. It was change or die, I guess." I felt sad, thinking about all those families whose men had plied the seas. "So what comes next? When petroleum runs out or is supplanted by the next technology?" We walked along, sobered by these thoughts.

The following day, we headed to Block Island to drop in on my mother, visiting friends for a few days. Fog had settled over the sea, giving everything an unworldly feeling. The breeze was gentle; we wanted to move cautiously and listen, so we kept our engine turned off. Only the rhythmic slap-slap of the waves on the bow marked our passage. We kept close track of our compass and the chart.

"Listen! I hear something." We stopped breathing. There it was: the faint whine of an engine.

"Hard to tell, but I think it's behind us. At least it's nothing big. Sounds like a small power boat. Keep watch." We peered into the dense curtain behind us as the sound grew lower in pitch and louder.

"There he is!" A dark shape loomed out of the fog, about fifty feet to our starboard quarter. Now we could see that it was an open fishing boat, about eighteen feet long, driven by a small outboard motor. They slowed as one of the three men aboard stood up and shouted to us through cupped hands.

"Which way to Block Island?"

Startled, Art and Herb pointed their arms in the general direction we were headed, while Herb looked down for a precise compass heading to report to them.

"Thanks!" they shouted, revved up their engine and were swallowed up in the gray curtain. We looked after them, stunned.

"If they manage to avoid colliding with a tanker and are lucky enough to hit that small target, we might see them in port. Otherwise, Spain is the next stop." We made it into Great Salt Pond harbor late that afternoon, but never did catch sight of our intrepid passers-by. I hoped Providence was looking out for fools that day.

The weather was hot July fourth, so hot that the oldest member of our crew wilted. Soon, it became apparent that he was suffering from heat exhaustion, and Herb worked hard to get his father-in-law back to East Hampton. A local airplane charter came to the rescue and the sick Grandad was airlifted home.

After that, we three sailed through the infamous Race where the fishing is said to be the best but the tidal currents are ferocious. Calculating slack tide with care, we sailed through handily, threading our way through the huge flotilla of fishing vessels.

Once, when I was at the helm, we noticed a very small stick in the water. "What's that?" I asked. "Is it a lobster pot, way out here in this deep water?"

"I don't think so," said Art, "it's leaving a wake." As we looked to port, the stick rose up, breached the surface, and materialized as an immense submarine, just across our bow. Herb wanted to lob a rifle shot across their bow for coming so near, but cooler heads persuaded him otherwise. We watched as the monster suddenly accelerated, going away, we estimated, at about twenty knots. To say we were impressed would understate it. None of us had ever come so close to one of our nuclear submarines.

It was a fitting finale to our adventure aboard the John Jay.

INVICTUS

Some fool wrote: *I am the master of my fate, I am the captain of my soul.* He was, at best, half right.

"Got a strange assignment today." Art was serving dinner.

"What was that?" I poured tea.

"The president named me to a new task force to investigate and report directly back to him. It's very hush-hush."

"Can you tell me?"

"Sure. You don't work for Baxter. He wants us to nose around and find out where there might be an accounting discrepancy in inventory control. About time. I've been sure something—let's say—unusual was afoot. Now we're supposed to find out all the details. Top priority."

"Mmmm. Where do you start?" I buttered a roll and bit into it. I knew of the audacious mission of the company. It was referred to as 20/20. That is, annual 20% increase in sales, 20% increase in stock price. Incredibly, the goal had been met for several years now. Art's conservative realism told him the bubble would burst.

"I gotta hunch. Going to poke around Distribution tomorrow. I think the answer's not so mysterious, and I wonder why he's sending us to do the dirty work."

The following two or three weeks got pretty hectic. This new task force, piled on top of his regular daily routine, gave Art a lot to do. I noticed that he seemed harried and he certainly talked less about his job. Halloween came and went, leaving me as always with an unsettled feeling in the pit of my stomach.

The task force—six men of middle-management level—were meeting now to put together their report. The facts were politically incendiary and they haggled over phrasing and perspective. How could they couch it in terms acceptable to the top brass? Who, besides the president, would see it? What did the man want from them? Art, leader of the group, held their feet to the fire. However they reported, it would be the truth, he told them. If they could find any amelioration to dress it up, he would accept that. Just not lies.

"Truth is," he told me, "the guy knew from the start. He is the reason. At his direction, inventory is being shipped out and marked as sold goods. That improves the bottom line. After quarterlies are in, the goods come back. Sometimes it's only a paper transfer."

"But that's crooked! Why would he send you on such an errand?"

"Good question. Maybe he wanted to see how our investigation uncovered it so tracks could be covered. Or maybe he expected us to make up a plausible story that would cover his tracks with the investment analysts."

"How are you going with it?"

"We're reporting what we found. Let him dig himself out. We didn't concoct this scheme."

The report was presented. The president personally thanked each member of the task force for a thorough job completed responsibly. All was well.

Within several weeks — each for a different stated reason — all members of the task force were unemployed. Each left the company with a stellar record of promotions, bonuses, commendations. Doors were shut, tracks covered, ranks closed.

Not one of them was inclined to blow a whistle. All of them were concentrated on finding a new job and they knew that whistleblowers were unemployable. Being captain of your own soul gives little comfort in a cold world.

LOCOMOTIVES AND COBOL

In 1975, Gerald Ford had taken the oath of office after Nixon's resignation, inflation had reached into the middle teens, and national production was sliding south. Gloom headed every business page. The unemployment rolls were increasing, but in spite of everything, I think of 1975 as a very good year.

Art had no office to go to every day, but he was certainly employed. His first move was to get new business cards, this time announcing that he was a Management Consultant.

"That, my dear," he said as he showed them to me, "is loosely translated as unemployed executive." Optimism led him to have invoice forms printed under his letterhead.

For years, the American Management Association had coaxed him out as often as possible to run seminars and give speeches to regional and national meetings. Now they closed in and snagged him for assignments as far away as Mexico City and Monterey to the south, Halifax to the north, and Phoenix and San Diego out west. Art was in his element; teaching was in his soul.

While the fees were modest, our combined incomes met our needs perfectly well. We were putting less away, but our investments continued to grow on their own. Our extravagance was sailing, but the Wilmette Yacht Club was no Houston Yacht Club. Here, we sailed our little Arrow-class boat with much less expense than vacations away from home would have incurred. Art was traveling a lot anyway.

I missed him when he was gone, but he returned with enough energy to sweep me off my feet when he came in the door. I even smiled when he greeted me with, "What's for dinner and when?"

Art's reputation in business circles kept him in touch with developments on the street. Many colleagues called him frequently to bring him up to date. One call the next spring woke his curiosity.

"What a great concept!" he exclaimed after he hung up.

"What's up?"

"A new group is getting underway, combining the commuting rail and bus lines of six counties from Milwaukee all the way around to South Bend. They're going to call it the Regional Transportation Authority. Of course, that sacred cow, the Chicago Transit Authority, will remain autonomous. No politician would dare touch that."

"So it's a good idea. Do I detect a note of excitement here?"

"Yeah. They think they want me to head up the purchasing function."

"Oh swell. You've bought rice and you've bought sulfur and potash. You've even bought sterile plastic intubation bags. But locomotives? Do you know about them, too?"

"Hell, honey, I can buy anything. Pencils, rails, locomotives. It's all the same thing you know." I didn't know, but I trusted.

That he was selected astonished Art, because such spots always went to the politically well-connected. You had to have, as they said, a 'Chinaman', someone powerful enough in city, county or state political circles to protect your back. Art was naked, but he was competent and someone in the inner circle was bright enough to appreciate the need for that.

Art's first day was a revelation. The RTA had rented offices in Marina City, those two iconic 'corn-cob' towers on the river.

"I have a nice office," he told me. "And a desk. No chair yet. But there were two pencils on the desk. It's a start."

"And a staff?"

"Anybody I can snag off the street. I've got a budget. It's a clean slate—I can build whatever I want. They're short on organization, but that will come. I'm part of the financial group." The sparkle in his eyes was brighter than ever.

I marveled at his enthusiasm. New situations without precedents intimidated me, but it was the opposite for Art. He loved the creation and the training and mentoring that went with it.

Within months, he had built a staff to be proud of and furnished the offices with enough equipment for efficient operation. There were forty bus lines and six major railroads to juggle. The rail cars he ordered from Bombardier in France developed problems in the test phase; it drove him crazy to wait while they fumbled. He ordered Canadian rail stock by the mile as lines were renovated and expanded. Art and his boss, Dick David, got along famously. Yes, 1975 was looking good.

It may have been the suffocating sameness of my job, or maybe my tendency to abandon one activity for a new one.

"Sweetie, it's none of those things. You finally have the self-confidence to spread your wings. I'm all for it. So what are you going to take on now?"

"Oh gosh, that's the problem. I haven't the slightest idea. I'm still fit for nothing much."

"You're trainable."

I shook my head doubtfully. "I wonder if I should answer that ad?" He waited for me to go on. "It's a women's career consulting firm. They test you and help you decide what's next. How do I know if it's legitimate?"

"You take a flyer, that's how. Go there and judge for yourself."

I took a personal day from work and found the consultant. After a few group tests with other women, a psychologist drew me aside.

"I have a hunch, after reviewing the work you've done here. Did you ever think about programming?"

I was bewildered. "What's that?"

"Just sit here and do this test, then we'll talk."

The test was pretty easy, just a few questions about simple logic and number matching exercises. I handed her the paper. After scoring it, she explained a little about programming computers, but I still had little idea what it was about. She told me I had a near-perfect score.

"Does that mean I'd be a good programmer?"

"Actually, no one knows. The test hasn't been validated. But I can tell you this: employers are blown away by it. They're very optimistic when they see such scores. Programmers are in very short supply. Why don't you enroll in a basic college course and see what you think?"

Lake Forest College was offering Saturday classes in Basic, one of the languages of the computer. I enrolled and was immediately entranced. The challenge of writing out coded instructions for what seemed simple tasks was a game.

Situation: you are sitting in a chair facing the wall, ten feet away.

Task: write instructions to get you standing, touching the wall.

It looked simple, but my first try took fifteen minutes. I forgot to lean forward in the chair before putting weight on my feet. One at a time, lift left foot, move it forward six inches, put foot down, shift weight, and so it went until at last, I was touching the wall. I was hooked.

In time, I enrolled at the local junior college, where I they told me the work was very hard. I think they meant very hard for someone approaching fifty; the other students were approaching twenty. I learned COBOL—which stands for Common Business Oriented Language—and two or three other related skills. After finding out that my teachers had no actual business experience, I determined to find out from someone out there in the real world how I should proceed.

All this time, I pursued my new education clandestinely—Dr. Peterkin knew nothing of it. Guilt was part of the secrecy, since I was aware that my boss was under fire from the school board. I felt disloyal to be considering abandoning ship, but suddenly, opportunity knocked.

I had told a friend about my plans and she spilled the beans. One night she was sitting next to her friend at the opera, gossiping about her other friend who had become so serious about school that she wasn't fun any more. "But you know her, I think. Kit Fournier." And then my friend said her heart sank. She realized she had betrayed a confidence to just the wrong person: the president of the board of education. She confessed to me.

"Art, as long as the cat's out of the bag, I think I'll contact him. He's a good guy, not one of those who are after Dr. Peterkin. He's a vice-president of Washington National Insurance Company. Maybe he'll help me, and at the same time keep my secret." I wrote a letter to Dr. Anderson: *Is there any way you could introduce me to someone in the data processing department of your company who might advise me about what courses would be most useful in the real world of business?* I explained Dr. Peterkin needed no alarms, since I expected any move would be many months or even years ahead. A few days later, Dr. Anderson called me at home in the evening.

"Kit, I talked to my friend in the company who is vice-president for data services." I gulped, surprised that he would go to the top. "He says he won't give you advice, but he will arrange for you to be tested at the company. If you can pass the test, he'll hire you and the company will do the training at their expense."

"Oh boy!" I exclaimed when I hung up the phone. "Now it's time to make the commitment or stop dreaming. I know I can pass the test. What should I do?" I explained the offer to Art.

"Kit, leaving the sheltered atmosphere at the school is a tough prospect. And I understand your hesitancy about loyalty. You need to decide who is your first priority — there's no shame in that."

I took the plunge. Shaking in my shoes, I presented myself at the imposing front door of the company, found the personnel department and took the test. On January 17, 1976, I signed employment papers. Leaving was easier than I thought;

no one had any bad feelings about it. In fact, the staff gave me a grand farewell party. I drew a deep breath and moved on.

There were eight of us in the training class. Our instructor was an exceptionally bright and gifted young man, Fred Stanton. All of them were younger than my children, but my advanced age seemed to make no difference to them—I was accepted as one of the gang in nearly every circumstance. The only exception occurred at a party one of the class gave. We attended, all with our significant others. Conversation was lively, but Art and I became aware that we were being cut out of an activity at the other end of the room. People kept moving around and talking softly. Art and I looked at one another in puzzlement until we smelled the familiar sweet scent of marijuana wafting through the air. I guess it would have been like offering a joint to your mother, wouldn't it? We laughed afterward.

The work was intense, but absorbing, and the homework kept me up past my bedtime every night. I lived, breathed, and ate programming. That was the time that Art threatened to sue IBM for alienation of affections. The weeks flew by and suddenly we graduated, to take our places at desks on the data processing floor in the big building. We had a few days off to catch our breath before starting the real work.

It was good to have those days, because I needed to travel to Michigan to help care for my new grandson. He was born on the Ides of March; Sue and Tim named him Douglas Arthur. I understand now that all first grandbabies are exceptional, are wonderful, are more special than any before or since. Then, I knew this only about Douglas—big and blond and beautiful.

VIRGIN DREAM

"Art, do you know a big anniversary is coming up in April?" I loved obscure calculations and little-known facts.

"Yeah? Like what?"

"Our wedding anniversary!"

"C'mon, sweetie, I remember that one. It snowed that day. December, I think."

"Hey, that's right! Now add twelve thousand, a hundred seventy-four days, and what do you get?" At his mystified glance over the newspaper, I continued, "you get Sunday, April 17th, 1978. We'll have been wed a third of a century. How 'bout that!"

Art shook his head and continued reading.

"We have to celebrate. I have it all figured out. This one's on me. I've been saving up from my salary and I'm taking you on a vacation."

He put the newspaper down now and grinned at me. "I'll drink to that! Where are we going?"

As our plane slipped into a landing pattern over Charlotte Amalie, capital of the U.S. Virgin Islands, I caught my breath. Spread beneath us was a perfect aquamarine sea, so clear that the bottom was visible in every detail.

"Unbelievable" breathed Art.

Our sailing friends, Dorothy and Herb Bailey, had joined us for a bare-boat-charter cruise in the waters shared by the U.S. and British Virgin Islands. After a taxi had taken us to our comfortable hostelry, we all headed downtown to check out the local scene.

"I'm looking for a straw hat," I said, and I left the street of tourist shops to find a place where the locals might buy their own necessities. The others stayed behind.

I entered a modest little store that seemed of offer everything, a sort of down-at-the-heel Woolworth's. As I moved slowly along, checking out the offerings, I was aware of many eyes following me. I was the only white person there.

"What can I do for you, Lady? Are you lost? Maybe you need be uptown." Her voice was soft, as all the islanders seemed to be, but suspicious.

"No," I said, "I want to buy a straw hat, and I think this one is just right." I held it up. Plain, it had a little brown shell decoration on the band. The price tag inside said $4.95, and I left it there for years to remind me of simpler, more affordable days. In this economy frame of mind, I paid for the hat and quickly walked back to 'my side of town', where I made a foolish decision I would regret for a long time to come.

Art was idling on the sidewalk; as I came along, he was nearly obscured in the brilliant sunlight. Taking me by the arm, he pulled me inside a small white cave of a jewelry shop.

"Look what I found!" His voice was urgent, excited. "Would this make a handsome ring!" There, on a little velvet cushion, the jeweler was holding up six small emeralds. About the size of the diamonds in my wedding ring, they were perfectly matched for size and color, brilliant deep green. "What a beautiful partner for your wedding ring! What do you think?" When it came to buying for me, Art left behind his usual purchasing agent's caution.

"Oh, Art, they are lovely, aren't they! But you and I don't know about gems. And really, I don't need such an extravagance. You are dear, though."

I should have bitten my tongue. He gave one more try, then shrugged, and we walked out into the sunlight. A third of a century had not been enough to teach me what I needed to know about this man. In years to come, he would point out emerald rings. None had that perfection of color and clarity, all were very much more expensive. Twenty years later, without asking me, he finally consulted a jeweler, mounted a search for perfect emeralds, and had them set in a platinum band. Too late, I understood. Sometimes, when someone says, 'the pleasure is all mine', it really is.

The next day, we were off to Road Town on Tortola Island in an amphibious plane, a new adventure for me. Flying in small planes was always a delight, but taking off and landing on the water was indescribable.

The well-organized charter company gave us lists of suggested supplies. Dorothy and I checked off what we thought we would need and joined the men in the briefing room. All the skippers and crews sat for extended lectures on navigation techniques. Most of the advice boiled down to watching the bottom. Channel markers were fairly reliable, as were depth sounders. The speaker advised, "A good eyeball on the bow is better than anything when you're traversing tricky areas. Keep in mind: coral reefs abound."

Down at the dock, deckhands toted crates of food and beverage onto the deck. Dorothy and I went below to see to stowing it all. Obviously, we had ordered too much food, and certainly far more beverages than we could possibly need.

"Maybe we can put some of it in the dinghy," suggested Dorothy. "It's just hanging there on the davits, and we probably won't need it right away." But no, all of it tucked into the many lockers and the spacious refrigerator. Finally, Herb started the engine, gear was given one more look, the lines were cast, and we were off to lunch at Cane Garden Bay.

The thirty-nine foot Pearson handled well, the breeze was moderate, sun shining, and all was right in the world. Herb, the senior sailor, made most decisions about where to sail next, and that was all right with Art. This was a vacation and he had left his executive hat at home. Although tasks were distributed among the crew, most of the work on the wheel was left to the men. I got my turn when we were safely in the middle of Drake Channel and far from trouble.

Art and I drew ever closer, nestling tenderly at night in our double bunk. His comfort and self-possession were endearing to me, even though I had not entirely abandoned my impulse to share the command. Art was satisfied to learn from Herb's greater sailing experience.

The days were lazy and incomparably beautiful. The evening we anchored just off the Rockefeller compound, we were careful to follow the instructions in the guide book: quiet please, just lie at anchor making a beautiful picture for the guests ashore, no laundry is to be hung, do not come ashore. Oh well, the sunset was as beautiful for the peasants afloat as for the gentry on the beach. We laughed about social relativism; if we were to be part of the lowly masses, where better than aboard a big sailboat floating in clear tropic waters? As the stars winked on, we poured glasses of Grand Marnier and meditated on the meaning of it all.

The radio weather channel seemed to be an endless loop. "Wind south-southeast, 8 to 10," intoned the voice every day. And it was quite reliably so. Occasionally, we could see a sudden rain shower in the distance, coming our way, but by careful sailing we managed to duck out from under, seldom getting any drops. One day, Herb decided to sail south out of the protected channel into the ocean, around the corner, to explore a remote 'hurricane hole'. The wind piped up and the waves were high, giving us one day of fairly brisk sailing. At the end, we were exhilarated, but tired.

We learned that the climate of intense sun and constant wind was enervating. Even though I was careful to wear my straw hat and the tropic gauze pajamas I had made, the rays penetrated everything. Sheltered under the canvas bimini stretched over the cockpit, we were hit by sunshine bouncing off the water. My fair skin darkened. In fact, when I returned to my office, an African American colleague put his hand down next to mine and commented, "You could pass, Honey, you could really pass!"

One afternoon, we set a course for the Bitter End Yacht Club, famed for a lovely harbor and an excellent kitchen. Taking a short cut under the slanting late-day sun was pretty risky, but I was assigned to stand on the bowsprit to guide us in. The water changes color with changes in depth and it is usually fairly easy to see a sudden coral reef coming up. At the end of the day, however, sunlight hits the water at a sharp angle and makes the bottom much harder to read. Herb set the sails inefficiently to slow us down and I peered ahead, signaling right or left with my hands. It was tense work; no one wanted to fetch up on one of those coral bars. Could take the bottom right out of a boat, though hopefully not at this slow speed.

After an hour and a half, we sailed into the harbor and deep water, triumphant. When we were safely moored, everyone went below to get presentable for the club dining room. Showers, combs, razors, all were pressed into service until the four bedraggled crew were buffed and polished. We ladies were decked out in long dresses, the gentlemen in white trousers and guyabaras. Herb and Art handed their barefoot ladies down into the waiting dinghy. High-heeled sandals were hand-held until we reached the dock.

When we swept into the dining room, we imagined ourselves personifying the Beautiful People. Perhaps we were, but we were also ferociously thirsty and hungry. A pretty feature of the tropics is the beverages: glasses: tall, filled with ice and the most delectable combinations of pastel colored, exotic fruit juices. And rum. Always rum.

We toasted the day and settled back to relax and enjoy. How refreshing it was! Being slower than the men, perhaps because they were engrossed in chatter, Dorothy and I had swallowed only a third or so of our drinks when we exchanged knowing glances and set them back on the table. This was powerful medicine, to be enjoyed with care. Not Herb and Art; they were thirsty. Empty glasses were swiftly replaced and those dispatched gratefully.

"Well," said Dorothy quickly, "we'd better get something to eat. The soup table is across the room, just over there. It's pumpkin. Sounds great, doesn't it? Let's go." How she and Herb made it I never knew; I was focused on Art.

He hissed in my ear, "Point me to where it's at. I can do it. Just get me there." His voice was thick and unsteady. In the space of ten minutes, Art had tied on a very quiet, dignified drunk. How fascinating, I thought, should I laugh or be embarrassed? I've never seen him like this before.

Putting one foot in front of the other, he slowly made his way to the soup table, weaving only slightly. His concentration was impressive. His dexterity being below par in this condition, I undertook to transport two bowls of soup back to the table, leaving Art to study his way back without my guiding hand. Determination brought him through. Even in an alcoholic fog, Art could keep his eye on his goal and, by exercising all his mental strength, get to where he was going.

By the time we had finished the splendid meal of local grouper, laced with lime juice and unfamiliar spices, Art had regained a good semblance of normalcy. He could again join in the conversation without tripping over his tongue.

Late in the evening, we weary sailors headed back in the dinghy to board our boat, rocking gently at its mooring in the harbor. Somehow, we managed to clamber aboard and stumble down the companionway into our bunks, the regular ritual of Grand Marnier in the cockpit forgotten for once.

None of us could really believe it, but in five days we had nearly completely consumed all those beverages. Garbage bags were bulging with empty cans and bottles. The refrigerator was alarmingly sparse. We actually had to return to be restocked for the rest of the voyage. It was all part of the plan, but none had really believed it. Sun and wind do remarkable things to appetite and thirst.

After re-provisioning, we headed for the remaining sights in British waters, and then it was down the Drake Channel to St. John's Island, a U.S. territory. We had to check in at the Cruz Bay immigration office, on the second floor of an aged, sagging building near the waterfront.

For all the years I had loved being on the water, I was still uncomfortable in the water. A poor swimmer, I never fully recovered from the trauma of summer camp challenges. Now, I tried to join the others who were snorkeling in these lovely, tranquil coves, but it was no use. I retreated to sit in the shade of the cockpit bimini while the others splashed happily, marveling at the grandeur of the underwater scenes. I could only imagine.

We climbed on the rocks at The Baths, where, coming down to the beach, Art spied the sunbathers. He readied his trusty movie camera, but I, laughing, restrained him.

"No," I told him firmly, "you cannot take pictures here."

"But," he protested, grinning, "the sights are so beautiful. I need to take home pictures of this."

Leading him away from the oblivious topless sunbathers, I ran with a very disappointed Art back to the dinghy and safety from wrathful sun-worshippers. Art always remembered that moment when his blushing bride saved him from taking great shots.

Reluctantly, we four sailors pointed our craft toward the marina for the last time. The dock was crowded with boats, and it looked like a long wait for a berth. We started to drop anchor, but suddenly paused. Crackling over the VHS radio came the command, "Captain, drift back ten feet and then drop your hook very fast. Lie there until boarded."

Doing as we were told, we saw, even then, a dinghy speeding toward us. In one quick motion, the black man secured his craft, swung aboard the sailboat, and took the wheel. Deftly, he gunned the engine in reverse, while he directed Herb in handling the anchor line. Herb payed it out, the sailboat glided backwards until it found a narrow opening between boats at the dock. A line thrown around a cleat, and we were secured. All agreed: it was an awesome demonstration of boat handling skill.

"Just snug up that anchor line, Captain, and you're home."

We all stepped off onto the dock, and the first leg of the journey home.

It was still April. When our plane landed at O'Hare Field, there was two-year-old Douglas with his parents, waiting at the exit ramp. His little voice piped up, "Here's Grama Kit! Here's Grampa Art! Home from the Carinbean."

And so we were. Goodness, it was cold! Our straw hats and sandals were unequal to the Chicago chill; we felt a little ridiculous. Luckily, Susan had come prepared with two winter coats. We rode home in comfort.

ENGLAND
O to be in England
Now that April's there

Robert Browning had it right, although in fact, it was May when Tim invited Susan, Art, and me to travel to London. He was going to a lawyers' conference, and he wanted us to tag along. His wife's advanced pregnancy might have suggested that a couple of parents-in-law could be a wise back-up. Whatever the motivation, Art and I accepted, applied for passports, and packed far too many clothes. None of us had ever crossed the Atlantic before.

We rode the train from the airport to London, struggling with big suitcases and clothes bags. On both sides of the train tracks, we watched the countryside roll by—lovely gardens surrounded snug little cottages. Blossoms cascaded over stone walls, nestled in the angles of houses, spilled onto garden walks.

This beauty caught me by surprise. I remembered my father's dour reflections on his visit there in the winter of 1938. I had taken his distaste seriously, but he was a very lonely young man on an all-winter solo business trip to Belgium. England had been a quick diversion that proved no more endearing than the rest of his bleak sojourn. This England, on a crisp, bright spring morning opened my eyes to the delights of travel. Nothing I had seen at home looked at all like this.

We delighted in all the common tourist activities, chatting with Beefeaters at the Tower, watching them feed the ravens, gawking at the crown jewels. We bought teapots at Harrod's, tea at Fortnum and Mason. At lunch, I ordered a pot of tea, but the waiter explained, "We offer coffee at lunch, madam."

"Well, when do you offer tea? I thought English people drank tea."

"You would have to visit a tea shop for that in the afternoon, I am afraid, madam." I never did locate a cup of tea, except at breakfast, when tea was strange to me.

Art led me down the Thames to Greenwich. It was his dream to see and touch Chichester's round-the-world sailboat, the *Gipsy Moth IV*, to walk the grounds of the Royal Naval College, to stand on zero longitude from which place all global positions are calculated, to see the Royal Observatory where world time begins. We did all that, and I was surprised to be moved by the sight of the little *Gipsy Moth*, rigged with very little concession to the fact of a solo crew.

"Look at this, Art. He had no lifelines. The man must have been mad."

"Or a pretty good sailor, Kit. He already had experience—he was 65 years old when he set out on this voyage."

Our sailing had been entirely in very protected inland waters, but suddenly this graceful ketch brought to life the glories and perils of blue-water sailing. No wonder the queen had knighted him, and what a wonderful touch that she had used the same sword with which the first Queen Elizabeth had knighted Sir Francis Drake. On the river cruise back to London, we spied a luxurious yacht anchored in the river, flying the Stars and Stripes.

Days were filled with a kaleidoscope of experiences. We walked the huge Hampton Court gardens, gazed upward in awe to the ceiling of Westminster Abbey, listened to the familiar chime of old Big Ben. At last, I saw the infamous marbles, 'acquired' by Lord Elgin in 1801 for the British Museum, those lovely fragments of the frieze around the Parthenon.

"Art, we had copies of these marble sculptures all around the tops of bookcases in my high school senior library. I always dreamed of seeing the originals. No wonder the Greeks want them back!" Sadly, they no longer displayed their original bright colors, but the white marble was beautiful.

A fast train carried us to Oxford one day, with a stopover in the Cotswolds region. No London visit is complete without theater; we enjoyed the venerable 'Mousetrap', still running 22 years later when Susan's son Douglas traveled there.

One evening, we four enjoyed a concert in Royal Albert Hall, then found a small Italian restaurant on the second floor in an alley. It was named for its address: 14½. Afterward, we returned to our hotel on the underground. It was the last train for the evening, and a pair of Bobbies had been dispatched to sweep all the stragglers from the station. They started up the long flights, herding us four Americans along. Suddenly, I decided to race one of the young men to the top. I was on the stairs, and he hopped over the railing to the escalator. As I climbed at top speed, he simply strolled on the moving staircase to keep pace. Unaccountably, I increased my pace. He strolled a little faster, keeping even. At last, I reached the top, huffing and puffing, while the smiling policeman stepped easily off the escalator. He had not broken a sweat, while I was exhausted, laughing. I had a new appreciation of just how deep London subways are. The others attributed my strange performance to the dinner wine, but I claimed it was only my natural foolishness.

Of course, like most tourists, we squeezed far too much into far too few days. We flew home, knowing that next time we should carry only what we could actually carry. Art and I vowed to return one day and explore further, this time branching out to Wales to trace Adams family history. It never happened.

Michael Adams, due nearly eight weeks later, was born early, June 9,1980.

ALLONS Y[6]

"Have you ever been in Baltimore?"

I thought for a moment, remembering the time I had looked out of the train window on the way to Washington with my father, years ago. A dim picture of row houses with their white marble front stoops lined up on every street was all that came to me.

"I've been through Baltimore," I offered.

"Hell, everybody's been *through* Baltimore. Have you ever been *in* Baltimore?" I had to admit I had not. Art had been there recently. More than once, in fact, but I wasn't paying attention. I was too busy at work to notice his frequent comings and goings.

Illinois politics had reared its ugly head again, and after six years of very successfully making sense out of the chaos that had been Chicago area commuting, the RTA was dismantled. Most of the managerial level people had been rescued by their 'Chinamen' and safely placed in other political jobs. Art was once again a Management Consultant. It was the summer of 1982, and Art had passed his sixtieth birthday.

Even though his regular paychecks stopped coming, we were unconcerned. Tired of supporting what he called 'an expensive warehouse', we had long since shipped off to our daughters all their remaining belongings, pared down, and moved to a townhouse more conveniently located to public transportation. Art was contentedly describing himself as retired, but occasionally consulting. He knew he was not going to connect with another job and that seemed to suit him just fine; he liked being retired, within walking distance of our sailboat. Sometimes a consulting assignment sent him off to another part of the country for a few days, but never for long. When he was not traveling, I liked finding dinner cooking

---

[6] Translates as "Let's Go."

when I returned home from work. So what was this about Baltimore, I wondered?

"Why do you ask about Baltimore?"

"Because I wanted to know if you thought you would like to live there."

"What?! Who?! What's going on?" Suddenly, I felt as if I had skipped a chapter in the book.

"Well, I didn't want to tell you, because it seemed pretty remote. The chief purchasing job in Baltimore is open and they've been romancing me a bit. I just thought it might be an opportunity to return to our roots. What do you think?"

"I think it sounds interesting and I want to know more. But what do you mean about our roots?"

"You and I were brought up on the East Coast. Even though we've been away for a long time, wouldn't you like to go back to where you came from for retirement? Back home?"

For nearly forty years I had understood where my home was and it had nothing to do with geography; I would follow him wherever he went.

"Sure. What's the current plan?"

"They've asked me to come back for a final interview with the mayor and I think they're going to offer me the job. Pack your bag and we'll go take a look at the town."

As our plane dipped over the city of Baltimore, I looked down on the Inner Harbor. Sun sparkled on the water, boats at the marina bobbed merrily in the wind. I could see people strolling along the broad walkways, enjoying the splendid autumn day. My heart began to beat faster; something about the scene caught my imagination. When Art led me to the waterfront, I was hooked. We had arrived from our hotel by an elevated walkway over the busy streets. What a civilized city, I thought, nothing like Chicago. It was nearly November, and the air had a soft freshness about it.

"Art, do the boats stay in the water all winter? Don't they freeze?"

"No, they don't freeze. It gets cold here, but not cold enough to lock in the boats. In D.C. they have circulating pumps around the hulls to keep the water moving, but I don't think that's necessary here. Remember, the water's somewhat salty."

Recalling those frigid days when we had waited too long to put up our boat and suffered mightily on the trip to a winter storage boatyard, I breathed a sigh of relief. What a great place to have a boat!

Falling in love has very little logic — it's a mystery of the heart. We had lived in many places, and each had its charms; I was in love with Baltimore.

"God, I hope you get the job!"

Art turned to me with an amused smile. "You really love packing up and moving that much? All those boxes, all that mess?"

"Just get us here, and I'll take care of the moving, O.K.?"

Art's interview with Mayor William Donald Schaefer was surprisingly devoid of the usual questions about experience or knowledge. Mr. Mayor wanted to talk about his hero, the mayor of Chicago, Richard J. Daley. How does he keep everybody in line? What's his technique for handling the press? Is he really as popular as the press says he is? At the end, Mayor Schaefer turned to his finance czar.

"Is he satisfactory to you? Yes? O.K., get it done."

The city of Baltimore had hoped to avoid underwriting the cost of moving us from Chicago; they had no budget to cover it. Art made it clear: no pay, no move. Once the mayor had put his stamp of approval on the deal, it was a bad idea to back up, so in the end a way was found and the deal was closed. Art reported for work at City Hall on November 2, 1982. For him, a major consideration was that the city had already closed the contract with a company to equip the city with television cable.

"That," he said, "would be a political nightmare I want no part of. My predecessor got that done before he retired."

Once Art was settled into his new office, he discovered that the cable contract had been contested and thrown out by the city Board of Review on a technicality. Mayor Schaefer appointed Art to head a blue-ribbon commission to go through the entire process again.

"Get all the CEOs you can muster to join you: Bell Telephone, Baltimore Gas and Electric, all the majors. They won't be a lot of help with the work, but they're unassailable and non-political. You noticed the deadline coming up in a couple of months? Meet it." Mayor Schaefer was decisive and he brooked no excuses. Art rolled up his sleeves, assembled phone numbers and set to work.

In the meantime, back in Illinois, I worked frantically to wind up my responsibilities at work. It had been only two years since my employer paid the tuition for me to return to college and earn my bachelor's degree. How could I bail out without tying up all the loose ends, at the very least? I had been promoted to handle all the data processing for the New York subsidiary, and I needed several months to settle design issues. Art agreed to live in a rented apartment until I could break away. When one of us felt too lonesome, Ozark Airline flew me to Baltimore for a weekend.

"Boy," exclaimed Art during one evening's phone chat, "my phone bill is getting pretty big. You better hurry up."

"Mine, too," I said, "but I'm almost there. Maybe next month I can wrap it up. Then I'll get the boat ready to travel."

That part came a little sooner than I planned. The boatyard called me. "Mrs. Fournier, that last storm was too much for your boat's tarpaulin. Tore it right off, and now the cabin is knee-deep in water. Froze up, I'm afraid."

"I'm on my way. Have a crew ready to give me a hand, please." I pulled on my snow boots, grabbed an axe and shovel and backed the car out of the drive into the cold night. When I climbed the ladder, shoveled snow out of the cockpit, and opened the cabin door I gasped. In the beam of my flashlight, I could see a smooth skating rink where the cabin sole should have been. The water was almost to the tops of the cabin benches. Maybe with a little judicious ice-breaking I could feed a pump below the surface of the ice and empty the cabin. I pulled on my leather mittens, buttoned my collar against the chill wind, and carefully swung the axe. My flashlight rattled from the blow, but the axe bounced. Another smack, harder. The axe glanced off and went crashing down into the blackness. I trained the light beam down and saw the axe lying there, out of reach. Did I dare to step on the ice? Would I break through? Where was that crew they promised me, anyway?

"Mrs. Fournier, you're not going to get anywhere that way. The temperature is below zero and the water is frozen all the way to the bottom."

"Am I glad to see you! What am I going to do?"

"Let me put heaters in here and we'll see if we can get it loosened up. We just needed to have you look at it and approve the plan."

"Do whatever it takes to get her back in service, and I'll check with my husband to see what he wants to do beyond that. Be careful with the heaters, though. Don't want to melt any fiberglass." I drove home with visions of a cracked hull bouncing around in my head. Damn this Chicago winter, anyway! By the time I called Art, he was already in bed, but he came alert when I described the situation. I was close to tears.

He soothed my ruffled feelings, congratulated me for my efforts, and said he had the answer. "When they drain the cabin, I'll hire a truck to haul her down here to warmer weather. Leave it to me from here, Darling. We didn't name her Allons Y for nothing. I'll find her a berth tomorrow and get the yard moving up there." Within a week, our sailboat was rolling to her new home just off the Patapsco River, in Maryland.

Allons Y on a summer day in Wilmette, Illinois

By early spring, our townhouse was rented, the movers hired, and my job wrapped up. My boss in the New York subsidiary, Martin Mandato, urged me to come to New York to work for him there.

"Martin, I am moving to Baltimore and that's the fact. I love working for you, it has been grand, but now it's goodbye. I'm going to have to find a job there. Keep in touch." I really did hate leaving the company, but New York was a world away from Baltimore. Oh well, I would manage.

Art had driven Mother's car to Baltimore and the movers loaded our other car into the big truck with the furniture. Mother and I waved farewell to the Midwest and took off for BWI. I would not see Chicago again for many years.

BAWLIMER LIFE

Never mind how it's spelled. Don't pay attention to the AMTRAK conductor, who cries "Baaall-tee-more" as the train slows, coming into the station. Local folks know to say Bawlimer. I never got it quite right, though my affection for the town of the Baltimore Colts, the Baltimore Orioles, and the Inner Harbor just kept on growing. Art and I consulted a very pleasant young man, a real estate broker. Patiently, I described our needs to him: at least three bedrooms, as long as there was an additional den, a living room, a kitchen, of course, and two or three baths. I stressed that a separate dining room was a definite requirement, as we had a large and beautiful set of dining room furniture. We wanted another townhouse, but would consider a free-standing house. Art was mindful of Mayor Schaefer's question: "You will live in the city, won't you, Al?" (As closely as they worked together for years, Art would be forever Al to the mayor.) The requirement was a political one—Art's choice, of course. We looked in the city, but saw nothing good. Art read the real estate section of the Baltimore Sun, and came up with a likely townhouse candidate, but the broker was a little doubtful. He was willing to go there, but we understood from the outset that something was wrong.

"Art, I like it. The third bedroom is a bit small, but it's only for when the kids visit, and the downstairs den is very spacious. Look how private the two patios are. And the price is very reasonable, too. What do you think?"

The broker interrupted my train of thought. "Mrs. Fournier, there is no dining room here. True, the living room is large, but it would hardly work with your formal furniture, now would it?" He made a move to leave.

"Oh, that's OK. I'll just give our dining room furniture to one of our daughters. We can buy something newer, smaller. How about it, Art?"

The broker stood there, mouth open, shaking his head, while Art agreed that it was a good buy. I have always thought it was out of spite that the broker never found a way to warn us that this was an entirely Jewish enclave. That fact, apparently, accounted for the lower-than-market price — the range of buyers was narrower. We signed the contract and found out soon enough who our neighbors were in this townhouse complex adjacent to Pikesville, Maryland.

In the many neighborhoods we had called home, we always felt culturally comfortable, even when our liberal, Eastern views were different from the norm. We thought we were sophisticated, but suddenly we had become the neighborhood token gentile family. Soon, we learned there was a token African-American family, too. One of each. Now what?

It may have been our interest in boating that made the difference, maybe not. Even among those who had no idea we were sailors, we were welcomed into the neighborhood. Two families, the Rosenblooms and the Foxes, latched on to Art, coaxing him to join the Coast Guard Auxiliary and the Maryland Yacht Club. Even though we never kept our boat at the yacht club, Art and I were part of the gang. We flipped hamburgers at the cook-outs, were asked to come along when there was a cruise, sometimes in our own boat, sometimes in one of theirs. Hilford Caplan took a special interest in Art's membership in the Auxiliary, while his wife, Annette, welcomed me.

Where was the storied clannishness, the closed circle I had heard about all my life? Such myths vanished in thin air; these were gracious, generous friends that lasted a lifetime.

Before I engaged fully in Baltimore life, Art and I traveled to Hampden, Massachusetts, to meet our new grandson, Adam Arthur. I think he was the most beautiful baby born in 1983, even without taking a grandmother's bias into account. I rocked him and changed him, dressed him and sang lullabies to him. Art helped with the remodeling of their country house, a process that would continue for years.

When we were at last settled in our townhouse with stylish new Danish furniture, I went job hunting. The best offering was with the data processing department of the First National Bank. I got a job as analyst and moved into a little cubicle all my own. Surrounded by beige fabric panels, I sat in my contoured beige office chair at a large beige desk under a bright light. A black telephone was my only accessory. Although the office was on the twenty-third floor, right downtown, there were no distracting vistas of the Inner Harbor or the bustling streets below. Only tedium.

The bright spot in my day was lunch. Only four or five blocks to the harbor, and I was restored to life. Sunshine sparkled on the water, sailboats bobbed at the marina docks, and water taxis skimmed back and forth. Inside one of the buildings at the waterfront was a shop where I could buy thick slices of French bread topped with bubbling melted cheese. I walked along, munching this fat-and-carbohydrate-rich feast with a smile on my face and a spring in my step. Sometimes, Art would walk down from city hall and we met for half an hour. We stopped to watch the old man clicking two spoons on his knee to the rhythm of the band playing on the sidewalk nearby. We stepped aside as rollerbladers whizzed past.

Those interludes were worth all the boredom of a dull job. Well, almost. The work day was eight hours long, lunch lasted an hour.

One afternoon, my phone rang. It was Martin Mandato, a voice from the near past. "How do you like your new job, Kit? We miss you here in New York."

"Martin, it's a living. Worse than before, but I'm surviving. What's new?"

"Did I tell you we miss you? Why don't you come work for me?" This conversation repeated about once every ten days, and while I enjoyed a quick chat with him, it didn't make me feel any better.

One day, he told me he was coming to Baltimore with his data processing manager to talk to me about coming back.

"But Martin, New York is a long way to commute. Don't be silly." They came, just the same.

"Kit, we have it all figured out. You won't have to come to New York any more than you want to. We'll get a terminal in your house with a dedicated line, and you can work right at home. What will it take to move you? What do you want?"

After I thought about what seemed a preposterous plan, I decided to kid him a little. What would it take, indeed? I pulled a number out of a hat, substantially greater than my bank salary, and I named that. Martin frowned. I *thought* that would back him off.

"No, I don't think so," he said. "The big advantage for you is that we'll reinstate your pension plan. Only three years to full vesting. But just to settle the deal, I'll up your bid a couple thousand. What do you say?"

I understood that I would be committing to three more years, and that Art might want to retire before that. I looked at him. He grinned and shrugged. "Up to you, Babe." I took in a deep breath.

"OK, Martin, I guess we have a deal." They went away happy but I was overwhelmed. What had I done? Could I prove myself worth all that money and trouble? I wasn't so sure.

The next day, I knocked on my supervisor's office door at the bank. He waved me to a chair. "Glad you came in, Kit. We want to talk to you about taking on a new assignment. As you know, your immediate boss has gone home on extended leave. Frankly, I doubt she will be back any time soon. After her baby is born in six weeks, and she stays home to be a mother, well, she told me not to hold my breath. So, how would you like a promotion to manage all the data processing for the trust department?" He sat back confidently, waiting for my happy reaction.

"Sir, I cannot tell you how honored I am." Actually, I was reviewing my low opinion of the trust department people I had met. "But the fact is I came in this morning to tender my resignation. My previous employer wants me to return, and I accepted."

"What would it take to persuade you to change your mind?" he asked, leaning forward.

I named my new salary. He whistled, stood up, reached across his desk, shook my hand, and wished me well. Said he was sorry, but that was a little out of their league. It's true that banks pay better in titles than money, and I knew there was no chance of their meeting the figure. After tying up a few loose ends, I left the bank with no regret, except for the lovely lunch hours.

My task for the New York company was to design a new customer billing system, a formidable assignment. Calculations of post-Tefra contributions, whose withdrawals are calculated on a LIFO (last in first out) basis, against pre-Tefra, that work the other way and have to be accounted for separately, even in the same customer account, kept my supply of scratch paper hopping. Oh, never mind! It's enough to say that it was all very complicated and esoteric. These manipulations culminated in screens that would be used by clerks in the home office to record money in and out. The screens needed to be clear and simple for clerks who had no background in the inner workings of the system. Designing these screens exercised my imagination, because I could not actually see them. The communication between me and New York was too primitive to bring up the results of my work on my computer terminal.

From time to time, I did commute to Manhattan to take a good look at what I had done, conferring with some of the clerks to be sure they understood the forms before them. The work was complex and challenging; I loved it. Traveling by AMTRAK to New York was a pleasure, two hours and fifteen civilized minutes, as the billboards advertised it. The president of the company, meeting me in the hallway, exclaimed, "Kit, you came all the way from Baltimore? How long did it take you?" "About as long as your trip in from Connecticut this morning, sir," I answered. To a New Yorker, two and a half hours each way can be standard. The office, at the corner of Fifth Avenue and Forty-second Street, was high enough to survey lower Manhattan. On a clear day, I could see Miss Liberty, a doll-like figure on a tiny island, boats chugging up the Hudson, and a commuter-helicopter landing beside the East River. This was a close second to melted cheese lunches.

Meanwhile, back at Baltimore City Hall, Art was turning the world upside down. Just under the wire, he had brought in a favorable cable contract that was accepted by the Board of Review. Now it was time to shape up what had deteriorated into a very sloppy purchasing function. Employees appeared at whatever hour suited them and spent much of the day complaining and bickering. Morale had reached bottom. His African-American deputy devoted much of her time to undermining his authority, angry that she had not been appointed to his job. One saving grace was Art's secretary, an experienced, skilled, loyal white woman, Ches Robbins. She provided a link to past practice and an oasis in the desert of strife. A few senior people, such as Ed Collins, formed the skeletal backbone of what he was determined would become an honest, efficient department.

He was caught in the crossfire of racial warfare in a city that now had a black majority. Art's concept of a day's work for a day's pay came as a revelation to many of the staff, and was often seen as discriminatory. Four times, he was sued in the Civil Service Court for racial discrimination, four times he was exonerated. Once, a complainant returned to him some time after her dismissal. She told him that she was sorry, that she had misunderstood the difference between discipline and discrimination.

One issue was his practice of withholding the paycheck of an employee who was chronically late to work. Paychecks were distributed as the first order of business on Friday morning, but withheld from tardy employees. One by one, they stormed his office, demanding their checks.

"You will have your check this afternoon," he said. "It will be a little late."

"You can't do that!" they sputtered.

"Ah, but you and the city have a contract. If you live up to your part of the bargain, the city will live up to its side. But if you're late, the city will be late. Just be glad the city is not as late as you have been this month!" In fact, the checks were given out before the end of the day, but the point was made. Some got the point, some did not.

Of the more than three hundred people under Art's wing, way too many were lazy, disgruntled workers who had never had a chance to take pride in doing competent work. The print shop was among the worst departments. Their work was running behind more than days—weeks—and getting worse. He got to know the people in that shop, and picked out one woman from the ranks. She was black, as were most of the others, and a tough old bird, he said.

"I challenged her to get them shaped up. She said she could do it if I would help, and I told her she had whatever she needed. They've caught up the backlog of work in just a month, things are humming along, morale is high, and they're proud. I gave them a little celebration and a small bonus."

Department by department, Art pulled it all together. Training upgraded the skills of those who aspired to do better. Challenges dropped on Art like rain. He had the misfortune to be in the path of the mayor's wrath over a school bus fight, although it was in no way part of his responsibility. Art learned from the outset that you never said 'not my job' to the mayor, so when he was charged with the burden, he took it. The bus companies had ruled the city by ganging up and threatening to strike just as school was about to start. By staggering contracts among companies, he brought order to negotiations and peace to that aspect of the city.

Baltimore provided moments of high comedy. Where else would the mayor don a striped bathing suit and straw hat and plunge into the seal pool of the still unfinished aquarium, holding on to his rubber ducky? He had promised the facility would be opened on schedule or he would dive in himself. Rumor had it that completion was held up until hizzoner took the plunge. Probably true, since Don Schaefer was a public relations genius. The swim got national press coverage.

When the city had no money to fix potholes, he declared, "Then we'll sell 'em!" Potholes went for $10 to $25, depending on size and location. For that money, the buyer would get a repaired pothole and the initials of his choice painted in a heart on the street. The drive was started just before Valentine's Day and holes went like hotcakes. Art bought one for me; they were very chic.

Even though the mayor was a straightforward man of plain speech, the city hired a high-powered interior designer to furnish executive offices in City Hall. One day, the mayor returned from a trip to Annapolis to find his office redecorated. Where before were untidy piles of papers, now sleek cabinets lined the walls. In the center of the room was a very expensive executive table in place of a desk. There were no drawers, only a pen set and a telephone on top. The mayor's legendary temper exploded. No amount of justification made the slightest impression on him; he wanted a REAL DESK, this at the top of his voice.

Staff retreated, and his secretary put in a call to Art. "Art, we need a desk for the mayor. He wants a real, old-fashioned desk. And he wants it now."

Art had a pretty good handle on the mayor's personality, and he understood the mission. He sent a staff member down to the city warehouse to search, but nothing turned up. Suddenly, Art had it. His friend Paul, the City Jail warden, had a big, old roll-top desk in his office. Art lifted the phone. "Paul, I need for you to do me a favor."

"Sure, Art. Whatever you need."

"I need your desk."

"You need what?"

"Your desk, Paul. A couple of guys are on their way over to pick it up. Just pile your stuff on the floor, go over to the warehouse and pick out any desk you find there. We have some dandies. You can get it delivered tomorrow. But I've got to have your desk today."

"What's this heist about, Art?"

"The mayor. He needs your desk."

"Oh. OK. But you do owe me one."

The following week, Art sat in a reviewing stand for a parade. Mayor Schaefer appeared, climbed up to where Art was sitting, and clapped him on the shoulder. "Love the desk, Al. You got it just right." Art said he added some bawdy opinions of interior designers that he wouldn't repeat to me. That was a banner day in our household.

At Christmas, a Santa's House was erected at the Inner Harbor. Inside, Santa Claus greeted the children who came by the hundreds. First to don the red suit was the mayor, then city executives had their turn. This was corny stuff and many rolled their eyes. The point is: it worked. This charismatic leader took the people out of a tired, broken old city into a new place of hopeful possibilities.

Still Art's deputy and her cohorts waged guerilla warfare. On his blackboard appeared incredibly filthy racist graffiti. He declared that he would prevail, but I could see that the emotional cost was enormous. Despite his sense of accomplishment, the combat was wearing him down. What began as a happy adventure degenerated, and the soldier was battle-weary.

Just before his sixty-fifth birthday, he announced his retirement, to the mayor's dismay. Although he could stay until his seventieth birthday, Art walked away. Shortly after his departure, Mayor Schaefer was elected governor, a new mayor moved in, and Art's deputy was appointed City Purchasing Agent. The waters closed over Art's reforms as if he had never existed.

TROUBLE IN PARADISE

When did it begin to come apart? I suppose that parents of married children seldom know the answer to that. The little wedges that wriggle their way between husband and wife go along unrecognized—or at least unacknowledged—for some time. Susan knew that we shared her hope for a successful marriage, and to preserve the illusion she papered over the cracks whenever we visited. From the beginning, we were disturbed by Tim's propensity to drink more alcohol than we thought wise, but we kept quiet. Certainly the births of Douglas and Michael gave the couple strong common interests. Tim struggled through a troubled career start, but at last managed to hang out his shingle as a sole-practitioner lawyer. Susan, a quick-study, became his paralegal assistant and office manager. We knew their road was bumpy, but had no idea how bad it was.

Near the end, Tim came to visit us alone, clearly to solicit our support in his decision to sue Susan for divorce. His thirst for alcohol, now quite naked, saddened us. When he returned to Michigan, Susan had already filed. It became Tim's stated goal to destroy his wife, and if needed, take down the whole family. His behavior appalled and frightened us, especially Art, who traveled to Michigan to give Susan support in the courtroom. The proceedings were incredibly ugly, involving a court order for Tim to stay away from the street on which she lived. We feared for her safety; Tim was a violent man.

The marriage officially ended in 1988, sixteen years after it had begun.

03 80 03 80

Three years later, Annie made the decision to separate from Larry. Unwisely, we tried to persuade her to reconsider, to work it out, to smooth it over. Two broken families in our midst seemed like more than we could bear. Our own sadness prevented us from realizing that these marriages were not about us. Though we were all close — and therefore vulnerable — we needed to let go.

The instruction book for parents contains no chapter about how to let go of your children. The trick is to let go without letting them go.

Somewhere in the process, we began to learn where the boundaries were: we were no more entitled to participate in their life decisions than they were in ours. All we could do was love them and hope for their love in return. We watched helplessly as Annie struggled to reconcile her need for her own life with her commitment to her promise. Her inner strife lasted six years; the divorce was final in 1997, twenty-three years after that rainy day in the rose garden.

CB ED CB ED

On March 17, 1990, Susan married Gordon Campbell. He was a man she had known in business for many years, and we liked him right away. His business was economic development, but his personal goal was to nurture Susan's two sons. The boys had suffered at the hands of their father, and Gordon helped each find his way to an independent life. The family moved to Indiana, giving Art and me relief from worry about Tim's violence. Gordon was more than a dozen years older than Sue, and an habitual smoker. His health began to cause some concern, but we were startled by her phone call in January, 1998.

Susan and Gordon with Mike and Doug

"Mom, could you get Dad to pick up the extension? I need to talk to both of you." I signaled Art to get the kitchen phone. "I'm calling you from the hospital. Gordon has been diagnosed with cancer and it is very far advanced. There is no hope to turn it around, only a slim chance that he can make it to Michael's graduation in May." Her voice was desolate. After a few minutes of halting conversation—we did not know what to say—we promised to be in touch again soon.

Gordon went home and Susan tried to juggle his care with her job, an hour's drive each way. She needed to continue the job that provided the health insurance they were now depending on. Art and I were distraught. My mother needed me in Williamsburg, our daughter needed us in Indiana.

After one particularly sad phone call, Art turned to me. "She needs me to be there. You stay here and keep the home fires burning. I'll catch a plane and take over Gordon's care at home." The next day, he was gone. We talked every day, and I tried not to cry, knowing it would only make the situation worse. What could I do?

I had just finished reading a book about coping with illness. It was filled with hope, and I wondered if that would do Gordon good. Since his eyes were affected by his illness, I knew he could not read. But he could listen. I set up a recorder, sat down at the microphone, and began on page one. As each cassette was finished, I hurried to the post office, hoping it would give him some benefit.

Art needed to take a breather, and he flew home for a few days. I arranged for added help for Mother at home, and the two of us drove the car back to Indiana. On March twenty-second, five days after the eighth anniversary of their marriage, Gordon died.

His funeral was a major event in their small town. He had brought new industry and new hope to a part of the Midwest that was sinking in the 'rust-belt' recession. His going left a gaping hole in all our lives.

WANDERERS

A rt's retirement was a pleasure to me. That old woman's joke about marrying him for better or worse but not for lunch had no place in our Baltimore house. In the middle of the day, he called down to my office, "Lunch is on the table, Hon." I trudged up the stairs to find the table set with steaming bowls of soup—his favorite—or tuna salad with hard-boiled eggs.

Sometimes I worked far into the night to unravel a mathematical puzzle. I logged my hours to be sure I gave my employer just enough. That way, I could steal away on Friday for a weekend on the *Allons Y*, discovering new rivers and harbors on the Bay, or sailing up the Patapsco River to the Inner Harbor.

"When are you going to give it up and be a bum like me?" Art asked.

"When I'm vested and have the system running."

"Too long. Vested is enough. You're not the only programmer in the world, and you have all the designs in place, right?"

"Right. But what's your hurry? What would you do different?"

"Get out of town, Babe, soon as we can."

"What do you mean? Am I going to be a migrant again?"

"Look. Maryland's taxes are tough on old folks. We could profit from crossing a state line—almost any state line. Besides, I never want to see snow again. How about Florida?"

"I don't like Florida. You want to leave the Chesapeake Bay? That's crazy! People come from all over the world to sail these waters and we're lucky enough to be right here."

We agreed to begin a search in Virginia, the only state that made any sense for us. By the end of the year, I would own my pension, and summer was already well under way.

I remember finding a house on a bluff, overlooking a river. Maybe it was the Rappahannock, or it might have been the Piankatank. Below us, water sparkled in the sunshine, lapping against a sturdy dock. The flower garden outside the kitchen door was ablaze with cosmos and hollyhocks. True, the house needed some work, but it seemed possible to us, and the price was certainly favorable. The nearest town was several miles away, though.

"What about Charlotte?" Art asked.

"Look at this garden. I think she'd like it, don't you?"

"Kit, we're going to travel. We'll be gone a lot. Who would look after her?" I drew in my breath. Of course. He was right. Could we leave even a healthy, independent nearly-ninety-year-old woman to fend for herself in a strange countryside? No. Right there, we redrew our parameters. Neither Kilmarnock nor Urbanna appealed. We even explored a retirement community there.

"How about Williamsburg? It's at least near the water. They have good medical facilities."

"And the kids love it. They would visit us there!"

We found Chambrel. Neither one of us yearned to live in 'an old folks home', but we toyed with the idea. No conversation topic had ever been off limits between Art and me, but neither of us expressed what I am sure both thought: it would surely be only a brief arrangement, and then we would be free. Chambrel required no long-term financial commitment, only monthly rent. But would Charlotte go for it?

Mother listened to our idea, and I think I saw her swallow hard. "Well," she said, "we could take a look, couldn't we!" She promised to be realistic in her assessment, and we put her to the test. She would stay there overnight while we found a motel. She would be on her own. I worried, because Mother was very shy. It seemed to me taking up residence there required some openness, some outgoing impulse.

One afternoon, we walked through the door to Chambrel's big living room. Three women sat there talking, but when they saw us, rose to greet us. No, they rose to greet Mother. They ignored us altogether.

"Do you play bridge?" She was a short, slender woman, dressed with New York style. Her glasses were framed in cherry red, her shoes were scandalously high-heeled. Mother smiled and replied that she did. "You're in!" cried Marge Hughel. "We've been waiting for a good fourth." Soon, all were engrossed in introductions, comparisons of previous lives, small talk. After a word or two, we slipped away to our motel.

In the morning, we returned to tour the grounds and look over the apartments. We settled on a two-bedroom, light and airy one that we thought would do nicely. Mother seemed happy about her new-found friends. As always, decisive Art was glad to keep moving forward. We would be Chambrel residents by Thanksgiving dinner.

Back in Baltimore, I phoned Martin Mandato to lay out our decision and plan for my departure. He told me he was pleased for us, that he would take care of the business details. I could go at my convenience. He kept from me the fact that he had held on to my position against strong pressure from the president. The company was in financial difficulty and belt-tightening was a necessity, but Martin honored his promise to see me through to vesting in my pension. Soon afterward, the company was sold, and Martin lost his job as vice-president and treasurer. His bravado concealed all this from me; I learned it much later from the data processing manager. All my design work disappeared; it had been for nothing.

Once more, we diminished our store of worldly goods. Both daughters arrived — I believe I remember a trailer — and took away some of our now-unneeded furniture. Much more went into a Williamsburg storage locker.

I suppose it may have been our consolation prize to ourselves that we put *Allons Y* up for sale and began to hunt for our dream boat. Now we were finicky, looking for comfort and luxury but speed, too. Motor-sail types turned out to be more motor than sail, slogging through the water like floating elephants. One even boasted a clothes washer! We moved to Williamsburg without a boat.

At last, in a remote creek in Poquoson, our dream boat finally appeared: a ten year old Pearson 365 (meaning she was thirty-six and a half feet long) in beautiful condition. Her ketch rig made her easy for us to handle and her four-and-a-half-foot draft made cruising in shallower waters possible. The Chesapeake has wide water spread very thin. One blustery afternoon, we sailed her home to York River Yacht Haven on Sara's Creek. I was glad the salesman, young Dan Bacot, came along with us, for he knew the water and had more large-boat experience than either of us. Handling her big wheel in a blow scared me more than a bit.

Maintaining marine varnish requires more patience and determination than we had. We found out how much work it was to strip the trim down to bare wood, but it was finally protected by teak finish. We were proud owners of the handsome lady that became *Sérénité*. Art wanted another French name, but this time vowed it would be something that would be correctly pronounced over the VHS radio. He was tired of hearing "Allens Why! Allens Why! Come in please!"

"This will be a cinch. Everybody will recognize it, and it's pronounced the same in English. Just a little bit different spelling, that's all." He was too optimistic. We were going to hear "Sara-nite, Sara-nite, come in please!" Oh well.

Living at Chambrel provided for Mother the security that we anticipated and a daily bridge game. It granted me a vacation from cooking and housekeeping. Art joined the local Coast Guard Auxiliary and promptly began teaching basic boating courses. I found the Unitarian Universalist church that was just was beginning to meet in the public library. Our roots burrowed down.

Art was right about the travel, though. In the next three years, we visited California, Hawaii, and Michigan and we cruised up the Rhine and down the Danube.

TRAVEL DIARY

In sixteen years, beginning in 1984, Art and I visited eighteen different countries. In between, we managed to get to Hawaii and Alaska, as well as wandering around in the northeast and northwest parts of our own country. Still, Art complained that I was dragging my feet.

"C'mon, Babe, it's not too soon to start planning the next trip. We have a long list of places to go and not near enough time."

"Please! Let me get the suitcases emptied and the laundry done before you go off on some other wild good chase."

"Hey—how come it's always so hard to get you out of town, yet when we're out there, you do fine? You a homebody or something?"

"I just think we need to husband our resources a little. Neither time nor energy is boundless, you know. And besides, I like being home—touching base with people, going to church, looking out our own windows. Don't you?"

"Sure I do. But here's a chance to cruise both the Rhine and the Danube on one trip! It's a University of Michigan group, and the new president will be going along. Look at this!" He handed me a colorful brochure and I shook my head. Can't argue with passion, I thought. Echoes of Hawaii were still ringing in my mind, and it was true that those bags were waiting to be unpacked. I sighed and opened the folder.

Art's lust for new geography, new cultures, new knowledge drove him all his life. Curiosity made him a good student and an observant traveler; his retentive memory catalogued every place he visited and all the places he traveled in reading. Eric Hansen's *Stranger in the Forest: On Foot Across Borneo*[7] captivated him for weeks, although he never suggested

---

[7] (Boston; Houghton Mifflin,1988)

we go there. Some really exotic locales chilled him, generally on health grounds; he never offered me a trip to sub-Saharan Africa, although he did urge India. On culture grounds, I declined that one; so much poverty intimidated me. Art soaked up all the details of *The Greek Islands,*[8] (an evocative guide written by the author and poet Lawrence Durrell) in the hope that we would one day cruise in the waters of the Aegean Sea. He wanted to be prepared.

Unfamiliar situations have always made me uneasy. Although I have learned to meet new people with a semblance of sociability, it is only a very small, familiar circle that puts me at ease. My remarkably poor facial memory certainly doesn't help. Art's gregarious nature and insatiable curiosity carried me along, helping me with names and poking into corners of the world I never would have braved alone.

ဆ ၼ

Our second flight across the Atlantic took us to France. After a few days in Paris and a side trip to the Loire Valley alone, we moved on to Marseillan to join a cruise up the Canal du Midi. There were only nine of us, and a crew of five on a barge that had been converted from hauling cargo. All the other barges were operated by English companies; our *Athos* by Pierre Noubel, a native of Castlenaudary.

Sunday morning, the first town on our itinerary was Aigues Mortes (Dead Waters), the jumping-off place for Louis IX, leading an army in the first Crusade. We stopped outside a local church and eavesdropped on the sermon to local sinners. Art interpreted. "Listen! He's flaying the flock, telling them how they have sinned and what they will pay. Let's move on."

This strict Catholic practice came down in a line from days of the Inquisition. We saw Minervois where hundreds had been burned for refusing to recant, a mountaintop — Mont Segur — where the last holdouts were starved into submission

---

[8] (New York; Viking Press, 1978)

or death. Such brutality in the name of religion mystified me, coming as I did from a modern liberal heritage. Art was more revolted than mystified.

More cheerfully, we paid a visit to Pierre's parents in Castlenaudary. His father, a retired pharmacist, lived in a sixteenth century house in town. The windows on the street were shuttered—no wonder, since they were less than three feet from the sidewalk. I didn't expect the beauty and luxury we found inside. Oriental rugs and priceless antique furniture, leather-bound volumes in the library reflected the cultured people who lived there. Open windows looked out on sunny gardens with colorful flowers nodding in the breeze at the back of the house. Art had a conversation with Pierre's father about his signed commissions from Napoleon Bonaparte while Pierre's mother showed us her collection of glass, equal to any museum display.

On board the *Athos*, we lived in luxury, enjoying fresh-baked croissants from a bakery every morning. One of the crew bicycled to the nearest town to fetch them and loaves of still-warm bread for us, along with fresh peaches.

Unfortunately, a course of contagious stomach flu made its way through every cabin. Art spent a day laid low, though I escaped until we returned to Paris. There, I was sick for the two days until our return home. While I languished in bed, gazing out at the Louvre across the Seine from our small hotel, Art made forays of exploration. He reported on the Champs Elysées and the Arc de Triomphe, one day coaxing me out to the Pompidou Museum to laugh at the pool of outrageous sculptures. He dined on fine French fare, while the waiters could only coax me to down a little tea and bread, with just a taste of custard.

"Never mind," said Art, "we'll come back one day and really explore the city. Go down to see the Bayeux tapestry, too." I hoped, but we never did.

ಲ ೞ

Every now and then, Art's willingness to try new experiences got us into a little embarrassment, like the time we drove across England. We were going to Andy Rosner's wedding to Gina, his warm-hearted English bride, in Barnstaple, a North Devon town on the English west coast. We were to arrive in London, make our way from the airport to the train that would take us across England, where Andy would meet us. Still groggy from our long flight, we stumbled sleepy into the terminal. At the baggage claim, Art spied the Avis counter.

"Say! Why don't we drive instead?" We had certainly rented many cars in our time, and it seemed then to be obviously the best strategy. As I say, we were still sleepy. Renting a car in advance from the States would have saved us a good deal of money, but Art was a negotiator. After a few minutes' friendly conversation with the young lady behind the counter, he emerged grinning with the keys and a contract at the New York price.

As soon as we piled our luggage in and climbed into the little vehicle, we realized our mistake. Automatic shift was standard at home, but this car shifted manually. It was twenty-five years since our last experience with a manual shift. I would have returned to rectify the difficulty. Not Art. He would deal with what he had. In the dark of an early February morning, I tried to read the map while Art struggled to put the car in gear. Like most right-handed people, he had never needed to exercise the skill of his other hand. I, a sinister person living in a dexterous world, had little sympathy; life had forced a degree of ambidexterity on me.

"Damn lever is on the wrong side," he sputtered. "How am I supposed to shift gears with the wrong hand?"

"Shh. You don't need to shout at me. I'm having enough trouble reading the map. When you are quite done traveling around the drive in circles like some vulture, take the right fork up ahead and we'll get to the main road." He looked a little like an organist, crossing his right hand over to play the lever while fumbling around to coordinate his feet. Luckily, the traffic was light so far.

When we reached the main road west, four lanes each way stretched before us in the dawn. As the sun rose, more cars whizzed by at breakneck speed, honking their horns as they pulled around us.

"What's their problem?" complained Art. "I'm not going to speed like that. Why are they honking? There's room to pass." Suddenly, I recognized the problem—Art was clinging to the right shoulder as he would have done at home. Only, the right lane was the fast lane here. Once we got that squared away, the trip settled into routine. About noon, the route took us through a small city where the lanes were narrower and the traffic thick. Crash!

"What was that?"

"Oh blast! I've hit a parked car. Came too close. Look—the mirror is just hanging there. I've got to pull into a space and find the driver." Art jumped out of the car and strode into the pub, soon emerging with a burly Englishman. The two men examined the mirror. Art was apologetic, but the other man just snapped the arm of the mirror back into place, shook his hand, and returned to lunch in the pub.

"He said it was designed to break away like that. Seemed more annoyed about interrupting his lunch than fixing his car. Do you want to stop to eat? No? Good. We can make it in a couple more hours." We rolled on, Art finally getting the hang of it.

The next day was St. Valentine's Day. Andy claimed it was chosen so that he would never forget his wedding anniversary. All the guests trooped down to the registrar's office while the happy couple signed the book, a few words were said, and they were husband and wife. No churchy stuff for them.

Andy's mother, Maxine, repacked for her journey first to Italy and then up to Belgium. Art and I packed our suitcases into the little car and set off for the east. This time, I drove. Having seen that Art had conquered, I determined I could do no less.

Our stop at Stonehenge filled us both with awe. Gazing at that enigmatic construct of giant stones, I pondered what the Roman legions must have thought as they marched in formation over the distant hills to confront this wonder. We could wander among the monoliths, touching the cold stone, feeling ourselves pygmies among giants. Boiling, billowing clouds, bright at the edges and dark inside, rolled in the sky, hurled by strong winter winds to disappear over the horizon. We drove along in silence after that.

From London, we flew to Venice for a few days and from there to Florence. Maxine, wanting to bypass the city where she and George had spent idyllic days, substituted Milan and the opera, planning to meet us in Florence. We arrived in Venice in a cold rain, sniffed by dogs leashed by armed guards—not a friendly beginning. The rest of our stay disappointed us. Many museums were either closed or littered with scaffolding and drapes. Winter is the time of refurbishment.

We stopped at a jewelry store in St. Mark's Square to buy a necklace for little Jenny Katharine, our fourth grandchild—at last a girl. By now, she was only five months old, but I wanted something special that I could wear to her dedication service on Easter Sunday and put away for her sixteenth birthday. It turns out that grandmothers are more sentimental than practical—how could I guess that Jenny would grow up to be a tall, beautiful, athletic girl with no taste for a crystal necklace formed into lace? Maybe when she is old she will wear lavender scent and enjoy it then. At least she will know that we thought of her with love.

In spite of the chill, we loved Florence and wanted to stay much longer. Maxine joined us and we explored the city together. Art climbed to the top of Brunelleschi's Duomo, but we ladies were less brave. The ascent involved stooping along a steep stairway between the inner and outer domes in relative darkness until you reached the open cupola. Art assured us that the view was worth every step, and we took his word for it. I wanted to linger at the Baptistry doors forever.

In Ravenna, we took coins in hand and set out to find churches. Dark and ancient red brick in Romansque style, they looked forbidding from the outside. Inside, all was darkness. We fumbled for the coin machine, dropped in a coin, and gasped.
"Ooooohh! Magnificent!" we breathed in unison. The walls came alive in the sudden light. Bright mosaics dazzled our eyes, gold and silver tiles mingled with bright reds and blues to form pictures of remarkable beauty. These were the precursors to the great oil paintings we had seen in Florence. Nothing on the outsides of these buildings hinted at the treasures within.

Back on the train, we glided through the green Italian countryside, past neat farms and little villages. After stops in Sienna and Pisa, we stayed in Rome for several days. We traveled to Naples and on to Sorrento, took the ferry to the Isle of Capri, and rode up the Amalfi Coast. Never in my lifetime have I been more chilled to the bone. A cruel wind howled over the blue water, a sad surprise in this storied land. That record winter, it snowed in Sicily.

❧ ❧

In contrast, the next year we cruised from Rhode Island in one of the hottest summers on record. Aboard a small ship with about a hundred other passengers, we slept our way across Long Island Sound to wake at Hells Gate, entry to the East River and Manhattan.

"Oh Art, this is magical! Watching the city wake as first light turns the windows to bronze—I've never seen anything like it." We stood at the rail touching hands and breathing deep.

We floated down the river and around Manhattan to sail over and greet Lady Liberty, holding her torch above the Upper Bay. This was home to me, for I had traveled the Staten Island ferry countless times and gazed at the lady.

Art stayed up late when we reached Troy, up the Hudson River. He watched as the crew lowered the pilot house for entry into the Erie Canal the next morning. I was satisfied to go to bed still steeped in history of the places I knew and loved best.

Despite the ship's air conditioning, we sweltered in the 100° heat. Through the great locks of the St. Lawrence Seaway, we steamed down the St. Lawrence River, until we reached the Saguenay River. For an hour or more, we watched beluga and pilot whales feeding. Dozens of them swam around the ship consuming tons of fish.

Later, when we tied up at Pointe-au-Pic, the men of the town gathered at the dock. Clearly, we were the best show in the tiny, isolated town. Art walked around talking to them. He laughed when they told him how good his French was.

"Of course it is," he told me, "because I speak the same patois they do! The language I learned at home was born here in this land." He wanted to know more about his heritage, but that would wait for another time. The next day, we explored Québec City before boarding the bus for Rhode Island.

৪০ ೞ

When Art picked up the phone, something in his voice caught my attention. He was talking to a woman. There was no mistaking his warmth, his charm. I listened.

"Of course, my dear. I would be delighted. Whatever you want me to do. Yes. When, then? Yes, I'm sure I can make it. We'll talk again. Soon. Bye 'til then." When he put the phone back in its cradle, I was looking at him over my glasses, eyebrow raised. I didn't need to say a word. He savored the moment.

"W ell, I'll be damned!"

"That's all you're going to say? If you are going to sweet-talk some woman in my presence, the least you can do is explain yourself!"

"That was Diane. You know, Andy's mentioned her as a friend of his wife's, but I didn't realize she and Kent were an item. I guess they are, because she wants me to give her away at their wedding." I was nonplussed. For whatever reason, Di's family would not be traveling from England for the ceremony, so there would be no one to walk down the aisle with her. Kent explained to Di that Art was like a father to him and Andy since they had lost their own father to ALS. Kent suggested she call Art, even though they had never met.

"Well, then, I guess your sweet-talk is O.K. How very nice. Am I invited, too?"

Of course I was, and we flew out to Sacramento, California. The bride was a lovely young woman, and I thought her brave to dare to train a forty-year-old bachelor. She planned a wedding aboard a cruise boat on the Sacramento River, and the party would be complete with all the formal trappings, even to little flower girls. Art had some moments of doubt about her heartfelt wish that he dress in his officer's uniform of the Coast Guard Auxiliary, but he agreed that it would not be too egregious a violation of protocol.

The day was very warm with only a little breeze to relieve the blistering sun. Along the river banks, hordes of holiday revelers gathered to barbecue their picnics and listen to the jazz festival in full swing. It was Memorial Day weekend and the din was intense. The couple decided to continue upriver a little farther in hopes of escaping the loudest of the noise, but just as they were about to begin the ceremony, they realized the setting sun would be in everyone's eyes.

"Turn around," directed the groom. "and we'll marry floating downstream." The ship's captain swung the boat around, and we approached the noisy partygoers again. All at once, people on shore caught sight of the bride's gown and veil, and a great hoot went up. Throngs of jazz fans ran up to line the riverbank and cheer as handsome Captain Art walked solemnly up the deck with the bride on his arm. The words of their vows were lost in the background of jazz and cheering crowds, but their happy faces testified to the tying of the knot. The party aboard continued on into the night.

ৰু ७४

NO PROPERTY DAMAGE

"That it, Cap'n?" I poked my head out the cabin door and shouted over to the dock.

"Yep. That's enough provisions for a week, and we're only going to be gone three days. Unless we get shipwrecked."

Art handed crates of drinks and food over the rail, and I stowed everything below. It did seem like a lot, but experience told me too much was better than going hungry.

"Did you remember the charcoal?"

"Quit obsessing and start checking the lines for me, would you?"

Sérénité on another day

"Aye aye, sir." I clambered up the companionway to begin the departure check-off. Art climbed over the rail and disappeared down the ladder to the navigation table. He was checking his instruments, water and fuel levels, and listening one more time to the NOAA weather report. I wrapped the halyards around their winches, secured the sheets, brought up the cockpit cushions, the LORAN and VHF handsets, and put my navigation book on the bench. I unzipped the storm covers and stowed them, made sure docking lines were on top in the port cockpit locker, right below our life vests. These tasks completed, we returned to the stern cockpit bench and sat down.

"Well, lady, are you ready for one more little adventure on the Bay?"

"I am. And no matter what happens, I love you."

"Hey! Only thing going to happen is fun!" With that, he kissed me soundly and got up to start the engine. After a cough or two, the engine purred reassuringly, and I moved forward to begin casting off lines. As he backed out of the slip, I controlled the last line, and when we were free, threw it on the dock.

"All clear!"

As we chugged down Sara's Creek into the York River, the mother osprey screeched, warning us to stay away from her nestlings perched on top of a piling. I looked closely at the nest, made of branches and twigs, counting the babies.

"Art, there are four! Isn't that a big brood for ospreys?"

"Maybe. If they keep multiplying like that there won't be an unoccupied piling or navigation aid left on the Bay." The Coast Guard, prohibited from disturbing nests, patiently erected second markers when the birds took squatters' residence on the first ones. Fortunately, their sense of territory prevented another family from moving to the new space.

Sitting in the cockpit, I sighed happily. The sun was shining, a gentle breeze rippled the water; it looked like a perfect day ahead. Art winked at me and I knew he felt the same sense of joy and freedom.

"OK," he said, "let's get this barge under sail." As he brought the bow up into the wind and shifted the engine to neutral, I jumped forward to seize one halyard and haul up the mizzen. Once it was secured, I gave a tug to the jib sheet, unfurling it from its home on the forestay. Art shoved the wheel over to fall off, the canvas filled, and we were sailing. When he cut off the engine, peaceful silence fell. It was not quite silence, of course—as we slipped through the water, a gentle swish-swish floated back from the bow wave. Other than that, the sparkling world was at peace. Since we knew our way out to the bay, I had no navigation duties yet. I sat down next to him and buried my face in his shoulder.

"See? I told you. Only fun." After a while, Art relinquished the helm, knowing how much I enjoyed taking charge—here and elsewhere. When the sun was overhead and we were fully shaded by the bimini, Art spoke the familiar words: "What's for lunch and when?"

Turning over the wheel, I descended to the galley and lifted the lid of the refrigerator. I made a salami sandwich for him and a peanut butter for me with German rye bread. A serving of potato salad, a few chips, and a slice of tomato filled our plates.

"Want iced tea or O'Doul's?" I called. As usual, for lunch, he chose the beer. Because our rule was no alcohol until the boat was secured for the night, the beer was tame, but cold and refreshing. I carried the plates and bottles to the cockpit, and we settled down for a hearty lunch. The breeze was freshening, so Art loosed the sheets just a little. Sailing inefficiently, we were nevertheless upright and comfortable. We had plenty of time to reach the cove we had chosen the night before.

As if by magic, gulls appeared, wheeling and screeching, begging for a share of lunch. How they smelled the salami from long distance, I never figured out, but Art took pity on them, tossing crumbs into the air. Not one reached the water, so quick and agile were the birds. When I cleared away the lunch dishes, the gulls got the message and swooped off to find other benefactors.

The *Sérénité* was a grand ketch, nearly thirty-seven feet long, but her galley was not equipped with a dishwasher. Somehow, cleaning up the kitchen at home never seemed as pleasant as it was here. Art called it my doll house, where work was more like play.

At about four o'clock—I never did get used to the maritime 1600 hours—I spotted a buoy ahead that I had in my notes. It was time to navigate, for our cove would be up a river about a mile ahead. I turned on the LORAN and punched in a way-point. This wonderful device told me how far away and in what direction that point was located. The night before, using a chart of the area, I entered the latitudes and longitudes of the crucial places I wanted to locate. Today, LORAN would lead us to the cove. I remembered the days before LORAN, when every landing place was to the west, right in the path of the lowering sun.

"Remember that time we almost ran aground trying to find our way into Salt Ponds at sunset?" recalled Art. That heart-stopping moment was still clear in my mind when, intent on trying to identify what looked like a buoy in the shining streak ahead, I had failed to watch the depth sounder. When it read five feet—and falling—Art swung the bow sharply away and saved us from a struggle at the end of a hard day. Our boat needed four and a half feet of water.

Going from marker to marker was like connecting the dots. At the last one, Art started the engine. Taking in the sails was simply a matter of hauling on lines and securing them. I called from the bow, "Turn right and find a good spot to anchor." I lifted the lid on the anchor locker and pulled up the heavy iron weight, chains clanking.

"What's the mark up ahead?" queried Art.

"Don't know. Come up on it and let's see. Watch your depth, though." The floating mark was unfamiliar to me, following no convention I knew about. "Must be a swimming buoy," I called, "you know, to keep boats off the beach. Best to stay outside it."

Art circled back a little way and instructed, "Drop it now."

Feeding the anchor under the lifelines, I quickly let it down the side and into the water, paying out the anchor line until it hit bottom.

"OK," I called, "she's down. Back off and I'll snug her up." When I felt the anchor tug at the line, I let out some more line and cleated it down. The line was marked every six feet to allow me to judge how much to let out, depending on the depth and other conditions. After a quick calculation, the skipper always told me how much line should be out, and I was proud when I could say, "Done!"

Inside this cove, we were protected from the brisk wind on the river — only a gentle breeze blew from shore,.

Art went below and emerged carrying two real beers, icy cold. I did not remind him about the nice jackets to catch the drips, I just lifted the bottle and exclaimed, "Another successful landing. No one injured and no property damage."

"I'll drink to that!" And he did. Soon, he busied himself with attaching the barbecue to the stern rail and arranging a few lumps of charcoal. While he lit it, I lifted the cockpit table and set its leg down. Soon, linen, wine glasses, utensils and dishes were in place; I favored eating dinner in style. Even a glass-enclosed candle waited for a flame. Water for corn was bubbling on the stove, while potatoes were sizzling in the frying pan. Sliced tomatoes and cucumbers were marinating in a basil-laced vinaigrette. Art was just putting the hamburgers on the barbecue when I peered out from the companionway. My gaze went beyond him.

"Art, look! Back there! A whole fleet of sails. Aren't they beautiful in the rosy light!" Suddenly, the boats changed course and spinnakers came down.

"Omigod," he exclaimed, "it's a race. And we are in the race course!"

Sure enough, the entire fleet, probably more than a dozen of them, were heading right for us. We looked at each other in sudden dumb horror. The mysterious mark was a RACE MARK!

"Is it too late to move, Art?" I asked, already knowing the answer was yes. Having been racers ourselves, we appreciated the enormity of our trespass, but we could do nothing, only hope for the best.

As the boats roared toward us, I grabbed my camera. Might as well record the scene, I thought, before they murder us. Despite our dire situation, we had to admire the sight.

"It must be something like watching the horses bear down on you at the Preakness," I breathed, "wild but awesome."

"Just hope one of these horses doesn't break a leg steering around us," responded Art, standing stock still.

The first boat up came within arm's reach, the rattling of rigging loud in our ears. Suddenly, one sailor called out, "A little mustard and pickles, hold the ketchup. I'll pick 'em up on the way back!" And he roared by. He had come almost close enough to help himself off the stern pulpit.

We watched as the next two, dueling and nearly even, headed straight for us, neither one giving an inch. The upwind boat was trying to force the other to fall off below us, but he was not giving way. I held my breath, transfixed. At the last moment, the downwind boat fell off and slid by our port rail. Did I hear profanity? Maybe not. Surprisingly, all the boats that sailed past us seemed friendly. Maybe they guessed we were as dismayed by our predicament as they were. In just a few minutes, all the boats had rounded the mark and headed off, reaching for the next mark, We had witnessed Thursday night races out of the local yacht club.

"I sure hope there isn't another class coming after them! Do you see any more?" I did not.

"If the hamburgers are done, I'll pour the wine and we can sit down to dinner."

Art raised his glass and offered a toast, "No one injured and no property damage."

"I'll drink to that," I laughed, and sat down.

Somehow, the most ordinary dinner on the water is more delicious and satisfying than an evening at the finest restaurant. When we had finished our ice cream, Art stood and observed that it was time to prepare for the night. I took a bearing on a flashing buoy and another on a yard light on shore. Later, I would check them again, to be sure our anchor was staying put. Even if the yard light went out, I had the flasher.

Art took the little sail out of the sail bag and we worked together to raise it on the mizzen mast. The very small steadying sail I made for this purpose worked beautifully to keep the boat from swinging in the wind. Art turned on the masthead light while I walked around the foredeck, making sure everything was secure. When the dishes were done, Art drying and stowing while I washed, we put on a CD of Mozart and returned to dream in the cockpit while the stars winked on, one by one.

"You were right about the fun," I murmured.

"I thought you were scared."

"Who me? Nah."

I lied.

BREAKING OUT

Although our life at Chambrel ambled along in a comfortable way, Art was discontented. The three-year holiday from housekeeping was all very well, but we were settling into a life of old people. Art longed to have me to himself, to be a householder again. He reasoned that Charlotte had by this time made friends and was happily playing bridge. For her, the down side was the long walk to the dining room. She was growing more frail, and the social interaction in the dining room was more difficult with her increasing deafness.

Art and I began a search for other housing; it would be rental, for Art swore he would not again own real estate. We found an attractive townhouse in Kingsmill and then broke the news to Charlotte.

"Mom, you can move down the hall to a new apartment, just the right size for you. You'll have plenty of space for a bridge table right in your own living room, and we won't be underfoot when you want to get up a game. Everything will be closer, and your window will look out on the fountain at the entry. You can keep an eye on the comings and goings."

Guilt enhanced my salesmanship, but Charlotte reacted with enthusiasm. "It sounds exciting," she said. "How many rooms will you have? How will you furnish it?"

"Well, remember we have quite a lot stored. And some of the furnishings here won't fit in your new place. We'll get them out of your way. And it will be fun to go shopping again."

"What will you do for bedspreads in your new guest room?"

"Mom! I don't even have beds any more. We'll get to that."

"You need bedspreads. What color do you want me to make?"

"No, Mom, that's a very big project. You don't want to get into that. Don't worry about it, I'll get something."

"You'll have to decide on colors and buy the fabric for me. Let me get started thinking about patterns."

She heard not a word. At ninety-three, she wanted to hand-quilt yet two more bedspreads. I just shook my head in amazement. Mother never allowed herself to express the slightest dismay over our move, but entered into the spirit of adventure. Characteristically, she concealed any hint of despondency from those she loved the most.

A year later, her friend Marjorie told me, "Charlotte confided at the time that she felt as if she were being divorced, but she didn't want to spoil your fun." I understood, but I was sorry Marge shared it with me. I had been sure which path I would take, but the conflict of loyalties lurked like a dark shroud in my heart.

When the stored furniture was moved to Kingsmill, we started a shopping list.

"Have to have a couch, and we can look for a television. Guest room needs beds and bureau." Art wrote all this down, and we planned a foray into the market the next day.

Setting up housekeeping in Kingsmill reminded us of our earliest days together and rekindled neglected sparks of romance. The morning after our first night there, Art appeared in the kitchen while I was making breakfast. All unsuspecting, I asked, "What's that you're drinking?"

He just grinned and held out the glass. "Cuba Libra. Want a sip?" I laughed until tears rolled down my cheeks.

When spring broke forth in a month, we discovered a neglected garden outdoors. With care, Art pulled weeds away from a lovely andromeda bush while I cleared the rampant mint across the patio, freeing azaleas from its smothering cover. We felt whole again.

Everyone we knew had two cars.

"What do you think, Art? Should we get another car?"

"What? Feel your style is cramped? When was the last time we had a real conflict over car schedules?"

"We have worked it out pretty well, that's true. But our neighbors, the Mirmelsteins, were kidding me the other day about how we always do everything together, and I just wondered if you were burdened by that. I'm not, and I certainly don't yearn to spend money on another car. But if it would make you feel more free to do what you want, maybe we should consider it?"

"I think we're flexible enough. Sure, you're tied up in the church building project and I have SCORE appointments, but it works, doesn't it? We pick the same Christopher Wren classes usually. I think we should stand pat." And we did.

That summer, Art decided it was time to plan a long-dreamed-of adventure. We would cruise the Intracoastal Waterway in *Sérénité* from the York River to Miami, Florida.

21 LESSONS

We would take months to upgrade the boat's equipment, get a thorough engine inspection, gather the charts, learn cruising lore from other experienced skippers. The cruise would begin next year, in the fall of 1993.

At Yacht Haven Marina, we backed the *Sérénité* out of her slip and maneuvered around the docks to the back of the boat yard. The big crane waited. Handlers lowered stout straps while a diver swam under the hull to place them just right. At his signal, the crane began to haul on the lines, lifted her, gurgling and dripping, above the water, swung her around, inched her forward to the cradle, and let her down gently as a baby.

"Art! Look at that slime! There are even barnacles on the propeller shaft! I thought she'd be cleaner than that. Why do we pay divers to scrub the hull then?"

"Because if we didn't, she'd be hauling a lawn's worth of grass, that's why. I think she looks pretty good, considering we don't use dangerous poisons any more."

All winter, men cleaned and polished the hull. A surveyor came from the Northern Neck to evaluate the engine's condition, to inspect rigging. We ordered a new inflatable dinghy, along with all sorts of safety gear. Art and I cleaned and oiled the teak brightwork, I varnished the bamboo rollers on the stays.

One sunny day, when the check-list was complete, the men slicked up the bottom with a fresh coat of paint, the crane lifted the boat and laid her in the water. Art started up the big diesel engine, and we motored back around to the slip.

We practiced sailing by Loran, letting the magical box guide us safely into harbors. Loran was my particular delight, since I navigated. Approaching a westward harbor, say Salt Ponds, at the end of the day was a nightmare. The setting sun in our eyes obscured any buoys leading to the harbor entrance, and it was a matter of luck to avoid running aground. Now, I needed only to locate the buoy on the chart, set its location as a waypoint, and let Loran guide us to it. The accuracy was close enough that I could see it when we were within a few yards, and make small corrections if needed.

By October, we had completed preparations. The boat, having been inspected from stem to stern, was pronounced cruise-worthy. We stowed rations into every nook and cranny, stuffed the refrigerator full. Emergency equipment of every conceivable sort was secured close at hand. We were ready. We were confident. We were excited. Let it be said that we were about to learn more than we had ever imagined. Afterward, I wrote an account of our adventures and called it *21 Lessons from the ICW, Sailing and Learning, Southbound on the Intracoastal Waterway*. Here are the lessons, along with later observations:

Art and I have 30 years of Great Lakes, Virgin Islands charter, and coastal sailing experience under our hats. Most of it has been benign – we don't go looking for reckless adventure – but we have encountered a few wild moments over those years. Our dream of the Intracoastal Waterway Cruise from our home dock on the York River, off Chesapeake Bay, to Florida has been on the drawing board for two years. We have read and heard many stories about its easy and beautiful possibilities. Given that our ages bracket seventy years, we decide to do it now, aboard our comfortable 36-foot sailing ketch Sérénité. We are planners and list-makers; before we leave, a diesel mechanic goes over the engine and gives us a list of spare parts to carry. We are ready. It turns out that we are ready to learn lessons.

LESSON ONE
October 10th, the Great Adventure starts with the bang of a wet firecracker. Sunday dawns cold, wet, and windy. We hesitate. One or two bravely set forth into the storm and we soon follow. Into the teeth of the northeaster we pound until, after an hour and a half, we find ourselves still in the York River. The seas are building higher and deeper. Now the wind blows a steady 25 and often over 30. A quick check of our travel arithmetic proves there is no way to reach

safe harbor by dark at this rate. We turn and run for home, reaching Sara's Creek in one hour flat. So much for beginnings.

Monday is no better. When Tuesday dawns with a thunder-storm, we feel really anxious; however, by eight o'clock the rain has stopped and we are casting off lines. Now the low has passed by, giving us a northwest wind. Yesterday's northeast wind would have pushed us toward the lee shore at Poquoson, but today's wind is safer, if no less intense. When we reach downtown Portsmouth, it is enough for today. After a pretty good dinner in the marina restaurant, we bed down for the night.

Lesson 1: Wait for safe weather.

What I did not put down on paper was our initial relationship, both to one another and to the cruise. Art was taking, I felt, an unnecessarily conservative approach. The weather was really less dire than he thought, and he was being just a bit chicken. I was slow to accept changes in the plans. When we got out on the river, on that first attempt, battling unfavorable wind and seas, I realized I could do the arithmetic as well as he. If we had progressed less than ten percent of the first day's journey in an hour and a half, turning back was the only choice. I felt chastened and ready to follow the more reasoned, conservative path. Art's moderation was vindicated, the chain of command reinforced.

LESSON TWO

Wednesday dawns sunny and nearly windless, although the temperature is only 47 degrees. By mid-morning, we arrive at the Great Bridge Lock and need to wait only fifteen minutes to enter. The crew (that's me) knew the lock would only change our level a few inches; therefore, our 25-foot docking lines are neatly laid out on each corner. It turns out the bollards are set very far back from the water's edge; our lines are too short. We quickly splice on second lines. Courteous line handlers pass our bow and stern lines around bollards and hand them back. They are probably used to a fumble or two, but our faces are a little red.

Lesson 2: Have plenty of lines ready, long and shorter

The trip down the Elizabeth River brought welcome change. At rush hour, the railroad bridge was closed, as well as the Gilmerton Highway bridge. Art had a chance to practice stalling, loitering, waiting, without losing control. I was glad not to be at the helm.

LESSON THREE

After a gentle drop of only a few inches, we are on our way again. Only now, without the ebbing tide of the Elizabeth River, we make much better time. North Landing bridge opens only on the half-hour; time has become the enemy. Still 30 miles to go, and it is half-past twelve. At six miles per hour, we will arrive around five-thirty, but we may fall short of that schedule. This is not the ideal cruising plan, for it is calendar driven - two days lost already. Thanksgiving and return plane tickets are dogging us.

Lesson 3: Let nothing persuade you to be driven by the calendar.

We had yet to enter the stress-free mode of sailboat cruising. Remnants of shore-side anxieties still pushed us.

LESSON FOUR

Now we are zooming down the Currituck Sound — if six miles an hour is zooming — toward Coinjock. We will make it by five-thirty, aided by sail. Hooray!

No, it turns out that 'hooray' is premature. The jib will not furl as good jibs are supposed to do when you don't need them any more. We pull into Midway Marina with sail flapping, looking pretty wild. With the help of a bosun's chair, three strong men, two winches, two halyards, and a lot of encouragement, the intrepid first mate — that's me — ascends four stories to the attic to check it out. The jib halyard is wrapped around the stay and jammed in the track. With the aid of tools, I pry it loose to the accompaniment of cheers all around. A welcome hot shower aboard, home-cooked dinner, and off to bed.

Thursday ... In the morning, Art inflates the new dinghy and we slide her into place behind the mother ship. Such a quiet day, we decide to tow her behind us across the Albemarle Sound. Big mistake. She starts off docilely enough, but soon I look back and there she is gasping and gurgling, half-drowned and struggling to stay up. The calm morning has become the lively noon, wind piping up to fifteen. I cannot handle her tow lines, so the captain takes over, while I assume the helm. Single handed, he tows the bloated baby up the lee side to the bow, secures the tow line, attaches a halyard to her hoisting harness, lifts and tilts out much of the water, hauls her aboard, tilts out the last gallons, tips her upside down and lashes her to the deck. On top of the forward hatch, of course. We will learn to regret this last part, but for now, ignorance is bliss.

**Lesson 4: Know how to tow your particular dinghy.
And when.**

Here, distinctive roles had begun to emerge for us two sailors. I actually enjoyed climbing the mast; the view from above was exhilarating and I felt no fear at the height. Art's superior physical strength was matched by his fortitude. Whatever was needful, he would achieve it.

LESSON FIVE

Dinghy secured, we decide we can motor sail, if the wind in the sound comes from the right direction. Tentatively, we unfurl the jib, about a third of the way. Jammed again. But we rise above these little troubles and hoist the main. Sailing at last! Although the sky looks threatening and the seas are building, we arrive at the Alligator River a little ahead of schedule and without rain. The mainsail comes down and, miraculously, the jib furls.

What a surprise the Alligator River is: wider than a mile, certainly. We keep on, making over fifty miles before finding a nice cove just beyond Newport News Point to take our anchor. The grill is stern-mounted in a jiffy and we sit gazing at a pink-puff sunset as the red coals turn to gray. What a feast we have here: steak, fried potatoes, asparagus, and sweets for dessert. Perfect. At length we are in the cabin, and as the last notes of our romantic music tape fade away, we hear a new sound. Is it our neighbor's wind generator? A passing motorboat? The captain unzips the screen door to take a look.

Whoosh! An enormous black cloud of something bursts through the opening, alighting on every surface in wriggling masses. I retreat to the V-berth, while the captain mans the gun. Backing toward the safety of the forward cabin, Raid gun blazing, he slams the door shut to wait for the carnage to end. What a scene! Enough dead and dying creatures to sweep up in a dustpan, vacuum into the Dust Buster, wipe off the ceiling. The companionway screen sags from the weight of them. A flashlight confirms our fears; the cockpit is black. They line the bimini. They are everywhere. Not to worry. In the morning, we will crawl out the forward hatch and come around from outside to sweep up the mess. How could we exit through the screened opening, sagging with the weight of thousands of the little creatures? There. I said we would regret the inflatable covering the forward hatch. Tomorrow's another day to face problems.

Lesson 5: Expect bugs.

What a shift in mood this was! From sweet romance to a scene plucked from a horror movie, this was a test of maybe the most valuable ingredient of cruising: a sense of humor. And we had it, all right. When the last of the bugs inside had been dispatched, we fell into the V-berth clinging together in breathless laughter. Morning was soon enough for the reality of our situation.

Lesson Six

Friday ... The morning is bright and lovely, even if we do spend an hour cleaning up last night's invasion of the midge flies. Did I mention that the refrigerator has essentially stopped operating? A block of ice keeps everything from spoiling for the moment. Oddly, we really are having fun. Up anchor after a good breakfast of eggs (can't let them spoil). Swampy forests crowd the shores above the dark brown water; then suddenly, the land opens up to farm pastures. They say cows come down to drink, but we see none.

The bridge at Fairfield Highway is scheduled for opening on the hour and half-hour. We are going to miss the next opening unless the bridge tender is feeling generous, seeing us steaming down the canal. Our radio request unheeded, the gate closes before we can reach it. We slow down, but the wind picks up, blowing us – what else? – hard toward the bridge. No way to go slow enough, Art decides to turn around. The cross-wind, stronger than he judged, pushes us.

There goes Art's projected book, How I Traversed the ICW without Going Aground. *Oh well, they say it's not if, but when, on this route. Darn! We are aground and caught by a submerged snag of branches. Luck is with us, and with strenuous backing and swinging, we break free. I peer into the bilge looking for a leak while Art listens for vibration from a bent shaft. All is well.*

Lesson 6: Turn into wind and current to stall at bridges, but carefully.

Another hallmark of successful cruisers is the ability to solve problems without assigning blame. We knew we were less than perfectly skilled in boathandling and we accepted the shortcomings without rancor.

LESSON SEVEN
And still the bridge stays shut. It is time to open now, for sure. I give two deafening long-shorts on the air horn while Art maneuvers upstream. At last, several minutes after the hour, a voice blasts over Channel 13.

"I got me a bridge swingin' here and I need some traffic to go through it."

We turn tail and roar through, without a nod to the bridge tender. He is writing our boat name in his book. Then we see what the game is: behind us, far behind, are two sails. He waited for them. A full seven minutes after we passed through, I look again. The bridge is still open, and a power boat is charging down the canal. The heartless bridge tender has suddenly found compassion, too late to help us.

Lesson 7: Retain your sense of humor.
You will need it.

There is nothing like a common enemy to forge an alliance, and bridge tenders were, for the most part, the enemy. I was hitting my stride in navigation, doing the calculations that would bring us to bridges right on schedule. It was challenging, but I glowed with the feeling of success.

LESSON EIGHT

We reach Behaven in good time to shower and bed down early on this, the fourth day of our ICW cruise. Weather forecast for the next several days sounds wet and windy. In the morning, a nice old man strolls down to look at our fridge, checks the freon level, pronounces it OK, is obviously mystified by the 12-volt compressor, and shrugs. We pay a $40 fee, top off the fuel, and – no better off – leave the dock later than we would have wished.

Lesson 8: Know the qualifications of any who undertake to fix your boat.

LESSON NINE

The wind is piping up, but we will motor. My trip up the mast has not solved the jib-furl problem and the wind is too far forward to do well on only the other sails. Besides, we are pushing hard at this point; despite our repeated vows to relax, we have a schedule in mind. The waves get higher and the clouds spill across the horizon in ominous gray rolls. With the weather channel reporting strong thunderstorms, the captain decides we will not anchor tonight, as there are no excellent shelters available. We will push on to Oriental. He increases engine speed and we fly.

Coming around the bend from the Pamlico River to the Neuse River, passing by Maw Point shoal, we are taking the waves broadside, but charging ahead. Soon all will be calmer when we head downwind. Suddenly, all is calmer. Much calmer. Too calm. The engine's roar has quieted to a purr and slowly died away. Only the whistle of the wind and the slap of the waves can be heard. She will not restart. The waves will eventually ground us on Maw Point.

Fire drill. Life jackets donned, harness buckled, captain forward, raise the main. Piece of cake, as we can now sail handily downwind on the Neuse River. Somehow, though, one more problem caps the day: the halyard has fouled and we cannot raise the sail. Helplessly, we drift toward Maw Point. As Art prepares to drop anchor, my heartbeat drowns out the wind.

Lesson 9: Have sailing gear tested and in good order at all times.

The emergency called for previous training; there was no time to think through the steps. Art's experience with the Coast Guard Auxiliary guided him through the process and his natural fortitude kept him moving rapidly, but surely. I, without such extensive training in emergency management, was frightened but able to follow his instructions. This was truly a situation that could have been a disaster, even life-threatening.

LESSON TEN

Just then, a big power cruiser comes steaming up behind us. Angels in a stinkpot — but we will never say 'stinkpot' again. The master boat handler backs the 44-footer down on our lee bow almost close enough for us to hand a tow line to his crew. Gently, gently, he eases ahead, the line grows taut, and we begin to move forward.

What a ride we are having! Loran shows over seven knots, now eight. (Embarrassing to realize how much faster we will reach our destination by tow. Best not to bring up that part.) In an hour, the Whittaker Creek channel lights come into view. Just outside Oriental, this is where the yachting action is.

Here we come. But slow down, slow down. We glide a mile. How will we get safely to the dock? It's a tricky entrance, following a pair of range markers. The dock-master talks us in by radio as we glide too fast, too fast. We don't want to ram our rescuers! The signal is given from the dock, and we are cast free. Still gliding fast, Art steers the bow neatly around the corner and then U-turns into the slip. I hand forward and spring lines over to waiting hands, and we are docked. The timing is so perfect we don't even strain to halt Sérénité's forward glide. She knows she is in the barn, and she comes to a gentle stop.

During the night, mist becomes deluge, Texas style. All night long, we rock and roll and listen to sheets of water pounding the deck. Shortly after breakfast, the storm is spent, sunshine and soft breezes wipe away all bad memories. Of course, it is Sunday, so no work will start until tomorrow. Nothing to do but hang around and be boat bums. Unaccustomed to this new lazy role, we do our best, but manage to fit in two loads of laundry and a good grocery shopping.

Monday brings the engine man, who finds our fuel filter packed with water and sludge, despite our care in filtering fuel from the pump and adding algaecides. The filter was new thirty-five engine hours ago, when we started, but the engine is choked and starved.
Lesson 10: Be sure to check the condition of your fuel and filters often.

Art hated to admit it, but the responsibility was the captain's. On reflection, he realized he should have had the tank pumped and cleaned before the cruise began. We realized that reliance on the boat yard staff was insufficient. After all, those men were not going on the cruise.

"Did you fill up on a Monday?" asked the mechanic.

"No. Why?"

"Because if you did, that could be the main cause here. The weekend boaters fill up on the weekend. By Monday, the supply tank is running low. Any sludge in the bottom will be sucked up by the pumps."

We made a note to remember that.

LESSON ELEVEN
Monday morning, the marina mechanic starts pumping air into the fuel to stir up the sludge, at the same time pumping it out into buckets. Of course, we keep a full tank; probably we had more than forty gallons. It makes for a noisy, smelly, gunky afternoon, but at last the tank is empty and presumably cleaner.

The effort to apply a fix to the jib problem depends on a part to be air-expressed from Florida. We wait all day Tuesday, but the part never arrives. Early Wednesday, we cast off lines and set forth across the Neuse River in dead calm with Loran leading us right to the *marks. Too late, we realize what a sin is complacency. Too long, we follow a range before turning to the next mark, and sloosh! We are stuck in the bottom. Firmly. Really stuck. Reverse gear produces only swirling water but no movement. A shrimp boat, hovering nearby, allows that he will tow us back to the channel. For $150. We thank him kindly, but no, we will ready the dinghy to go overboard and kedge off.*

Lesson 11: Pay close attention to range markers. They're serious.

It was disheartening to find that greed still lived, even here on the water. Not every boater was a fellow-traveler, some were predators. It was tempting to generalize about commercial fishermen.

LESSON TWELVE

Suddenly, another sailboat — one of the boating brotherhood — approaches and offers help. We urge him to take care to avoid getting into the same fix, but he presses forward. Art heaves him a line, both engines strain forward at full throttle. Finally, we lurch ahead and are free.

We trudge on down the waterway. We have read about a channel to an abandoned factory, suitable for anchoring. Although I picture a bulkheaded ditch, the channel turns out to be a charming little creek leading to a boat builder's factory, now out of business. The night is warm and incredibly starry, although the ever-present swamp mosquito keeps us locked inside.

In the morning, we find ourselves at low tide, sliding gently over the mud. Our overnight neighbor asks for depth readings as we depart in the rising water, and I keep radio contact all the way back to the main channel. They draw six feet and will enjoy a very long breakfast before crossing the bar.

Soon, we are pushing along in the hot south wind and sunshine, going full speed. The captain has determined we will reach Wrightsville Beach tonight. When I protest that I cannot handle the helm at high speed in narrow channels, he promises to do it all by himself.

Our route this morning takes us through the Marine base at Camp Lejeune, right down the firing range. The Coast Guard has told us they will have no information about the shooting schedule until eight o'clock; we push on, hoping to avoid a delay. When the range goes 'hot' delays can last for hours. We try to close our minds to the tales we have heard of boaters watching shrapnel splash in the water all around them as they try to slip through after the warning signals have sounded.

There are young Marines roaring by in inflated boats, some on the shore in military vehicles, obviously undergoing training. But no artillery fire is heard, no patrols warn us off. When we reach the other end, yellow lights have gone on, indicating that traffic through the camp must now stop.

Lesson 12: To avoid delay, try beating the gunnery crews out of bed.

LESSON THIRTEEN

Iron Man Art does it again, almost entirely alone. Ten hours against an ever-strengthening wind. Fifty miles may sound inconsequential to a car driver, but it feels like too much to me. It is good to arrive at the marina in Wrightsville Beach, where we will stay for two nights. Our friends will meet us tomorrow. Heaven only knows what we put together for dinner; we are early to bed.

During the night, our warm, strong south breeze has shifted to a chill, blustery north gale. Autumn has roared back. Seapath's floating docks are a pleasure; no adjustments are needed to account for the very strong tidal currents in Mott's Channel.

At a little before four in the afternoon, our friends knock on the hull. They treat us to a brief tour of the beach town. The ocean is wild. An evening of refreshment at their house is followed by a delicious restaurant dinner. Overwhelmed by their generosity and open hospitality, we sleep comfortably in a Real Bed with No Rocking.

Lesson 13: If you are offered a night off, take it.

LESSON FOURTEEN

Had the adventure begun to wear thin? No, even though we were glad of the respite, the little holiday in the real world, both of us were eager to move on. Heeding our host's warning about Snow's Cut, I finished my meticulous notes about the navigation to come. I developed a system for recording way-points and relating them to the chart and was getting pretty good at it. My uncertain vision through the binoculars worries me a bit, but I compensate by studying hard. It is just as well.

After an elegant breakfast, they deliver us back to the marina, advising us to leave as late as we can to avoid the greatest tidal currents in Snow's Cut. Incoming tide on the Cape Fear River cannot be helped. Accordingly, we cast off shortly before eleven. Fridge problems still dogging us, after another mechanic has picked our pocket. (Some lessons are learned only slowly.) The sharp northeast wind is, mercifully, pushing us, and we tool along at good speed. The infamous Snow's Cut lies ahead, waiting to ensnare us. At last, we turn in, only to find ourselves sheltered from the wind, cruising past many loungers on the beach, fishing and sunbathing. What is so hard about Snow's Cut? Soon, we emerge from the sheltering bluffs to find ourselves in a rough, open, confusing, twisting channel. I try to understand and follow the range marks, feeling panicky. This is definitely a bad place to find the bottom. The solid captain is calm and confident, threading his way through to the Cape Fear River ahead.

The river is well named today. It is wide and wild, heavy with commercial traffic and peppered with buoys, range markers, day marks, and only pilots know what else. On a calm day, this navigation would be an absorbing task. Today, a strong tide is surging in from the sea, opposed by winds coming downriver at a steady 25 knots, gusting to 30. Where tide meets wind in these conditions, steep and choppy seas build. Our little craft weighs 17,000 pounds, but she might be only a walnut shell. Bucking and yawing, she is a true handful. I read off the course changes and search for the next buoys while Art keeps Sérénité on the right path. More than a little lark; it is fifteen miles. Art fights the seas for more than three hours, and he does a masterful job. While a sail would help steady our boat, we are not confident enough of our balky jib furl to try it. The mainsail is out of the question in such wind and seas. Ocean seas may be bigger, but these are steep and nasty. It is definitely our second major challenge of the trip, and Art meets it with admirable strength and endurance.

**Lesson 14: Anticipate difficult passages;
lay out compass courses.**

In every life, a few passages stand out forever from the rest. The memory of Art gripping the wheel, braced with feet spread apart, eyes sweeping the water ahead for commercial traffic and obstructions, jaw set in determination, was one of those passages. Those perilous miles called for all the skill, stamina, and character he could muster. In a very primal sense, I accepted him as my heroic shield.

LESSON FIFTEEN

We are glad at last to come into Southport Marina and tie up. I think even Sérénité is relieved to nuzzle the bottom at low tide; the water is only four feet deep in our slip, and our keel is four and a half feet down. She rocks happily in the mud until the tide lifts her again at three o'clock in the morning.

Sunday, we scoot out at first light and half-tide, lest we be stuck by the next low. Shivering in the early morning light, we are on to Myrtle Beach to find out how the rich golfers live.

On the way, we pass two inlets, both reputed to be dangerous. Today, both Lockwood's Folly and Shalotte inlets are mercifully peaceful. Even though the tide is very low, we have enough water. We can see out to the ocean, though, and can only imagine what it must be like when an easterly storm piles the surf through these narrow passages.

The cold northwest wind keeps us bundled up in long underwear and mittens, but no surf or tidal surges bother us. As the day wears on, the sun grows hotter. My turtleneck begins to cling and bind, but we are too busy to go below and change. How fascinating it is to watch the golfers cross over the waterway in overhead trams! We reach Myrtle Beach in tee-shirt weather, sporting woolen shirts and long underwear, looking foolish and feeling hot.

**Lesson 15: Dress in removable layers in changeable
weather.**

LESSON SIXTEEN

After a pleasant evening, we again set out on a beautiful morning, wiser in our choice of clothes. Art does need gloves at first, but soon we are warm and comfortable. Condominiums and fine houses line one side of the waterway, while the other is almost entirely wild, untouched marsh. At Barefoot Landing, we pass a shopping mall filled with factory outlets and restaurants. Strange. The famed Waccamaw River is lovely, as its reputation would have it, although by now we are pushing on ahead too fast to fully enjoy the ride. As we near Georgetown, clouds roll up on the horizon and a little rain spatters down on my laundry, drying on the lifelines. Wind sharpens.

The marina proves to be the equivalent of a truck stop, but we are glad to tie up. This has been our longest day. During the night, the forecast storms break forth, rocking and shaking our floating home. Morning brings thirty-knot gusts and more rain. It is a day to clean, organize, and plan strategy. Between showers, we walk the streets of Georgetown, South Carolina, and restock the larder. The historic houses that line streets near the waterfront bear plaques with dates as early as 1740. Ancient trees bend over the sidewalks. By eight-thirty, we are ready for a long day tomorrow, breakfast set out and clothes ready to jump into. We fall asleep to the creak and crunch of fenders and fender boards on the dock.

Sure enough, Wednesday morning brings a beautiful sunrise and gentle breezes. We fall into a long parade of boats; the fine morning has turned loose a flood of stranded snowbirds like us. In a tidy line, we troop down the channel toward the Minim Creek Canal. This will be another long day, all the way to the edge of Charleston; the Skipper turns on the juice. One by one, we pass most of the parade, although the passing is amusing, somewhat like a Tom and Jerry cartoon, set back in ultra-slow motion. This is a relatively easy day and we have a chance to try a few minutes of sailing. While the jib is fairly ineffective, we feel satisfied to see it flying.

As we float past McClellanville and Andersonville, Hurricane Hugo's effects come into view. Palm trees have been topped, large cypress trees upended, and all the docks are made of new wood. Down Mathews Cut, down the Harbor River, through Price Creek, we are flying now. The navigator – that's me – calculates time from speed and distance over and over again, judging whether we can slow the pace a little.

At last, the new high bridge from Isle of Palms to the mainland appears on the horizon. It is clear that we can make the last opening of the famous Ben Sawyer Bridge before it closes for the four-to-six o'clock rush hour. Triumph!

Lesson 16: By carefully watching clock and speed, you can gauge bridge openings.

LESSON SEVENTEEN

We steam through the bridge, turn right into a development of condominiums, and we have arrived. For the second time since we embarked we serve dinner in the cockpit and enjoy a spectacular sunset. Just then, the flying bombers arrive in swarms, and we retreat to the screened cabin. While the wind pipes up during the night, we sleep soundly.

Thursday. How hard it is to keep track in this unreal, never-never land. We have done a lot of homework. Charleston harbor is said to have formidable tides, especially with an opposing wind. We have consulted Reed's Nautical Almanac and found that flood slack is at eight in the morning. Open water is less than two miles away.

In the harbor, Art follows the compass courses we have laid out. Visibility is excellent, with the sun just rising over Fort Sumter, lighting the low skyline of the Charleston battery. Each buoy shows up right on schedule, although the wind is now gusting up to twenty, pushing ever stronger waves into our bow. Despite the lovely view, we are glad to reach Wappoo Creek, off the Ashley River, and turn into quiet water. Tide has now begun to flow against us.

At length, another lovely mile of fine houses glides by. Suddenly we reach a new major challenge. Just ahead, we can see giant whirlpools and swift eddies. I have seen this before, only it was the flow of the Niagara River; this is Elliott Cut. We have done good planning, for the current is against us, giving the rudder control. Sluicing down with the current, in control of these giant forces, is unimaginable. The cut is only about three hundred yards long, but it is very impressive. Art guides us through nicely.

Lesson 17: Plan for favorable tides in tough spots

LESSON EIGHTEEN

Soon, we emerge into the Stono River on the other side, none the worse for the adventure. I have noted, for I am the designated navigator, many ranges to follow up ahead. May I do better here than in Adams Creek! Although the water looks wide and inviting, the charts assure me there is more threat than invitation there. This is stressful work, requiring constant attention. During a lull, I duck below to pour fruit juice.

What is going on? We have a rising headwind, and yet the cabin smells strongly of diesel exhaust. Art checks all the dials and directs me to open hatches. As we keep going, the fumes increase. It is clear we have a serious and growing problem. So far, the engine sounds normal, the temperature is normal, water is pouring from the exhaust, and the bilge is dry. We search for a likely anchorage where we could regroup. It is, happily, only two o'clock. Of course, the wind is rising sharply, as it always does, keeping time with trouble. By now, black clouds are pouring from the hatches.

Suddenly, the engine purr changes to a clatter and the exhaust pipe runs dry. Art kills the engine and we roll a sail into action. She takes hold nicely, and we are sailing. The water is wide and deep here in the Wadmalaw River. But wait! Ahead lies another narrow twisting channel on the Dawho River, similar to the narrow ranges behind us.

Now we call Coast Guard Group Charleston. The voice at the other end sounds unperturbed, wants to know our home address and phone number. He is filling out forms. Eventually, he offers to call a private towing service to come from Charleston to get us. Our protestations that we are Coast Guard family fall on deaf ears. At home, a trusty 41-footer would have been dispatched immediately to our rescue. Here, we are just another dumb tourist. Art's many years of faithful service in the Auxiliary avail us nothing.

Lesson 18: Because of recent regulation changes, count on the Coast Guard only if you are in dire peril.

The air was thick with Art's salty denunciations. At home, he was a person of some merit, some power. Here, he was nothing, drained, helpless. He was furious. I jumped to the bow, opened the anchor locker, grunted and heaved until the heavy weight lay on the deck. At the skipper's command, I dropped it overboard, carefully paying out the line, wrapped around the cleat, as Art had taught me. When the anchor grabbed the bottom, the line strained and pulled; it took all of my strength to stop it, but finally I secured the line and we were safe for the moment. But alone and abandoned.

LESSON NINETEEN

Meanwhile, we receive a call from a local towing company, asking if we would like assistance. They can reach us in a little more than an hour. Charleston is more than two and a half hours behind us by fast boat. Of course we would like the locals to come! Soon, we are in experienced hands. The crew attaches a towing bridle and starts down the North Edisto River toward Bohicket Creek and from there into Adams Creek. The whole operation takes the remainder of the afternoon.

What a day this has been! After all our disasters, this boatyard and these people take on a fantastic air. The 1950's have passed and small town folks like Jimmy Stewart have always existed only on the big screen, right? The warm concern for our predicament and our state of mind cannot be genuine, can it? The foreman, Tony, goes so far as to invite us to join his family at dinner in a local restaurant. Both he and David, the owner, make it clear that our safety, comfort and needs are their paramount goal.

Lesson 19: Good things sometimes happen out there among boating people.

LESSON TWENTY

The captain and crew have conferred both at the depths of disaster and in the cool light of day. We have agreed to terminate the cruise. The journey has fallen short of our hopes and this latest incident has sapped the remainder of our enthusiasm, optimism, and money. Our limit has been reached.

We will spend the next few days readying Sérénité for a haulout, and scrubbing every inch of her interior to remove as much diesel smell as we can. Even the curtains get a sudsing.

During Friday night and Saturday morning, another fierce storm blasts through. Two trees are upended in David's yard by winds in excess of fifty miles an hour. The same storm has roared through Georgia, killing three people, and this is only Halloween. After the storm subsides to a slow drizzle, we retire for the night only to be awakened before dawn by still more huge gusts of wind and pounding water. A cold front is coming through, dropping the temperature to the thirties; high winds will prevent the haulout for a couple of days.

Lesson 20: Winter in the south is definitely no picnic.

LESSON TWENTY-ONE

We pack the little rental car, say reluctant good-byes to these good people, and set off on the last leg of the first half of the Great Cruise, amended. During the drive to the airport, we reflect on our experience. Nothing we read or heard prepared us for such frequent onslaughts of brutal weather – sustained winds above twenty-five and many times much higher, torrential rains, temperatures that reached into the low thirties. The mechanical problems, while alarming, are reasonable in a boat manufactured in 1979, even though we have labored hard to maintain her in top condition. They were, except for the mysterious jib difficulty, the result of advancing age. The water in many places we traveled was shallower and narrower than advertised; the Ditch is simply not dredged to a uniform twelve-foot depth.

Are we sorry we embarked? Certainly not! We had interesting times, beautiful days. We learned new respect for each other's capabilities and, better yet, to enjoy being together. We have discovered that we are not, after all, powerboat people. We yearn to come back to the wide Chesapeake where the sailing is some of the best in the world.

Lesson 21: You're never too old to learn who you are.

CANCER

Finally, I understand it isn't whether you have crises in your life—everyone does—it's how you cope with them. We sold our beloved boat, *Sérénité*, in 1994. Our tidy townhouse in Kingsmill was littered with life vests, foul weather gear, spotlight, and who could tell what all? I had rescued my favorite teak-and-holly cutting board from the galley, but the cozy, hand-made v-berth quilt had stayed aboard. Now we had free time to do… what? Art had been elected chairman of SCORE, the Senior Corps of Retired Executives. I was busy working on the church 'Home '95' building project. Just the same, an empty space loomed in our lives. The summer promised to be quiet and, I was afraid, rather dull.

Both Art and I took full credit for our good health; we knew we deserved it, because we were attentive to regular medical check-ups. It was time for Art's annual physical, and I found him a little unsettled when he returned home.

"John says there's a little nodule on my prostate gland he wants Roger Schultz to investigate. Would you make an appointment for me, please?" There is one thing about even a retired executive: he expects someone else to take care of secretarial details.

"Yes, Sir," I replied, "do you have a preference for morning or afternoon?" I teased him with my most efficient secretary voice.

"Just make it soon." His somber tone gave me pause.

After his appointment with Dr. Schultz, Art underwent a biopsy and we waited a week for the result. When it was time to go, Art asked, "Want to come along?"

"Wouldn't miss it."

As we walked toward the office, I squeezed his hand, and he squeezed back. After a few minutes in the consultation room, the doctor came in.

"Well?" asked Art.

"It's cancer," came the reply.

I felt the bottom drop out and I was falling, falling, my heart pounding. I reached for his hand, warm and steady; he gave mine a squeeze. There followed half an hour of explanation and reassurance, accompanied by the doctor's sketches of cell structure on his sketch pad. Supported by his hospital lab training, Art asked technical questions and I was soon lost in the discussion. It turned out there were several choices to be made, among them doing nothing. Art instantly rejected that thought.

"No, Doc, I want to bring up all the guns. Just have to learn a little more about which are the best guns. You've told me what you recommend. Let me do a little research first, and then we can move forward."

We shook hands all around, made another appointment, and were soon on our way home.

"God, Art, are you really as cool as you seem? I'm scared!"

"Of course I was scared at first. But now that I know what my choices are, I want to get to work. This is not the time to panic. I don't think it's a death sentence, but it's definitely a challenge."

In the next few days, Art contacted several organizations active in prostate cancer research and treatment. The most valuable was in Grand Rapids, Michigan; they offered information in depth and quantity. Art undertook a crash course in malignant disease of the prostate, reading everything he could find, both popular and technical. Within ten days, he was ready to form a partnership with Dr. Schultz and do battle with the dragon. I could think of nothing else. Having no background in such matters, I felt like the outsider, abandoned and left behind.

"Art, would you like me to make gazpacho?" I knew the soup was his summer favorite.

"You bet! Any time you want, Love." As he always did, he helped me chop the vegetables. He jostled me, he rubbed my back, he kissed my neck. Working with him, side by side in the kitchen renewed my sense of calm and confidence. Together, we could lick anything.

We could, couldn't we?

That evening, we ate our rustic supper of home-made bread, cheese, and gazpacho while I learned more than I ever wanted to know about the variety of cancer treatments available. There was cryogenic treatment, in which the affected tissues were frozen, highly experimental and not yet backed up by any significant studies.

"Forget that," Art grunted. "They're not going to freeze mine off!"

Evidently, we were going to be discussing this accompanied by Art's ribald sense of humor. For once, I did not protest; instead I wondered how he managed to maintain lightness.

"I see by this one paper," he went on, "they're beginning to experiment with planting seeds of destruction. Seems to be a promising avenue."

"They are doing what?" I was alarmed.

"Radioactive seeds at the site of the cancer. It may work well, but mostly if cells are all still inside the capsule. The procedure is very controversial."

"Isn't surgery a choice? Get rid of it once and for all!"

"Well, there's an ancient surgical choice. Been used for a long time. Castration. You see, prostate cancer lives on testosterone, so if you remove the source of supply, poof, it's gone. That was the theory, anyway. But now they know the adrenal glands also produce testosterone. Less, but enough to nourish the little cells. There's medication they can give to suppress even that, but I don't relish the side effects of castration. Singing soprano somehow just isn't me!"

"Well then, what?" He was teasing, saving his decision for last.

"I'm inclined to go for radical surgery followed by radiation. There are risks, of course. To me, the worst possible outcome is incontinence; I don't think I'd be able to manage that. I have read that a meticulously careful surgeon can minimize the possibility."

To my surprise, he was less concerned about possible impotence. "Trouble with you," he told me, "is you never frequented 'The Block' in Baltimore. Your education is very narrow. Those sex shops offer a lot of hope to old men." He continued by updating me on the practical aspects of paraphernalia available from such shops as well as, he assured me, from his physician. His descriptions were bawdy and graphic, and in spite of myself, I ended the meal laughing.

When we returned to talk with Dr. Schultz—I was now a junior partner—he approved of Art's decision.

"It's what I would do," he said, reassuringly, "and my ability to preserve nerves in the surgical area is actually quite good."

I asked, hesitantly, "Doctor, why are you going to do fine microscopic surgery and then let the radiologists hit it with a baseball bat? It doesn't make sense!"

"No, they're not going to bludgeon him. The x-rays will be very narrow and carefully mapped to target exactly where we want them to hit. It's additional insurance that we haven't left any stray cells behind." He stroked my hair gently and smiled down at me.

Apparently, this was a slow and painstaking process. First, Art had to store up a supply of his blood, in the unlikely chance he would need it. Two units were comfortable backup. The first unit was drawn right away, but the second had to wait a month for regeneration. Then, of course, another wait until his blood was back up to a good level. Surgery was scheduled near his 73rd birthday at the end of August.

The day came to pack up and head for the local hospital. Art packed his toothbrush and I packed my knitting. We drove in silence, but when I parked the car, he leaned over to kiss my cheek. Mercifully and efficiently, the paperwork had been completed in advance by telephone and we were allowed to go right up to the surgical suite. After he had undressed and donned his hospital gown, the nurse handed me a plastic bag containing his belongings.

"Here you are," she said, "it's safer if you take them now. When he goes to his room you can put these things in his closet." She left us alone.

"Well, Babe, don't sweat it. Schultz is good and I'm going to be OK. Don't run away with any of those interns while I'm gone."

"Art, this isn't a teaching hospital. There are no interns here!"

"Well good. That's a load off my mind." He winked at me.

"You just behave yourself and don't pinch any nurses." I gave him a sound kiss, slipped out of his hungry grasp, and closed the door behind me. The pulse at the base of my throat was pounding.

Like Madame de Farge, I knitted away the hours of crisis until the needles blurred and my hands shook. No one had told me how long it might take and I worried. Finally, as the trees were making long shadows in the late afternoon, Dr. Schultz came into the room, still in green surgical gown and cap, his mask hanging from strings around his neck.

"He's fine!" His hearty tone was upbeat. "The disease was pretty much contained, except for one seminal vesicle. We took that one out, too, and the rest looks clean. He is in recovery now, and when he is fully awake the nurse will take him to his room. Do you have any questions?" I shook my head, still dazed. "See you in the morning, then." He patted my shoulder and was gone.

The following days are a blur in my mind. I know I spent all the daylight hours in his room. He slept. Nurses took vital signs, meal trays came and went. He ate little, spoke little. But he smiled at me—I remember that.

In a few days, he was sitting up and receiving a few visitors. Although he denied having pain, I could see creases of tension around his eyes. When the catheter was removed—he breathed a sigh of relief—the doctor told him to go home. Healing continued for several weeks while he regained strength. Then radiation began.

The special equipment required was unavailable then in Williamsburg; we had to drive to Riverside Hospital in Newport News, about half an hour away. I went with him, remembering the doctor had warned that radiation brings increasing fatigue with it. Although he seemed fit, I looked forward to the time when he would need to ask me to drive for him. I waited in the waiting room, still knitting, watching other patients come and go. Some were wheelchair bound, others bald. Many were clearly very sick. Art came striding out, smiling broadly.

The first night, when he undressed for bed, I gasped. "What in the world is all that marking on you?" There were crosses of black, red, and green on his hips, groin, and buttocks.

"They put those marks on and then they chant strange incantations." He was grinning mischievously.

"No, really?"

"Those are target marks. After careful measurement, they decide where they want to aim the beam. I'm supposed to wash around them so they'll stay visible until next time."

"But your underpants are a mess! The markers have smeared color all over them."

"Deal with it," he shrugged.

After trying to scrub out the dye, I gave up and went to the store. I found handsome bikini numbers in green, in red, and in navy. At least markers wouldn't show on those!

Delighted, Art started a betting pool with the nurses. They had to guess the color of his underpants before he undressed. Other patients might be having grim treatments; Art was stirring up hilarity among the staff. Radiation was to last for twenty-three days, every day. About halfway through,

Art suggested he drive by himself. Although I protested, he said he didn't like my wasting two or three hours every day.

"Are you sure you feel all right? It may get worse, you know."

"Hey, I'm fine. If I get tired, I'll tell you. Right now my only complaint is I'm getting sunburned in pretty surprising places." Special skin cream soothed that, and I applied it twice a day. He continued to drive by himself until the end, still feeling quite well, but beginning to experience a little nausea. It ended just in time.

As the following days went by, and Art began to pick up steam, I felt the tight band around my chest had been snapped apart. I could breathe again, and sun broke through the clouds.

"So what's next?" he queried, raring to go again.

Just before Thanksgiving, we raised wine glasses in a farewell toast to prostate cancer.

"Well you did it!" I offered.

"No," he responded with a wink, "we did it."

THANKSGIVING

"Hello? Hi, Annie, what's up?" Hearing from our New England daughter was always a delight, but this developed into a mild surprise.

"Mom, we're all coming down for Thanksgiving, so plan to put us up for a long weekend. We'll get there on Tuesday."

As I put the phone down, I called to Art, "Are you ready for a lively holiday? Your New England kids are driving down for five or six days! I didn't think they'd come so soon after your radiation. Can you handle it, all three of them?"

"Great! What's for dinner?"

"Art! It's only two o'clock! Too early to get into that."

"No, silly, what's on your menu for Thanksgiving? I think the question is: can you handle it?"

"I guess so," I replied tentatively. Actually, I had been looking forward to a quiet time, maybe a restaurant dinner, just Art, Mother, and me. My reverie was interrupted by the phone ringing.

"Hello? Hi, Suzy, what's up?"

"Mom, we're all coming down for Thanksgiving, so plan to put us up for a long weekend. We'll get there on Tuesday."

The same message, word for word! Susan laughed. "Don't worry, we'll do all the cooking. You have the weekend off!"

That meant seven guests for nearly a week, and my coping skills were still reeling.

"Never mind," soothed Art, "they're adaptable, and so are we. It's good we have three bedrooms!"

"And air mattresses and pillows and sheets and blankets," I added. "Oh golly, we'd better take inventory." As I started upstairs, the phone rang.

"Art, would you get that? Now I *am* glad we have only two children." I continued up to sort bedding. When he put the phone down and joined me in front of the linen closet, he was grinning.

"What?"

"Another guest."

"No!"

"Yes! Maxine."

"Ohmigod! How wonderful! How awful! Oh how can we?"

Maxine was my dearest, oldest friend, and I was thrilled she would be coming all the way from San Francisco.

"What about her sons and their wives?" I asked fearfully.

"Kent and Andy are going to Hawaii or something, so she's at loose ends. She arrives on Wednesday."

Every now and then, I surprise myself with a brilliant inspiration. "I know! We'll check in at the local Howard Johnson, we three old folks. That way, we can leave the confusion behind, have breakfasts out, and show up when the house is getting organized."

The plan worked like a charm. While the house was being trashed by the busy bustle of seven people, we elders took our ease in comfort. Mid-morning, we sauntered in to the fragrance of holiday delicacies cooking.

Wednesday morning, anxious about the Thursday menu, I asked, "Shouldn't I be shopping, girls? I don't even have a turkey!"

"Not to worry, Mom. We told you we'd take care of it. We ordered a bird a week ago. Last night, we got everything we'll need. If you and Dad want to get Maxine at the airport, that'll keep you busy and out of our way."

We drove Maxine right to the motel, where we all talked well into the night. After breakfast in the little restaurant next door, we returned to our house in Kingsmill.

"Mmmm! Smells good! What's for dinner and when?"

"Daddy, how many years have you been asking that same old question? Dinner's what we say it is, when we call you to the table."

"Honey, these kids got no respect," he complained, as they pushed him out of my kitchen.

At last, we were summoned to the table. Wine was poured all around, and Susan lifted her glass. "Our anniversary gift to you, Mom and Dad. We couldn't come in December, what with school schedules, so we all decided to do this instead. We couldn't think of what else to get you."

Surrounded by all those we loved the most, this was the best gift to celebrate our fiftieth year of marriage. Art's eyes met mine across the table, and he blew me a kiss.

"Sit down, everybody," said Annie, "while we bring in the sacrificial bird." The big platter came, and bowls of mashed potatoes, and beans, a casserole of sweet potatoes, steaming gravy, Annie's favorite ripe olives, and cranberries.

The children listened, wide-eyed, while the grown-ups told family stories of long ago. My mother, Charlotte, asked, "Do you remember Thanksgiving dinners at the farm?"

"Oh yes! But I think there were more of us. Weren't Uncle Dave and Aunt Barbara there, too, with their girls?"

"Remember how Skipper always had to scrape the potatoes? He didn't believe in peeling. Wasted too much good potato." Charlotte's father was a cherished memory. Maxine remembered our two families having Christmas dinner in the Everglades.

"My those were rustic cabins, weren't they! But it was a good time. That was before you were born, Jenny. Do you boys remember?"

The younger ones remembered a little, but Douglas had been ten and the events of that Christmas were clear in his mind.

When the turkey had shrunk to a skeleton, the dishes were cleared away and dessert brought in.

"What is this wonderful pie? Is it pecan? Is that pumpkin underneath?"

"Yes," answered the cooks. "it's both. Pumpkin pecan. And there's mince, too, especially for Grama."

"You know, Art, I think we did pretty well with these women. They've become superb cooks!"

"If you can't talk and cut pie at the same time . . ." The pies had been placed in front of me.

"Mother can always cut pie without mangling the first piece."

"Not another bite," groaned Charlotte, pushing away her empty dessert plate. There were nods all around, and the meal was over.

When I started to carry dishes to the kitchen, the girls barred the door. "The children want you to join the card game with Grama in the living room. Go! Scat!" I obeyed.

In a little while, I heard bustling around at the front door, but my attention was drawn to the game of hearts. Before the hand was over, we heard many voices in a hearty "Happy anniversary, Fourniers!" Into the room streamed a parade of many good friends from church, bearing funny gifts, hugs, and kisses. They had left their own holiday feasts to wish us well.

When Art had poured champagne for everyone, I lifted my glass and said, with a catch in my voice, "Life doesn't offer any more than this. Thank you all."

Art replied, "I'll drink to that!"

The boys brought in chairs for everyone, and we all found conversation enough to fill the evening. When, at last, the guests filtered away, we three elders were sent on our way, too. Susan's husband, Gordon, drove Charlotte home.

"No, you can't help with the dishes. We have plenty of slaves here. Go to bed. See you tomorrow."

We were glad to put our bodies down, knowing we were, indeed, elders. Maxine left the following day.

When the two families drove away that weekend, the dishes were put away, leftovers safely stored, linens neatly folded in the laundry, and the whole house vacuumed. We stood in the doorway with arms around each other, waving farewell.

"Good kids," he murmured, holding me close.

I buried my face in his shoulder.

When our real anniversary came in December, Art took me to the Bray Dining Room in Kingsmill for a candlelight dinner. I wore the black Chinese silk dress he had bought for me at Gump's, years before.

"You're every bit as beautiful tonight as you were the first time you wore that dress. I'm really impressed it still fits so well."

"And you are still the handsome flatterer you always were, Sir." I smiled.

The pianist played the Anniversary Waltz as the waiter brought us a vase of red roses. The card read, "All our love to the best parents in the world from your daughters."

TURKEY

On the day before my birthday in 1997, we landed at the Istanbul airport. About six months ago, we were halfway around the world in Thailand; Art's wanderlust continued unabated. Our group of forty checked into a moderate hotel across the Golden Horn from the ancient city. In the morning, we piled back into the bus to start our adventure.

"Mustafa," I said, speaking to our native guide, "why is there so much difference between the women we saw last night in the neighborhoods around the hotel and the girls and women we see on the street this morning?"

"O.K.," he explained, "when women are at home, they wear Muslim dress. It's a religious requirement. Those you see this morning are going to work or to school, and they wear Western dress. That's a legal requirement. Kemal Attaturk, the father of Turkey, envisioned a secular society for our country, not a theocracy. They say he was an admirer of Thomas Jefferson. Whatever he was, he instituted laws of separation between religion and government that still stand today."

There was no mistaking the central role of religion in this city's history—as we rolled across the Galata Bridge, we saw minarets on every side. They were as numerous as banks in Williamsburg. The largest of the mosques were museums, open to visitors from everywhere. First, we entered the Hagia Sophia, known in Turkey as the Ayasofya, and I was amazed to learn that this was originally a Christian church.

"Art," I whispered, "if I had been paying attention in the sixth grade, I think I would have known that. I should have taken this field trip then!"

When the church became a mosque under the rule of the Ottoman Turks in the fifteenth century, mosaics depicting connections between royalty and divinity were carefully covered with plaster. In contrast, Crusaders often stole or destroyed the treasures they found, both Christian and Muslim.

After three days of exploration, we packed our bags to be loaded on the bus for Ankara. Art and I had been careful to deposit our extra cash, travelers checks, and passports in the hotel safe. Now it was time to retrieve them, and I stood at the counter, stuffing everything into my capacious handbag. We started for the bus, when Art said, "It's a long way to Ankara. What say we stretch our legs a little with a stroll down the avenue? The bus won't be leaving for another fifteen minutes."

For a brief moment, I thought of putting my purse on the bus first, but thought better of it, not yet being entirely comfortable with this bus full of strangers. I slung the strap over one shoulder, and we started out. Another woman from the group joined us, and soon she and Art were deep in conversation. Since the sidewalk was narrow, I dropped behind. When we were a couple of blocks from the bus, I called to them, "Let's go to the next corner and turn back. Don't want to be left behind!" They nodded.

Suddenly, I felt a sharp blow, my purse was snatched from my shoulder and out of my hand, and two young-looking men were running pell-mell down the side street.

"My purse! They have my purse!" My voice must have carried, because here came Mustafa after us at a dead run. I pointed down the street, and Art and the guide ran in hot pursuit. It was no use, of course—the thieves were long gone, vanished into the maze of narrow alleys. The defeated and winded men huffed back up the hill.

"Are you hurt? Did they hurt you?" Art looked anxious.

"Not really. My shoulder aches a little, that's all." I was trembling with fright, never having been a crime victim before.

"We must go to the police to make a report," said Mustafa. "I will first explain to the other guide and then you will follow me." For the next hour, we sat in the little police station while endless paperwork was executed. The room was close and very dirty, but the policemen seemed sympathetic. Mustafa had to translate their questions for me, get my reply, then translate it for the clerk, who was writing everything down. They wanted to know the contents of the purse, and it was only then that I began to realize the magnitude of our loss.

Art and I had always been careful to split our belongings between us and to pack some cash and travelers checks in our bags, as well. This moment of vulnerability had slipped in, unnoticed. My purse contained both passports, all our travelers checks, and nearly all of our cash. One credit card was gone, along with all my medications—luckily, none of that was life-threatening. When we returned to Baltimore for the drive home, I realized the car and house keys were gone, as well. I have never felt such guilt. The 'if onlys' drummed a rhythmic beat in my head for days.

Art managed to be more philosophical. "Damned nuisance," he observed, "but at least you are not hurt. Everything can be replaced eventually, and we'll figure out how to do without until then."

As we finally trudged back to the bus, I cringed to think what the other passengers must be suffering. How angry they must be, I thought, to be held up like this. I was wrong. We climbed into the bus to universal hand-clapping, and queries about how we were. A spokesman rose. "We've agreed that we will all chip in to a pool, so you can enjoy the rest of the trip. If there is anything any of us can do, please let us help." I was touched beyond measure, and felt a sudden stab of pain that this was the group with whom I had hesitated to leave my purse.

Art saved me from tears by declaring, "Not to worry! Think I'd let her have everything, even for a minute? Not a chance!" He pulled a different credit card from his wallet and waved it triumphantly. I poked him in the ribs and we both sat down as the bus pulled away from the curb. Our next stop was Ankara, the nation's capital and the location of the American Embassy, many hours away. We would take care of the missing passports there, get American Express to send their messenger with replacement money, and be back in business.

We checked into the Sheraton Hotel and spent the evening exploring the mall next door. We bought a voice recorder with Art's credit card.

"Well," I said, at least I can take notes again, but nothing can replace my record of the Code of Hammurabi. When we saw the actual tablets with Hittite writing on them, I took pictures and recorded some of the laws. All gone."

"Never mind," said Art. "It's all up here where nobody can take it away." He tapped his forehead.

Back at the hotel, I placed a collect call to American Express and got a connection to someone in Salt Lake City. Her voice was soothing, but her words were disappointing. No, despite their commercials that said otherwise, there would be no messenger at my door. She would arrange for a refund, but I would have to go to an American Express office in Ankara. At morning check-out, we were accosted by the hotel manager demanding we pay $80 for the telephone call.

"But it was a collect call!" I was exasperated. I turned my pockets inside out to emphasize that I had no money to pay. Art kept very quiet about his credit card and turned a stony face to the man. We had reached an impasse; the man blocked our exit.

"Come, come" called Mustafa, returning to herd his laggard sheep. When he realized the problem, Mustafa promptly paid the bill and led us to the bus. We boarded, and the bus headed for the day's sightseeing, taking a detour to drop us off at the American Embassy. Our other guide got off with us to see that we gained entrance.

At the gate were about two dozen people—I took them to be Turkish. A few were women, all were trying to get through the closed gate, but without success. Art strode up to speak to a guard standing inside the iron gate while I surveyed the scene. A small guard house stood inside nearby, a path led from there up a small rise to a large white house set far back. My gaze returned to the guard, and I realized he was as impassive as a guard at Buckingham Palace. His eyes did not flicker, he gave no indication of having heard Art at all. He looked Turkish, too, and I wondered if he understood English. Finally, our guide stepped forward and spoke to him in Turkish. An argument ensued for several minutes, but at last the gate opened a crack, just enough to allow Art and me to pass through. Our guide was blocked. He called out a farewell and told us he would be back to get us after a while.

As I heard the gate clank behind me, a uniformed woman approached and gestured for my purse. (I had found a small purse in my luggage—it held nothing but a linen handkerchief.) She opened it, inspected it, and tossed it behind her on the ground, gesturing us to proceed up the path to the house. When I reached for my purse, she blocked my way and said in clear English, "You'll get it when you come out." Angry, I turned away to join Art, already heading for the house.

Inside, we were confronted by another uniform. He asked the reason for our visit, Art told him to replace stolen passports, he took our names and pointed to two empty seats in the bare waiting room. Three others, including a young child, were already seated, apparently Turks. One man still standing, was American. He told Art, "I was in the airport, just arrived. My shoe had come untied, so I put my wallet down on my suitcase and bent to tie the shoe. In a flash, the wallet was gone." The guard shushed the two men, and all of us sat down to wait.

The clock on the wall showed eleven o'clock. Had this been the waiting room for a professional, I believe I would have left quickly to find someone else to consult. Someone cleaner, for one thing. The walls were smudged, the paint peeling, and several gouges in the walls spoke to poor maintenance. The chairs were worn and dirty and, after a time, very uncomfortable. The guard was sipping coffee from a mug, making loud slurping sounds, and maybe that's what made the little boy thirsty. He whispered to his father, who spoke to the guard, who pointed down the hall to a water fountain. Father and son walked there quietly and returned without another word. I thought they looked frightened. More time passed. It was nearly one o'clock and my stomach was beginning to waken, although the odor of bodies too long confined was spoiling my appetite.. I stood at the desk and inquired, "How much longer do we have to wait to speak to someone?" The guard simply shrugged indifferently. The door that seemed to lead to the inner sanctum was locked, electronically controlled by the man at the desk. Once or twice, someone came out and left the building, but no more supplicants arrived. We waited.

I whispered to Art, "What if I fainted? What then?"

"Hell no!" he hissed back. "Want to lose your place in line? They'd simply haul you outside by the feet." I thought it was true, and settled back to wait.

I think it was about two o'clock when the door opened and a woman called out "Sylvio and Katharine Fournier!" We sprang to our feet and followed her inside. There, the woman thrust several papers at us, gave us pens, and disappeared. At least we were now at the counter of a real office with real people working. It seemed like progress.

We completed the passport applications, proud that we were able to provide the numbers of the missing ones and photographs for the new ones. At last, a woman came to the counter, took the papers, and asked my husband for the money to pay for new passports.

Out of patience, he said in a low, angry tone, "If you had paid attention to our application, you would know that we have no money. All of it was stolen. I can write you a check or give you a credit card, but we have no cash." She told us that only cash would be accepted and we would need to make arrangements to get some cash.

I spoke up. "May we speak to your supervisor, please?" Her eyebrows shot up in astonishment at the effrontery, but one look at Art's face seemed to convince her to go get someone else to talk to us. We waited. After nearly half an hour, a man approached with a sociable, affable demeanor. He introduced himself as the vice-pooh-bah. I'm sure that's not what he said, but I was beginning to think Gilbert and Sullivan. For the first time, this man was all schmooze. "I am so sorry about your predicament. It is really too bad. We will certainly get you new passports within a few days." Then he looked at our photos and explained that they failed to meet the required standard. We would have to have others taken. As he told Art how to get to the studio, I was thinking brother-in-law.

"You don't understand," I said. "We are on an organized tour. The bus will leave for the south this evening and we need to be on it. We need passports now." He shook his head.

The upshot was that Mustafa returned to fetch us and was allowed to enter. A brief conversation with pooh-bah settled it all. We would go to the photographer, who would deliver the pictures back to the embassy. The bureaucrats would move at whatever speed suited them, an agent known to Mustafa would pick up the finished passports and deliver them to Istanbul in time for our departure. The tour company would foot the bill and, needless to say, charge it all back to us. So it was settled.

But what about the American Express money? We did find the office and, after several back-and-forth faxes, the local people found the right papers to give us—a hunting license, as it turned out. American Express had no cash or ability to issue checks, just an order for a bank to issue the checks. For the rest of our trip south, east, west, and finally north in Turkey, we presented the papers to banks. None would honor the order. We learned later that American Express had bailed out of the country, owing to the explosive inflation rate there, but they did not tell us that.

The surprising thing is this: the remainder of the trip was delightful and memorable, quite unmarred by our experience. In fact, I learned the joy of travel with empty hands. At a town farther down the line, Art was able to get some cash from an ATM and we soon forgot trouble as we rolled along the ancient Silk Road to Ürgüp, a town in the province of Cappadocia.

Before we left that area, we had acquired a heavy box of tiles from a local factory. Art sighed deeply at the prospect of hauling it around, but really, the bus did the work. At another factory, we succumbed to the blandishments of the rug merchants. Until you have met a Turkish rug merchant, you don't know what it is to be romanced. Art enthusiastically urged me to order the one I really loved—which was pretty costly—instead of one more reasonable but less handsome. I was a little nervous about giving them all that money with only a paper receipt written in Arabic to show for it, but Art said, "Not to worry. The tour company has vouched for them, and if you don't take a chance once in a while, what good are you?" I wrote my initials on the back of the rug and gave them our home address. The salesman promised that it would arrive on our doorstep within six weeks, and it did, still displaying my initials in red.

After we climbed around in the bizarre hills of the region—unlike anything we had ever seen before—the bus took us through Konya and on to Greek lands. I was about to learn fully that western Turkey's early history included occupation by Greeks and then by Romans. All the sites on the lower shore of the Dardanelles were Greek ruins.

We took the ferry across and stopped at the beach of Gallipoli. This was the place where, in World War I, it cost more than 300,000 casualties to convince the British to withdraw. The Turks buried the dead there with honor, and Kemal Attaturk had a monument placed, celebrating the bravery of those soldiers who had tried, but failed, to breach the Turkish lines. Before we left that sad place, handkerchiefs were mopping the tears from all our cheeks.

At last, it was on to Troy and remembering the tales of Homer. An enormous wooden horse stood outside the entrance to the excavations, and someone asked how they had kept it in such good condition all these centuries. I think Mustafa had heard this question before, but he answered as kindly as he could. We stood on the parapet, gazing down on the Meander

River, imagining the slaughter of the Trojan Wars on the plain that stretched beyond.

The bus drove still northeast, toward Istanbul and our last night in the same hotel as before. Our passports were waiting. After dinner, Art said, "Let's go for a walk."

"You're kidding."

"No really. We can't leave without having a drink in the Pera Palas, that hotel made famous in *Murder on the Orient Express*."

I gathered my courage, and we set out. He was right: if you let the horse throw you and you don't get back on, you'll always live with fear. The hotel was built in 1892 to house the rich and famous who rode that luxury train. We walked around, admiring the Victorian décor and ended in the Orient Express Bar, where two gin-and-tonics cost 350,000 lira each.

In the morning, we flew to Baltimore to retrieve our car for the drive home. It took some negotiating with a car dealership to get the necessary authorization for a locksmith to replace the key. At home, I was finally able to get replacement of the travelers checks, and a complaint to the president of American Express extracted a check for $80 to pay for the phone call. Insurance took care of the rest.

After I unpacked our bags and finished the laundry, I was still angry about our treatment at the embassy. I wrote a letter to our congressman, laying out every detail of the long, ugly encounter. Within only a few days, I received a telephone call from Ankara. It was the embassy — possibly the vice-pooh-bah himself — apologizing for the shabby treatment they had given us. He assured me that the policy for handling visitors had been thoroughly reviewed and that basic structural changes were even then falling into place. I observed that I hoped they would reconsider the official attitude toward foreign nationals who came seeking entrance. Whether they were admitted was unimportant, but that they were treated as valued human beings instead of cattle was vital to our national interest. The man in the embassy was conciliatory. I wonder.

SPAIN

"I guess this means we're getting old, huh?"

"What? Not me!"

"You said we'd save the cruises until later, and now all you show me are brochures about cruises. You tired?"

"My knees are tired, that's all." Art rubbed them thoughtfully. "So what do you think? We've never been to Spain." He had handed me an enticing invitation to cruise from Barcelona to Lisbon, with stops at Mediterranean islands and a side excursion to Morocco. Tired knees or not, he was ready to go.

Two days in Barcelona hardly scratched the surface. We were on our own, though, and I noticed that Art was walking slower than usual as we tramped around the city. I know he was glad when it was time to board the big ship in the harbor. For several days, we cruised around the Balearic Islands, exploring Mallorca and Menorca. Then we hopped over to the mainland again to visit towns I had only dreamed of, like Almería, Málaga, and Cadiz before heading south to Tangier and Casablanca.

"Art, I thought I had seen mosques. Great mosques, beautiful ones. But did we ever see anything like this?"

"No," he said, "because there isn't anything like this anywhere."

"Is this the same effect the Taj Mahal has on people?" We stood silent then, gazing up. The beauty, grace, and cool delicacy of this breathtaking building nearly brought me to my knees. We were under the spell of the great Hassan II Mosque in Casablanca, the largest religious structure in the world, outside Mecca. One-hundred-thousand people can gather within its walls and courtyard. It incorporates the most modern details, like heated floors, electric doors, and laser beams shining toward Mecca at night, yet the building casts a spell that evokes centuries of poetry and music. Blue waters of the Atlantic lap at its feet.

Then we steamed north to Gibraltar, where the Barbary Apes tried to steal Art's hat. If the legend is true — that Britain will relinquish control of Gibraltar only when the apes die out — the Spanish can just give up. Those monkeys are thriving.

Our last stop in Lisbon introduced us to the naval history of this nation of great explorers. I would have learned more except for my preoccupation with Art's knees. Obviously suffering, he said nothing, but limped gamely after the group, always bringing up the rear. I dallied behind sometimes to cover the annoyance of always the same laggard. Characteristically, Art wanted to explore the city's public transportation. We took the subway to the zoo and enjoyed a peaceful afternoon riding the elevated tramway, looking down on the animals. It was February, and few other visitors had come out. When our few souvenirs were safely tucked into suitcases, we headed for the Marco Polo airport and home. Art's knees were throbbing

BIRTHDAY AND FAREWELL

My mother was born in the nineteenth century. Now approaching the twenty-first century, she was nearly one hundred years old. She bid fair to inhabit still a third century. Imagine! It was time for a birthday party.

"Oh no," she said, "just a little cake will be fine. Don't make a fuss."

"Mother, we have decided to give you a big celebration at the church. We will hang from the rafters as many of your quilts as we can gather from near and far. How many do you suppose you've made in the last thirty years?" She was scandalized.

"You'll do no such unseemly thing," she told me. "It would be bragging. I can't do that."

"No, Mother, it is Art and me and all the rest of our family bragging. We have a right to brag—you are a fine artist, and your work deserves an exhibition." Only a little persuasion was needed; I think she was secretly pleased, even if a little embarrassed by all the attention.

Counting what she and we could remember, there must have been more than forty-eight in all. Some had been given for charity auctions, at least two were sold. The one in Germany wasn't going to be shipped all the way to Virginia, though her granddaughter, Polly, assured her it was the best one. We assembled twenty-six others, from crib to king size, invented a way to hang them, climbed up a sixteen-foot ladder, and decorated the sanctuary. Despite painful knees, Art worked along with Susan and me. Our minister, Randy Becker, was both enthusiastic and hard-working, insisting that the show remain in place for some time to give the whole community a chance to see it. Smaller quilts showed better at eye level in the lobby, and some examples of other needlework came along, too.

The afternoon of the party, I took Mother through it all in a wheelchair. She shook her head. "Did I really make all these? I don't remember that one." Even she was amazed at her productivity; in about twenty-five years she had amassed a body of work that would have been impressive in two lifetimes.

Guests arrived by Chambrel bus and car, and Mother insisted she had to greet them in person. She sat by the door for several hours, shaking hands and talking to each one in turn, urging them to sample the beautiful birthday cake. It was astonishing to see how energized she was, staying until the last guest had departed. I drove her home, helped her undress and get into bed for a nap.

That evening, she rose and dressed to join a family dinner in her honor. Dave and Barbara had come from Ohio, three of their daughters and two grandchildren came, too. Annie and Susan each brought their two, and our circle was complete except for Polly. Eager to miss nothing, Mother rose on Sunday morning to join the clan at brunch before everyone went their separate ways. At the end, she was exhausted, but she knew how her family treasured her.

ဆ ၄ *postscript* ဆ ၄

Mother's life ended a little more than three years later. Her body, like the wonderful one-hoss shay, just disintegrated. Art was already gone, and I knew she now needed more care than Chambrel could provide. My first impulse was to revamp my townhouse to accommodate her needs, but Susan argued vehemently against the plan.

"Mom, do you know what 24/7 care really means? You would wear yourself out. You'd never be able to hire enough help." Reluctantly, I agreed that we had to try a nursing home, at least for a little while.

At the same time, Annie was diagnosed with thyroid cancer, and she needed my support. I moved Mother to Patriot's Colony, mentally reserving my thought about bringing her home. I would deal with that after Annie's surgery was over. Surely I could manage it somehow

While I was in Massachusetts, Susan called. "Grama has a broken hip. No, she didn't fall; the doctor said it was a spontaneous fracture. I got her to the hospital and they x-rayed it. The doctor felt that surgery was not an option, but that it would heal by itself, given time. She is back at Patriot's Colony."

My heart sank. By this time, Annie was mending, and I was on my way home the next morning. All the way, I felt guilt like a heavy blanket lying on my heart. What could I have done differently? I had no answer. It was too late for could-have, should-have.

I walked into her room on a dreary Thursday afternoon. My friend, Beverly Baldwin, was sitting with Mother, and the thought crossed my mind that they don't call my church the beloved community for nothing. Mother lay in the big bed, small as a child. Her face was pinched by pain, and I noticed how her sharp elbows wanted to poke right through the papery skin. Her crown of lovely white hair lay straight and stringy on the pillow. She reached out her hand to hold mine.

"Can I go now?" she asked, gently. Blinking my eyes to hold back the tears, I said, "Of course you can, Mother. I told you before I left that you were to work on your own schedule, not mine or anybody's. You go when you're ready." When she asked about Dave, I said he was on his way. She closed her eyes and slept.

For the next two nights, I stayed in her room to be sure the morphine was enough to suppress her pain. She refused both food and drink, but most of the time seemed fairly comfortable. The bad times were when the nurses came to move her, preventing bed sores, they said.

"Wouldn't bed sores be preferable to this?" I asked them, but they persisted. Mother groaned and cried out, but they did the best they could.

Dave arrived Friday and had some time to be with her; she had saved the last of her strength for him. He went back to my house to sleep, and I drove there to fix him some breakfast.

By the time we returned to Mother's bedside, she was gone.

KNEES

Once back in home territory, and with the centennial birthday party over, Art sat in his easy chair and declared loudly, "Enough with the knees! I've had it!" Then began the search for a surgeon, one who specialized in knee replacements.

"Art, are you nuts? Why?"

"Because if I have only one knee replaced, I might never have the nerve to do the second one. Might as well get it over with."

Art's friend shook his head doubtfully. "Think about it, though. With just one, you could get around with crutches sooner. With both, you'll be helpless."

"That's O.K. The little woman here will wait on me hand and foot." I stuck out my tongue at him—though I knew he was probably right.

The surgeon in Richmond readily agreed: both knees were good candidates for replacement. I shuddered to remember the loud crunching sound Art's knee made when he lifted a leg in bed and bent the knee. The operation was scheduled for shortly after Mother's birthday party.

At Henrico Hospital, Art surveyed his room. "This is pretty nice," he noted. "Could give a party here." The spacious private room occupied a corner on the second floor and large windows looked out on the landscaped grounds. Every room in the wing was similar to allow plenty of space for the exercising and apparatus that would be needed.

When he was suitably groggy from the medication that dripped into his vein, two orderlies came to roll him away. I gave him a quick kiss and he was gone.

I had waited for Art's surgeries before, but in less dire circumstances. Half a dozen times, he had to have the palms of each hand opened up and smoothed out. Dupuytrens contracture, a disorder passed from father to son, caused scar tissue to grow under the surface of both hands. The result was disfigurement and eventual disability, but surgery kept the worst of it at bay. The aftermath— pain for a few days and an impressive bandage—was intense but transient. In those times, I learned about Art's ability to endure pain; it might make him cranky, but he did not complain. His disdain for anyone who 'rode the sick book'—a concept from his army days—allowed him little slack.

After several hours, the patient was wheeled back into the room and gently lifted onto his bed. Dr. James came to assure us both that everything had gone well and we could expect an uneventful recovery. Even though I was relieved, I still planned to spend the night at a nearby hotel. Art woke long enough for me to feed him a little supper from the tray that came, but his conversation consisted mostly of grunts and head shakes.

"Do you hurt?" Little moves from side to side.

"Are you awake?" Chin up and down a bit.

"Want to waltz me around the room?" He was asleep again.

I found my way to the hotel room and slid into the Jacuzzi tub. The knotted muscles in my neck and shoulders began to let go, and by the time I was in bed, I could sleep. My dream was indistinct—something about a storm, loud roaring, couldn't find him in the dark. I woke in a sweat, went to the bathroom, drank a little water, looked at the clock, and climbed back into bed. It was a long night.

When I walked into his room after breakfast, a therapist was already moving his legs and listening to the patient say "Stop that!" I was alarmed until he looked over at me and winked. "They just can't leave well enough alone."

The therapist stood up and said defensively, "I was only checking to see that you still have two of them." They were, I could see, just developing a relationship. In the next few days, that relationship was tested. She demanded more of Art than he was ready to give, and I admired her firm insistence that he could endure more than he thought possible. She brought a machine that guided his foot forward and back on the bed, bending his knee up and down. Art took to calling her Torquimada. She smiled back at him, and I wondered how much medieval history she knew. Or had she heard it all before?

Art's pain increased as the effects of anesthesia wore off. He was supplied with a morphine pump that he could use to self-administer medication, and that helped. Still, I grew more uneasy. The staff said he was 'doing just fine', but I noticed a subtle change in his outlook—for the first time, he was anxious. This man who always met every challenge, had become agitated, fearful. Of course, since the nurses did not know him, they assumed he was only expressing his personality, but I knew better. Something was wrong here, and I had no idea what it was.

There must be a course in nursing school that teaches spouse-soothing. I had been the victim of this treatment before but never figured out a remedy. Art fidgeted with the sheet, moved his head from side to side, licked his lips. None of these behaviors was remarkable to the staff, and they denied it was an effect of morphine. What then? With each day, he seemed worse to me; with each day, the staff and doctor saw appropriate progress. He was to be moved to a rehabilitation center nearby in Richmond the next day.

When I went home that night, I vowed to capture the doctor in his morning rounds and persuade him to stay until I arrived at the hospital. To be sure, I telephoned the nurses' station at six before I left for the hour-long drive back to Richmond.

"Mrs. Fournier, the doctor has discharged your husband, and he will be going to the rehab center this morning. You will find him there when you get to Richmond."

I was panicked. "No! Please don't let him go before I get there! He is not ready—he's too sick. Please!"

"Now Mrs. Fournier, he is fine. The doctor saw him last night and signed the order. Just be calm. You'll see. I know it's a stressful time for you but don't worry. We see these cases all the time, and he is O.K. Honestly."

Sure, I thought as I raced up the interstate, you see these cases all the time and it's so routine you no longer really see them. Something is very wrong and when I get there, I'll convince them somehow. But when I got there, Art was gone. The nurse gave me driving directions and I flew back to my car.

At the rehabilitation center, they knew he was coming. I was ignorant of the complicated routine the hospital went through to call an ambulance, wait for it to arrive, fill out who-knows-how-much paperwork, transfer him to the vehicle that would drive him away. The process consumed a good hour, while I paced the floor of the rehabilitation center.

At last, the doors opened and a litter was wheeled through. Art's face was ashen, his eyes closed. As I bent over to kiss him, he stirred a little, reached up to stroke my hair. The ambulance people wheeled him to a room and gently transferred him to the bed. They backed out of the room and disappeared. A nurse came into the room and told me a doctor would be in momentarily to check Art in. Soon, the doctor appeared and began to take vital signs. The pulse was enough.

"Mrs. Fournier, your husband's pulse is nearly 180. He has no business here. Should be in intensive care. There is a hospital just down the street, but I think it's safe enough to send him back to Henrico where they are better equipped to handle a cardio case. Only a couple of miles. We must get the ambulance back here quickly." He spoke to a nurse, who ran down the hall to the front desk, then he turned back to me. "Do you know why Henrico discharged your husband this morning?"

I explained that I urged them to keep him until he could be evaluated, but apparently the train of protocol was rolling down the tracks and running away. The doctor shook his head and sat down; he would stay with Art until the ambulance returned and Art was loaded aboard.

The next time I saw Art, he was in the emergency ward, hooked up to a heart monitor, fluid dripping into his arm. The diagnosis was atrial fibrillation, a common malady, they told us. For the next ten days, Art lay in a bed, not in the orthopedic wing, but the cardiac wing. For a couple of days, he rested while the new medication took effect; I sat and knitted, trying to look calm. As his heart settled down, Art's anxiety did, too. He was getting back to his old self when a familiar face appeared at his door.

"You chased me down here with that dratted machine? Dammit. No rest for the weary!"

The physical therapist came in and began to set up her equipment. "A fine welcome, Mr. Fournier, that's all I can say. Didn't you miss me? Here, put your left foot in and we'll get started."

Nearly two weeks later, Art was again discharged, but this time to go home. We were to continue the work of rehabilitation ourselves, with the help of home visits. Soon, we enjoyed the fresh spring air on halting walks around the neighborhood. Art's rhythm was stabilized, although sometimes he could feel his heart stutter a bit. Every day, Art walked farther and grew more restless to get going again. It was allons y, all over again. Where to next?

DIGGING ROOTS IN THE GASPÉ

"Dad, I got a weird e-mail yesterday. Think it's a hoax? I don't know how they got my name." Susan handed it to Art.

"Hmm. It's an announcement of the Fournier family reunion. Invitation to attend. Oh, I see why you're suspicious. Says to fill out the form and send a check. Probably a scam."

"Maybe not," I chimed in. "Maybe you could find out something about your family if we went." I knew Art was itching to be on the move again. This might be just the ticket. We could travel at our own pace—I could do the driving. I asked, "Where's Montmagny, anyway?"

We looked for Montmagny on the map of Québec, and found it on the south shore of the St. Lawrence River. The prospect was so intriguing that Art determined to find out whether there was really a reunion afoot. How to do it?

"If I could talk to the mayor, he would know. How do I find him?"

Susan and I looked at each other and said in unison, "The internet!" In only a few minutes, we had found the mayor's name and with some additional clicks got his home phone number. That evening, Art dialed the number and found the mayor at home. I knew he was speaking in formal French, but my earlier listening skill was lost altogether.

When he hung up the phone, Art was smiling. "It's legitimate, all right. He says that reunions of various kinds are sort of a cottage industry in Montmagny. Said he'd see us there—he's giving a welcoming speech." I promised to send off the check for the banquet and look into the hotel choices mentioned in the e-mail.

The small town of Montmagny was bustling along the main street; we found the hotel, just on the edge of town, and checked in. Everywhere were signs and images of white geese because this town is the center for watching the annual snow goose migration. Thousands of birders come from hundreds of miles away to see the great birds on their spring and autumn journeys. We were disappointed that late August was too early for this spectacle.

In the morning, we followed directions to the meeting place, and wondered whether we would make connection with a cousin or two. We had no idea. From as far as British Columbia and California, Fourniers had gathered in a migratory event of their own. Five hundred of them crowded into the local school. To my dismay—and Art's delight—very little English was spoken. It was a Franco-cacophony of deafening proportions. Art was in his element, speaking his language and telling his old jokes to a new audience.

We learned that, despite the common occurrence in North America of the name Fournier, more than half the attendees were descended from one Louis Hébert and his wife, Marie, both born in France around 1575. Louis arrived on the shore of the St. Lawrence with Samuel de Champlain's second voyage in 1604. The first Fournier, an émigré from Normandy named Guillaume, married Louis's granddaughter, Françoise Hébert. Eight generations later, Art's name became a leaf on the family tree.

The last evening, we dressed for the banquet and found our way to a nearby steak house, reserved for Fourniers. As we expected, the mayor spoke to the crowd, but then, the room darkened, a spotlight shone on the stage, and a couple dressed in seventeenth century costume appeared. The mayor introduced the guests of honor—Monsieur et Madame Louis Hébert. In a body, the entire crowd rose up, applauding. A few whistles rent the air. Suddenly, the spotlight found Art and the band struck up *Happy Birthday*. Five hundred voices sang out in French a greeting for Art's seventy-eighth birthday.

When the reunion was over, Art wanted to explore and try to find out something about his forebears. All he knew for sure was that his father was born in a little town called Val

Brillant in the middle of the peninsula that is the Gaspé. Beyond that, he had only vaguely remembered place names from family stories he had heard.

Almost miraculously, we did find the church that held the entry of his father's baptism in 1897. Of many, this looked like the oldest church. We made a lucky choice. After long negotiations with first a nun, then a priest, then a man who had charge of the archives, the old book was laid on the table for us to see. There, in fading ink, was the entry, a few days after the baby was born in September. Art touched the page with his fingers and lingered over it for a moment. Then he thanked everyone and we went outdoors to photograph the building.

For several days, we circled the Gaspé, finding delightful hotels overlooking beautiful water. We did not find any more genealogical information. Finally, one kind soul in a town hall explained to Art that the government had gathered up all that kind of record and placed it at Laval University in Québec City. Frustrated, Art exclaimed as we left the building, "Why in the world didn't somebody tell us before this?"

"Ah, but think what we would have missed," I said. "Let's make tracks for Québec City, then."

At the university, we found the library and a helpful librarian who put us on the right track. We started with Art's grandfather, Theophile. By following marriage records, we were able to trace his lineage all the way back to Louis. The books listed all the brothers and sisters and fathers and mothers. I had a small notebook and a pen. When Art found the entries, I scribbled names and dates. Then we moved back a generation and I wrote some more. Before the afternoon was ended, my hand ached and my eyes blurred, but we were triumphant. We had everything we had hoped for.

Behind all those names and dates there must be place names and stories. Those people had cropped up in dozens of tiny towns and villages, and we were left to wonder why.

"They were poor, I know that from stories my grandfather told when I was a boy. I suppose they were moving around to try to find work to sustain them. Those were hard times. That's why they came to the United States, although some did return to Canada after a few years. I wonder why? None of these towns offers much."

"Maybe because it was home," I said.

LOSING HEART

For once, I chose the destination. Captivated by a TV miniseries about the Lewis and Clark expedition, I lobbied for a trip up the Columbia and Snake Rivers. I wanted to follow the end of their trail in the far Northwest, a territory I had never seen.

"Looks good to me. Let's go. But you'll never catch up with me," said Art. "I've already been in most of that country. All fifty states." He added that last proudly, the realization of a long-time goal. That he was relinquishing his position of leadership here never occurred to me.

Starting from Portland, Oregon, we sailed on the *Spirit of Endeavor*, a small cruise ship, all the way to Washington, where the Snake River flows into the Columbia. The country is dry here, and thinly inhabited. We made our way up the Snake to *Hell's Canyon*, in Idaho, where we boarded small, powerful boats to take us crashing through the precipitous twists and turns of the narrow canyon. Along the steep rock walls, mountain goats leaped from crag to crag, seeking scarce grass to munch. Petroglyphs looked down on us, ancient writings of long-disappeared inhabitants.

The Oregon Trail passes through Washington near Walla Walla. At the Whitman Mission, we climbed a small rise and looked out on wagon tracks, still visible on the prairie after more than 150 years.

Back on the Pacific coast, we traveled to Fort Clatsop to see how those intrepid explorers passed the winter. The buildings were spare and damp; I couldn't imagine what hardships they endured, after years of arduous travel through the wilderness. Although traders from the Orient sailed into coastal ports, the expedition never saw any before they turned around and headed home to the Atlantic coast. Our trip home in late October — on a jetliner — was fast and painless.

Our garden—small though it is—needed to be put to bed for the winter. The last of the weeding and trimming and a good mulch cover waited for us. Art usually tended the garden by himself. Long ago, we parted company on this one activity. Nothing I did satisfied Art, but we did work together on the major fall and spring chores. This year was different.

"I'll get around to it. Just not today." Today he was watching television. And tomorrow. A small black cloud floated over my horizon. The winter passed.

"Art! You're sleeping in front of the television again. Are you feeling O.K.?"

"Hey, leave me alone. I'm an old man. Got a right to snooze. Yeah, I'm O.K."

Every day was the same: he dozed, off and on. Oh lord, I thought, maybe it's true, maybe he is suddenly an old man. He had passed his seventy-eighth birthday, after all. But this man was energetic, optimistic, forceful—he wasn't old. I didn't want him to be old. I did not feel old. I was angry that he felt old.

In the spring, I tried to nag him into activity. "Let's go tackle the garden, dear. It's really looking ragged." He shook his head.

At last, the obvious struck me: maybe he *was* sick. With persistence, I coaxed him into Dr. Mincks's office.

"Art, considering your recent heart episode, I think it's time for a really thorough cardiac workup. There's a well-qualified group at Henrico hospital, and I think you should make an appointment." Art's experience with that hospital put me off. We actually discussed traveling to Cleveland, where the cardiac clinic was widely respected.

"I don't know, Babe, dragging you all the way out there for what's probably just a simple checkup seems a little extreme. What if they want to admit me for a couple of days? You'd have to check in at a hotel all alone. And if they wanted to do something, there would be follow-up. I don't think this is a big enough deal to warrant all that. Let's go to Richmond.

They'll give you enough reassurance. I'm telling you, there's nothing wrong with me." We went to Richmond.

I never figured out why they put him through all the fancy tests — the stress echocardiogram, complete with intravenous dye, the scans. I believe they were heading in the direction of angioplasty from the start. Finally, it came to that. The doctor explained that they could get a really definitive look that way, and if they found blockages, they could probably just reduce them with a balloon. Late one afternoon, Art waved goodbye as he was wheeled toward the vascular surgery laboratory.

Waiting in a hospital dredges up memories of other times, other crises that surge forward down the halls of the mind leaving traces of echoes as they flash by. I paced. I found the cafeteria and bought a bowl of soup. Why is hospital soup so uniformly tasteless?

At last, the woman at the waiting room desk signaled me to go back to his room. There he sat, alert and smiling. "See? You worry too much. Wasn't bad at all. Here comes the doc."

The doctor pulled up a chair, and right away I knew the news was bad. "Mr. Fournier, we got a very thorough look at your arteries. Unfortunately, you're not a good candidate for the balloon. Of four arteries, one is completely blocked, another is about ninety percent closed, and the third is more than fifty percent. We recommend a surgical bypass. Lucky that we found this situation, because you are a ticking time bomb that could have gone off any time. You will want to go home and think about it, talk it over with Mrs. Fournier. But don't let it go for a long time." He rose from his chair.

"I've thought about it. Let's go." Art sounded like his decisive old self. "What are you doing first thing in the morning, Doc?"

Sitting down again, the doctor questioned him. "Are you sure? This is a pretty big decision."

"Of course I'm sure. What's to think about? How about tomorrow morning?"

"As a matter of fact, most cardiac surgery is unscheduled. We work pretty much on an emergency basis, when a patient comes in with a heart attack. So my morning is open. We can slot you first thing, if you want to stay here tonight."

"Good. That way, they won't have to change the sheets."

After a few words about possible complications and negative outcomes from bypass surgery, the doctor shook hands with each of us and left the room. I was shaken, but Art seemed cheerful. "Look at it this way. The surgery is routine; they do hundreds every day. Just be glad it's not a transplant."

The same hotel still offered a Jacuzzi tub. I slipped into it, wishing for Art to join me. In the middle of the night, I wondered if he was sleepless, too. Probably not.

In the morning, I arrived just in time to kiss the patient goodbye and warn him not to give the nurses a hard time.

"Who me?" He grinned, and then they wheeled him away.

Hours later, the surgeon came to report that everything went routinely, that Art would be fine in a few days. Numbly, I gathered up my books and knitting and found the place where he would recover. Still unconscious, he lay there hooked up to tubes, wires, and catheters. At the foot of his bed, a heater fan blew warm air under the blanket. He was so wrapped up that I could scarcely recognize him.

Just as promised, Art was sitting up in a few days and making good progress. He began to connect to the outside world, and one day said, "I guess we'll have to cancel our trip. Bet you didn't think of that."

"You're right, I didn't."

"What trip?" It was the doctor asking.

"Oh, we've booked a trip to Norway in late July."

"Tell me about it."

"Well, we were to fly to Copenhagen for a few days, then Oslo, then up to the top of the country—Kirkenes. There we would have boarded a ferry to travel down the coast to Bergen, stopping at all the ports of call on the way."

"Sounds good. Do you have trip insurance?"

"Yes, why?"

"Then hang on to it. The trip sounds quite possible, and you have nearly eight weeks to recover. I think you can do it. If not, you can always pull out later."

Art looked determined. "We're going!"

Doubtful as I felt, I remembered General MacArthur. "I guess we are."

July twenty-seventh found us boarding a plane for Denmark. Art's recovery had progressed just as the doctor said it would. Stamina was a little slow in returning, but Art's outlook had come from the shadows into sunshine. We strolled Tivoli Gardens in the evening, admired the little mermaid in the harbor, and traveled to Elsinore to feel the ghosts of Shakespeare's *Hamlet* gliding along the high walls.

The day we flew to Kirkenes, the mountains stretched under us as far as the eye could see. In the clear air, flying lower than most long-distance flights, we saw the whole Norwegian geography. Here and there, a valley sheltered a small bright green farm with buildings tucked under the shadow of looming mountains. Snow lay on most of the peaks.

Art was doing well, and I was encouraged. Since we were traveling more or less independently, we could move along slowly, savoring each new experience. We were only a couple of months beyond the longest day, and my sleep pattern was disturbed by the constant daylight. Art slept peacefully. At three o'clock in the morning, I crouched at the cabin window gazing out at the passing scenery, swathed in dusk. When the ship docked, both of us watched to see what cargo was exchanged: machine parts, tractors, crates of some kind of foodstuff, but we couldn't tell what. A lot of fish. Passengers came and went—this was the ferry lifeline along the western coast of Norway.

At Bergen, we checked into a hotel for two nights. Early in the morning, we boarded the train bound for Oslo, but got off at a little town halfway there. Then we found a much smaller train headed for the fjords, down precipitous canyons, past rushing waterfalls. In the afternoon, we climbed aboard a ship that took us down a river through spectacular scenery, and finally to a bus that wound through rich farmland tucked into valleys among craggy mountains. We were back in Bergen before nightfall, though I couldn't tell you what the clock said. We took the funicular up the mountainside for an evening concert and later watched the sunset. I think it was close to midnight. We fell into bed and slept.

In the morning, rain was falling. We had experienced two days of sunshine in Bergen — they offer only a few successive days without rain for the whole year. That was one of the loveliest cities we had ever visited, and both of us were sorry to leave, knowing we would never return. Art slept most of the way home to America.

THE GIFT

'New York, New York! It's a wonderful town!' The song in joyful shout never fails to send a thrill up my spine. This magical town, this mythical Oz, may be the location of impossible dreams for some. For me, it is the repository of all my youthful memory. New York is my home town.

I sat forward in the plush theater seat with my seven-year-old feet, clad in white socks and shiny black patent leather Mary Janes swinging in the air in time to the music. The sounds swelled up from the great theater organ far below, filling the space around me, the largest indoor theater in the world. Looking down from the second balcony, I could barely see the stage until Mother handed me her mother-of-pearl opera glasses. There in front of my eyes, the huge stage rose out of nowhere and glided into place, lines of dancers swaying to and fro. I did not know I was witness to the first holiday show at the Radio City Music Hall, I only knew that I was transported to a place of dreams. Like every little girl, I wanted to inspect all of the ladies' rooms, and each was more wonderful that the last. Black or green marble fixtures, warm-air hand dryers — I stored away each detail in my velvet box of memory.

Into the Third Avenue elevated train — razed long ago — wafted the strong smells of roasting coffee. Sometimes, if I was very good, Mother would give me a penny for the peanut machine in the station. I pushed the coin into the slot, turned the handle and held out my hand for a cascade of salted nuts. The cars screeched and whined as they careened around curves on the way uptown.

When I was a very young woman, I guided tours for the National Broadcasting Company in the RCA building, ate my lunch looking down on the city from its observation deck. The next year, I strolled hand-in-hand down war-dimmed Fifth Avenue with my soldier sweetheart. Forty years later, we again strolled that same street together.

I moved to the Mid-West and left my childhood behind, but I never lost deep feelings of nostalgia for my home town. Art knew that.

It was December, and I knew that Art and our daughter, Susan, were deep in conspiracy. They bent over the computer, but when I approached, the screen went dark.

At last, Art asked me, "Wanna take a little trip?"

"But we just got back from a very big trip!"

"Oh that was months ago. Time for another."

Although it was four months since our return from Norway, Art had since encountered a heart rhythm problem that had prompted his doctor to install a pacemaker. Since then, Art had begun to regain both strength and confidence, but I was wary of any ambitious plans.

"Like where?"

"This will be short and sweet—an anniversary celebration. A little visit back to your childhood."

"Let me guess, then. New York?"

"Yep. They've finished refurbishing the Music Hall—it had grown pretty seedy. Returned it to its former glory. I think you ought to go up there and inspect the work. The Christmas show will be on." He was grinning. I wrapped my arms around his neck and kissed his cheek.

"Oh I love New York at Christmastime! What a great gift! Thank you!"

So it was settled. We would leave by train the following Wednesday and stay in a business hotel close to Penn Station for just two nights. We would see the show on Thursday, and I began to think about getting last-minute tickets for something on Broadway for Wednesday.

Almost before light, we piled our two small bags into the car. Susan had agreed to drive us to Richmond. It was clear but chilly and I was glad to have my heavy winter coat buttoned around me. When the train pulled up to the platform, Art was satisfied to let me find a redcap to handle the luggage, and I took Art's arm. He seemed a little unsteady, but we soon settled comfortably into our seats. The train quickly gained momentum, leaving the city behind. Just after we left Washington, we made our way to the dining car. Sure enough, there were linen tablecloths and napkins, little vases of flowers on the tables. A white-coated waiter held my chair. The fare turned out to be—instead of the elegant offerings of the distant past—defrosted, microwaved, portion-control concoctions. Art dozed much of the rest of the way into New York.

It was late afternoon when we alighted in Pennsylvania Station. I fastened the two little suitcases to my wheeled cart, pulled it behind me, while Art and I walked together toward the escalators to the street. I could feel excitement rising in my chest—the sights and sounds of the big city pulsed through my head. Suddenly I realized that Art had slowed to a stop, and I turned to urge him forward through the crowd. Ahead of us were banks of escalators, all except one flinging hordes of commuters down from the street. It was rush hour in Manhattan, ever the same. Both of us had battled it many times. I looked into his face and saw stark fear there. He seemed to have shrunk into his overcoat.

"C'mon," I said. "Hang onto my hand and follow me. I'll break trail. You don't have to do anything but stay with me." I maneuvered him behind me, the cart at my side. I gripped his hand tightly. Up the moving staircase we went, packed in almost too close to breathe. Out on the street at last, we saw snowflakes floating down in the beams of headlights.

"OK? You OK?" He nodded dumbly. I took a deep breath and led him across Seventh Avenue. Got to move faster in the big city if you want to survive, I thought. He was shuffling along, trying to keep up. "Only two blocks more and we'll be there. Can you do it?" He nodded wordlessly.

We entered the hotel and rode the escalator to the lobby.

"You sit here and I'll check us in," I told him, finding a comfortable chair. I had never registered the two of us at a hotel before. Gone were my romantic ideas about finding a great little restaurant and last-minute tickets to a Broadway show. The hotel restaurant would work just fine, and I would forage in the neighborhood for food for breakfast. Thank goodness the hotel room included a decent kitchen.

"I'll be fine in the morning," Art assured me. "But now I'm tired and I think a little TV and then bed."

Usually, the night sounds in Manhattan lent excitement; this time, they brought a sense of dread. All night, fire trucks and ambulances shrieked of pain and fear. Art's breathing was deep and steady.

After a slow breakfast of orange juice, toasted bagels, marmalade and coffee, Art revived. "Remember that first breakfast?" He was grinning at me. "Where's my rum coke?" His hands reached under my nightgown as I leaned over to pour another cup of coffee. I kissed his forehead.

"Behave yourself. We're heading out of here to recapture it all. Get dressed." And we did.

None of the choices of transportation were promising. Seventh Avenue is one-way southbound, and the side streets offered little hope for a taxi.

"Don't be silly," said Art, "we don't need a cab. We'll walk over to Sixth Avenue and catch the bus." With those brave words, we set out. Within a few yards, Art stopped. The biting wind took his breath away. He was fumbling with his scarf, trying to cover his face. I draped it over his nose and mouth, tying it at the back, just as I had with little children, years ago. We continued on, step by step, Art lagging behind. When I looked back to wait for him, my mind conjured up pictures of sick old men huddled in doorways out of the wind, pictures from my childhood excursions to the city during the Great Depression. In what seemed half an hour, we finally arrived at the bus stop and climbed aboard. A woman rose to offer Art her seat, and he took it gratefully, breathing hard.

At Fiftieth Street, we left the bus and ducked into the back door of the RCA building. I was sure it had another name now, but it was ever RCA to me. As we walked slowly down the corridor, I pointed out the drugstore where I saw Frank Sinatra that year I worked in the building, the jewelry shop that made my gold ring, the murals by Diego Rivera that caused such a political stir. All the time, I was searching for a place to sit down, but loungers were discouraged here.

"Let's take the elevator down to see the skaters." I punched the button. Surely, there would be someplace to sit. Maybe the restaurant would be open. Chairs were arrayed around the viewing windows, and I found him a place to sit. His face was as gray as his thin hair, his shoulders stooped. Our Music Hall tickets were for the five o'clock performance, and it was clear that Art would fade long before that. He rested while I pretended to shop in the Christmas store nearby, but when I returned, he looked no better.

"OK, buddy, back to the hotel. This is enough for now. We'll come back in time for the show. Can you make it up to Forty-ninth Street?"

"No way. You are not spending your day in New York in a hotel room. That's not what I had in mind at all." His face showed his disappointment. This excursion was his gift to me and now I was spoiling it. It was up to me to rescue the plan.

"I'll put you in a cab if you promise me you'll have lunch in the hotel and take a nap this afternoon. Do you think you can trust me to spend a whole day on Fifth Avenue shopping up a storm?" He smiled weakly and told me to go for it. I piled him into a cab, gave the driver the address, and asked him to take care of Art. "He's feeling sick," I said.

"Not to worry, lady." And they sped off.

I stood there on the street, pondering what to do. A whole day stretched ahead and I would need to give a good report. First, to plan dinner. Maybe the Rainbow Room. It was a tourist trap, but it was right here. I walked over to make a reservation, only to see that the whole place was reserved for a private party tonight. I remembered our daughter Annie's recommendation. It was just up a few blocks between Fifth and Sixth, and we could take the bus after the show. I walked. The restaurant, typically Manhattan, was down a few steps from the street, small and cozy. The menu looked good. Now what?

I started walking down Fifth Avenue. With the wind behind me and the sun shining, I felt warm enough to loosen my coat. Nothing was what I'd expected. All I could think of was Art, alone in a hotel room, but I couldn't cry. Not here. I headed for Saks and the perfume department. Instead of the rose scent I favored, which they did not carry, the sales girl talked me into a bottle of something else that was outrageously expensive. I bought a bottle; it didn't matter.

I cut across to Grand Central Station to view the laser light show I had read about, taking careful note for my report. Next came lunch in the Birdcage at Lord and Taylor's, a favorite treat when I was a little girl. It was crowded and noisy, the dainty little tea sandwiches gone. I bought silly Christmas socks for the girls. The holiday windows were festive, but I couldn't focus on the details. I remembered our fortieth anniversary, when we had strolled the avenue late at night, enjoying the windows. Hard to think this was sixteen years later. I kept walking.

What's Macy's like nowadays, I wondered? It was all chrome and glitz and rather tawdry. Now I was close to the hotel, so I just kept walking until I was there. I had walked three miles — probably more — the day was gone and I had a little shopping to show for it. I took the elevator up.

Art was lying on the bed, head propped up with pillows, watching CNBC, the business channel. "Did you leave anything in the stores or did you buy it all out?" His color was good, the sparkle back in his eyes.

"As a matter of fact, I did."

"Left some, or bought it all?"

"I came away with memories enough for a lifetime. I kept getting mixed up between today and all my yesterdays. And I did bring home a couple of things. Here—smell this." I held out my wrist. He took my hand, sniffed, then pulled me down to him. I rested my head on his chest and breathed, "Thank you for giving me a wonderful day."

Slowly, we dressed for the evening, then went down to brave the elements again. By this time, darkness was enveloping the city. A few snowflakes swirled in the air, but the wind had abated. I tied the scarf again, and we trudged slowly toward Sixth Avenue.

Once again, we got off the bus, this time to join the crowd surging toward the entrance to the Music Hall. Art gave me the tickets, and I led the way through the lobby. Our seats were on the main floor, near an aisle—just as well, for Art was flagging. To be truthful, I cannot remember the show, except for the great organ console gliding forward, music filling that immense arched theater. The Rockettes performed, Santa Claus appeared. It was a blur beyond my conscious mind. I was plotting our next move. Could we find a taxi after the show? Would the dinner menu offer something that met Art's very low sodium requirement? Should we have anything alcoholic or would that only make things worse?

Miraculously, even though we were among the last to exit the theater, we did find a cab that took us right to the restaurant. Art solved the drinks question by ordering a perfect Manhattan and a dry martini. When I declined the waiter's offer of wine with dinner, Art explained to him, "I married her because she's very economical. One drink. Easy keeper." We ordered Dover sole bonne femme, and I wondered how many ordinary French farm wives ever cooked Dover sole, but Art observed that any woman who could turn out fish like this was, in fact, a bonne femme. After a crème brûlée of delicate perfection, we gathered ourselves to go out into the night.

Art wouldn't let me tie the scarf until we were safely outside in the dark. The street was deserted, and the likelihood of finding a cab here was thin.

"Maybe on Sixth," I said optimistically, and we started to walk.

"But that's one-way north!"

"Sure, and he can go around the block. We'll see." It was an unfortunate hour; cabs would be just getting their fares to the theaters in Times Square, instead of cruising here. We saw none.

"Can you make it one more block? The buses may still be running on Seventh Avenue." In Manhattan, the streets are close together, the avenues far apart; I was asking a lot. The night was bitter, but we both knew there was little choice.

Slowly, painfully, we struggled toward the distant corner, knowing we would need to cross to the other side of the avenue when we got there. Art put his head down and we kept going. He found shelter in a doorway, while I kept watch at the curb for any likely vehicle. The avenue was mostly deserted, but I noticed that across the street and down a little way was a hotel. I walked back and asked Art if he could make it over there. He was shivering and tense, but he nodded. We went. I put a bill in the doorman's hand and asked him to get us a cab a quickly as he could while we waited in the shelter of the entrance. With a few shrill blasts on his whistle, he summoned one out of the night. We stumbled into the warm interior and clung to one another while the cab sped south.

In the morning, I fixed a breakfast of orange juice, cereal and milk, muffins and coffee, packed our clothes, and led the way to Penn Station, across Seventh Avenue, two blocks north. The avenue was quiet. When we reached the train, Art was breathing hard and coughing. I was beginning to let the tension go.

Art slept most of the way to Williamsburg while I knitted the brown yarn I had bought in Norway to make him a sweater. Susan met us at the train.

"Well," she asked, "how was it?"

' Marvelous," I said heartily.

She looked at her father's haggard face and then at mine. She gave me a hug.

The next week, when we visited Art's doctor, I described our trip and expressed concern, but both the cardiologist and his nurse-practitioner reassured me.

"He is doing just fine. Coughing up blood is common for a heart patient—it looks worse than it is. You shouldn't worry. Your concerns may affect how he feels about it."

This once strong and powerful man was a stranger to them, but in fifty-six years, I had grown as close to him as his rib. No matter what they said, in my heart I knew he was dying.

GOODBYE

Christmas came and went, but our focus was the next medical appointment. Nearly every day, it seemed, we were seeing someone about something. Art's chronic cough, 'common for a heart patient', brought up a little blood. The throat specialist could find nothing to explain it. Through it all, the cardiac nurse kept up a soothing, upbeat patter. He was doing just fine, the pacemaker was doing its job, every patient's experience is a little different. Not to worry.

The cardiologist wondered out loud whether the faulty valve was allowing blood to spurt back into his lungs, maybe have to be repaired. Furious, I raged: Crack his chest again, when you could have taken care of it when you were in there? What is wrong with you! Shut up, you fools! This dear man is dying, can't you see that! But I said nothing. My head was splitting with the explosive silence of my protest. Like a dutiful patient's wife, I smiled and nodded in the right places. "Yes, of course, we can be here next Tuesday. At eleven? Fine."

Every day, as Art napped in his chair, I walked my habitual mile. With each step, I mumbled verses from half-remembered poems. In innocent adolescence, I had been struck with Edna St. Vincent Millay's dramatic yearnings over lost love. *Well, I have lost you, and I lost you fairly, in my own way, and with my full consent.* No! No! She had no idea what love was. You can't just let it go with consent. She didn't know. I was angry now. Art was dying, and I would *not* consent, I would *not* approve, no matter what. My grieving had begun, and it was only January. I clung to him in bed, reluctant to roll away to let him sleep.

Did he know, too? I did not think so. He kept on seeking answers, jollying with the nurses, attending to the regimen they dictated. Maybe I was wrong; I had always been ready to cave in before the battle was over. No, I was right; I felt it in my bones.

Art's vision was giving him a problem, and the ophthalmologist told him his lenses had clouded. Cataract surgery was pretty simple; they could do one a week and his vision would return to normal. The cardiologist was willing. Surgery was scheduled for February thirteenth and twentieth.

The first surgery went well, although now his glasses were useless for reading with that eye. Never mind, Dr. Hodges would be able to write a new prescription within a few weeks. The day of the second surgery, Art seemed less well. "OK. Don't worry about it, I'm OK." If his tone was sharp, I put it down to anxiety. When we arrived, he asked for a wheelchair from the car to the hospital door, and I went to fetch one.

"Just saving my strength, that's all," he insisted. When he was released from surgery, he again asked for a chair, said he didn't feel so hot. I took him home, where he quickly dozed off. In the morning, after the check-up with Dr. Hodges, I took him right to Dr. Mincks.

"John, he's feeling kind of peaked. Would you take a look?"

"Well," said Dr. Mincks, "I think we may be dealing with a little pneumonia here. Let's get a picture of this."

The x-ray showed a spot on one lung. Art protested that he was sick of hospitals. Sympathetic, Dr. Mincks thought he could manage it with outpatient medication. We went home with a bottle of pills.

By suppertime, Art was sinking alarmingly. I called the hospital. "My husband needs to be admitted. Will you please take care of the admission papers? No, we are not going to the emergency room. Right to the medical ward. You want a diagnosis? It's pneumonia. No, we don't need to have the emergency doc confirm that. We already know. He is too sick to wait in the ER." A few more minutes of wrangling and I announced that we would come in through the front door and if it was locked they had better have a security person there to open it. I hung up and got Art ready. I bundled him into the car and headed downtown. His temperature had risen. At the front door, we were met by a guard with a wheelchair. I rolled him to the elevator. In his room, the nurse started an IV.

On Thursday morning, Dr. Mincks came in and sat down by Art's bed. "Art," he began gently, "I've had a chance to go over the x-rays with the radiologist. You do have pneumonia, but he agrees that there are some other spots in the picture that were absent in your last x-ray, just a few weeks ago. We need to look into it."

"John," I asked, "is there any possible explanation that you know of for those spots other than cancer?"

"No, there is not. But we need to be sure, to find out specifically what it is. I'm going to order more extensive x-rays, and then we'll talk some more."

Art had little to say, although he seemed to be alert and listening. When the doctor left, a visitor entered.

"Doc doesn't want to let well enough alone. He's going to get more pictures. I don't think he knows what my problem is."

Then I realized with a start that Art had not heard him. This was unknown territory for me. After a few minutes of small talk, the friend started to leave, and I walked with him out in the hall. "Les, I don't know what to do." I was glad to have this friend, a psychologist specializing in counseling families with serious illness. " John believes it's lung cancer; I think he's going to look for metastasis. But Art wasn't ready to hear him. What should I say?"

"For now, let him lead. He will hear when he can."

The next twenty-four hours told the story. It was lung cancer that had spread widely to Art's liver. Dr. Ellis, the oncologist, stopped at his room to discuss it with us. "This type is so aggressive that as soon as half a dozen cells have gathered, it is already too late. There is no way to know how long you have, weeks, months. Not many months, at best, I'm afraid."

Art heard that. He was stunned, although I could see that he was not surprised.

"Darling," I whispered, "we've had fifty-seven years of loving each other. We have been so lucky."

"Yes," he said sadly, "but I want more!"

The next day, he said, "You need to make arrangements with a nursing home. They won't keep me here much longer."

I was appalled; imagining him among strangers made me feel sick. "I want you at home," I protested. "I want you close to me every moment that we have." I think he was relieved.

So it was settled. Now all I had to do was make it happen. He would be released in a few days, after the pneumonia was under control, and that gave me time enough. A band of angels from the church came and emptied the first-floor den of all my sewing equipment, all our books. They left only the telephone and computer. Everything was neatly gathered in the guest room. The little chest of drawers was brought down, the television placed on top. All this happened under Susan's direction while I remained at the hospital.

Charlotte was grieving, too. She and Art had a close mother—son relationship, strengthened by their shared intense interest in financial investments. I spent some time keeping things smooth at Chambrel, but I could talk to Mother about it only in the most factual terms. We hid out grief under a blanket of bland conversation.

Susan, who had lost Gordon just three years before, was burdened enough at the impending loss of her father. We spoke of everything except how we felt. Telling Annie was very hard to do, but she made immediate plans to come with her children. The hospital's hospice service activated to send daytime nursing aides and a hospital bed, and the private hospice service chimed in with equipment and supplies.

On the first day of March, the ambulance backed up to our door and three strong men carried Art in, helping him gently into bed. He slept then. I sat beside him, resting my head on his outstretched hand.

Susan had long-standing plans to be away with Michael for several days, and I insisted they must go. Annie would be here to help. To keep confusion to a minimum, Annie and the children slept at Susan's, only a few steps away at the other end of the building. That gave the children an opportunity to watch television or lounge around without being underfoot. Jenny was less than fifteen, Adam close to eighteen. They would be helpful when strength was needed, but I counted on them for no more.

Recovered from the acute phase of what was probably minimal pneumonia, Art rallied somewhat.

"Art, I can wheel you to your favorite chair in the living room. C'mon. Do you good to see something different.!"

He slipped into the wheelchair, and I pushed him into that sunny room he loved so well. After a few minutes, he said, "Enough. Back to bed." One trip sufficed; he never wanted another. For the rest of his days, he watched the financial channel on television, and he slept.

Although I had vowed that no one in my family would ever again have to endure a deathbed signing of wills, that is just what happened. A misstep in what we thought was meticulous planning called for the emergency services of our lawyer. On March fifth, he came with several of his staff to present and witness a new will and trust agreement. I watched Art struggle with his signature while fury rose in my throat over this grotesque procedure. He was losing the use of his hands; his speech began to go next.

Art could not move himself in bed, and the children proved to be more valuable than I could have imagined. They learned how to move him gently but efficiently, and they were tireless in their attention to his needs. Adam sat with him for a long time; whether they spoke much or not, I never knew, but left them alone to commune as they would. Adam needed to return to school, but Jenny and Annie stayed the week.

Every night, Art had to be tended to once or twice. A monitor set up between my bedroom and his allowed me to hear him when he stirred. The first time I heard him moan, I grabbed my robe and ran, still groggy. It was a mistake. I picked myself up at the bottom of the stairs, having slipped somewhere along the way. Frightened, I realized that one careless move like that could create a complicated disaster. After that, I took care to turn on lights, put on my robe, and walk down, holding the railing.

Soon, he could not even use the bedside commode, but he still struggled to do for himself, humiliated by the need to be nursed. For a time, I could join in his pretense to care for himself, but I ached for him. If he needed to be turned or lifted, I phoned Annie. Both women came instantly and among us we managed to straighten him out without hurting him or ourselves. By now, it was clear that Jenny was fully a woman, capable of taking on any task asked of her. She was gentle and loving, yet strong and competent.

The church food brigade took action. Every day, meals were brought on schedule, never too much, always delicious. Elizabeth Pickell came to sit with him one evening; she brought her guitar and her experienced massage therapy hands. Another time, Chris Marie came, diffidently, to stay with him. I told her she could skip conversation, but just be there. When I returned home from a meeting, they were deeply engaged in swapping lies about their military experiences. His speech was thick and slurred, but Chris seemed to understand.

Les Dubnick appeared and asked Art's permission to take his wife to lunch. Permission given, I had a diverting hour at *The Trellis*, a chance to catch my breath and talk a little about my feelings. When we returned, Les reported to Art that he had brought his wife home safe and sound.

In his halting voice, Art said, "I want to talk. Get everybody in the house here."

"Jenny, too?"

"Yes."

Annie, Jenny, Les, and I stood arrayed around his bed.

"I want you all to promise to help me die. I'm ready to go and I don't want to linger on. Will you all promise? Please? Please!" I thought my heart had stopped, and for a moment there was silence in the room. I think we all nodded in assent— I know I leaned down and whispered, "I will do what I can."

With many tears, Jenny and Annie finally took their leave, saying last tearful good-byes. Fred Adair, a sensitive and caring friend, drove them away. Susan and Mike had returned to take up the traces.

Art was now beginning to gulp for air. It was a race to see whether his liver malfunction would overtake his lung difficulties. Morphine was there on the medicine table. I filled the medicine dropper and dripped some into his mouth. He swallowed a little and retched. The doctor had warned me that Art might tolerate only small amounts at a time. I tried again, but again only a few drops went down. He was very agitated and tense, clenching his fists and flailing about in the bed.

In the late afternoon, dusk was gathering. "There, my dear, just lie back and let go. Go to sleep. I love you and I want you to go. Sleep, sleep." I held his hand and began to sing softly. *Sleep, my Love, and peace attend thee, all through the night, Guardian angels God will lend thee. . .* Sad that my voice was cracking, I continued anyway, crooning softly. I sang songs I had sung to him when we were first courting, songs about love. Little by little, his arm lost its tension. He thrashed around the bed less, seemed to be coming to peace. Time to sleep. I sang and sang, over and over.

About two o'clock in the morning, Susan led me away. "He's sleeping peacefully at last, Mom. You need to rest. I've made up beds for us in the living room on the couch. Come."

She had set up the monitor there, too, so that we could hear if he called. Soon, both of us were asleep.

In about an hour, Susan woke to listen. All was quiet. Perfectly quiet. Not a sound. She rose to go to him, came back and roused me. "He's gone, Mom. He has stopped breathing."

It was over.

Art and Kit 1998

POSTLUDE

The past is a kaleidoscope, shifting and tumbling as you turn the wheel. Have I told the truth? Who can say with finality what is truth? Does it reshape itself to meet today's need? The truth, when it happened, differs from the truth told much later, understood from the distance of time and experience, sharp edges worn away by the passing years. The second truth is no less real, and was more serviceable to my needs as I chronicled this story.

Is this life supposed to teach us something? Are we destined to leave it wiser than we were? What changes took place between these lovers? How did our two threads become one?

At the beginning of this tale, Art was a foreigner in American life. Even though all towns have their own unique qualities, Lewiston had one more. In addition to being divided by class, it was divided by language and culture. He was on the short end. Or was he? His family left him no legacy of money or power, only integrity, hard work, and steadfastness. It was enough. He developed more than changed. The great mystery is the source of his capacity for patient, enduring love.

I was a whole different case. I began with a legacy of money — some, at least — and with whatever implied power goes with that. Integrity was certainly part of my heritage, but the hard work and steadfastness passed over me without leaving a mark. My image of myself deteriorated by reflection from my classmates and mirror. I glowed, even through my illness, with that spark of energy which comes across as, well, sexy. That, and native intelligence, were what I started with.

Over the years, Art continued to achieve his goals, just as he always had. He was confident of that, even in those early days on the road, when he was sick with fear. Like a soldier, he fought through his fear, assured that he would win the war. He never allowed himself to feel the stranger, never less than his surroundings. He was, as a friend said of him, comfortable in his skin. He sought change, he honored it.

Through the turbulent sixties, I saw the harvest of anarchy and rebellion in confused young people and realized that Art's respect for order and discipline had some merit. I gravitated in his direction at the same time that he loosened his stern and single-minded view of adolescence. We could, at last, see life through nearly the same prism.

My understanding of myself ebbed and flowed with the tides of the particular sea I was swimming in. My early view of myself as wonderful and quite special soon shattered. When a new possibility stared back at me from the eyes of that man, I began to grow. Prompted by his persistent encouragement, I ventured into the world and found some acceptance from others and some comfort within myself. I was not destined to be, like him, comfortable in my skin, but I could detach myself from dismal dependence on approval from others. I learned to look inward and to trust myself.

In the end, neither of us took full credit for triumphs. Blame for our failures ultimately became irrelevant. Our lives, both of them, were what they were: brilliant and ordinary, rich and mundane, above all, responsible. What was the point of it all?

Each of us is a weaver of the Great Tapestry of existence. Most of our threads are small and inconspicuous, although occasionally one large strand displays a different design. Some threads are weak or corrupt and leave a ragged rent in the fabric that other threads may mend. Thus, the tapestry grows, generation upon generation.

I have this view of interlacing of the human experience, and I feel responsible to contribute in creating a splendid work. I see our daughters weaving their own special cords, one with unexpected images of beauty, the other with ordered rows that bring compassion to meager lives. Our grandchildren, learning how to throw their shuttles, work with ever-growing skill to design their special parts. Art left his thread straight and strong, woven with humor and compassion. And mine? I only hope that when viewed from a further range my little piece will be seen to embellish the whole. My thread grew stronger and more resilient but will soon run out. My work is nearly done, and now I can say to Art, in the poet's[9] words: i am, through you, so i.

೪ ೫ ೪ ೫ ೪ ೫

---

[9] e e cummings